Researching Practice

PRACTICE, EDUCATION, WORK AND SOCIETY

Volume 2

Series Editor

Professor Joy Higgs,

The Education for Practice Institute,
The Research Institute for Professional Practice, Learning & Education
Charles Sturt University,
North Parramatta, Australia

Advisory Editorial Board

Professor Della Fish
The University of Swansea, Wales

Dr Debbie Horsfall
The Social Justice Social Change Research Centre,
University of Western Sydney, Australia

Dr Stephen Loftus
The Education for Practice Institute
Charles Sturt University, Australia

Professor Pam Shakespeare
Centre of Excellence in Teaching and Learning
The Open University, United Kingdom

Dr Franziska Trede
The Education for Practice Institute
Charles Sturt University, Australia

Researching Practice:

A Discourse on Qualitative Methodologies

Edited by

Joy Higgs
Charles Sturt University
Australia

Nita Cherry
Swinburne University of Technology
Australia

Rob Macklin and Rola Ajjawi
Charles Sturt University
Australia

SENSE PUBLISHERS
ROTTERDAM/BOSTON/TAIPEI

A C.I.P. record for this book is available from the Library of Congress.

ISBN: 978-94-6091-181-1 (paperback)
ISBN: 978-94-6091-182-8 (hardback)
ISBN: 978-94-6091-183-5 (e-book)

Published by: Sense Publishers,
P.O. Box 21858,
3001 AW Rotterdam,
The Netherlands
http://www.sensepublishers.com

Printed on acid-free paper

All Rights Reserved © 2010 Sense Publishers

No part of this work may be reproduced, stored in a retrieval system, or transmitted in any form or by any means, electronic, mechanical, photocopying, microfilming, recording or otherwise, without written permission from the Publisher, with the exception of any material supplied specifically for the purpose of being entered and executed on a computer system, for exclusive use by the purchaser of the work.

CONTENTS

Series Introduction: Practice, Education, Work and Society ix
Joy Higgs

Foreward xi
Joy Higgs, Rola Ajjawi

Section 1: Framing Qualitative Research on Practice in the 21st Century

1. Researching Practice: Entering the Practice Discourse 1
   Joy Higgs

2. Doing Qualitative Research in the White Spaces 9
   Nita Cherry

3. The Origins of Qualitative Research: The Importance of Philosophy 19
   Stephen Loftus and Rodd Rothwell

4. Philosophical Frameworks and Research Communities 31
   Joy Higgs and Franziska Trede

5. Understanding Qualitative Research in the Context of Cultures:
   Methodological Consequences 37
   Gavin Melles

6. Writing Contemporary Ontological and Epistemological Questions
   about Practice 45
   Angie Titchen and Rola Ajjawi

7. Theoretical Frameworks and Literature: Framing and Supporting
   Qualitative Research 57
   Joy Higgs and Franziska Trede

8. Using Lenses and Layers 65
   Robert Macklin and Joy Higgs

Section 2: The Qualitative Research Journey: Connections, Transformations and Challenges

9. Researching Ethically? 75
   Susan Groundwater-Smith

CONTENTS

10. Research as Praxis: Growing as a Person through Research 87
    Nita Cherry

11. Researching in the Face of the Other: Doing Decent Research 95
    Robert Macklin

12. Relationality and the Myth of Objectivity in Research Involving
    Human Participants 105
    John A. Bowden and Pamela J. Green

13. The Place of Qualitative Research in Helping Voices be Heard 113
    Rosemary Leonard

14. The Voice of the Researched in Qualitative Research: Rigour and
    Research Practices 123
    John A. Bowden and Pamela J. Green

15. Being Critical and Creative in Qualitative Research 133
    Joy Higgs and Debbie Horsfall

16. Enacting Internal Coherence: As a Path to Quality in Qualitative
    Inquiry 143
    Stacy M. Carter

17. Interpreting Quality in Qualitative Research 153
    Carol Grbich

18. Demystifying Data Analysis: A Kaleidoscope of Decision Making,
    Congruence and Evolution 165
    Joy Higgs

19. Qualitative Data Analysis 173
    Carol Grbich

Section 3: Qualitative Research Approaches

20. Hermeneutic Research: Exploring Human Understanding 185
    Franziska Trede and Stephen Loftus

21. Phenomenological Research: Understanding Human Phenomena 197
    Sandra Grace and Rola Ajjawi

22. Making a Thesis Text in Creative Practice-Based Research:
    Razzle Dazzle 209
    Inger Mewburn and Robyn Barnacle

23. Arts-Based Research for Teachers, Researchers and Supervisors 217
    Jill Franz

24. Ethnomethodology: The Situated Study of Professional Practice 227
    Natasha Wardman and Sue Saltmarsh

25. Action Research 237
    Nita L. Cherry

26. Critical Inquiry 247
    Franziska Trede and Joy Higgs

27. Collaborative Inquiry: Process, Theory and Ethics 257
    Donna Bridges and Sharyn McGee

28. Poststructuralist Research: Dipping into the Social Worlds
    of Multiplicities 269
    James Latham and Robert Jones

29. Doing Mixed Methods Research 279
    Branka Krivokapic-Skoko and Grant O'Neill

30. Pursuing Feminist Research: Perspectives and Methodologies 289
    Anita Monro

31. Research in Indigenous Spaces 299
    M. Elaine Duffy and Wayne (Colin) Rigby

32. Hermeneutics as Meta-Strategy 309
    Joy Higgs

Section 4: Looking Forward

33. Future Positive? 323
    Nita Cherry

Contributors 331

JOY HIGGS

SERIES INTRODUCTION

Practice, Education, Work and Society

This series examines research, theory and practice in the context of university education, professional practice, work and society. Rather than focussing on a single topic the series examines areas where two or more of these arenas come together. Themes that will be explored in the series include: university education of professions, society expectations of professional practice, professional practice workplaces and strategies for investigating each of these areas. There are many challenges facing researchers, educators, practitioners and students in today's practice worlds. The authors in this series bring a wealth of practice wisdom and experience to examine these issues, share their practice knowledge, report research into strategies that address these challenges, share approaches to working and learning and raise yet more questions.

The conversations conducted in the series will contribute to expanding the discourse around the way people encounter and experience practice, education, work and society.

Joy Higgs, Charles Sturt University
Australia

FOREWARD

Practice as a lived phenomenon, is accessed through the individual and group perceptions of practitioners, practice partners and society, and requires relevant and credible research and writing strategies[1] to contribute to the advancement of practice. Qualitative research is expected to generate insights, and deeper understanding of practice and to impact directly or indirectly on practice.

Research itself is a practice and like any other social activity, has an associated discourse. In this book we contribute to the discourse on qualitative research methodologies and reflect on research contexts, goals, communities and approaches. Each of these aspects of research is shaped by the culture of research communities. A key requirement of being a researcher within the qualitative tradition is to critically embrace the influence of different cultural contexts on the knowledge generated. This book examines various cultures and traditions of qualitative research.

This book is divided into four sections. The first section explores the issues that frame qualitative research on practice in the 21st century. Chapter 1 enters the discourse on researching practice. Researching the messy world of practice (or the white spaces) is the topic of Chapter 2. Chapters 3, 4 and 5 explore the historical, philosophical and cultural contexts of qualitative and practice-based research respectively. Coherent and rigorous qualitative research is not a matter of following recipes or protocols but stems from judicious and informed choices about philosophical (Chapter 4) and theoretical frameworks (Chapter 7), the type of questions we wish to research (Chapter 6) and the lenses that we all bring to our research (Chapter 8).

Section Two is concerned with locating the questions, practices and issues of qualitative research on practice in researchers' journeys and presents a number of themes – connections, transformations and challenges. Ethical research is a priority for all researchers (Chapter 9). The connections between researchers and the researched throughout the research journey is a dominant theme explored from different perspectives in Chapters 11 to 14. Through these connections, transformations can occur where the researcher grows as a person through the research practices (Chapter 10). Being critical and creative in qualitative research is the topic of Chapter 15. Reflexivity (awareness and sensitivity to self and others) is increasingly being advocated as a marker of quality; this and other criteria for interpreting quality in qualitative research are explored in Chapters 16 and 17. Finally in section two, the challenge of qualitative data analysis is 'demystified' and examined (Chapters 18 and 19).

Section Three makes accessible a range of qualitative approaches commonly used to research practice in which the themes of connections, transformations and challenges are further explored. These methods include: hermeneutics (Chapter 20), phenomenology (Chapter 21), arts-based research (Chapter 23), ethnomethodology (Chapter 24), action research (Chapter 25), critical inquiry (Chapter 26), collaborative inquiry (Chapter 27), poststructuralist research (Chapter 28) and feminist research

FOREWARD

(Chapter 30). Other important strategies and issues are explored in this section including making creative thesis texts (Chapter 22), mixed methods research (Chapter 29) and researching in Indigenous spaces (Chapter 31). Common to all the qualitative research approaches presented in this section is the critical place of interpretation (Chapter 32).

The final section contains one chapter that explores future considerations in qualitative research and examines the positives and considerations of future research.

Joy Higgs and Rola Ajjawi

NOTES

[1] See also Higgs, J., Horsfall, D., & Grace, S. (Eds.). (2009) *Writing qualitative research on practice.* Rotterdam: Sense Publishers.

JOY HIGGS

1. RESEARCHING PRACTICE:

Entering the practice discourse

To set the scene for this book three key elements are brought together in this chapter. The first is the purpose to focus on research that enhances practice through understanding, interpretation and change. The second relates to the artefacts of research, being knowledge and practice effects. Of particular interest here is the cyclical and ephemeral nature of both of these artefacts. Knowledge, of course, builds on existing knowing, enters into the field of knowledge – the discourse – and changes that discourse; then in turn this same knowledge is challenged and often changed by new waves of incoming knowledge. Practice, broadly speaking, is what we do, and more specifically what we as practitioners do in particular practice communities and how others engage with this practice; such practice is constantly evolving. And, paradoxically, practice needs to be known (our foreknowings and pre-judgements) before we can conceptualise and imagine the questions we want to ask of practice, before we can identify the dimensions we want to change in it, and before we can address the puzzles we want to solve about it. Third, there is the living and lived dimension of research. Practice is a lived phenomenon. It is accessed through perceptions and experience; it is understood through interpretation; it is framed and shared through language; and in turn it transforms those who seek to appreciate (understand and value) it. In the book we explore both the points of reference of the practitioners as well as the perspectives of researchers. In this chapter I focus mainly on the practice of research.

ENTERING THE PRACTICE DISCOURSE 1:
BRINGING IN THE INQUIRING SELF

The researcher as an inquiring self is the concept and phenomenon highlighted in this section. This concept includes being an inquirer about the topic or practice concerned, being awake (see Chapter 33) and receptive to what is being investigated in the world, and critically challenging self as person and researcher in this inquiry process. Each of us brings many dimensions of self to the inquiry process in relation to person, researcher and practitioner. And we are all variable and evolving in relation to these dimensions. The symbol for infinity, the lemniscate, is used to portray this endless variability in the images below.

In Figure 1.1 multiple lemniscates reflect how the researcher's goals, interests, world view, ways of relating to others and practice background (etc.) are brought into each research episode.

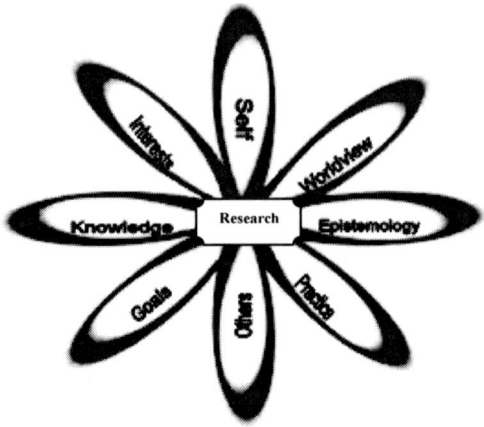

Figure 1.1. Multiple dimensions researchers bring to research.

In Figure 1.2 the interaction of several individuals (both researchers and participants) is illustrated. Of particular importance in these interactions are the ways researchers engage with others and establish ethical partnerships as well as productive research-oriented relationships. The values, interests and stances adopted by researchers (see Figure 1.1) are integral to these interaction choices and patterns.

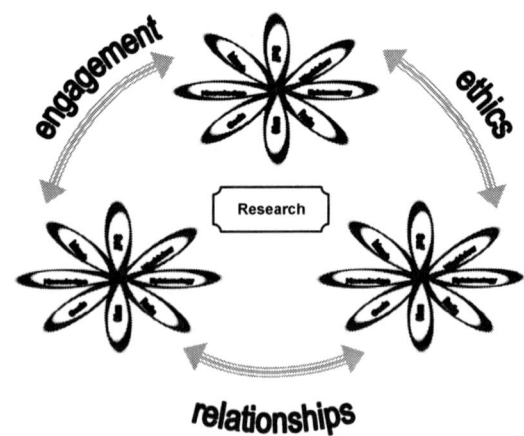

Figure 1.2. Multiple researchers interacting.

RESEARCHING PRACTICE

The encounters implied by these interactions can be virtual and real-time, remote and immediate, intellectual and emotional, easy and difficult. To do work together is always different from working alone, and if the work is meaningful it calls forth – sometimes demands – dialogues that are robust, challenging, enlivening and stretching. Arguably, the growth of individual and collective research practice depends on these encounters, encouraging those involved to crystallise implicit assumptions, to articulate them in ways that others can understand, to listen to others and to work out which practice issues really matter.

ENTERING THE PRACTICE DISCOURSE 2:
WORKING IN RESEARCH COMMUNITIES

In Chapters 3 and 4 the importance of researching within philosophical frameworks and the impact of working within different research communities and cultures of inquiry are examined. Such communities may reflect overt aspects of interaction of researchers working on particular projects, or they may have more distant and even implicit frames of reference that influence research strategies, modes of engagement with the research participants (see Chapters 9, 11, 12).

There is an inevitable connection between the type of research questions we ask and our philosophical frames of reference (see Chapter 6). In turn, the methodologies selected for the research are influenced by individual interests as well as norms and practices of the research community. Figure 1.3 draws these various notions and practices together. This figure depicts the way that a research team, with the team members' various individual and collective characteristics, goals and modes of engagement, operates within a research community. The culture and paradigm of the research community frames the team's decisions around their philosophical and methodological frameworks (see Chapters 3 and 4).

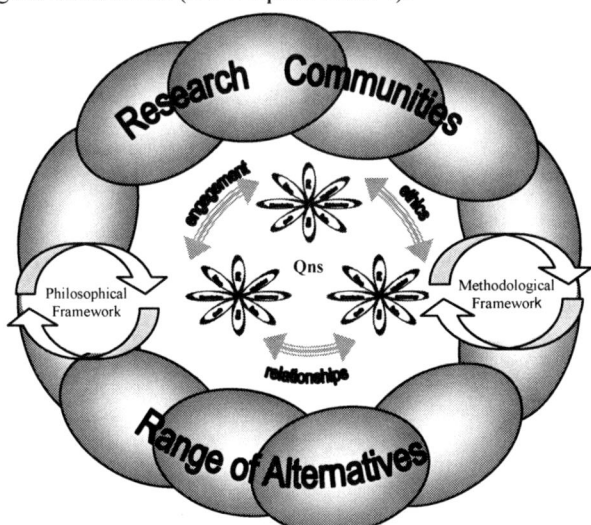

Figure 1.3. Working in research communities.

ENTERING THE PRACTICE DISCOURSE 3: BEING PART OF THE HISTORY OF IDEAS

Professional knowledge is located within the wider history of ideas (see Berlin, 1979) and the broader knowledge of society. Knowledge which has evolved within a practice includes both the history of the ideas contained in the practice and the history of how people have shaped those ideas and shaped the practice. This knowledge can assist us to better contextualise our understanding of contemporary research and professional practices, and to work more effectively on developing future knowledge and practice. Understanding human practices requires an appreciation of the contribution of history to their development. We need historical knowledge of the nature of any professional practice if we are to recognise its imperatives, constraints and possibilities. Moreover, we need an understanding of the evolution of research practices (see Chapter 3) if we are to appreciate how to research credibly.

Figure 1.4 depicts the location of research projects and the associated research community in the world of ideas. This world is shaped by the history of ideas and is manifest in the literature of the relevant field. The term *discourse* recognises the way that language, themes, dominant messages and interpretations frame our ways of knowing, knowledge making and acting in the world.

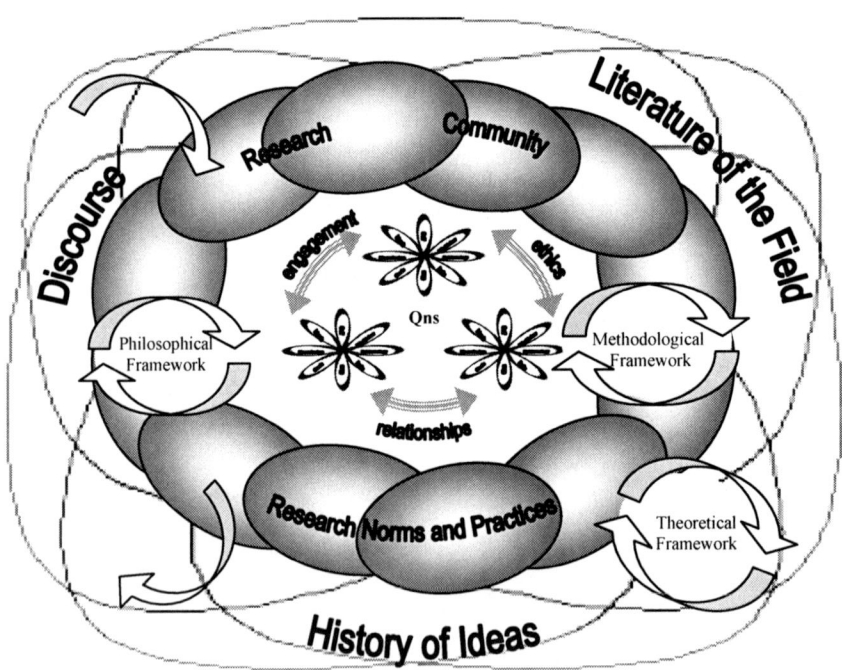

Figure 1.4. Being part of the history of ideas.

The theoretical framework (see Chapter 7) of a research project is drawn from existing literature to highlight key knowledge pertinent to the project and identify the theoretical lenses (see Chapter 8) chosen to shape the research questions and interpret the research findings. Higgs and Andresen (2001) created a metaphor for knowing and knowledge: a picture of threads of understanding being woven into tapestries and carpets to illustrate, respectively, collective and individual knowledge bases. This imagery arose from a view of the historical evolution of knowledge as resembling a never-ending tapestry, a product of centuries of human thought, and seeing the theoretical framework for a research project as a virtual carpet. Students are encouraged to enact their research by dancing on this carpet.

Cherry[1] provided the example of a student who was researching the question of whether mentoring is something that can be arranged or something that simply happens in ways that are hard to predict and manage. The student searched the business, nursing and education literature and found that this question had been asked many times. This literature provided the theoretical framework for the student's research. It influenced the research strategy; data collected reflected the first-hand experience of people who had mentored or been mentored. The themes identified from the data collected were examined, suggesting ideas that had not been previously been pursued in the literature on mentoring. Further literature searching led the student to the psychoanalytic literature on unconscious interpersonal dependency, which resulted in revision of the theoretical framework and provided a valuable lens for reflecting on the research findings. In this example we see both the importance of creating a theoretical framework and the value of seeing such frameworks as evolving practices and scaffolds responding to the dynamic nature of research and knowledge creation.

ENTERING THE PRACTICE DISCOURSE 4:
FROM, IN AND FOR PRACTICE

We focus in this book on researching practice. Research can generate empirical and theoretical knowledge. Such knowledge, it can be argued, emerges from practice and is created to explain, explore or extend practice. The concept of the primacy of practice is the recognition and contention that within the development of knowledge practice is what comes first, and theory is developed from it. This places practice at the centre of this debate.

So what is practice? Higgs, McAllister, and Whiteford (2009, p. 102) defined practice as "the enactment of the role of a profession or occupational group in serving or contributing to society". To unbundle this seemingly straightforward notion it is useful to look at the categorisations of Kemmis and McTaggart (2000), who distinguished five different notions of practice based on different approaches to research into practice:

1. the behaviour of individual practitioners as perceived by outside observers
2. patterns of social interaction among practice participants as perceived by outside observers

3. the intentions, meanings and values which constitute practice as perceived subjectively by individual practitioners
4. the way the language, discourses and traditions of practice are perceived by communities of practitioners as they represent their practices to themselves and others
5. historically, the evolution of practice as an social form which is reflexively transformed and restructured over time.

From these ideas we see the complexity of practice as purposeful actions, a multifactorial form of occupation and role in society, a way of being and doing in the world within a frame of reference of a particular profession or occupation and a phenomenon that is variously viewed, experienced and owned by different groups of people including the practitioners, the clients or partners in this practice, and the community or society which recognises, allows and monitors this practice. Figure 1.5 is an image of this complex set of parameters. It portrays a fluid, dynamic arena comprising multiple players and dimensions engaging in periodic encounters, yet being consistently influenced by the interactive, evolving whole.

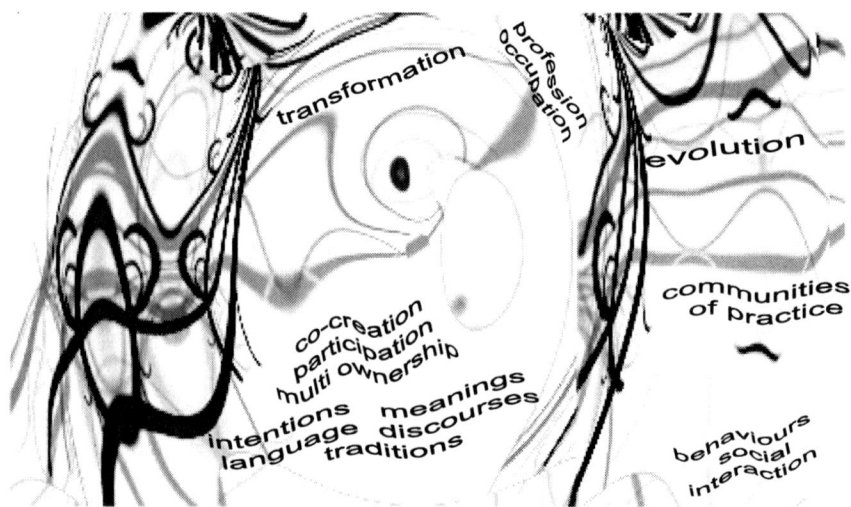

Figure 1.5. Practice dimensions.

To enter the discourse from within practice requires a practitioner's perspective; thus it is the task of practitioners or researchers who take the time to become part of that practice discourse. This gives credibility to the goal of writing about, for, and from within practice.

In Figure 1.6 the acts and experiences of research are placed in this "living sea" of practice, becoming another process – inquiry – in the midst of practice that is transformed by the practice context as it (the inquiry process) seeks to know this practice and offer ways and ideas for practice transformation.

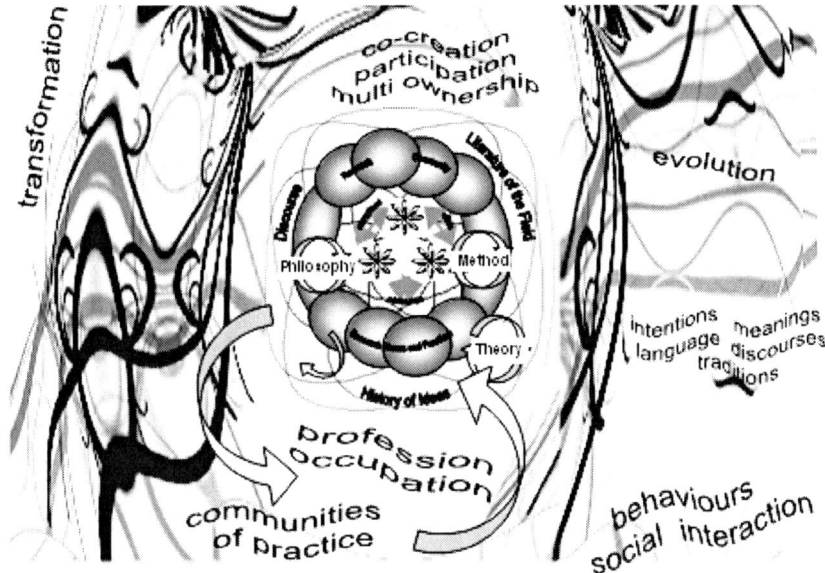

Figure 1.6. Practice-based inquiry.

CONCLUSION

To enhance practice through understanding, interpretation and change, researchers are well served by entering the practice discourse as discussed in this chapter. In parallel the researcher is practising research through knowing self and bringing this inquiring self into the discourse, working in research communities with other researchers – alongside practitioners and practice partners – recognising the contributions and reciprocal influences that emerging knowledge and the history of ideas have on one another, and valuing the primacy of practice as source, purpose and influence of research. Throughout this chapter there are many such interchanges reflected in paired circular arrows, demonstrating the inter-connectedness in the various contexts, purposes and practices of research and professional practice. These themes are reflected in many chapters in this book.

NOTES

[1] Personal communication.

REFERENCES

Berlin, I. (1979). *Against the current: Essays in the history of ideas* (H. Hardy, Ed.). London: Hogarth Press.

Higgs, J., & Andresen, L. (2001). The knower, the knowing and the known: Threads in the woven tapestries of knowledge. In J. Higgs & A. Titchen (Eds.), *Practice knowledge and expertise in the health professions* (pp. 10–21). Oxford: Butterworth-Heinemann.

Higgs, J., McAllister, L., & Whiteford, G. (2009). The practice and praxis of professional decision making. In B. Green (Ed.), *Understanding and researching professional practice* (pp. 101–120). Rotterdam: Sense Publishers.

Kemmis, S., & McTaggart, R. (2005). Participatory action research: communicative action and the public sphere. in N. Denzin & Y. Lincoln (Eds.), *The Sage handbook of qualitative research* (3rd ed., pp. 559–603). Thousand Oaks, Ca: Sage.

AFFILIATION

Joy Higgs AM PhD
The Research Institute for Professional Practice, Learning & Education
The Education for Practice Institute
Charles Sturt University
Australia

NITA CHERRY

2. DOING QUALITATIVE RESEARCH IN THE WHITE SPACES

INTRODUCTION

This chapter explores the potential for qualitative researchers to contribute to productive engagement with the opportunities and challenges presented by living and working in the age of complexity (see Oliver, 2000). It describes the features of the practice challenges that reside in the white spaces of complexity – the spaces where data and know-how are either limited or ambiguous and conflicting – and suggests that these translate into some distinct opportunities for qualitative research. Building on the seminal contributions of Van de Ven and Johnson (2006), who suggested six broad strategies for engaged scholarship, and Weick and Roberts' (1993) concept of decision-awareness, it explores a number of design features that can be helpful in pursuing these opportunities. It then suggests some of the protocols that can contribute technical and ethical rigour to a wide range of cultures of research inquiry.

THE WHITE SPACES

Freed (1992) has suggested that this a time of relentless innovation: a time in which human imagination and ingenuity have unparalleled access to global resources of all kinds. The opportunities, challenges and dilemmas associated with this era have, in turn, come to be described as the "age of complexity" (Oliver, 2000). Arguably, there are four dimensions of this era that are particularly striking.

The first is what David Perkins (2006) has called *troublesome knowledge*. This is knowledge that is potentially ground-breaking or transformative but brings with it enormous dilemmas as to how it is to be used wisely and ethically. An obvious example is the human genome project, and another is access to the means of euthanasia. The second dimension is the sheer speed and volume of knowledge creation, and the impact of continuous and rapid change, in all arenas of life and work. The third dimension is a paradoxical one. On the one hand, knowledge is characterised by very high levels of specialisation in research and knowledge, and with that, very divergent ways of dealing with some difficult issues (like the state of clinical depression).

At the same time, we see the collision and convergence of industries and disciplines, as is the case with many biotechnologies. This has led to such blurring of the boundaries that we can be said to be in the postdisciplinary age. The fourth

J. Higgs, N. Cherry, R. Macklin and R. Ajjawi (eds.),
Researching Practice: A Discourse on Qualitative Methodologies, 9–17.
© 2010 Sense Publishers. All rights reserved.

dimension of this age of innovation is that despite the plethora of knowledge, some problems and opportunities seem beyond obvious solutions or even rules for helpful engagement, beyond existing skills, and sometimes beyond even imagination and optimism.

Graphic designers draw attention to the white spaces[1] that lie outside symbols and marks on a page. These white spaces start at the boundary of what we know or can express and so provide a powerful metaphor for the potential of the unknown. Emmett (1998) suggests that it is here that we can go *searching among the absences*. Elsewhere, the present writer offers an exploration of the possibilities of the white spaces for learning and practice development (Cherry, 2008).

Many of the issues that occupy the white spaces are what Conklin (2003) calls *wicked problems*, while other issues are what could be called *juicy opportunities*. Some of the distinctive qualities of wicked problems and juicy opportunities are that little data about them are available, or the data that do exist are ambiguous, even contradictory. They are often systemic, and the connections between causes and symptoms are not at all obvious, so that seemingly small events have enormous consequences, and individuals or groups can find it difficult to accept and sustain accountability for dealing with them. When such issues are perceived as threats, they can become the focus of power, politics and force, or subject to efforts to achieve quick closure, rather than sites for robust and sustained engagement and debate.

Engagement in these white spaces can come more readily to some people. Entrepreneurs, artists and philosophers find fulfilment in holding open difficult questions that would overwhelm others. For many people, however, engagement with the truly complex comes at a tremendous price, not the least of which is the great anxiety which comes with the uncertainty of not knowing what to do. Much of the implicit and explicit expectations of practitioners and researchers is that they reduce and manage uncertainty, not create or sustain it. Arguably it requires energy to deliberately lean into the white spaces, and hold the tension of "not-knowing", plus the capacity to be buoyantly confused for significant periods of time.

In this zone of complex practice, where knowledge and skilful practice remain in the white spaces, the same compelling challenges that face practitioners also arise for researchers who are prepared to venture into the space. So how can we strengthen the capacity of qualitative research to impact on practice in the white spaces? How can qualitative research help us to acquire and use the knowledge, skill and confidence to engage with the white spaces?

Choices about what to do and how to do it in the zone of complexity are the result of processes of judgment made by individuals and groups who must cope with the emotional, ethical and spiritual – as well as the intellectual – dimensions of their choices and actions. Men and women not only engage with the particular, the specific situations of complexity, but over time, integrate knowledge with habit and skill to form their characteristic approaches to complex practice. These are the human challenges facing practitioners and those who contribute to complex practice through research.

THE OPPORTUNITIES FOR QUALITATIVE RESEARCH

It has been argued that qualitative research has a particularly helpful role to play here, that it gives us the means to engage fully with the complete range of human experience and ambition, in a broad range of settings. One of the most influential and seminal writers about research, Gareth Morgan (1983) has said that the most significant research questions need to be lived, and that research itself can be understood as a practice journey. In research, he says, we meet ourselves.

All of this suggests that qualitative research has at least four great opportunities to impact on contemporary practice. The first and most obvious opportunity is to throw light on the substance of issues that reside in the white spaces, to study the dynamics and issues that are in play, and that are the focus of people's energy and effort. The second opportunity is to offer – and perhaps to model – strategies and tools which are helpful in engaging with the human issues we seek to research. These include strategies to hold paradoxical or differing perspectives in creative tension; this is a skill which one could expect to be foremost in the tool-kit of researchers of any kind. The third opportunity is to explore how practice actually develops under conditions of complexity, for better or worse, and to examine how we might assist its development under those conditions. A fourth – and intriguing – opportunity is to throw light on what Weick and Roberts (1993) called decision-awareness.

This means bringing into sharp relief the moments or periods when decisions and choices are being made in practice situations, either implicitly or explicitly, and making them the subject of research. It means shining the light on decision making in the white spaces. These four areas offer critical and pressing opportunities for qualitative researchers. They are all examples of what Schön (1987) called indeterminate zones of practice, characterised by uncertainty, uniqueness, conflict and confusion, contrasting sharply with what he called the canons of technical rationality.

It can be argued, of course, that it is in the zone of complex practice that qualitative research has always made its mark. Qualitative researchers have been prepared to roll up their sleeves and engage with, rather than discount, lived experience, and they have helped practitioners construct theories of, and for, their practice. Qualitative researchers have also demanded what Law (2004, p. 4) called a broader and more generous sense of method: methods that are adapted to the study of the ephemeral, the infinite and the irregular. Qualitative researchers have developed and argued for a wide range of cultures of inquiry, with different but equally defensible truth claims (ontologies) and methods of knowledge creation (epistemologies).

However, qualitative research has also been seriously criticised for the sometimes limited quality of the work undertaken and for the limited effectiveness of its application:

> Several special issues in leading academic journals have highlighted growing concerns that academic research has become less useful for solving practical problems and that the gulf between theory and practice in the professions is widening ... There is also increasing criticism that findings from academic as well as consulting studies are not useful to practitioners and do not get implemented. ... Academics are criticised for not adequately putting their

research into practice. ... Practitioners are criticised for not being aware of relevant research and not doing enough to put their practice into theory. (Van de Ven & Johnson, 2006, p. 802)

These are serious criticisms. It is not the intention here to dwell on the limitations of qualitative research, but rather to explore how qualitative research can rise to the challenges posed by practice in the white spaces.

DESIGNING STRATEGIES FOR ENGAGEMENT WITH THE WHITE SPACES

There has been no shortage of ideas about how to do research in the white spaces. Starting with Ernest Boyer (1990), many have called for a deeper form of research that involves active collaboration between researchers and practitioners who co-produce knowledge on important questions and issues, and learn together. This is rather different from viewing organisations simply as data collection sites and funding sources.

The idea of *engaged scholarship* has been helpfully elaborated by Van de Ven and Johnson (2006), in an attempt to deal with the criticisms previously noted. They first advise us to stay with the big questions or problems, ones that are fuzzy, messy and confusing, They suggest that a good indicator of a big question is that it gets both scholars and practitioners excited – or alarmed. Big questions ask us to stick with real life rather than proxies, to be immersed in experience, get our hands dirty, witness first hand the things that we propose to understand and influence.

Their second suggestion is to deliberately create robust collaborations between people with divergent experiences and perspectives. This means involving insiders and outsiders, people with different knowledge backgrounds, and stakeholders with different and conflicting interests. This contrasts strongly with the common practice of rounding up and interviewing panels of so-called experts who are often chosen for their similarity, convenience of access, or because they represent a particular viewpoint.

Van de Ven and Johnson's third idea is to attempt more extended studies. This can be as basic as taking the time to build personal relationships over time with key players. It can mean gaining a much deeper appreciation of the genealogy and provenance of the framing of the problem or opportunity, and asking: who says it is an issue? why is it an issue now? and for whom? It can mean more longitudinal studies, contrasting with the many particular and disconnected cross-sectional studies that are more common.

Their fourth idea is to spend more time distilling the trends in the literature. They argue that more research needs to be aggregated to form practice-based wisdom through meta-analysis and that more journal space needs to be given to meta-analyses and systematic literature reviews. They point out that such regular consolidation happens in medicine and the law but is lagging behind in other fields. We can't keep expecting PhD students to accomplish in their literature reviews what the disciplines can't manage to do for themselves.

Their fifth idea is to employ what Harrison (1997) has called *intellectual arbitrage*. This is the idea of using dialectical methods of inquiry, where understanding of a problem is built by deliberately testing and contesting divergent ideas and building robust alternative models of any problem or opportunity. Constructive conflict is intrinsic to this kind of inquiry, and, as the authors point out, is very different from detached and consensus dependent approaches. It means highlighting, valuing and learning from the lack of agreement about the phenomenon in question.

This idea of arbitrage might sound a bit idealistic but actually goes to the heart of robust scholarship. Arguably, good scholarship is about holding oppositional ideas in play: not just trying to decide that something is probably true or not, but asking "could it be like this? or like this? or like something completely different again?" Complex practice is full of paradoxical tensions, and holding opposite or different ideas in tension is key to engaging with it. As it happens, that is also what good scholarship is about.

Their last suggestion reprises Morgan's (1983) advice to us from years ago, to focus on designing methodologies that are fit for purpose. In essence, this is about not letting the problems of practice get hijacked by single focus methodologies. And about resisting the temptation to squeeze the research problem into methodologies that don't fit.

Similarly, McWilliam (2004) insisted that design needs to be customised, deeply appreciative of the particular question being framed, the needs (and power base) of end-users of the research, and the constraints of time, place and funding. Attention to research design means careful positioning of the research, asking: will it work here? is it worth it in this case? who does it privilege? who benefits? The present writer suggests that to create useful options for action we might need to design a portfolio of mixed methods, which between them are fit for the purpose. It could mean creating or adapting specific tools with defined and rigorous protocols. Building research approaches and tools is itself a focus for research, and graduate research students can be supported to make original contributions in this way.

In addition to these six ideas, engaged scholarship puts a high value on developing theories of practice, theories for practice and theories from practice. Qualitative research is often accused of being a theory-free zone, with a bias for description rather than explanation. Practitioners are said to be more interested in best practice that actually works, rather than being bothered by why it works.

Although some have taken up the challenge of connecting theory and practice, (Lynn, 1996), this remains a significant challenge. Engaged scholarship asks us to place competing and possible explanations and theoretical frameworks side by side and then compare them. Before we can do that, maybe we need to be more rigorous in asking some basic questions, like: where did that idea come from? why do I do what I do? what theories inform what I do? This requires serious attention to establishing the provenance of ideas: the minds and hands through which they have come into and passed through the world.

ANOTHER IDEA

But as well as the six ideas already mentioned, there is a seventh possibility that is in many respects the most interesting. This is the idea of focusing more qualitative research on that zone of potential decision-awareness to which Weick and Roberts (1993) have drawn attention. This is the point at which the practitioner is making choices – which might be conscious or not – about what to do and how to do it. This is the point at which the attitudes, habits, beliefs, skills and knowledge of the practitioner, however acquired, come together to guide and shape action. Surgeons might need to be exquisitely aware of their decisions moment to moment – at least one hopes they are – but that kind of awareness (or mindfulness, as Weick and Roberts called it) might not be habitual for managers, educators and a vast range of other practitioners.

It is in the space of mindfulness that the opportunity is created to notice, or invent, or choose other options. It is the point at which we might acknowledge that we need to think again, allow ourselves to be buoyantly or optimistically confused in the best Socratic tradition, to enter a time of constructive not-knowing. It is the space of learning, in which new knowledge might be crafted, tested, discussed and disseminated. For researchers to authentically enter this space, they must themselves be mindful.

Different writers have found different words for this space, and some of them are very beautiful words: it is the space in which we are invited to "look again" (Bleakley, 1999) in which "the present becomes remarkable" (Travis, 2002), in which we "make the familiar strange" (Emmett, 1998); it is forgetting the name of the thing one sees (Wechsler, 1982), and it is problematising what we have previously taken for granted.

This space entails a challenge to tacit knowing: to make it explicit. Anne Cunliffe (2002) has studied how managers work and learn in uncertain environments. She suggests that between tacit knowing and explicit knowledge is an area of muddy water in which lurk possibilities for learning, and from which constructing new understanding may open up. She sees learning as a process in which we are "struck" by what is beyond ourselves, even rattled, and then moved to make sense of our experience in different ways. The moment in which we are struck often embodies a trigger for clearing the muddy water.

The writer of this chapter suggests that research has the potential to make it easier for us to recognise and profit from these striking moments. Going even further, research might also involve creating the potential for striking moments to happen. This is not an uncommon approach in action research, but might be something that could be considered by other cultures of inquiry as well, as a deliberate design strategy.

PROTOCOLS FOR RIGOUR IN ENGAGED SCHOLARSHIP

As we have seen, engaged scholarship offers some powerful design strategies for engaging with the wicked and powerful issues that occupy the white – and dark – spaces of knowledge and practice. Such strategies demand equal attention to the protocols that bring rigour to research. To speak of rigour is to go to the heart of many debates about the nature of knowledge and what counts as research. Most cultures of research inquiry have distinctive protocols that articulate (albeit with varying degrees of clarity and agreement) how the research is conducted and how it might be evaluated.

It is contended here that the design strategies of engaged scholarship demand that we revisit, re-examine and articulate what we believe are the sources of academic rigour in qualitative research. This might mean seriously questioning one's own research practice. For this writer, that means transparency about our key assumptions and thinking process right though the research journey, not cleaning up the confusions and messes we encountered and made along the way. It means holding oppositional ideas in play, as already mentioned.

It means articulating our protocols at the start and then evaluating how well they worked and how much we held to them along the way. And it means contextualising our work in a helpful way, highlighting what triggered the researcher's interest, the social context which framed the language and key constructs being used, and the genealogy of the issues. It also means establishing the connection between a particular phenomenon and other system dynamics in which it is embedded. This is the critical skill of being able to "zoom in" and "zoom out", like the skilled weavers of tapestry who must work in fine detail in close-up and also walk away and view the entire work from a distance.

Engaged research also demands a deeply ethical stance, one that that goes deeper than just filling out the form for ethics approval. We need to live the question ethically, examine our values and particularly the value bases of what we think we "know" and how we come to know it. McWilliam (2004) noted that postmodernism has shifted the discussion from: what is the nature of reality? to: what is the nature of my interest in it? That's a different framing of what it is to be objective. McWilliam also suggested that we need to accommodate both interest and disinterest in the one design. Disinterest can be helpful to us, allowing us to be untroubled by other people's praise or blame or disturbance, rising above seeking to please.

This space of ethical and technical rigour has been claimed by ideas like reflexivity and critical subjectivity, the notion that despite our being socially constructed we can be capable of thinking and acting in ways that challenge particular or local constructions. In one of the great formulations of critical subjectivity, Bleakley (1999) asks us to develop an individual and collective consciousness about how we "are" in the world that is both critical and holistic; that is, reflexive (able to think against itself), ethical, aesthetic, worldly (rather than personal) and ecological or sensitive to difference. And as a result we can learn in richer ways how develop our culture and our private and public discourse.

IN CONCLUSION: THE RESEARCH CHALLENGE

Being able to engage with the unfamiliar, the complex and the frightening, in ways that are not dysfunctional, being able to learn from a position of not-knowing: these are demanding capabilities. To be creative and enjoy the space in the research process seems to be asking a lot. As suggested at the start of this chapter, this is the space in which we can regress as well as grow. It is a space that requires practice, experience and mental effort. In 1987, 20 years ago, Schein predicted that we would need to wait until a generation of practitioner/scholars had been trained in appropriate skills before we could hope to fully engage with the complex issues of change and practice.

The European Community's expert group (see Knight & Page, 2007) looking at higher education and research has proposed that researchers should have a set of core competencies. These include reasoning, critical thinking, problem setting and problem solving of various kinds, creativity and curiosity, team-working and collaboration, information handling, working across subject boundaries, trans-disciplinary practices, leading and being entrepreneurial, ethical practices, and leading and facilitating conversation and communicating in diverse forums.

That list looks a lot like the skills of master practitioners in many domains of practice. If the qualities and tools needed for effective engagement with complex practice day-to-day, month-to-month and year-to-year are similar to the ones needed to research them, then it's fair to ask: what can researchers learn from master practitioners? This stands in contrast to the more commonly asked question: what can researchers teach practitioners? Sustained and deep engagement with the juicy and wicked dilemmas and opportunities of the white spaces through qualitative research gives us the way to do justice to both questions.

NOTES

[1] This usage of the term "white spaces" is not to be confused with the unused White Space spectrum between TV channels.

REFERENCES

Bleakley, A. (1999). From reflective practice to holistic reflexivity. *Studies in Higher Education*, 24(3), 315–330.
Boyer, E. L. (1990). *Scholarship reconsidered: Priorities of the professoriate*. Princeton, NJ: Carnegie Foundation.
Cherry, N. L. (2008). Symbolic self curation: A reflexive activity for practice, life and scholarship. *Creative Approaches to Research*, 1(1), 19–37.
Conklin, J. (2003). *Dialog mapping: An approach for wicked problems*. Chichester: Wiley.
Cunliffe, A. (2002). Reflexive dialogical practice in management learning. *Management Learning*, 33(1), 35–61.
Emmet, P. (1998). *Janet Laurence: Gatherings*. Sydney: Craftsman House.
Freed, G. (1992). *Fifth generation innovation*. Occasional Paper, Australian Centre for Innovation and International Competitiveness, The University of Sydney.
Harrison, P. (1997.) A history of an intellectual arbitrage: The evolution of financial economics. *History of Political Economy*, 29(4), 172–187.
Knight, P., Page, A., & Knight, P. T. (2007). *The assessment of 'wicked' competencies Report to the Practice-based Professional Learning Centre*. Retrieved November 27, 2008, from http://www.open.ac.uk/pbpl/activities/details/detail.php?itemId=460a62435af49&themeId=460299b584ed5
Law, J. (2004). *After method: Mess in social science research*. London: Routledge.
Lynn, M. (1996). Negotiating practice theory (or, I've got the theory, you've got the practice). In J. Fook (Ed.), *The reflective researcher*. St Leonards, NSW: Allen and Unwin.
McWilliam, E. (2004). W(h)ither practitioner research? *The Australian Educational Researcher*, 31(2), 113–126.
Morgan, G. (Ed.). (1983). *Beyond method: Strategies for social research*. Beverley Hills, CA: Sage.
Oliver, R. W. (2000). *The coming bio-tech age: The business of bio-material*. New York: McGraw-Hill.
Perkins, D. (2006). Constructivism and troublesome knowledge. In J. Meyer & R. Land (Eds.), *Overcoming barriers to student understanding: Threshold concepts and troublesome knowledge*. Oxford: Routledge Farmer.

Schein, E. H. (1987). *The clinical perspective in fieldwork*. Newbury Park, CA: Sage.
Schön, D. A. (1987). *Educating the reflective practitioner*. San Francisco: Jossey-Bass.
Travis, T. (2002). Print and the creation of middlebrow culture. In S. E. Casper, J. D. Chaison, & J. D. Groves (Eds.), *Perspectives on American book history: Artefacts and commentary*. Amherst, MA: University of Massachusetts Press.
Van de Ven, A., & Johnson, P. (2006). Knowledge for theory and practice. *Academy of Management Review, 31*(4), 802–821.
Wechsler, L. (1982). *Seeing is forgetting the name of the thing one sees: A life of contemporary artist Robert Irwin*. Berkeley, CA: University of California Press.
Weick, K., & Roberts, K. (1993). Collective mind in organisations: Heedful interrelating on flight decks. *Administrative Science Quarterly, 38*, 357–381.

AFFILIATION

Nita Cherry PhD
Faculty of Business and Enterprise
Swinburne University of Technology
Australia

STEPHEN LOFTUS AND RODD ROTHWELL

3. THE ORIGINS OF QUALITATIVE RESEARCH:

The Importance of Philosophy

INTRODUCTION

The field of qualitative research is large, is used in several academic disciplines and encompasses a range of distinctive approaches. However, in this chapter we attempt to provide a brief overview of the development of qualitative research, together with a summary of what we regard as some of the key trends and issues that have characterised developments within the field over the years. In our opinion many of these issues arise from philosophical differences and, therefore, we devote some attention to exploring these differences.

Qualitative research is named as such to contrast it with quantitative research. Briefly, this is the difference between a focus on text as opposed to a focus on numbers. For many years now, a lot of people have associated serious scholarly research exclusively with the kinds of activity that occur in laboratories or via mass surveys and questionnaires. Such laboratory-type research generally produces numerical (quantitative) data that can be mathematically and statistically interrogated. In contrast, qualitative research generally produces data in the form of texts. Occasionally qualitative data can be in the form of text analogues, such as artworks or performances.

Beyond this it is often said that the major difference between the two approaches is that quantitative data is used to measure and *explain* the mechanics of how some phenomenon works, so that cause/effect relationships can be established. On the other hand, qualitative data is interpretive and aims at understanding a particular phenomenon in greater depth so that it becomes more meaningful.

However, even this differentiation can be a source of controversy. Scholars such as Gergen (2009) argue that seeing the world in terms of cause/effect relationships is already to assume that we live in a mechanistic Newtonian universe where everything must be seen in cause/effect terms. As Gergen points out, there are other ways of conceptualising the world around us. These controversies have typified the differences between quantitative and qualitative approaches to research for many years.

THE LEGACY OF DESCARTES

The origins of the qualitative/quantitative debate can be traced to the work of Descartes in the seventeenth century (1637/1968). Descartes sought to find a firm base for indubitable knowledge. In his famous *Meditations* (1641/2009) his goal was to subject every thought and so-called accepted truth to a process of radical doubt, with the view of arriving at certain and indubitable knowledge. The outcome of this doubting process is summed up in his famous oft quoted dictum "Cogito ergo sum" (*I think therefore I am*) or to paraphrase, all one can be absolutely sure of is the fact that one is a thinking thing. This "thinking thing" Descartes related to spirit or mind or the mental, and it was of a different order to that of the material world. So he proposed that there were in fact two realms of being: the material word and the spiritual or mental world, and each required its own means of investigation – the mind revealed through an act of thought of one's consciousness, and the material world identifiable or revealed by means of mathematical formulae, themselves creations of God.

Descartes gave the world dualism and it has dogged philosophers of science ever since, though with remarkable results that have made possible the technological advances of the modern world. However, it can be argued that this technological success has also seduced many people into thinking that all scholarly inquiry must therefore be based on mathematical measurement. Some good examples of materialist dualism can be found within the field of academic psychology.

In the Western world during the twentieth century, psychology was dominated by behaviourism and its successor, cognitivism. The proponents of both were of the firm opinion that a quantitative approach was the only valid and scientific way of advancing the study of psychology. However, throughout the twentieth century a growing number of voices have criticised this Cartesian approach. For example, the great, Russian psychologist Vygotsky pointed out that an experimental approach misconceived and distorted much of importance.

> Blind transportation of the experiment, the mathematical method from the natural sciences, created in psychology the outward appearances of science, under which, in reality was hidden a complete powerlessness before the phenomena under study. (Vygotsky, cited in Van der Veer & Valsiner, 1991, p. 149)

The philosopher Wittgenstein (1958) expressed similar sentiments to Vygotsky when he said that an experimental and quantitative approach misunderstood the very phenomenon being studied and distorted it in order to force it to fit into a laboratory setting. Examples of this are the numerous attempts to "measure" clinical reasoning skill (for a critique of this field see Loftus, 2009). Wittgenstein went further, pointing out that the foundations of the mathematical method, so dear to the quantitative approach, are not the numbers that appear to offer so much stability and security but mathematical axioms (Wittgenstein, 1956/1978). Axioms are statements in language and as such are open to interpretation.

It is possible to combine quantitative and qualitative methods in research, and such mixed methods can be powerful research tools. However, it is important to realise that the marriage between the two is not without problems because of the underlying philosophical differences and assumptions. What often seems to happen is that a research project will include some interviews or focus groups to clarify the findings from mass surveys. Qualitative research in these circumstances has been subsumed within the quantitative approach to measure and explain cause/effect mechanisms, without any clear understanding of what each approach truly offers.

EARLY DEVELOPMENTS

The 1920s and 1930s saw a number of developments that made many people begin to question the Cartesian approach to scholarly inquiry within the social world, where people can be expected to make sense of their circumstances. For example, there was the well-known Hawthorne effect that defied explanation from a strictly mechanistic and Cartesian approach to inquiry. Between 1924 and 1932 a number of experiments aimed at improving worker productivity were conducted at the Western Electric Company in Hawthorne, Chicago (Roethlisberger & Dickson, 1964). The results were confusing because no matter how the many variables were manipulated worker productivity improved.

It can be argued that these quantitative experiments showed that a simplistic and reductionist approach failed to engage with the meaning and the interpretations the workers made of being in an experimental situation. A more interpretive approach could have been expected to open up inquiry in a way that would begin with the assumption that human workers have agency and the ability to make sense of their role within experimental settings rather than simply behave like rats in a maze responding simplistically to a change in stimulus.

It was during this time that the most reductionist of the sciences, physics, began to accept that the role of the observer could profoundly affect the outcome of an observation. In quantum mechanics Heisenberg's uncertainty principle compelled physicists to question the very possibility of prediction based on accurate measurement. With a growing number of misgivings such as these, an increasing number of scholars in the social sciences began to look for alternative ways of conducting research that would not be subject to the distortions and assumptions of the quantitative approach.

Grbich (1999) wrote of two periods in the history of qualitative research. The first, before 1965, was strongly influenced by anthropology. Anthropology has traditionally been a discipline that documented primitive societies (e.g. Malinowski, 1923). Anthropologists would do this, not by conducting experiments, but by spending extended periods of time immersed in those societies, participating as much as possible in an attempt to understand how those societies worked "from the inside", from the viewpoint of the local people who made up these societies.

The result would be an ethnography that documented the findings in detail. This approach has now been taken up in modified form by many other qualitative researchers more generally, where it is often referred to as participant observation. Modern variants include critical ethnographies that focus on power relationships and postmodern ethnographies that focus on how the discourse of a community shapes the ways participants understand what is going on. It was gradually realised that the ethnographic approach could be used by researchers who wanted to look at any social setting. By adopting such an attitude and approach to Western societies and "making the familiar strange", investigators began to produce insights that would be missed by a purely quantitative approach (e.g. Katz, 1998, in medical anthropology).

The so-called Chicago School was notable for adopting and popularising ethnographic methods in the 1920s and 1930s, when they were used to study urban sociology and later criminology. Also in the United States, at Columbia University in New York, Paul Lazarsfeld developed a range of well-known qualitative methods and data analysis techniques. For example, Lazarsfeld invented the focus group. These qualitative techniques were used in the fledgling discipline of communication studies, but were quickly taken up and popularised by the marketing industry as a means of establishing what people liked and wanted. They are still widely used today in these settings.

LATER DEVELOPMENTS

Grbich (1999) described a distinctive shift in the mid-1960s in people's attitude to qualitative research. This period saw the publication of a number of significant texts that did much to question the dominance of the Cartesian approach to inquiry. In 1962 Thomas Kuhn published the first of several editions of his book *The structure of scientific revolutions* (1962/1996). This book caused a sensation at the time and for a short time outsold the bible. Kuhn introduced the notion of paradigms and paradigm shift. The essential idea is that scientific activity is conducted from within a paradigm with its own discourse. A paradigm is the set of assumptions, beliefs and practices that form the foundation of inquiry. The paradigm provides the theoretical lens with which the world is examined. Scientific inquiry is guided by the theoretical foundations of the paradigm and these are not questioned by scientists working within the paradigm.

Kuhn considered that adherence to the theoretical givens of the paradigm made scientific work (normal science) possible, as without it scientific work would be random. The paradigm, in a sense, determines what kinds of research question are acceptable and what acceptable answers might look like. Kuhn claimed that over time anomalies would occur that were incompatible within the paradigm. A paradigm shift was said to occur when so many anomalies accumulated within a paradigm that there was a relatively sudden and radical change to a completely new way of thinking, a new paradigm. Kuhn also maintained that when scientists undergo such a paradigm shift they themselves talk of life after this experience as being like living in a new world.

In discussing Kuhn's notion of paradigm shift, Geertz (2000, p. 163) mentioned that "scientific change does not consist in a relentless approach to a waiting truth but in the rollings and pitchings of disciplinary communities". This is a profound challenge to the Cartesian assumption that measurement and application of scientific method guarantee pure unadulterated versions of the truth. It is a challenge because, for a long time, many scientists have believed that the scientific method allows them to research reality in a "pure" form, with no contamination from culture or subjective judgments made by the observers. Kuhn's notion of paradigm challenges this idea, insisting that reality is always seen through the theoretical lens provided by the paradigm. There is no question of the facts speaking for themselves. The facts always need to be interpreted and they will always be interpreted through the lens of the paradigm. More than this, there is an implication that what counts as a fact in the first place is also determined by the paradigm. Therefore, inquiry is always value-bound; there are no neutral interpretations. Kuhn's paradigms have much in common with the notion of tradition as used by Gadamer.

About the same time as Kuhn published the first edition of *The structure of scientific revolutions*, Hans-Georg Gadamer published the first edition of his own magnum opus *Truth and method* (1960/1989). There is more on Gadamer elsewhere in this book (see Chapter 20). He criticised the prevailing Cartesian idea that rigorous scientific method was guaranteed to produce something called the truth. Like Kuhn, Gadamer pointed out that our pre-existing beliefs, our tradition, strongly shaped what could be seen as legitimate inquiry. Gadamer's work can be seen as part of an ongoing philosophical response to the domination of Cartesianism, beginning with the development of phenomenology by Husserl in the early 20th century (Husserl, 1931).

Husserl sought to bring philosophy back to the human world from abstract metaphysical speculation and from domination by the physical sciences and into contact with the interacting human world by exploring the way the world is experienced by human beings or by human consciousness. Husserl's idea was that human consciousness is not, as Descartes would have it, unrelated and of a different order to the material world of matter, but is always, even before one reflects upon it, in fundamental contact with the material world. Consciousness was not, for Husserl, a thing in itself but always consciousness of something – one is not just conscious but one is conscious of some *thing*. One is always interacting with the world even before one is aware of it. As Merleau-Ponty (1962) described it, Husserl's phenomenology tries to give a direct description of our experience as it is, without taking account of its psychological origins or the causal explanations which the scientist, the historian or the sociologist might be able to provide. According to Husserl, phenomenology is an attempt to establish the structure and meaning of experience, which in turn can lead to a clearer understanding of the phenomena in question. There is consequently a vast range of phenomena that phenomenology can examine, which is why it has become a popular means of conducting qualitative research (see Chapter 21).

Phenomenology has branched off in many different directions since Husserl's time and many of these branches have become popular foundations for many qualitative research projects. There is the hermeneutic phenomenology of Heidegger (1927/1996), which has been used to produce useful insights into expertise in nursing care (Benner, 1984). Svenaeus (2000) used Heidegger's hermeneutic phenomenology to explore the experience of health and Gadamer's philosophical hermeneutics to explore the practice of medicine. Loftus (2009) used philosophical hermeneutics as a foundation to explore clinical reasoning. Gadamer placed much emphasis on the linguisticality of human experience. In other words, Gadamer emphasised the importance of language in shaping the theoretical lenses humans use to interpret what they experience. By using these insights, Loftus showed the extent to which clinical reasoning depends on skills with language such as the ability to use rhetoric and narrative forms.

Other qualitative research approaches based on phenomenology include disciplines as diverse as ethnomethodology (Garfinkel, 1967), conversation analysis (Sacks & Jefferson, 1992a, 1992b) and phenomenography (Marton & Booth, 1997). Phenomenography, for example, has proved to be enormously popular within educational circles, and is used to explore and articulate the common misunderstandings people develop of a phenomenon they are studying. It has a practical goal of providing insights that can then be used to customise education that will target the common misconceptions people are likely to have and so make education more effective.

Another well-known and popular qualitative research approach that began in the 1960s is grounded theory (Glaser, 1967), developed by Barney Glaser and Anselm Strauss as a means of "grounding" theoretical perspectives within data from the empirical world. According to Grbich (1999) it is highly likely that the phenomenological tradition was a strong influence, together with the Husserlian concept of "back to the things themselves". In other words, any new theory development must be clearly related to data gathered from the social world. Grbich traces the theoretical underpinnings of grounded theory to the work of scholars such as John Dewey and George Mead. Dewey (1934, 1937) was concerned to emphasise links between the involvement and interaction of the researcher with who and what was being researched.

Mead (1934) provided a social philosophy that emphasised the location of human experience within social interaction. This philosophy was later termed *symbolic interactionism* because it focuses on the ways in which people use signs, symbols and language to construct meaning. Grounded theory is currently popular but is not without its critics. It has been claimed that in practice it places too much emphasis on technique and is therefore not too different from the positivist science it seeks to replace, and that it is sometimes used to reaffirm the biases of the researcher rather than generate new theory (Grbich, 1999).

Other approaches to qualitative research that began to become popular in the 1960s were those based upon postmodernism and poststructuralism. Post-modernism is essentially a reaction to modernism, where modernism is seen as the view that there is one (usually Cartesian and scientific) best way of viewing any phenomenon or issue. The postmodern view is that there are many voices that can have different and equally valid views on many issues. For example, in the world of healthcare a modernist view would be that the biomedical and scientific view of the doctor is paramount. A postmodern view is that the voices of patients and their families, carers and other health professions need to be taken into account (e.g. Morris, 1998). Patients might not have the scientific understanding of a doctor but can be expected to have important views on their illness experience and what it means to them. There are clear parallels here with other approaches to qualitative research, such as the anthropological, the phenomenological and those based on narrative inquiry. These issues become important in cases such as end-of-life care and the care of people with chronic disease. For example, it was clear from research in a clinic that managed chronic pain that the health professionals working there recognised that they would have no success with many patients unless they made efforts to find out what meaning patients attached to their pain (Loftus, 2009). It was also clear to the same health professionals that the management of these patients needed to include a lot of time, effort and resources to directly addressing the meanings that patients associated with their health problems. The simplistic application of biomedical procedures alone would invite failure. The postmodern view can also include research into power relations. To stay with the healthcare example, a postmodern approach might address the financial constraints placed on the provision of care by budget holders. This opens up an important dimension of inquiry in a world where the provision of healthcare might be seen as determined by strictly biomedical considerations.

Closely related to postmodernism is poststructuralism (see Chapter 28), which arose as a reaction against structuralism. Ferdinand de Saussure (1916/1983) developed structuralism, wherein language was seen as an abstract system of signs. The word, written or spoken, was the signifier, with a relation to a concept or meaning called the signified. A common example to illustrate the difference is the use of the terms "morning star" and "evening star". Both are signifiers that appear quite opposed to each other, but both refer to the same signified, the planet Venus.

During the 1960s and 1970s poststructuralism was developed by a number of theorists, most notably Jacques Derrida (1982). The poststructural challenge was to the fixed meaning of signs. The poststructuralists pointed out that in different contexts meanings can change dramatically, and therefore claimed that there was a need for deconstruction to expose the hidden discourses and power relations at play. A potential influence on poststructuralism is the later work of Wittgenstein, not published until the 1950s, in which Wittgenstein wrote of the different forms of life (contexts) in which humans live, each with its own particular language game (Wittgenstein, 1958). The meanings of words can vary from one language game to another.

Closely related to the postmodern and poststructural approaches is critical theory. The critical approach has been described as a distinct paradigm (Higgs, 1997). Higgs described three paradigms of research. One is the quantitative, that seeks to measure. The second is the interpretivist, that seeks to understand, and the third is the critical, that seeks to illuminate power relations with the aim of moving towards a more just society. The origins of critical theory go back to Karl Marx (1906). The critical theory approach became established as a distinctive research tradition at the so-called Frankfurt School, which was based in the Institute for Social Research, in 1924. Well-known names associated with this organisation are Max Horkheimer and Theodor Adorno (1972). The institute was associated with Marxism, but the degree to which the Frankfurt School can be said to be truly Marxist has been debated ever since (see Crotty, 1998).

Jürgen Habermas is another well-known scholar within the critical theory, publishing a landmark book *Knowledge and human interests* (1972). Habermas saw critical theory as a form of reflective self-knowledge that sought to free people from the strictures of culture and society. Here, there is a strong emphasis on power relations between people in different sections of society, which can provide powerful insights. For example, persuading young people not to smoke is often seen as an exercise in providing information about the dangers of smoking to health. However, Trede and Higgs (2003) reflected upon the use of a critical theory approach to research, and pointed out that research needs to look at the reasons behind behaviour. For example, the reason many young people take up smoking could well be a gesture of resistance and independence, in which case additional health education would probably be a waste of time and resources.

DISCUSSION

The distinction between qualitative and quantitative method in science is now accepted by most of the scientific community. In general, we no longer hear very much of past prejudices such as "hard" versus "soft" science or objective versus subjective. The distinction is based on the old Cartesian notion that mathematical formulae somehow provide God-given access to the workings of the material world and that the human mind is notoriously treacherous and misleads us about the way things are in that world. We can study the human world in many ways that do not deny the existence of a subjective world. However, there is an attitude that human behaviour can be studied only by reference to the action of the brain and other biological phenomena. That approach has sometimes been labelled "scientism" or "reductionism" and is underpinned by the desire to eliminate reference to any non-materialist phenomenon, or even to reduce all subjective phenomena to objectively identifiable processes. However, it can be argued that in doing so science goes far beyond its legitimate area of inquiry.

Many philosophers and thinkers such as Davidson (1984) and Rorty (1991) saw no problem in describing human behaviour in terms of several different and valid explanations of the same process. On the one hand we can understand human actions on the basis of their objective states or (simplistically perhaps) as brain states. Such an approach will surely provide valuable information about human action. On the other hand, we can understand why human beings act in certain ways by asking them what motivates them and why they do what they do, and we can also observe them interacting with others. This, as we know, can provide valuable knowledge for understanding people and for improving their conditions of life.

To accept the notion of several valid explanations of an identical form of behaviour means we can escape charges of reductionism and of soft science, because both can be seen to have their legitimate place in the study of human behaviour and human society. This approach may also open up the future possibility of some sort of interaction between the two.

However, despite these observations there is currently in existence, especially in the area of the health sciences, the notion of a hierarchy of scientific methodology. In many formulations of evidence-based practice (EBP) what is presented is a list that places methodologies into hierarchies as a basis for ranking research evidence in terms of objectivity, rigour, etc. For example, the Australian National Health and

Medical Research Council claims that research evidence may vary in level, quality, relevance and strength. It adds that these factors are important in considering the weight or degree of confidence given to particular research evidence. On the surface, this is obviously correct and good advice. However, the point goes beyond the ranking of any research in terms of its methodological soundness and rigour – it is implied that soundness and rigour are inherent in certain methodological practices or study designs and by implication not in others.

Although research evidence is only one component of EBP, what is rarely discussed anywhere is the basis of this research hierarchy – it is taken as a given not requiring any justification. This assumption is inherent in a philosophical position (positivism) that conflates its quantitative methodology with the methodology of science. In our opinion, this seems to be a common assumption among many EBP writers, despite the fact that most scientists and nearly all philosophers of science have long ago written off positivism as logically invalid as well as methodologically and historically incorrect (e.g. Feyerabend, 1975).

Denzin and Lincoln (2005) described the backlash against EBP as being part of the last of eight *moments* of qualitative research, that range from the "traditional" through to the "fractured future" (p. 3). Their interpretation of the history of qualitative research explores a range of sociopolitical aspects. It is quite clear from their discussion that qualitative research has always been controversial, even if only in hindsight. For example, they argue that much early anthropology and sociology (the first or traditional moment) was used as a basis to exploit colonised peoples and provided some intellectual justification for racism. Denzin and Lincoln further argue that the current moment (the fractured future) is concerned with a wider agenda that seeks to provide a forum for "critical conversations about democracy, race, gender, class, nation-states, globalization, freedom, and community" (p. 3). In this chapter we have focused most of our attention on the origins of qualitative research from a philosophical perspective.

It is also possible to discuss the same origins of qualitative research from a sociopolitical perspective, which would have a quite different emphasis. The point, made earlier by Davidson (1984) and Rorty (1991), is that all forms of knowledge are devised for particular purposes, whether quantitative, qualitative or critical/ sociopolitical. It is important to be clear from the beginning exactly what purpose a research project is meant to achieve, whether it is to explain, to understand, to liberate, or to do something else entirely. It is worth remembering the warning of Harré (1978), who pointed out that all too often what looks like a mistake in methodology is actually due to a deep confusion about the nature of the phenomenon being researched. That is why it is so important to have some understanding of the philosophical basis and the origins of any research approach.

REFERENCES

Benner, P. (1984). *From novice to expert: Excellence and power in clinical nursing.* Reading, MA: Addison-Wesley.

Crotty, M. (1998). *The foundations of social research: Meaning and perspective in the research process.* Sydney: Allen & Unwin.

Davidson, D. (1984). *Inquiries into truth and interpretation*. New York: Oxford University Press.
Denzin, N. K., & Lincoln, Y. S. (2005). Introduction: The discipline and practice of qualitative research. In N. K. Denzin & Y. S. Lincoln (Eds.), *The SAGE handbook of qualitative research* (pp. 1–32). Thousand Oaks, CA: Sage.
Derrida, J. (1982). *Margins of philosophy* (A. Boss, Trans.). Chicago: University of Chicago Press.
de Saussure, F. (1916/1983). *Course in general linguistics* (R. Harris, Trans.). London: Duckworth.
Descartes, R. (1637/1968). *Discourses on method and other writings* (R. Kennington, Trans.). Harmondsworth: Penguin.
Descartes, R. (1641/2009). *Meditations on first philosophy*. New York: Classic Books America.
Dewey, J. (1934). *Arts as experience*. New York: Minton Baloch.
Dewey, J. (1937). *Logic: The theory and inquiry*. New York: John Wiley.
Feyerabend, P. (1975). *Against method*. London: Verso.
Gadamer, H.-G. (1960/1989). *Truth and method* (J. Weinsheimer & D. G. Marshall, Trans., 2nd Rev. ed.). New York: Continuum.
Garfinkel, H. (1967). *Studies in ethnomethodology*. Engelwood Cliffs, NJ: Prentice Hall.
Geertz, C. (2000). *Available light: Anthropological reflections on philosophical topics*. Princeton, NJ: Princeton University Press.
Gergen, K. (2009). *Relational being: Beyond self and community*. Oxford: Oxford University Press.
Glaser, B. (1967). *The discovery of grounded theory: Strategies for qualitative research*. New York: Aldine.
Grbich, C. (1999). *Qualitative research in health: An introduction*. Sydney: Allen & Unwin.
Habermas, J. (1972). *Knowledge and human interests* (J. J. Shapiro, Trans.). Toronto: Beacon Press.
Harré, R. (1978). Accounts, actions, and meanings - The practice of participatory psychology. In M. Brenner, P. Marsh, & M. Brenner (Eds.), *The social contexts of method* (pp. 44–66). London: Croom Helm.
Heidegger, M. (1927/1996). *Being and time* (J. Stambaugh, Trans.). Albany, New York: State University of New York Press.
Higgs, J. (1997). *Qualitative research: Discourse on methodologies*. Sydney: Hampden Press.
Horkheimer, M., & Adorno, T. (1972). *Dialectic of enlightenment*. New York: Continuum.
Husserl, E. (1931). *Ideas: General introduction to pure phenomenology*. London: George Allen & Unwin.
Katz, P. (1998). *The scalpel's edge: The culture of surgeons*. Boston: Allyn & Bacon.
Kuhn, T. (1996). *The structure of scientific revolutions* (3rd ed.). Chicago: University of Chicago Press.
Loftus, S. (2009). *Language in clinical reasoning: Towards a new understanding*. Saarbrücken, Germany: Vdm Verlag Dr. Müller.
Malinowski, B. (1923). The problem of meaning in primitive languages. In C. K. Ogden & I. A. Richards (Eds.), *The meaning of meaning* (pp. 296–336). New York: Harcourt, Brace and World.
Marton, F., & Booth, S. (1997). *Learning and awareness*. Mahwah, NJ: Lawrence Erlbaum.
Marx, K. (1906). *Capital: A critique of political economy: The process of capitalist production* (S. Moore & E. Aveling, Trans.). New York: Modern Library.
Mead, G. (1934). *Mind, self and society*. Chicago: University of Chicago Press.
Merleau-Ponty, M. (1962, English translation). *Phenomenology of perception*. Routledge.
Morris, D. B. (1998). *Illness and culture in the postmodern age*. Berkeley, CA: University of California Press.
Roethlisberger, F., & Dickson, W. (1964). *Management and the worker: An account of a research program conducted by the Western Electric Company, Hawthorne Works, Chicago*. Cambridge: Harvard University Press.
Rorty, R. (1991). *Objectivity, relativism and truth*. Cambridge University Press.
Sacks, H., & Jefferson, G. (1992a). *Lectures on conversation* (Vol. 1). Oxford: Blackwell.
Sacks, H., & Jefferson, G. (1992b). *Lectures on conversation* (Vol. 2). Oxford: Blackwell.
Svenaeus, F. (2000). *The hermeneutics of medicine and the phenomenology of health: Steps towards a philosophy of medical practice*. Dordrecht: Kluwer Academic.

Trede, F., & Higgs, J. (2003). Reframing the clinician's role in collaborative clinical decision making: Rethinking practice knowledge and the notion of clinician-patient relationships. *Learning in Health and Social Care, 2*(2), 66–73.

Van der Veer, R., & Valsiner, J. (1991). *Understanding Vygotsky: A quest for synthesis.* Cambridge: Blackwell.

Wittgenstein, L. (1958). *Philosophical investigations* (G.E.M. Anscombe, Trans., 3rd ed.). Upper Saddle River, NJ: Prentice Hall.

Wittgenstein, L. (1956/1978). *Remarks on the foundations of mathematics* (G. E. M. (Anscombe, Trans., Rev. ed.). Boston: MIT Press.

AFFILIATIONS

Stephen Loftus PhD
The Education ForPractice Institute
Charles Sturt University
Australia

Rodd Rothwell PhD
Faculty of Health Sciences
The University of Sydney
Australia

JOY HIGGS AND FRANZISKA TREDE

4. PHILOSOPHICAL FRAMEWORKS AND RESEARCH COMMUNITIES

Research is a means of generating knowledge; it is framed by the positions and practices adopted by different research communities and cultures of inquiry. In this chapter we commence with an analysis of the nature of research as knowledge making and proceed to discuss the nature of the philosophical frameworks and research communities or traditions that guide research. We take the position that ways of knowing differ in the natural, social, and critical science fields and that these ways of knowing are influenced by the motivations, interests, values and world views of researchers, research communities and research cultures.

WORLD VIEWS – ONTOLOGIES

To do research – to generate knowledge – a key initial question we need to address is: What can we know? This question leads on to further questions: What is reality? What is our/my world view? In philosophy these questions comprise the field of ontology. In qualitative research, ontology, or what can be known, is socially constructed, dialogued, experienced or perceived by people. This ontological stance asks researchers to use words and images to describe and interpret experiences and perceptions of their lived worlds. In Figure 4.1 we present five ontological perspectives that underpin different research approaches.

The five perspectives on world views with relevance to research are critical, social constructivist, hermeneutic, constructivist, and positivist/empiricist. Each emphasises a different ontological stance. The critical perspective focuses on understanding the world through social interests, whereas the constructivist perspective focuses on reality being constructed through people's experiences and perceptions. The social constructivist perspective focuses on meaning making and claims that reality is constructed by historical and social influences. A hermeneutic perspective represents knowing through being in the world rather than separating people and nature; both are seen in an interdependent relationship. In contrast, positivist/empiricist ontology separates people from nature and claims that the world is objective and exists independently of people knowing about it.

Critical theory focuses on the social world: people are socially located, knowledge is always influenced by social interest (Habermas, 1968/1972).	The hermeneutic view arises from the ideas of Heidegger (1962), Merleau-Ponty (1956) and Gadamer (1975). Knowing is seen as a kind of being, as a concrete form of being-in-the-world and as pragmatic, involved activity or "know-how" that is more basic than, and that occurs prior to, reflective thinking. This knowing is embedded in unarticulated common meanings and shared background practices of groups of people. This knowing has no mental representation and may be embodied, that is, known by the body without cognition. This view of people and the world is a relational one (Benner & Wrubel, 1989).	In the constructivist view, knowers are seen as conscious subjects separate from a world of objects; subjects who use knowledge, who have theories about their practice and who behave according to tacit rules and procedures. In qualitative research, in general, multiple constructed realities are recognised to occur (i.e. different people have different perceptions of reality through their attribution of meaning to events, meaning being part of the event, not separate from it) (Lincoln & Guba, 1985).
The social constructivist view is that reality and knowledge are socially constructed. That is, reality exists because we give meaning to it (Berger & Luckmann, 1985). Different cultures have different social constructions of reality. Within the interpretive tradition, the world and reality are interpreted by people in the context of historical and social practices.	In the positivist/empiricist research tradition, the world is objective, since it is said to exist independently of the knowers, and it consists of phenomena or events which are orderly and lawful.	

*Figure 4.1. Various ontological perspectives
(from Higgs, 2001; Higgs, Trede, & Rothwell, 2007).*

EPISTEMOLOGIES

Building upon researchers' world views we can ask the following epistemological questions: How can what exists be known? What means can I use to access this world as I know and frame it? In qualitative research, epistemology, or how can we know something, is based on the position that we can know and understand phenomena through experiences and dialogues with others that lead to meaning making. Figure 4.2 presents various epistemological perspectives. Some ontological perspectives invite certain epistemological approaches, while ruling out others. For example, empiricist researchers accept that the world exists independently of people experiencing or discussing it; thus adopting dialogues and lived experiences as an epistemological strategy would be rejected by these researchers. The seven text boxes in Figure 4.2 represent epistemological stances in various philosophical traditions. These examples emphasise that each philosophical tradition guides researchers to different tools for exploring ways of knowing. For example, historical realism, which belongs to the critical paradigm, understands the world through historical, political, and socio-economical lenses and the way these lenses

PHILOSOPHICAL FRAMEWORKS

The (historical) realist is concerned with social structures, and how macro- and micro-political, historical, and socio-economic factors influence our lives and how we understand our lives.	Constructivists view knowledge as "an internal construction or an attempt to impose meaning and significance on events and ideas". In this perspective "each person constructs a more-or-less idiosyncratic explanatory system of reality" (Candy, 1991, p. 251).	The social constructionist approach (McCarthy, 1996) construes knowledge as a changing and relative phenomenon and examines the social and historical constructs of knowledge in terms of what knowledge is socially produced and what counts as knowledge.
To positivists or empiricists, knowledge arises from the rigorous application of the scientific method and is measured against the criteria of objectivity, reliability and validity.		

The idealist approaches of Dilthey (1833–1911) and Weber (1864–1920) focused on interpretive understanding (Verstehen), accessing the ideas and experiences of actors, as opposed to the explanatory and predictive approach of the physical sciences (Smith, 1983). Dilthey presented understanding as a hermeneutic process involving constant movement between parts and whole. This perspective results in a focus on human behaviour as occurring within a context, and the understanding or knowledge of human behaviour are considered to require an understanding of this context.

Three strands of feminist epistemology have been identified (Schwandt, 1997): (a) feminist empiricism – knowledge arises from experiential or observational data and seeks to portray social reality; (b) feminist standpoint epistemologies – knowledge arises from the lived socio-political experiences of women – a world view not accessible by men; (c) feminist postmodernism – knowledge is linked to power and struggles against oppression, and opens up discourses to multiple voices.	The epitome of knowing in the creative arts paradigm is professional artistry. Eisner (1985) conceived of such knowing as connoisseurship. He described it as a way of paying attention, and adopted the accompanying notion of criticism as a way of disclosing or expressing what has been seen.

Figure 4.2. Various epistemological perspectives (from Higgs, 2001; Higgs et al., 2007).

influence people's ontological perspectives. The positivist/empiricist perspective, in contrast, understands the world through objective, detached lenses that focus on selected variables and exclude others.

PHILOSOPHICAL FRAMEWORKS AND PARADIGMS

Knowledge generation through research occurs in research communities and can be described as working within paradigms or cultures of inquiry. We use the term *paradigm* to denote the philosophical stance of a community of researchers (including ontological and epistemological perspectives) along with their methodological norms, expectations and ethical practices. Research paradigms are independent of research topics. For example, researchers in agriculture may not all share the same philosophical framework. Cultures of inquiry (see Higgs & Cherry, 2009) have developed over time in particular disciplines and contexts; they favour certain combinations of ontology and epistemology and reflect interest in particular issues, values, topic areas and applications. This construct includes emancipatory and advocacy cultures, practice-based inquiry, action-based cultures, hypothetico-deductive cultures, narrative inquiry, theoretical inquiry, ethnographic cultures, arts-based inquiry and phenomenological inquiry. The goals of research communities are significant in framing and reflecting researchers' values, interests and beliefs. Figure 4.3 provides examples of research goals together with specific philosophical frameworks which provide a fitting match.

Each of these different research communities has sub-communities. The interpretive research paradigm, for example, embraces ethnographic, phenomenological and hermeneutic philosophical traditions. The critical research paradigm includes traditions of feminism, participatory action, and action learning. Research goals are closely connected to research interests (see Habermas, 1968/1972), and their related ontological and epistemological perspectives. Together they build the philosophical framework for a research project. For example, if the goal is to richly describe and understand experiences, then the research project fits the phenomenological, interpretive tradition. The goal of transforming practice and practitioners fits within a participatory action research tradition in the critical paradigm. The goal of understanding cultural workplaces fits within an ethnographic tradition in the interpretive paradigm.

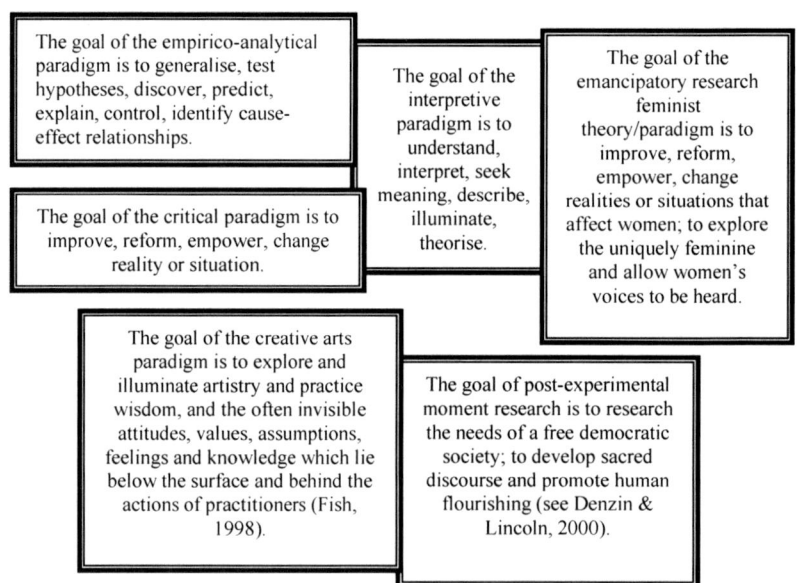

Figure 4.3. Paradigm research goals.

The central element of research paradigms/communities is the capacity of human beings to sense and make sense of their worlds and to use the tools or strategies they consider valid to know this world. A researcher working in the empirico-analytical paradigm would view reality as external and objective and use empirical data (specifically, data gained through the senses) to generate technical knowledge of this world. Such an approach is typical of the natural and biomedical sciences. A researcher working in the interpretive paradigm seeks to understand the human world by exploring the multiple realities people construct to make sense of their lived experiences. Here the definition of the term empirical is expanded to include experiential data. The critical paradigm researcher also explores human experiences, seeking through understanding of social, cultural and historical influences on human lives and society to understand and to promote change in the human world through critical, emancipatory knowledge and practices.

CONSIDERATIONS IN ADOPTING A PARADIGM APPROACH

To identify a suitable philosophical framework researchers must consider what reality is, what counts as evidence, and how it is to be gathered. The adoption of a paradigm approach becomes apparent through its strong interdependence with decisions about research questions, ontological and epistemological stances, the goals as well as the values and interests that shape the research project. All these dimensions of a research project need to inform each other and be crafted to fit together coherently. Researchers should draw on the philosophical literature to articulate what they are exploring and why, how they construct meaning from their data, and what assumptions underpin their research (see Chapter 3 for the origins of qualitative research). In qualitative research, researchers can choose to explore a phenomenon by focusing on what it feels like, what it looks like, how it is perceived and understood, or how it influences people, practices and society. The researcher's interest in bringing to bear a particular focus of inquiry is a guide to the optimal paradigm for the project.

Researchers draw on the body of literature of philosophers in arguing for their philosophical framework. For example, researchers conducting a philosophical hermeneutic study in policing could draw on Gadamer, among others, to defend their philosophical framework, despite the fact that Gadamer wrote nothing about the police force. It is important to differentiate the body of literature that informs the theoretical framework from the body of literature that informs the philosophical framework. The scholarly discourse of the content literature is discussed in more detail in Chapter 7. Suffice to mention here that these frameworks are interrelated and a research community can include researchers who share the same philosophical paradigm but conduct their research in different disciplines, and a research community can be understood to comprise researchers who not only share a philosophical framework but also research in the same discipline. Trede (2008), for example, in studying the relevance of the critical paradigm for physiotherapy practice, was part of the critical paradigm research community. Yet she was rather an outsider to the physiotherapy research community which predominantly conducts research in the empirico-analytical paradigm. This was inevitable, because the critical paradigm challenges the dominant and established disciplinary discourse (see Morrow & Brown, 1994).

CONCLUSION

Identifying, articulating and following your chosen philosophical framework and research community is a vital component of producing a credible and rigorous model or theory at the end of your project. Included in the philosophical framework are discussions of ontology, or what can be known, and epistemology, or how can it be known. Defining reality and what counts as knowledge points to the criteria against which you (and others) will judge the quality of your project. The philosophical framework also indicates and justifies data collection and analysis methods. To conduct research credibly outside of the dominant research discourse (the empirico-analytical paradigm and associated quantitative research approaches), it is important for qualitative researchers to clearly articulate their chosen philosophical framework.

REFERENCES

Benner, P., & Wrubel, J. (1989). *The primacy of caring: Stress and coping in health and illness.* Wokingham: Addison-Wesley.
Berger, P., & Luckmann, T. (1985). *The social construction of reality.* Harmondsworth: Penguin.
Candy, P. C. (1991). *Self-direction for lifelong learning.* San Francisco: Jossey-Bass.
Denzin, N. K., & Lincoln, Y. S. (2000). Introduction: The discipline and practice of qualitative research. In N. Denzin & Y. Lincoln (Eds.), *Handbook of qualitative research* (2nd ed., pp. 1–36). London: Sage.
Eisner, E. W. (1985). *The art of educational evaluation: A personal view.* London: The Falmer Press.
Fish, D. (1998). *Appreciating practice in the caring professions: Refocusing professional development and practitioner research.* Oxford: Butterworth-Heinemann.
Gadamer, H.-G. (1975). Hermeneutics and social science. *Cultural Hermeneutics, 2,* 307–316.
Habermas, J. (1968/1972). *Knowledge and human interest* (J. J. Shapiro, Trans.). London: Heinemann.
Heidegger, M. (1962). *Being and time.* New York: Harper & Row.
Higgs, J. (2001). Charting standpoints in qualitative research. In H. Byrne Armstrong, J. Higgs, & D. Horsfall (Eds.), *Critical moments in qualitative research* (pp. 44–67). Oxford: Butterworth-Heinemann.
Higgs, J., & Cherry, N. (2009). Doing qualitative research on practice. In J. Higgs, D. Horsfall, & S. Grace (Eds.), *Writing qualitative research on practice* (pp. 3–12). Rotterdam: Sense Publishers.
Higgs, J., Trede, F., & Rothwell, R. (2007). Qualitative research interests and paradigms. In J. Higgs, A. Titchen, D. Horsfall, & H. Armstrong (Eds.), *Being critical and creative in qualitative research* (pp. 32–42). Sydney: Hampden Press.
Lincoln, Y. S., & Guba, E. (1985). *Naturalistic inquiry.* Newbury Park, CA: Sage.
Morrow, A., & Brown, D. D. (1994). *Critical theory and methodology.* London: Sage.
McCarthy, E. D. (1996). *Knowledge as culture: The new sociology of knowledge.* London: Routledge & Kegan Paul.
Merleau-Ponty, M. (1956). What is phenomenology? *Cross Currents, 16,* 59–70.
Schwandt, T. A. (1997). *Qualitative inquiry: A dictionary of terms.* Thousand Oaks, CA: Sage.
Smith, J. K. (1983). Quantitative versus qualitative research: An attempt to clarify the issue. *Educational Researcher, 12,* 6–13.

AFFILIATIONS

Joy Higgs AM PhD and Franziska Trede PhD
The Education for Practice Institute
Charles Sturt University
Australia

GAVIN MELLES

5. UNDERSTANDING QUALITATIVE RESEARCH IN THE CONTEXT OF CULTURES:

Methodological Consequences

As researchers, we conduct qualitative research in a wide variety of contexts, addressing an even broader range of questions, some of which explicitly name culture as a focus of interest. The term *culture* itself, while familiar, however, does not have an univocal meaning, and thus a preliminary step for researchers is to explain exactly what they mean by the term. Fields such as anthropology, cultural studies, and sociology all offer us guidance here, providing different and sometimes convergent images of our object of interest. Once we have explained the particular purchase on culture that our research purports to address, we must then explore the methodological consequences this choice entails. By consequences, I mean that commitments to a particular version of culture will demand choices and modifications to the methods associated with the epistemological, ideological and methodological position(s) we take. Exploring and defining these consequences is the second substantive task for the qualitative researcher. In this chapter, I offer a preliminary discussion of the scoping of the term culture for qualitative research. I follow this with a consideration of the potential methodological and representational consequences of doing culture in research, focusing on the discovery of culture through qualitative research, methodological adjustment to culture in such contexts, and approaches to the discursive production of culture in research contexts. In addition to reference to "classic" qualitative texts and exemplar studies, I include where relevant some reference to my own work of addressing culture in the contexts of qualitative research.

CULTURE(S) AND QUALITATIVE RESEARCH

Qualitative research is often conducted in contexts where culture is significant as either background or foreground to our project. In the backgrounded situation, we may talk of cultural contexts and demographics of participants, for example, as influencing what people say and do. In cases where culture is foregrounded and a topic in its own right qualitative research may discover how culture is done or constructed. In fact, of course, these two broad distinctions do not exhaust the plurivalence of the term culture, a term which until recently also referred to the privileged intellectual baggage of social class. Raymond Williams (1976), for example, viewed high culture as merely the socioeconomic, ideological and material aspirations of a privileged minority, whereas culture is just the everyday workings of life. This is a position much closer to that of qualitative research in the traditions of cultural studies and sociology.

The ambiguities and politics of the term have provoked some to avoid it. Yet avoiding engagement with "culture" in a post-colonial world, Duranti (1997) suggests, makes it problematic to "understand similarities and differences in the ways in which people around the world constitute themselves in aggregates of various sorts" (p. 23). Thus the pragmatic need for a term that can signal while not foreclosing on difference should, I believe, motivate the use of culture in qualitative research. Ultimately, engaging with and re-presenting cultural difference through research and writing can contribute to enlarging our individual and social conversations about the "other", as Richard Rorty (1991) observed with respect to the work of anthropologists like Geertz (e.g. Geertz, 1973).

Williams (1976) also pointed up three important considerations about the term *culture* for qualitative researchers. First, it is a pluralistic term – not culture but culture(s). Second, culture has intra- and intercultural significance, as it potentially refers to class and other distinctions within society as well as to ethnic difference in commonsense terms; the intra- and intercultural scoping of the term respectively nominate the conventional separation of focus on culture in cultural studies/ sociology and anthropology. Third, meanings and positioning on culture are inevitably bound up with ideological research positioning, including positions whose advocates are reluctant to challenge the purported neutrality of research.

Inspired by anthropology's legacy, sociology and cultural studies, qualitative research generally treats culture as a dynamic social and historical construction of shared beliefs and norms within groups in society. Sensitivity to these nuances and complexities in the formation of culture means that qualitative researchers should be sceptical of culture as a generalised *tertium comparationis* which ignores the researchers' own cultural assumptions and commitments in categorising the "other" (Hasse & Trentemoller, 2009). Qualitative researchers also, I believe, eschew approaches to objectified cultural dimensions used to plot difference, as in organisation and management studies (e.g. Hofstede & McCrae, 2004). The ideological end of such work is to treat it "as an independent variable that can be manipulated through management interventions in order to achieve organizational goals" (Hudelson, 2004, p. 345).

Thus, culture, as it is evoked in qualitative research is socially constructed and discursively and materially sustained. Culture and society emerge and are sustained through social interaction.

> Two major objectives of qualitative research are to describe and analyse both the processes through which social realities are constructed, and the social relationships through which people are connected to one another. It is within, and through these relationships and processes that organizations, institutions, culture and society emerge and are sustained. Social structures are, in other words, built from the "bottom up". They are interactionally constructed realities and patterns of social relationship that may be studied using a variety of qualitative methods. (Miller & Dingwall, 1997, p. 3)

This account of culture as social practice and interaction has methodological consequences for qualitative research, which I attempt to clarify in what follows.

SOCIOLOGICAL, CULTURAL AND LINGUISTIC TAKES ON CULTURE IN QUALITATIVE RESEARCH

I suggest that anthropology, sociology and cultural studies provide three broad interrelated perspectives on culture relevant to qualitative research. A useful "anthropological" starting point is Carol Grbich's (1999) definition of culture relative to qualitative research in health:

> A culture is generally defined as a group of people with shared knowledge, beliefs and ways of living. Cultural explorations can range from longitudinal anthropological studies of the health practices of a large cultural group, such as a tribal or community group, to investigations of the culture of a hospital ward, seen from the perspectives of administrators, health professionals and patients. An investigation of the lifestyle of a group of drug-addicted homeless youth in an inner city suburb is another example. Requirements for identification as a "culture" generally include some shared beliefs or feelings of identity, and a common location tends to be involved. (pp. 10–11)

Grbich's definition highlights the shifting scope of the term and the assumption that collective practices, both material and discursive, are informed by shared beliefs. Thus, culture may address intercultural "ethnic" difference but may also refer to the norms, values and practices of groups in society, such as hip-hop culture. Qualitative research projects engage with particular local manifestations of such culture(s) in schools, neighbourhoods and institutional environments, and such studies demand attention to the symbolic and material resources employed to constitute world(s). Giddens (2001), for example, observed that culture "comprises both intangible aspects – the beliefs, ideas and values which form the content of culture – and tangible aspects – the objects, symbols or technology which represent that content" (p. 22). Shared beliefs, identities and practices therefore constitute key focal areas for qualitative research, and such work will inevitably involve some or all of the ethnographic inventory of observation, interview and other techniques (Atkinson, 1990).

A relevant definition of the intersection of culture and qualitative research familiar to cultural studies, overlapping with sociology but foregrounding ideology is that of Alasuutari (1995), who claimed,

> In my view, qualitative analysis deals with the concept of culture and with explaining meaningful action. To me cultural studies means that one takes culture seriously, without reducing it to mere effect or reflection of, for instance, economy. On the other hand, cultural studies treat culture and systems of meanings in connection with questions of power and politics. This means that one should not be content with just making new observations about qualitative data with the methods borrowed from the humanities. Such observations must be put to use in explaining or at least problematizing social phenomena. (p. 2)

This need to "problematise" social phenomena, including culture, by connecting meanings and practices with power and politics is not unique to cultural studies, but neither is it necessarily pursued in some forms of qualitative research that prefer to remain neutral on these questions, such as classic grounded theory (Glaser & Strauss, 1967) and ethnography (Hammersley & Atkinson, 1989).

METHODOLOGICAL CONSEQUENCES

Citing the ethnographies of working class subcultures (e.g. Willis, 1977) as exemplary, Alasuutari (1995) highlighted the potential of multiple research methods, including ethnomethodological approaches such as Gee's discourse analysis (and see Freebody, 2003), to achieve purchase on culture. The discursive turn in qualitative research has added a concern with the privileged place of language in social interaction. Gee (2005), for example, has offered a model of discourse analysis embracing language use and Foucaultian discourses mediated by cultural models (e.g. Shore, 1995) as a qualitative research practice capable of illuminating the nature and ideological consequences of literacy practices. Exploring interview and material data, Gee suggests that big D(iscourses) informing identity, material and behavioural choices are intricately associated with little d(iscourses), i.e. language use in interview and other contexts. In sum, culture is both a discursive (linguistic) and non-discursive, i.e. material, construction. This position has methodological consequences for qualitative researchers. In the following section I to explore some of the methodological consequences of taking culture seriously, in its various senses above. Since it is impossible to exhaustively cover what these consequences are I illustrate what I take to be some of the significant issues that others have faced in addressing culture. Where possible I also refer to some of my own recent work, not because it is exemplary in any way but because it is familiar in the relevant sense.

Culture(s) in Institutional Settings

There are many practical domains of life, including health and education, where interventions are promoted or hampered by understandings of culture. Qualitative research offers tools, such as the interview, to explore constructions of culture that can constitute barriers to programs aimed at improving the circumstances of specific social groups. Hinton, Guo, Hillygus, and Levkoff (2000), for example, examined constructions of dementia among Chinese-American families with a view to improving the recruitment of caregivers from this group for research. Through interviews it was possible to begin to identify some of the dominant cultural constructions of the meaning and significance of dementia which were previously under-acknowledged in this domain of health practice.

Cultural diversity in higher education offers cases where qualitative research can contribute to clarifying cross-cultural difference. For example, the supervision of international research students offers a domain where culture is relevant as a designation for the practice of research supervision, namely "research supervision culture", and as a reference to the potential cross-cultural misunderstandings that can occur between students and faculty, i.e. culture as ethnic and social difference. I explored these issues in relation to the supervision of international Bachelor of Medical Science students (Melles, 2007). Recruiting a cohort of 27 supervisors and conducting semi-structured interviews allowed me to uncover some of the struggles that supervisors had with coming to understand these students, and simultaneously to question the homogeneous deployment of culture in the literature as an explanation of barriers to research supervision. I concluded:

> This study suggests that supervision is not easily dichotomized into a set of issues around ESL Asian versus native speaking English students. Supervisors show sensitivity to the nuances of project demands and also appreciate the intellectual capacity and commitment of students in particular sites. Several respondents made explicit mention of the contribution the students brought to the department and to the social and cultural "mix" of research sites. On a practical level, the study suggests that some research sites may be more conducive to overseas student exchanges and that greater structure and direction, appropriately supported by faculty, may be beneficial for many students. (Melles, 2007, p. 23)

Culturing Research with/on the Other

One potential response to our desire to research the "other" and acknowledge their perspective is to relinquish control and allow the "other" to guide and eventually take over ownership and direction of the research. Action research, for example, encourages participatory research *with* rather than *on* co-researchers, with a view to practical change (e.g. Reason & Bradbury, 2001) and offers an albeit contested emancipatory message (Melles, 1998). Participatory qualitative research offers one response to sociocultural difference, but more radical research approaches may be necessary to adapt to the cultural concepts of Indigenous research.

Qualitative research and research in general operates largely on the assumption that the Western traditions with which we are familiar provide universal guidelines. Nevertheless, for research in New Zealand for example, indigenous cultural concepts or *tikanga whakaaro* (Barlow, 1991), may require somewhat radical change to existing research practices. Sensitivity to such cultural concepts and to the colonial baggage associated with research on culturally different communities was clearly signalled in Tuhiwai-Smith's (Smith, 1999) call for a decolonising of research methodologies to allow for the development of indigenous approaches to research. The complex network of issues facing indigenous researchers is not alleviated by simply bringing in some uncontested "insider" sense of what is appropriate. The author suggests:

> Many indigenous researchers have struggled individually to engage with the disconnections that are apparent between the demands of research, on one side, and the realities they encounter amongst their own and other indigenous communities, with whom they share lifelong relationships ... there are a number

> of ethical, cultural, political and personal issues that can present special difficulties for indigenous researchers who, in their own communities, work particularly as insiders, and are often employed for this purpose, and partially as outsiders, because *of* their Western education or *because* they may work across clan, tribe, linguistic, age and gender boundaries. Simultaneously, they work within their research projects or institutions as insiders within a particular paradigm or research model, and as outsiders because they are often marginalized and *perceived* to be representative of either a minority or a rival interest group. (p. 5)

Sensitivity to the politics and history of the cultural contexts we investigate is essential for capturing the origins, meaning and significance of such constructions. This ideological layer challenges the purported neutrality of some cultural constructions, emphasising instead the political and contested nature and significance of culture work and the need for research "emic" awareness of our cultural presuppositions (see Hasse & Trentemoller, 2009).

Consider the Discursive Construction of Culture

Ethnomethodologically inspired discursive approaches to the construction of culture have made their way into the qualitative research. David Silverman, for example, has long advocated attention to the interactional accomplishment of culture in medical clinics (e.g. Silverman, 1987), while simultaneously attending to the broader social and political discourses of medicine and health. Silverman (2006) has advocated a catholic and pragmatic use of a range of sources and techniques in qualitative research to examine the social construction of society, culture and institutions.

Taking culture seriously in the analysis of language use requires the qualitative researcher develops some expertise in attending to language in social interaction as a topic and socio-culturally constitutive resource in its own right. Central to Gee's (2005) work is the cultural anthropology's notion of cultural models. These are "presupposed, taken for granted models of the world that are widely shared (although not necessarily to the exclusion of other, alternative models) by the members of a society and that play an enormous role in their understanding of that world and their behaviour in it" (Holland & Quinn, 1987, p. 4). Interviews and attention to discursive specifics, e.g. choice of pronouns and lexical items (nouns and verbs), can reveal what such cultural models are and how they are discursively constructed.

I recently explored in qualitative focus groups the cross-cultural understandings of group work in higher education (Melles, 2004), discovering that some of the assumptions in the literature about the inherent difficulties of international students were either mistaken or overstated. As well as discovering conventional qualitative themes in interview talk, I explored the cultural identity work students engaged in within the interview setting, claiming that "students seek to fashion a culturally acceptable student identity through their talk; in some cases resisting existing assumptions about their identities as problematic second language learners" (p. 224).

This resistance to existing assumptions was visible both in what they said and how they said it, an analytical focus – what and how – compatible with the active interviewing approach (see Melles, 2005). Thus there is value and potential in qualitative studies engaging with culture to treat language use itself as more than a neutral channel to thoughts and beliefs, but rather constitutive of those thoughts and beliefs, as Wittgenstein (1953) taught us over 50 years ago.

ACCULTURATING QUALITATIVE RESEARCH

Anthropology, cultural studies and sociology offer a range of meanings and ideological commitments for culture in the context of conducting qualitative research. Although culture as a term is problematic and ideologically invested, there are pragmatic reasons for keeping it on the research agenda, particularly in practice-oriented domains of life such as medicine, health and education. How culture is constructed and used has practical consequences for how the world is "done", so to speak, on various institutional and social scales. Methodologically, qualitative research seems to be moving increasingly towards taking culture to be an interactional accomplishment, and this entails closer attention to the language of interaction in its material contexts. This social constructionist principle entails attention to both the *what* and *how* of research questions and, therefore, the what and how of "doing culture" (Turner, 2000). Ultimately, the commitments we have to exploring qualitative research in context(s) of culture have methodological consequences that need to be mapped out, including a questioning of our own (emic) presuppositions.

REFERENCES

Alasuutari, P. (1995). *Researching culture: Qualitative method and cultural studies.* London: Sage.
Atkinson, P. (1990). *The ethnographic imagination: Textual constructions of reality.* London: Routledge.
Barlow, C. (1991). *Tikanga whakaaro: Key concepts in Maori culture.* Oxford; Auckland: Oxford University Press.
Duranti, A. (1997). *Linguistic anthropology.* Cambridge: Cambridge University Press.
Freebody, P. (2003). *Qualitative research in education: Interaction and practice.* London: Sage.
Gee, J. P. (2005). *An introduction to discourse analysis: Theory and method* (2nd ed.). London: Routledge.
Geertz, C. (1973). *The interpretation of cultures: Selected essays.* New York: Basic Books.
Giddens, A. (2001). *Sociology* (4th ed.). Cambridge: Polity Press.
Glaser, B. G., & Strauss, A. L. (1967). *The discovery of grounded theory: Strategies for qualitative research.* Chicago: Aldine.
Grbich, C. F. (1999). *Qualitative research in health: An introduction.* St Leonards, NSW: Allen & Unwin.
Hammersley, M., & Atkinson, P. (1989). *Ethnography: Principles in practice.* London: Routledge.
Hasse, C., & Trentemoller, S. (2009). The method of culture contrast. *Qualitative Research in Psychology, 6*(1), 46–66.
Hinton, L., Guo, Z., Hillygus, J., & Levkoff, S. (2000). Working with culture: A qualitative analysis of barriers to the recruitment of Chinese-American family caregivers for dementia research. *Journal of Cross-Cultural Gerontology, 15*(2), 119–137.

Hofstede, G., & McCrae, R. R. (2004). Personality and culture revisited: Linking traits and dimensions of culture. *Cross-Cultural Research, 38*(1), 52–88.
Holland, D. C., & Quinn, N. (1987). Culture and cognition. In D. C. Holland & N. Quinn (Eds.), *Cultural models in language and thought* (pp. 3–40). Cambridge: Cambridge University Press.
Hudelson, P. M. (2004). Culture and quality: An anthropological perspective. *International Journal of Qualitative Health Care, 16*(5), 345–346.
Melles, G. (1998). Action research: Boundaries, tensions, and directions: Review essay. [Review of International action research: A casebook for educational reform (1997) and Action research as living practice (1997)]. *Australian Educational Researcher, 25*(2), 113–123.
Melles, G. (2004). Understanding the role of language/culture in group work through qualitative interviewing. *Qualitative Report, 9*(2), 216–240.
Melles, G. (2005). Beyond the romantic impulse for authentic data to coconstruction of meaning in interview-based educational research. *Qualitative Research Journal, 5*(2), 21–30.
Melles, G. (2007). Challenges to supervision of undergraduate ESL (English as a second language) Asian students in the Bachelor of Medical Science. *Focus on Health Professional Education, 9*(2), 11–26.
Miller, G., & Dingwall, R. (1997). Introduction. In G. Miller & R. Dingwall (Eds.), *Context and method in qualitative research* (pp. 1–11). London: Sage.
Reason, P., & Bradbury, H. (2001). *Handbook of action research: Participative inquiry and practice.* London: Sage.
Rorty, R. (1991). *Objectivity, relativism and truth: Philosophical papers.* Cambridge: Cambridge University Press.
Shore, B. (1995). *Culture in mind: Cognition, culture, and the problem of meaning.* New York: Oxford University Press.
Silverman, D. (1987). *Communication and medical practice: Social relations in the clinic.* London: Sage.
Silverman, D. (2006). *Interpreting qualitative data: Methods for analyzing talk, text and interaction* (3rd ed.). London: Sage.
Smith, L. T. (1999). *Decolonizing methodologies: Research and indigenous peoples.* London; Dunedin, NZ: Zed Books; University of Otago Press.
Turner, A. (2000). Embodied ethnography: Doing culture. *Social Anthropology, 8*(01), 51–60.
Williams, R. (1976). *Keywords: A vocabulary of culture and society.* London: Fontana.
Willis, P. E. (1977). *Learning to labour: How working class kids get working class jobs.* Farnborough, UK: Saxon House.
Wittgenstein, L. (1953). *Philosophical investigations.* Oxford: Basil Blackwell.

AFFILIATION

Gavin Melles PhD
Faculty of Design
Swinburne University of Technology
Australia

ANGIE TITCHEN AND ROLA AJJAWI

6. WRITING CONTEMPORARY ONTOLOGICAL AND EPISTEMOLOGICAL QUESTIONS ABOUT PRACTICE

INTRODUCTION

In this chapter we bring alive the complexity, sophistication and practical know-how of developing contemporary ontological and epistemological questions about practice. As experienced qualitative researchers who are not philosophers, we share our understanding of the philosophical traditions of ontology and epistemology, how we design ontological and epistemological research questions and how we help our doctoral students to attain a sufficient grasp of these traditions to create their own research questions. We draw on our experiences researching in the interpretive (AT, RA), creative and critical paradigms (AT). Our position situates qualitative research as an explicit, embodied, choice-rich journey of exploration that is grounded in and informed by a deep understanding of appropriate philosophical underpinnings and paradigmatic expectations. Framing research questions is about making the research process transparent and guiding the research approach. In this way, research can be seen as an explicit, embodied, choice-rich journey of exploration that impacts on the researcher and the research.

Epistemology is defined as "the philosophical theory of knowledge, which seeks to define it, distinguish its principal varieties, identify its sources, and establish its limits" (Bullock & Trombley, 2000, p. 279) or more simply "the theory of knowledge" (Crotty, 1998, p. 3). Epistemology is concerned with knowing through cognitive representation.

Ontology is defined as the theory or study of what really exists (Bullock & Trombley, 2000) and is concerned with the nature of reality and human being in the world (Guba, 1990). Reality and being in the world are often embodied and embedded in shared meanings, behaviours and practices, and although this embodiment is about knowing, it has no mental representation.

So why do researchers need to consider research questions in terms of ontology and epistemology? The aim of research is to generate propositional (theoretical/scientific) knowledge of an epistemological or ontological nature through a transformation of participants' mental representations and/or embodied, existential knowing. Researchers therefore need to be aware of these different kinds of knowledge/knowing and their sources in order to access them in their research. They also need to be cognisant of the different kinds of research "product" they want and the distinctive ways each kind of propositional knowledge is generated and verified in order for it to become accepted public knowledge (Higgs & Titchen, 1995). Table 6.1 provides examples of such questions, based on research publications of these authors.

The type of research question (along with the desired product) is central to choosing an appropriate research paradigm and designing and implementing a research methodology that is congruent philosophically, theoretically and methodologically. Congruence between these elements of the research is a marker of quality in qualitative research and is an important requirement if the research is to be judged credible by others. Further, deep understanding of the type of question asked, and therefore of the kind of knowledge sought, enables researchers take a sensitive, authentic and reflexive approach to the research and the participants.

But why do we have the word "contemporary" in our title? This is because, increasingly, postmodern researchers are "boundary riding", melding or blending the assumptions of different paradigms, asking both kinds of question in one study. Cross-paradigmatic researchers need to examine carefully the assumptions of the paradigms and approaches within them, and to build on similarities and reconcile differences (see e.g. Titchen, 2000).

Table 6.1. Examples of epistemological and ontological questions

Epistemological questions (concerned with accessing knowledge that has mental representation)	*Research "product" (concerned with creating propositional knowledge)*	*Research paradigm/ approach*	*Research aim/objectives*
Titchen (2000) What is the nature of the professional craft knowledge of experts in patient-centred nursing? (*) How do they describe what they do? What sense do they make of what they do? Given that this is their perception … why do they choose to do what they do?	A conceptual framework of patient-centred nursing from the perspective of the expert, grounded in contextualised, rich description (interpretive knowledge: a representation of participant's cognitions by researcher)	Interpretive Phenomeno-logical sociology	The generation of a phenomenological understanding of the nature of an expert's craft knowledge of patient-centred nursing and how she creates and uses it in everyday situations.
How can experts in patient-centred nursing be helped to become facilitators of less experienced nurses' acquisition of professional craft knowledge?	Principles for action, grounded in contextualised, theorised accounts of actions and their effects (emancipatory knowledge of how to overcome internal and external obstacles. Created by participant and researcher simultaneously to carry out change together)	Critical Action research	The development of principles for action from this phenomenological understanding and from the findings of the action research.

Table 6.1. (continued)

Ontological questions (concerned with accessing embodied knowing without mental representation)	Research 'product' (concerned with creating propositional knowledge)	Research paradigm/ approach	Research aim/objectives
Ajjawi (2009) How do experienced physiotherapists learn to communicate their reasoning with patients and with novice physiotherapists? What is it like to learn to think like a physiotherapist? What is it like to communicate a phenomenon that is embedded or pre-reflective?	A storied/ phenomenological description of participants' learning in the workplace (interpretive knowledge: a representation of participants' taken-for-granted knowledge)	Interpretive Hermeneutic phenomenology	The development of a way of understanding the development of clinical reasoning and its communication – phenomena that are often subconscious and pre-reflective
Titchen (2000) Main question as above (*) What is it like to be an expert patient-centred nurse? What is the meaning of being patient-centred? What are the salient aspects of the situation to which they attend?	A complementary interpretation of the nurses' human *being* (interpretive knowledge: a representation of participant's non-verbal, embodied, existential knowing)	Interpretive Hermeneutic phenomenology	As in row above

THE NATURE OF ONTOLOGICAL AND EPISTEMOLOGICAL QUESTIONS

Epistemological questions are created to help us find out what people know about the entity that we want to investigate, and how they know what they know, whereas ontological questions enable us to discover what exists and what reality is like (see Table 6.1). In other words, whether a question is epistemological or ontological in concern depends on the nature of the research phenomenon of interest and the type of knowledge sought. This differentiation gives rise to methodological considerations. For example, the entity of interest may be a physiotherapist's being, in terms of communicating that which is known only by the body. In this case, an ontological question directs the choice of a methodology that would facilitate the revelation, pointing out and naming of this pre-reflective, embodied knowing.

Thus the research product is a mental representation of what was previously embodied. Alternatively, participants may well have mental representations of their being in the context of communication. In that case the researcher would ask an epistemological question, leading towards a methodology designed for the development of abstract re-presentations of physiotherapists' mental representations. Thus epistemological questions shape the systematic study of the mental content of individuals' inner worlds, that is, the cognitive reality embodied in the processes of subjective human experiences. These questions are concerned with finding out what research participants can tell you about the entity. Therefore, methodologies and methods are developed which enable participants to tell you what is going on for them in the moment; promote their reflection; or foster articulation of what they take for granted or do not think is worth mentioning to you.

On the other hand, ontological questions lead to systematic and intuitive study of everyday, practical know-how, knowing gained through the senses and socialisation and meanings in background practices. So in our example the researcher would not ask physiotherapists directly about what exists in terms of their communication, because the researcher wants to access embedded, embodied knowing and being, and background meanings that exist before cognition has come into play. For instance, data gathered through observation and capturing everyday language and stories can be used to uncover and interpret hidden meanings "between the lines", as it were. The researcher is interested in what it is like, what matters, what is significant or real to and for the physiotherapists. In addition, methodologies and methods can be devised within the study to bring the uncovered knowing into participants' cognition, for discussion and co-creation of knowledge through critique and contestation.

HOW CAN WE COME TO UNDERSTAND?

In this section, we show how, through active learning, we can come to understand the framing of ontological and epistemological questions and how this framing impacts on the research process and researcher stance. Active learning is defined as learning, in this case about qualitative research, through reflection, dialogue with self, others and literature, and engaging in learning activities that make use of the senses, multiple intelligences and doing research activities with others (e.g. supervisors and colleagues) (adapted from Dewing, 2008).

Framing Ontological and Epistemological Questions

As introduced above, writing research questions that are likely to enable us to achieve the kind of research product we wish to create requires an understanding of the philosophical, theoretical and conceptual starting points. These starting points are necessary for sound methodological decision-making about research form and design. Paying attention to congruence between our questions and these starting points and our methodology will help us to shape a rigorous research question. In addition, considering context in terms of participants, the research topic and our

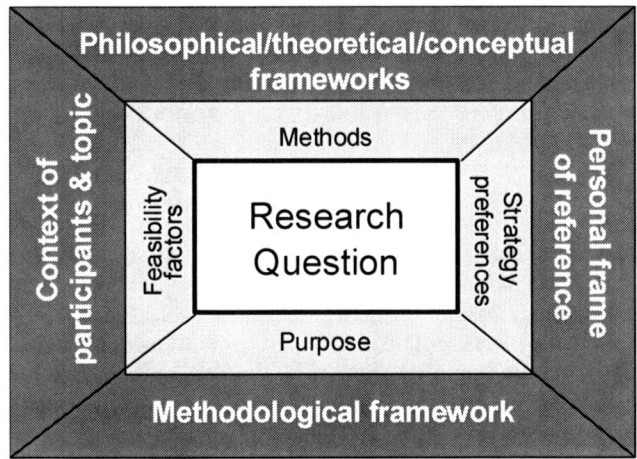

Figure 6.1. Framing ontological/epistemological research questions: Framework dimensions (adapted from Higgs & Llewellyn, 1998).

personal frame of reference will also influence our questions. These elements, comprising the dark outer frame of a research framework devised originally by Higgs and Llewellyn (1998, see Figure 6.1), are the focus of this chapter.

Shaping research questions through framing is often a lengthy, difficult journey that requires us to use different ways of knowing, as follows (see Higgs & Titchen, 2007):

Pre-cognitive knowing is ineffable knowing without mental representation. It is the knowing gained through the senses, that is, through perceptual awareness (intuition, aesthetics and embodied knowing), socialisation, emotions and spiritual awareness.

Cognitive knowing implies bringing our embodied, precognitive, "heart" knowledge to thought and to words; to know for oneself and to communicate with others. Cognitive knowing is the owned and conscious journey into knowing or meaning-making. It occurs, for example, when researchers name their practices and "map out" what they know and what they want to know in order to frame their development or inquiry direction and research questions.

Metacognitive knowing refers to our awareness of our cognitive processes and exerting control over these processes; it includes the cognitive skills that are necessary for the management of knowledge and other cognitive skills (Biggs 1988). "To perform well, one needs to be aware not only of the knowledge and algorithms required for the task, but of one's own motives and resources, the contextual constraints, and to plan strategically on that knowledge" (Biggs, 1986, p. 143).

Reflexive knowing is self-knowledge, self-awareness as a person and researcher in interaction with others and consciousness of the impact of that interaction on self and others.

Some 3 or 4 months into the first year of her study of professional artistry in the practice of person-centred, evidence-based nursing, Donna Frost (one of Angie's doctoral students) used her pre-cognitive knowing to begin her framing of her research questions. In terms of active learning, she was using her visual sense, analogy, creative imagination and dialogue with self.

Donna's story

Angie and I were engaging in supervision as we walked by a lake. Angie asked me if I had noticed a difference in the way different authors had approached ontology and epistemology. I realised that I hadn't! I thought there were pretty well defined ways of understanding ontology and epistemology. As we began a period of silent contemplation, I noticed that I didn't even know where to begin asking questions, or which questions were relevant to the discussion.

The water of the lake looked calm on the surface but cold and difficult to enter, and the trees and bushes on the edges were thickly planted and full of mystery. It was beautiful to look at. It felt to me like this represented the philosophical landscape. Although I had been looking at this landscape for some time now, I hadn't explored it myself. I hadn't swum in the water or explored the forests. As we walked, I saw a picnic table at the edge of the lake, under some trees and set a wee way back from the water's edge. I almost laughed when I saw it. It felt like I had been "sitting at that picnic table", having other people come and tell me their stories about their forays and travels into the landscape before me. I had been considering the philosophical landscape via their interpretations. Although this was enough to help me understand their travels and the decisions they may have made on the way, it wasn't enough to help me make my decisions about my own research.

I was worried about getting lost in the woods, finding myself out of my depth in the waters. But the picnic table now felt confining, no longer an adequate viewing point. I needed to get up and enter the landscape myself,

make my own explorations, draw my own map of my journey. I looked to Angie, my first guide along the way, and approached the water's edge. (Frost, October 2008, supervision notes)

Acknowledging her worry, and strengthened by naming her *pre-cognitive knowing*, Donna found the courage to start her framing journey through active dialogue with herself, Angie and the philosophical landscape (the literature) by intentionally posing questions to guide the dialogue. Thus she engaged in *cognitive knowing* as she analysed the philosophical differences between ontological and epistemological questions, how others had been influenced in their question making by *theoretical/ conceptual frameworks* and how the resulting *methodological frameworks* had been shaped. These dialogues were reiterative in nature, helping her to become aware of the subtle move she was making towards a *metacognitive knowing*. She noticed that not only was she engaging in analysis of *philosophical frameworks*, she was also beginning to critique and synthesise ideas from different research paradigms. In her first reading of Angie's PhD thesis (Titchen, 2000), in which the ontological and epistemological concerns of different types of phenomenology were compared and contrasted, Donna did not make her own connections between the nature of the type of question and the impact on the researcher and research process. However, on a reiterative reading, she wrote:

> Despite your clear style of writing, I've obviously not understood a lot of this material in the past as I felt ... as if I were reading these chapters for the first time. I am now recognising ideas and am more able to "hold" the different ideas in my head. [After this re-reading] I looked at your research questions and tried to figure out which were ontological and which epistemological in direction. And then I read [Table 5.1] and there I found some of your research questions used as examples and I could check out my own understandings ... So now I have started writing some possible questions ... as a step along the way. If I can recognise or learn what is significant about the questions and identify what kind of information the question will yield, it will help me with getting the questions sorted for this project. (Frost, February 2009, email).

The previous month, Donna had recognised that she needed to ask both ontological and epistemological research questions to get at nurses' professional artistry, and that this decision would lead her to melding two very different research methodologies in her research design. She demonstrated her *reflexive knowing* by her self-awareness that her knowing, doing, being and becoming would have to be very different as she sought to answer each type of question, but that she didn't know how she was going to do that or even how to word the different types of question.

In reiterative dialogue with Angie and herself over some months, Donna had examined the conceptual framework of her topic, professional artistry, in the research literature in terms of the context of participants. The research so far had shown that the dimensions and processes of professional artistry rarely had any mental representation in the minds of research participants; that these dimensions and processes were primarily embodied and embedded, and although they could be seen or felt they were not talked about. Donna could see that in this case there would be no point asking epistemological research questions.

Rather, ontological questions, in the tradition of hermeneutic phenomenology, would be necessary to access the embodied experience of practising professional artistry and to reveal the meaning between the lines of stories, everyday language and practices. But as she talked with Angie and other researchers engaging or participating in professional artistry research in other fields of practice, she identified that a few nurses were beginning to be able to talk about it. This suggested to her that she could possibly seek out such people as participants in the part of her research that would be guided by epistemological research questions and the philosophical, theoretical and methodological frameworks located in a congruent tradition like phenomenological sociology. This beginning to make conscious and congruent choices about the elements of the research framework (Figure 5.1) displayed Donna's developing metacognitive knowing.

Impact of Framing on Research Process and Researcher

In a similar way to Donna, Rola approached her research with pre-cognitive knowing as a physiotherapy clinical educator sensing the difficulties of articulating clinical reasoning (a phenomenon that is often subconscious and embedded) to her students and wanting to do it better. Starting the journey from this knowing, and with the help of her supervisor, she transformed her pre-cognitive knowing into cognitive and metacognitive knowing, enabling her to make conscious choices about the ontological and epistemological questions of the research and match the theoretical, philosophical and methodological frameworks (Ajjawi, 2009).

Rola's personal frame of reference as a physiotherapist and an educator also guided the choice of research questions. The motivation and interest stemming from her personal frame of reference fostered an authentic approach to the research along with an insider perspective on the context of the participants and the topic. By making her personal frame of reference explicit and unearthing her assumptions about the research and about herself as a researcher, practitioner and educator (reflexive knowing) she was able to be reflexive in her role in the research and to be conscious of the decisions being made and why.

One "product" of the research was a model of how experienced physiotherapists learned to communicate their reasoning. As Rola wished to create this model as an abstract interpretation of the participants' lived experience, and which responded to her epistemological questions, she had chosen hermeneutic (interpretive) phenomenology as her research approach. The other product comprised stories that spoke to the phenomenological and ontological questions of what is it like to learn to reason and to communicate reasoning as an experienced physiotherapist. Reflecting on the research now gives a clearer perspective on how the philosophical, theoretical and methodological choices resulted in the research product. This clarity can be used to guide novice researchers as they make their own ways through the research landscapes.

Principles for Coming to Understand the Framing of Questions and its Impact

We offer the following principles:

1. Acknowledge any fear of exploring the philosophical and theoretical terrain that you may feel, and find support to help you embrace the unknown.
2. Use an active learning approach to make the framing of research questions your own.
    a. Pay attention to your own ontology and epistemology as a person and researcher.
    b. Work with your body, imagination, creative expression and reflection in learning from experience.
    c. Actively compare and contrast different *philosophical, theoretical/ conceptual and methodological frameworks* and how they shape research questions (the tables in Titchen & Higgs, 2007, might be helpful).
3. Engage in *metacognitive* and *reflexive knowing* to examine your development of all *ways of knowing* that are central, not only to writing research questions but also to the whole research endeavour.
4. Be playful in developing an agile, curious, flexible and open mind.
5. Think through and record your learning intentionally and systematically, noting your use of the different ways of knowing,
6. Ask your research supervisor to support you in all the above and to pose salient questions to guide you in your dialogue with yourself and the literature.
7. Ask your supervisor and other experienced researchers specific, focused, but open questions about their practical know-how as you observe and work alongside them.
8. Adopt a critical friend who you can engage in discussions and "thought showers" about your topic.
9. Examine your data open-mindedly in terms of what questions are being answered. These questions might be different from your original questions, so you might need to reframe your original questions.
10. Remember that this is an iterative process or journey, where you will transform your knowledge and gain deeper insights as you progress through the research process engaging in active learning.

CONCLUSION

We conclude that writing contemporary questions of this nature is complex and sophisticated work, with the implication that is it the responsibility of research supervisors to help students to write questions that are going to facilitate the conduct of rigorous, quality research. The beginning of the framing journey for doctoral students is often a "rabbit caught in the headlights" experience. For example, taking the first steps into philosophical literature to understand ontology and epistemology often engenders the worry or fear that Donna expressed: fear of not being able to find our way through it and make it our own and fear of the spotlight on us (feeling naked, self-exposed) as we struggle to find our way. Supervisors and other experienced researchers can share their own experiences of such fear with students and reveal the wisdom they have accrued through embracing the fear and leaping into the unknown. This wisdom can also underpin the design of effective learning opportunities that help students to take that leap. As shown in her work with Donna, Angie enables students to uncover their pre-cognitive knowing of the starting point which gives them confidence to step into the framing journey. She follows up by encouraging students to use their imaginations to frame their experiences and understandings in the "landscape", wherever it might be.

Working alongside a supervisor or experienced researcher who can model the operationalisation of the above principles can be very powerful for students, especially if a co-learner or a critical companionship relationship is negotiated. Paying attention to the ontology of the student as a person, student and researcher, as well as to the student's epistemology, models the importance of paying attention in the living, real-time of the relationship. Experienced researchers, modelling the framing of research questions, sharing their practical know-how and pointing out their ways of knowing, can be very effective.

Thus the supervisor/experienced researcher helps students to swim with the flow of the river, rather than battle against it. Students learn thereby and gain energy from spiralling through turbulence by means of reiterative dialogues with self, others, practice and literature. Accompanying students through calm waters, storms and occasional whirlwinds and steering a steady course, yet never in a particular direction, can be deeply rewarding and joyful as students flourish and experience the delight of achieving congruence.

We leave you now with suggestions of resources that will help you to go deeper into the issues surrounding the framing of contemporary ontological and epistemological questions and their impact. Probing PhD theses can be an excellent way to engage in active learning and develop your metacognitive capacity. Like a detective, identify the nature of the research questions and then critique their congruence with the research framework (see Figure 6.1). You may have to work backwards from the stated philosophical position to identify the nature of the research questions. The tables in Titchen and Higgs (2007) might also be a useful guide in your detective work. Trede and Higgs (2009) have provided many examples of research questions framed for various traditions, paradigms and methods. The next step is to ask yourself what you have learned from these activities, and to determine whether you can use that learning in the creation of your own questions.

ACKNOWLEDGEMENTS

We thank Donna Frost for contributing her story to this chapter and we honour her courage in making visible the first steps of her framing journey.

REFERENCES

Ajjawi, R. (2009). *Learning clinical reasoning and its communication.* Saarbrücken, Germany: VDM Verlag Dr. Müller.
Biggs, J. (1988). The role of metacognition in enhancing learning. *Australian Journal of Education, 32,* 127–138.
Biggs, J. B. (1986). Enhancing learning skills: The role of metacognition. In J. A. Bowden (Ed.), *Student learning: Research into practice – the Marysville Symposium* (pp. 131–148). The University of Melbourne: Centre for the Study of Higher Education.
Bullock, A., & Trombley, S. (Eds.). (2000). *The new Fontana dictionary of modern thought* (3rd ed.). London: Harper Collins.
Crotty, M. (1998). *The foundations of social research: Meaning and perspective in the research process.* Sydney: Allen & Unwin.
Dewing, J. (2008). Becoming and being active learners and creative active learning workplaces: The value of active learning in practice development. In K. Manley, B. McCormack, & V. Wilson (Eds.), *International practice development in nursing and healthcare* (pp. 273–294). Oxford: Blackwell.
Guba, E. G. (1990). *The paradigm dialog.* Newbury Park, CA: Sage.
Higgs, J., & Llewellyn, G. (1998). Framing the research question. In J. Higgs (Ed.), *Writing qualitative research* (pp. 59–68). Sydney: Hampden Press.
Higgs, J., & Titchen, A. (1995). The nature, generation and verification of knowledge. *Physiotherapy, 81*(9), 521–530.
Higgs, J., & Titchen, A. (2007). Qualitative research: Journeys of meaning-making through transformation, illumination, shared action and liberation. In J. Higgs, A. Titchen, D. Horsfall, & H. B. Armstrong (Eds.), *Being critical and creative in qualitative research* (pp. 11–21). Sydney: Hampden Press.
Titchen, A. (2000). *Professional craft knowledge in patient-centred nursing and the facilitation of its development.* University of Oxford DPhil Thesis. Oxford: Ashdale Press.
Titchen, A., & Higgs, J. (2007). Exploring interpretive and critical philosophies. In J. Higgs, A. Titchen, D. Horsfall, & H. B. Armstrong (Eds.), *Being critical and creative in qualitative research* (pp. 56–68). Sydney: Hampden Press.
Trede, F., & Higgs, J. (2009). Framing research questions and writing philosophically: The role of framing research questions. In J. Higgs, D. Horsfall, & S. Grace (Eds.), *Writing qualitative research on practice* (pp. 13–25). Rotterdam: Sense.

AFFILIATIONS

Angie Titchen PhD
Knowledge Centre for Evidence-Based Practice
Fontys University of Applied Sciences
The Netherlands

Rola Ajjawi PhD
The Education for Practice Institute
Charles Sturt University
Australia

JOY HIGGS AND FRANZISKA TREDE

7. THEORETICAL FRAMEWORKS AND LITERATURE

Framing and Supporting Qualitative Research

INTRODUCTION

A core goal of research is to produce knowledge that enters the domain of texts called scholarly discourse or "the literature". This literature in turn provides the foundation for developing new knowledge. A field of research and its relevant body of literature have an interdependent relationship. In this chapter we explore the following questions:

How does existing literature provide a conceptual frame of reference for research?

What guides researchers in choosing literature to frame their current research?

How is literature used in supporting the credibility of research?

CONTEXTUALISING RESEARCH

Research occurs in multiple contexts and the combination of these contexts creates a unique framework for each research project. The following factors contextualise research:
- The interests and questions of the researcher
- The researcher's past experience with methods and topic areas in the chosen research field
- The phenomenon of interest
- The context of existing knowledge that pertains to the research, which includes both the broader *history of ideas* (see Chapter 1) and the specific *knowledge of the field* of the research topic area.
- The research traditions and theories of the research field or community. For instance, this includes typical (but not prescriptive) modes of research conducted in this field, expected forms of written reports and writing styles.
- The research paradigm that provides the philosophical and methodological framework (see Chapter 4)
- The conceptual or theoretical framework for the research, including work of the major researchers and scholars who have informed the discourse in the field of study in question. See "giants" below.

- The setting in which the research is being conducted (including such factors as geographical location, demographic parameters, populations, communities, actual people's lives).

THEORETICAL FRAMEWORKS

Part of contextualising the inquiry is locating the research in a theoretical context. This can involve situating the research within the discourse pertaining to the topic area, locating the research within the field of study, situating the research in the history of ideas, and identifying major "knowledge makers" in the field (Higgs et al., 2007). We use the term *theoretical framework* to refer to segments of the existing literature that have been selected by the researcher to create a conceptual or content frame of reference for a research endeavour. Although the term "theoretical" is used, this literature includes research and theory as well as other sources of knowledge and information such as the Internet and informal literature such as news media.

Anfara and Mertz (2006) have presented a convincing discussion on the viewpoint that research is not an atheoretical process; researchers hold theoretical positions prior to conducting their research. Anfara and Mertz view theoretical frameworks being the theory or theories that can be applied to understanding the phenomena being researched, and they exclude methodological or paradigmatic aspects of the research framework. This view is similar to ours in making a distinction between the philosophical framework that guides the research method (see Chapter 4) and the conceptual or theoretical framework that informs understanding of the phenomenon or content of the research.

The Purpose of a Theoretical Framework

The purpose of a theoretical framework is to provide the theoretical underpinnings, boundaries, justification, lenses and critical reference points for the research. The boundaries and content of theoretical frameworks are both inclusive and exclusive; signalling the interests of the researcher. Framing the field of study also contributes to its focus. Furthermore, the credibility of the research is influenced by the grounding of the emergent knowledge in an existing knowledge framework.

Examples of Theoretical Frameworks

Anfara and Mertz (2006) explored a range of different examples of theoretical frameworks and associated disciplines in their book *Theoretical frameworks in qualitative research*. Table 7.1 is derived from and extends their ideas.

Importantly, many topics can be examined from a range of disciplinary and theoretical frameworks. For example, a study of professionalism could focus on theoretical areas such as professional socialisation, transitioning from practitioner to academic, ethical dilemmas of decision making, or generic values that underpin professionalism.

Table 7.1. Examples of theoretical frameworks (adapted from Anfara & Mertz, 2006)

Theoretical Framework	Field or Discipline
Culture (Goodenough, 1981)	Cognitive anthropology
Transformational learning (Mezirow, 1978)	Psychology, Adult learning
Liminality (Turner, 1977)	Anthropology
Social identity theory (Hogg, Terry, & White 1995)	Sociology
Grief model (Kubler-Ross, 1969)	Psychology
Queer legal theory (Lugg, 2006)	Law
Theory for the moral sciences (Schwandt, 1993)	Ethics
Professional socialisation (Higgs et al., 2009)	Professionalism
Skill acquisition (Dreyfus & Dreyfus, 1996)	Social sciences
Clinical decision making (Higgs, Jones, Loftus, & Christensen, 2008)	Health sciences

The Construction of a Theoretical Framework

The following questions can be employed to create a theoretical framework.

What are the major content areas in the literature
that relate to my given research questions and topic?

What is the scope of the research – its focus, boundaries, language etc. –
and how does this impact on the scope, volume and sources of literature needed?

What are the key knowledge claims and themes
in the research and theoretical literature in my topic area?

What are the main reference points (e.g. core arguments, major theories, historical trends, current challenges) in the fields of literature relating to my research topic?

Are there particular lenses or perspectives (e.g. critical theory)
that I wish to use to frame my inquiry? (see Chapter 8)

In constructing my theoretical framework
how am I positioning myself as researcher and scholar?

What literature is needed to describe and explain
the context of my research?

In choosing the sources of my literature,
how confident am I of the quality and credibility of these sources?

Is my research question clearly located as a needed
and missing issue or topic in the literature?
On this basis does my research have clear value
to warrant its conduct and the time and resources
I and others need to commit?

Making Decisions about One's Theoretical Framework

Constructing a theoretical framework involves a series of decisions to be made relating to the questions posed above, in consultation with the literature, the research team and possibly experts in the field. A theoretical framework represents the content area, whereas the philosophical framework construes the methods adopted for the research. Theoretical and philosophical frameworks are closely related, and shape and justify each other; however, the focus here is on constructing theoretical frameworks only. A useful starting point for constructing a theoretical framework is to determine the topic, research question(s) and context of the study. For example, a study of clinical decision-making might focus on (i) expert medical practitioners in emergency settings of a metropolitan area, (ii) novice dietitians in remote areas of Australia sharing the decision-making process with clients presenting with chronic conditions, or (iii) collaborative decision-making in multidisciplinary teams. All three examples would explore the topic of decision making, but the different contexts and the different professional practice foci help to shape the theoretical framework. Further, a clinical-decision-making study could be pursued as single case studies, as the cultural practice of a professional group, as a questionnaire, or as an interdisciplinary community of practitioners. Although the latter are philosophical considerations, they also shape the inclusion and exclusion criteria for a literature search and the theoretical framework.

A study of novice dietitians sharing the decision-making process with clients presenting with chronic conditions in remote areas of Australia would include the following content: a specific literature section dedicated to dietetic practice in Australia: undergraduate training, including national standards and competencies, curricula and pedagogy; a section on decision making in the health sector, with a focus on the dietetic context; a section on novice practice and transitions from student to graduate to expert. In collecting this literature the researcher provides background and context for the study, identifies existing research and searches for key theories that inform practices and perspectives adopted by investigators.

Each of these theoretical framework sections needs to be related and discussed to inform the chosen research topic. This approach builds the justification for the study, including the identification of gaps and of the need for this particular research. It is equally important to state which other bodies of literature about decision making are excluded, such as decision making in other health care settings, or decision making as intra-personal clinical reasoning. Constructing the theoretical framework is an exercise of carving out the research topic and terrain. This boundary setting makes the study manageable and sets the basis for it to build on existing knowledge, as well as the basis for considering future research directions beyond the study.

It is desirable initially to read widely in order to confidently determine what is the relevant body of literature to be explored. Studying reference lists of pertinent books and papers is a useful navigation exercise to identify key thinkers and seminal works on the chosen research topic. Making note of relevant journals and key words used in other papers is a strategy to help construct a literature search plan. Creating a flowchart of literature search strategies will increase the clarity and credibility of the theoretical framework.

THEORETICAL FRAMEWORKS

STANDING ON THE SHOULDERS OF GIANTS

The metaphor of dwarfs standing on the shoulders of giants refers to the idea that we can expand our understanding (of a topic or phenomenon) by building on the ideas of major thinkers and researchers who have (already) contributed to the body of literature or the knowledge foundations. The best known use of this phrase was by the 17th century scientist Isaac Newton who famously remarked in a letter to his rival Robert Hooke dated February 5, 1676, "If I have seen a little further it is by standing on the shoulders of Giants." However, Newton didn't originate the saying. The 12th century theologian and author John of Salisbury used a version of the phrase in a treatise on logic called *Metalogicon*, written in Latin in 1159. A translation of this writing is:

> We are like dwarfs sitting on the shoulders of giants. We see more, and things that are more distant, than they did, not because our sight is superior or because we are taller than they, but because they raise us up, and by their great stature add to ours.[1]

The following outline illustrates a choosing of giants that informed the research of a colleague (Loftus, 2009) who was investigating the nature of clinical decision making and the language that clinicians used in these situations. The project was informed by the contention that clinical decision making should be seen as a socially constructed phenomenon. Core issues identified for the project were context, culture and language. To match the phenomenon and these topics Loftus selected several giants whose work informed this research: Vygotsky (1986), Wenger (1998) and Wittgenstein (1958). According to Vygotsky, language and consciousness are intimately woven within a matrix of social activity. In these social situations people are required to articulate their thoughts and justify their opinions, thereby providing an opportunity to observe and analyse cognition in action. Wenger (1998) addressed the issue of culture and context in constructing professional identity within a community of practice, which involves learning the norms and language of that community. For Wittgenstein (1958), the analysis of language needs to be contextualised. If the goal is to achieve a better and deeper understanding of complex and multidimensional human phenomena such as the use of language, a theoretical framework is needed that permits a relevant conceptualisation of the issues at stake. This research demonstrates a unique synthesis and extension of the work of the selected giants (or key theorists).

PLANNING LITERATURE ENGAGEMENT

In a major research work like a thesis, planning a literature engagement that is credible, selective, meaningful and manageable involves several activities:

– **Framing** your research by reading widely enough in the topic area of the research to know with confidence (a) what research and theory exist in the field already, (b) what the gaps are in the field that your research will address, and (c) what the key literature areas are that you wish to select to inform your theoretical framework, and include the giants whose work your research will stand on.

- ***Contextualising*** your research by planning your introductory chapters, clarifying your research goals, questions and audience, and identifying what literature is needed to present the context or background of your research to your readers.
- ***Selecting appropriate research strategies*** to address your research questions and the phenomenon you have selected to research. (Consider the strengths and limitations of strategies used by others to research the same or similar topics.) This task informs the philosophical and methodological frameworks of the research (see Chapter 4).
- ***Reflecting critically*** during the research on the adequacy of the literature already obtained, and extending the research to additional areas based on your emerging research findings and feedback, e.g. from conference presentations.
- ***Reviewing*** your research findings in relation to pertinent research, e.g. studies of relevant topics, related theories or models, practice trends.

Placing the literature meaningfully and strategically in a thesis or major research report is another challenge. Some guidelines are as follows:

- It is useful to provide *background* literature in the introductory chapter(s), orienting readers to your work and educating them about the context of the study if they are not already familiar with it.
- The critical appraisal of the *literature of the field*, the platform upon which your research is built, commonly requires one or more chapters (depending on the topic complexity) early in the thesis, prior to reporting findings of your research.
- In *hermeneutic* studies the literature of the field may become the text or "data", replacing the literature chapters with one or more findings chapters. Further, the literature of the field may also signpost and indicate the appropriate philosophical background and research approach.
- Literature pertaining to the *research methods* would normally appear in a methods chapter. If the thesis reports several studies there could be a methods overview section early in the thesis, with relevant "big picture" literature placed in the introduction or a general methods chapter, followed by more detailed methods literature in the chapters that report the individual studies. In substantiating the research methods used, literature relating to the research paradigm, research approach, data collection strategies and data analysis strategies should be provided, followed by a report on the actual methods, timeline, participants, ethics procedures, etc., provided in sufficient detail and transparency for the research process to be judged for credibility and rigour.
- In the *findings* and *conclusion* chapters, literature should be included that assists critique of these findings and the product (e.g. themes, model, theory).

CONCLUSION

The theoretical framework of a study is an important contributor to framing and supporting qualitative research. It provides a collection of concepts, theories and perspectives that inform the study and thus provides a set of lenses through which the research is designed and the findings are interpreted. A theoretical framework explains and exposes the problem under investigation and it offers a rationale for the approach taken in exploring the chosen topic. It also makes explicit what will be noticed and explored, and indicates which theoretical aspects are not going to be included in a study. Constructing a theoretical framework is a key aspect of ensuring the quality and credibility of the research. Constructing the framework requires a deep understanding of the extant literature in order to identify its gaps, provide a basis for reviewing findings emerging from research, contribute new insights to the body of literature, and suggest further research directions. Sound research draws on, refers back to, critiques, and extends the body of literature.

NOTES

[1] http://www.phrases.org.uk/meanings/268025.html. Accessed 5 December 2009.

REFERENCES

Anfara, V. A., & Mertz, N. T. (2006). *Theoretical frameworks in qualitative research*. Thousand Oaks, CA: Sage.
Dreyfus, H. L., & Dreyfus, S. E. (1996). The relationship of theory and practice in the acquisition of skill. In P. A. Benner, C. A. Tanner, & C. A. Chesla (Eds.), *Expertise in nursing practice: Caring, clinical judgment and ethics* (pp. 29–47). New York: Springer.
Goodenough, W. (1981). *Culture, language, and society*. Menlo Park, CA: Benjamin/Cummings.
Higgs, J., Hummell, J., & Roe-Shaw, M. (2009). Becoming a member of a health profession: A journey of socialisation. In J. Higgs, M. Smith, G. Webb, M. Skinner, & A. Croker (Eds.), *Contexts of physiotherapy practice* (pp. 58–71). Melbourne: Elsevier Australia.
Higgs, J., Jones, M., Loftus, S., & Christensen, N. (Eds.). (2008). *Clinical reasoning in the health professions* (3rd ed.). Edinburgh: Elsevier.
Higgs, J., Trede, F., Ajjawi, R., Loftus, S., Smith, M., & Paterson, M. (2007). Journeys from philosophy and theory to action and back again: Being critical and creative in research design and action. In J. Higgs, A. Titchen, D. Horsfall, & H. Armstrong (Eds.), *Being critical and creative in qualitative research* (pp. 202–214). Sydney: Hampden Press.
Hogg, M., Terry, D., & White, K. (1995). A tale of two theories: A critical comparison of identity theory with social identity theory. *Social Psychology Quarterly, 17*(1), 255–269.
Kubler-Ross, E. (1969). *On death and dying*. New York: Touchstone.
Loftus, S. (2009). *Language in clinical reasoning: Towards a new understanding*. Saarbrücken, Germany: Vdm Verlag Dr. Müller.
Lugg, C. A. (2006). On politics and theory: Using an explicitly activist theory to frame educational research. In V. A. Anfara & N. T. Mertz (Eds.), *Theoretical frameworks in qualitative research* (pp. 175–188). Thousand Oaks, CA: Sage.
Mezirow, J. (1978). Perspective transformation. *Adult Education, 28*, 100–110.
Schwandt, T. A. (1993). Theory for the moral sciences. In D. J. Flinders & G. E. Mills (Eds.), *Theory and concepts in qualitative research: Perceptions from the field* (pp. 5–23). New York: Teachers College Press.
Turner, V. (1977). Variations on a theme of liminality. In S. F. Moore & B. G. Myerhoff (Eds.), *Secular Rites* (pp. 36–52). Amsterdam: Van Gorcum.
Vygotsky, L. S. (1986). *Thought and language* (A. Kozulin, Trans.). Cambridge, MA: MIT Press (originally published 1962).

Wenger, E. (1998). *Communities of practice: Learning meaning and identity*. Cambridge: Cambridge University Press.
Wittgenstein, L. (1958). *Philosophical investigations* (G. E. M. Anscombe, Trans., 3rd ed.). Upper Saddle River, NJ: Prentice Hall (originally published 1953).

AFFILIATIONS

Joy Higgs AM PhD
The Research Institute for Professional Practice, Learning & Education
The Education for Practice Institute
Charles Sturt University
Australia

Franziska Trede PhD
The Education for Practice Institute,
Charles Sturt University
Australia

ROBERT MACKLIN AND JOY HIGGS

8. USING LENSES AND LAYERS

INTRODUCTION

All researchers look at the world they are studying through different and multiple lenses. Lenses change the way we see the world, providing subtle or gross differences in perspectives, and all have an influence on what we take to be important, significant or meaningful. As researchers this is our reality; we cannot remove our lenses. As qualitative researchers we accept, own and embrace the impact of our lenses rather than seek to ignore, deny, or restrict them. To work without lenses would be to work blind, but even more than this, metaphorically it would be to work without any of our senses. In presenting the arguments in this chapter we do this not to undermine qualitative research. We are not seeking to wreck our craft on the rocks of relativism. Rather, we seek to sensitise researchers to the reality of research and to provide insights into how researchers can work with lenses and also communicate what we do in authentic terms.

All qualitative research is situationally embedded; it is historically, culturally, philosophically, theoretically, emotionally, morally, physically, locationally, and temporally bound. There is no "non-lensed" view in research. As for qualitative research, it is inherently a situated interpretation of a phenomenon. It is impossible to conduct qualitative research in an "objective" way that somehow stands above interpretation; to search for some kind of Archimedean point that is unencumbered by time, place, culture, theory and the hopes, joys and fears of the individual researcher. Qualitative researchers are not erroneously conducting their investigations through distorting lenses; nor would they be doing better research if they could somehow develop techniques and methods that removed the influences of history, culture, emotion, personality, etc. This would be a return to positivism which would be both undesirable and impossible.

Lenses, like values, cannot be removed. All researchers look through multiple and evolving lenses, some of which are integral to their identity, thereby constituting an internal frame of reference; others are external and contextual, but both impact on the researchers' priorities and goals and shape the way the phenomenon under study is viewed and understood. Also, we must remember that our participants' lenses frame and shape the way they understand their own experiences and the way they report these experiences to us as researchers.

This is not a new idea. Many writers have discussed the way human endeavours – ethics, politics, religion, history, research – are impossible to undertake and discuss free from an overlay of interpretation that we as social, cultural and historical beings inevitably bring to it (e.g. Sandel, 1990). In the study of history, Hegel (1770–1831) argued that we cannot break out of the prison house of our own contemporaneity. In the sphere of political philosophy and ethics, writers such as MacIntyre (1981, 1988) and Walzer (1994) have claimed that morality is always embedded in historically and communally shared meanings. Ethical norms and principles are not objective universals but are always defined by and located in particular communities at particular times and particular places. Guba and Lincoln (1989, p. 65) argued as follows about qualitative research paradigms:

> Values permeate every paradigm that has been proposed or might be proposed, for paradigms are human constructions, and hence cannot be impervious to human values ... Thus nature cannot be viewed as it really is (even if one starts with the assumption that there exists a real nature out there to be assessed) but only as seen (constructed) through some value window.

In this chapter we describe and analyse the ways in which typical activities of qualitative research are undertaken through lenses that colour and shape how researchers see the world and derive meaning from it. The chapter is divided into four sections. We first look at the role of lenses in the initial stages of most projects, when questions are being formulated. Second, we look at how the different lenses researchers put on enter into the research framing process. Third, we discuss the way the lenses through which researchers and the researched look can affect what sense is made of participants' input in the actual interview process.

That is, in the midst of the dialogue between the researcher and the researched, located as they are in a particular time and place, the lenses each wear affect what is discussed and how it is responded to. Fourth, we discuss the way in which the interpretation of data is driven by people's unique lenses and that, as such, every person's interpretation will be different and that even one person's interpretation will change over time.

QUESTION FORMULATION

Formulating the research question is an early priority for most researchers. Before launching into articulating a research framework or conducting interviews it can be argued that we should have a clear idea about the question that we are seeking to answer with our research. This question will reflect a particular phenomenon and will direct the investigation in fundamental ways. At this stage the way we look at a phenomenon and the nature of the lens through which we view things have a profound impact on the type of question we formulate. As a result there is rarely an obvious or stand-out question that everyone who looks at a phenomenon will ask. There is no single "right" question.

Questions can be framed by multiple factors. Of particular interest are epistemological lenses, moral lenses, and the "collective lenses" created in projects where there are multiple researchers. Different researchers wear different epistemological and moral lenses, which will make them think and assume things about the nature of knowledge and the nature of right and wrong. These lenses inevitably colour the researcher's deliberations about what questions to ask of the world. Moreover, they are not lenses that can be simply put away. For example, committed feminist researchers share a concern with gender which is ingrained into their identity and structures the way they see the world. And people who implicitly assume that we can access the world as it really is might not even question this assumption and might dismiss out of hand any alternative view. They will therefore never formulate questions that reflect other views of reality.

Epistemological lenses influence the way we think about what we can know about the world and the assumptions researchers make about the nature of knowledge. Some views or lenses portray reality as knowable by humans as it "actually" is, objectively and unmediated by human interests or bias. From this perspective, it is argued, we can attain "a god's eye" view and thus learn things about how something "really is". At another extreme are epistemological lenses that deny our capacity to ever observe phenomena in an unmediated fashion; that is, our views of the world always occur through filters such as the personal, cultural and historical backgrounds of the research participants.

The epistemological lens being used colours the way a question is formulated. For example, if the investigation is of a dispute between two groups of people, the objectivist would see no difficulty in formulating a question such as "What is the *real reason* the dispute occurred?" For the more subjectivist researcher, however, there would be a recognition that not only are the reasons for a dispute likely to vary between the different parties involved in the conflict but also the researcher's own background would influence the way a question is articulated. The research question could be "How do the disputing parties *view* the cause of the dispute?" and "How have these views *been shaped by* their socio-historical circumstances?"

Researchers also differ in their moral commitments, and these commitments may be (but are often not) realised and acknowledged. Taking a particular standpoint, for example in relation to feminism, race or homosexuality, is typically reflected in the research question(s). A feminist, for example, when researching the dispute raised above, will view the matter through a feminist lens and is likely to ask questions that focus on gender and whether the dispute reflects and reproduces gender inequality or power differences. Even researchers who do not recognise in themselves or identify with an explicit moral commitment are likely to structure questions in ways that fit their broad moral lenses (e.g. taking the view that inequality in the world is inherently inevitable).

Another set of lenses can be seen to transcend the individual and are formed during dialogue between multiple researchers in a project. Here it is common to discuss, debate and perhaps even negotiate the question or questions that will structure the study. Questions are thus formed out of the dynamic relationship that the researchers have built among themselves over time (involving communication dynamics and potential power struggles), and the resultant questions are likely to be different from how any single researcher might have framed them. The group will form, or at least agree to support, a collective way of viewing and understanding the world that is tantamount to a unique group culture mediating between researchers and the questions they are seeking to devise. In this way different research groups studying the same phenomena are likely to have different presuppositions, assumptions, norms, beliefs and dynamics and hence are likely to develop different questions.

FRAMING THE RESEARCH

A key task in conducting research is to frame the research project. This framing involves drawing boundaries around the study in terms of what is to be researched and why, with whom, how much, when and how. Setting these boundaries is a question of choice and, as such, is also a highly lensed activity.

Looking at the "what" first (and how much), researchers looking at the same phenomenon do not automatically or naturally focus on the same thing. That is, they are likely to create different boundaries around what is being researched.

There is a much hackneyed parable about several blind men seeking to describe an elephant by touch which demonstrates this idea quite well. All the blind men touch the elephant in just one place and thus describe the creature in very different ways.

One describes a trunk, another a leg, another a tail and another a stomach. Each is studying an elephant, but each reports on it in different terms.

Different researchers are likely to focus on different features of a phenomenon. In the hypothetical research about a conflict between two groups, one researcher might focus most of his or her attention on the tactics that each group uses, another on the interests and agenda pursued by each, and another might give more attention to one of the groups. And while one researcher might seek to understand the conflict within its broader organisational or social context, another might confine his or her study to the dynamics of the immediate dispute. Each of these different foci represents a different lens and will be shaped by a different set of interests, perspectives, value, experiences and hunches. This a priori frame of reference inevitably shapes what the researcher studies, highlights and reports.

Boundaries are also created around definitional variations. This relates to both the topic or phenomenon being studied (e.g. what is a group? What does power mean (in this context)?) and the method. In case study research, for instance, understanding of 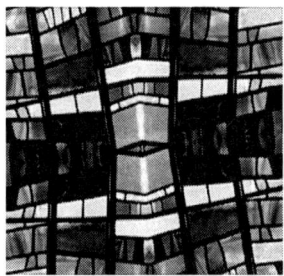 what constitutes a case may vary between researchers. Thus in studying organisational activity in a particular firm some researchers might identify the case as the complete organisation but others might narrow the focus to a division or a department, or even just one work process. The choices each researcher makes about what constitutes the case or unit of analysis will form the lens through which they view the case or organisation and will influence what they attend to or ignore. This decision has many consequences in relation to who is invited to participate in the study, the investigation strategies, the amount and type of data collected and the scope of the research findings.

The "what" of any study – another lens – is also influenced by the theoretical framework the researchers adopt. Thus, for example, the modernist sociologist who sees the world as a continual work of progress underpinned by widely accepted values and measured by clear objective criteria looks through a different set of lenses to the sociologist who takes a postmodern perspective and thus is far more circumspect about the inevitability of progress, the universality of values and the possibility of objective criteria. These underpinning lenses or assumptions will frame the research not only in terms of the overarching research question but also the whole approach that is taken. The modernist will likely be intent on uncovering data that accords with his or her claim of social progress, whereas the postmodernist is more likely to identify arguments for regression and disjuncture.

Turning to the "when" of research, historical timing creates unique lenses, as does the time researchers give to their projects. One can easily imagine that a researcher undertaking research into the stock market after the collapses of late 2008 and early 2009 will come to this study with a set of lenses very different from those a researcher would have worn in earlier years when the market was booming. The researchers'

a priori assumptions about what they will discover will be focused on different things, and these assumptions will influence what they look for and what they count as significant. What is happening in the stock market when they prepare to study it will have an effect on what they decide to examine. Regardless of how much they try to come to the study with an open mind their existing understanding of current market conditions will have a profound effect on how they frame and structure their study.

The amount of time a researcher can give a project is also clearly a form of lens that will influence what will be viewed. Different researchers face different imperatives when it comes to completion dates. Some qualitative researchers, who have extensive time to spend on investigating their phenomena, perhaps because they are undertaking a PhD, are able to examine in significant depth the important features, facets and dynamics of the phenomenon under study. They may also be able to return to the research site over and over in order to clarify points and ensure a deep understanding. For others undertaking research funded by industry grants or research with a policy focus, time pressures may be far greater. This could result in limited time in the field and a need for much greater clarity and tighter specification of data collection foci and timelines.

In relation to the "how" of research, qualitative researchers wear very different lenses to those who rely exclusively on quantitative methods. Qualitative researchers seek to collect data on what people say and think about a phenomenon and in doing so aim to accumulate a rich understanding of how people describe and experience their world in words and images, and rely on qualitative means of analysis. Quantitative researchers rely on quantitative analyses, for the large part of numerical data. These broad strategies thus reflect different data collection, analysis and reporting lenses and different expectations of the processes and products of research. Within qualitative research there are numerous methodological lenses that can be adopted, as illustrated in Section 3 of this book.

In many ways, the "why" lenses of research draw many of the other lenses together. At the framework setting stage, the raison d'être of any research project provides a key lens influencing the researchers' views of the phenomena under study. For some researchers the reason for conducting research is to understand the phenomenon, in which case they would choose to operate in the interpretive research paradigm, whereas for others changing the status quo is paramount and the critical research paradigm is the relevant avenue. Frequently researchers' theoretical, moral, political and paradigmatic frameworks can come together. Critical theorists, for example would argue that Western societies are not just, and that some privileged and powerful groups in society are able to influence and shape social structures and arrangements in ways that suit their ongoing interests and dominance. Their reason for undertaking research is to reveal this inequality and to empower people to question the current situation.

In summary, the frameworking stage of any project influences the direction and character of research in many ways and there are clearly many lenses operating at this stage. Each lens changes the way phenomena are observed and the way the

USING LENSES AND LAYERS

observations are conducted. There is no one way of setting the framework; it depends on the lenses through which people view this stage, which is influenced by the issues surrounding the what, when, how and why of the study.

THE RESEARCH INTERVIEW AND ITS LENSES

In interviews (along with other data collection methods used in qualitative research) the lenses of the researcher again shape the research process. Essentially, the researcher engages in a dialogue with the research participants in a particular setting created by the researcher. This dialogue, and hence the data collected, affect what is discussed and how it is responded to.

Before moving on to talk about specific lenses in the data collection context, it is important to point out that in this stage an added dynamic is that the researcher is not interacting with a passive research subject. In qualitative research the researcher is typically engaged in interviewing other human beings, who have their own agendas, beliefs, hopes and fears. In other words, the researched come to an interview with their own sets of lenses; they may choose to perform during the interview in yet another way, and this multiplies the complexity of the research act. The qualitative interview can be approached in many ways and so can be affected by an untold number of factors, in particular the questions asked, the relationship between the interviewer and the interviewee, and the spatial and locational context.

With respect to the interview questions there is no single list of appropriate questions for a particular study, nor is there a single right way to pace and deliver questions. Different researchers will construct different questions, bringing their unique set of lenses to the question construction process. Some researchers create more elaborate questions than others, some create longer lists and some are more comfortable with allowing questions to emerge out of the interview itself. Some of the variation here derives from the researcher's philosophical, theoretical and moral lenses and interests, whether they are consciously or unconsciously employed, and the data collection strategy. For example, Alvesson (2002) described a romantic view of the interview where the interviewer aims to establish genuine "equal" human interaction with the participants by building trust, rapport, and a meaningful dialogue involving shared revelations and interpretations that results in a co-constructed account of the topic under study. Another strategy is for researchers to ask open-ended questions and refrain from expressing their views, so that it is the participants' ideas that predominate. The focus here is on listening rather than sharing.

Different researchers also have different styles and competencies in data collection. Some may have finely honed critical skills, and thus when interviewing are capable of insightfully and quickly getting to the nub of the issue being investigated. Others, however, may have developed a strong capacity to draw out responses and reflections from the person they are interviewing. Sometimes negative factors such as stress, complacency and poor listening skills can bring lack of clear vision and limited listening skills to the interview. All these factors form the lenses through which

a researcher enacts the interview, and influence what the researcher discovers and understands about the phenomenon under study.

Conversations between two or more people are structured by the dynamic way people interact with each other, the way they catch each other's intentions and way of conversing, and the way they choose to flow with each other's waves of meaning. Different researchers and interviewees interact in different ways, thus creating conversations that are unique artefacts. We each bring different things to the conversation, but the conversation itself is more than the sum total of the lenses the parties bring. In the interaction between two or more people a unique artefact called the conversation is created that shapes what is understood about the phenomenon under study.

Another set of factors affecting the interview process consists more of what some might call externalities. These are not constructed from within the mind of the researcher or the interviewee. Rather, they are things such as the locational and spatial constraints on the interview, such as where the interview takes place.

Place has an effect and is another source of lenses. Conducting an interview in the relative comfort of a manager's office will afford the researcher different lenses than an interview conducted in someone's house or in a space that is busy, sparse or pressured. Our way of gazing at the world is affected by location. Every location has its own effect and probably different effects at different times.

ANALYSIS

Finally and briefly, data analysis, perhaps more than the other research stages, is a direct result of the way researchers consciously and unconsciously shape their research. Data analysis in qualitative research is a process and product of the researcher's frame of reference. Whereas some research approaches and traditions have a range of analysis strategies, in many cases analysis strategies are tailor-made to suit the research goals and informed by the research paradigm. The process of analysis is also organic and emergent; researchers adapt what they are doing as issues emerge.

Analysis begins with the first act of data collection. Each interview is interpreted as it progresses. The analysis is a driver of the research project, directing it, where it appears important to the researcher, into new areas, themes and concerns. The researcher builds the analysis around insights and adjusts the analysis questions around these insights.

The analysis process itself is replete with lenses. Perhaps most importantly, analysis must be understood as dealing with an engagement between the researcher and the text or narrative of interviews. It is thus open to the multitude of interpretations or lenses that readers can bring to any text or narrative. As a score of writers (e.g. Heidegger, 1962; Merleau-Ponty, 1962; Gadamer, 1975; Caputo, 2000) have argued over many years working from what can loosely be called a hermeneutic perspective, humans cannot read the world as disembodied, value-free, disinterested beings. We interpret the texts of interviews through the lenses of our history, language, culture, ideology, interests, preferences, personalities, hopes, fears and triumphs. Thus it is impossible for us as researchers to take ourselves out of the process of analysis; because of their ultimate uniqueness, every person brings a different set of lenses to the process.

CONCLUSION

In this chapter we have argued that different researchers see the world through different lenses and that this has a profound impact on what they ask about the world and on what answers they report. Even when it comes to the writing of research into papers or reports for publication, lenses will affect the outcome. Different writers construct their papers in different ways in accordance with the lenses of history, culture, skills, and what they perceive to be important. Even the ways they use language vary, structuring and shaping what they communicate in particular, unique ways.

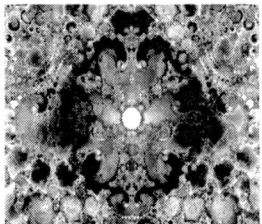

Researchers cannot remove their lenses, and despite their diversity these lenses provide us with the very possibility of being able to make sense of the world. But this also means that no lens brings us closer than any other to an objective view of reality. That is, no lens can enable us to knowingly reveal *the* truth. Rather, every lens can be claimed to reveal truths for a researcher. Such truths, if convincingly presented by the researcher, will be accepted by his or her peers and the broader audience as among the many possible truths about a phenomenon. And such truths will have longevity to the extent that they remain convincing and are pragmatically useful.

REFERENCES

Alvesson, M. (2002). *Postmodernism and social research*. Buckingham: Open University Press.
Caputo, J. D. (2000). *More radical hermeneutics: On not knowing who we are*. Indianapolis, IN: Indiana University Press.
Gadamer, H.-G. (1975). *Truth and method*. London: Continuum.
Guba, E. G., & Lincoln, Y. S. (1989). *Fourth generation evaluation*. Newbury Park, CA: Sage.
Heidegger, M. (1962). *Being and time*. New York: Harper Perennial.
MacIntyre, A. (1981). *After virtue: A study in moral theory*. London: Duckworth.
MacIntyre, A. (1988). *Whose justice? Which rationality?* London: Duckworth.
Merleau-Ponty, M. (1962). *Phenomenology of perception*. London: Routledge.
Sandel, M. J. (1990). *Liberalism and the limits of justice*. Cambridge: Cambridge University Press.
Walzer, M. (1994). *Thick and thin: Moral argument at home and abroad*. Notre Dame, IN: University of Notre Dame Press.

AFFILIATIONS

Rob Macklin, PhD
The Research Institute for Professional Practice, Learning & Education
Faculty of Business
Charles Sturt University
Australia

Joy Higgs AM PhD
The Education for Practice Institute
Charles Sturt University
Australia

SUSAN GROUNDWATER-SMITH

9. RESEARCHING ETHICALLY?

In some ways the title to this chapter belies its contents, for its question mark suggests that it is conceivable that one may undertake practice-based research unethically – that is, in a way that might do harm to those who participate. It is difficult to imagine a case where research is undertaken that would be deliberately unethical in its intent. It cannot simply be assumed, however, that full attention has been paid to the matter of ethical behaviour in either the imagination or conduct of the research. It is my contention in this chapter that to research ethically is to have concern for the impact upon the wellbeing of those who participate uppermost in the mind of the researcher(s), and for it not be a matter that is taken for granted.

To make this point clearly I commence the chapter with an anecdote from my own practice, in which a large independent girls' school catering for students from Kindergarten to Year 12 engaged me to conduct an enquiry. My brief was to investigate the ways in which the current assessment practices were commensurable with the beliefs about the ways in which students learn that were held by all the stakeholders, including the parents. The study was seen as an educational impact study, in that it was believed that prior to making changes to assessment practices it was desirable first to identify current policies and procedures.

As part of this complex investigation, which included both teachers and students in the research team, it was agreed that I would conduct focus group discussions with samples of parents from given age cohorts. Thus I found myself one evening holding several focus groups with parents of girls in the junior school. Since the discussions were not to be recorded I undertook to provide to each participant in any given group a portrayal of the meeting; a portrayal that could be amended, if necessary. This, I believed, provided an appropriate membership check. Parents were advised that once the portrayal was approved it would go into the case record and be available for analysis, but that the names of those participating would be confidential. All this appeared to be quite a smooth operation. However, one group had quite a robust discussion of the current practices. On receiving the portrayal, one parent promptly printed it out and made it her business to share with others, who had not participated, in the school playground the following morning. She also divulged the names of the other participants. Although the damage was not huge it reminded me of the sensitivity of this kind of work. Clearly, I should have been explicit about the boundaries and requested a more formal commitment on the part of the participants not to openly discuss the proceedings at this early juncture.

We cannot promise, in the conduct of practice-based research, or in any research involving human participants, to do "no harm", simply because we cannot conceive of the harm we might do. But we can work assiduously to minimise harm. Researching ethically is researching in such a way that we are sensitive to the consequences of our work, taking account of its impact on the various stakeholders and their needs, rights and responsibilities.

In this chapter I discuss a range of desiderata that need to be taken into account when giving due and proper consideration to designing and engaging in a research project that is linked to professional practice. Because my own experience is in the field of education many of my examples draw upon the range of practices found therein. However, I am mindful that those who choose to read the chapter might be engaged in other professional fields and communities, such as those found in health and social care, and I hope that they will find the parallels and congruences. Furthermore, I am aware that the focus is upon qualitative research practices, but argue that ethics associated with human research, whatever methodology is chosen, should adhere to the maxims and principles that I articulate here.

RESEARCHING ETHICALLY AS A REALISABLE GOAL

I intend to treat researching ethically as an aim or goal that "we deeply desire to realise" (De Ruyter, 2003, p. 468). Although some, such as Heyting (2004), would contest this position as one that is an approximation of an ideal rather than something that is realisable, I find it useful in that it suggests what might and should motivate the researcher, but also allows for a complex and imperfect world. Research that is worth doing is research that addresses the hard questions and has an intention to improve and transform the practices that are being investigated (Groundwater-Smith & Mockler, 2008). Giving due consideration to the ethical implications of research practice is vital to the research process itself. As Gorman (2007, p. 23) has noted in defence of university human research ethics committees, when treated and used positively their ethics review processes should enhance rather than detract from the research. In other words, researching ethically is the first step to researching well. As Hazlett, McAdam and Murray (2007, p. 671) have asserted, "quality lives in symbiosis with ethics". Ethical practice is the essential foundation upon which authentic research quality is built.

In their account of the connection between quality and ethics, Ahmed and Machold (2004) provided a set of domains for ethical accountability as a form of moral responsibility, voiced as maxims, these being:
- The maxim of no-harm (as far as is possible and predictable)
- The maxim of transparency
- The maxim of voice
- The maxim of equity
- The maxim of benefit
- The maxim of integrity
- The maxim of liberty
- The maxim of care (pp. 539–542)

Although these are cited in the context of management they have equal application in the conduct of practice-based research. It is worth considering each one.

No Harm

It has already been argued that we cannot guarantee that an outcome of research will or will not be harmful; but we can attempt as far as is possible to minimise harm. Research that sets out to deliberately deceive those who participate is inherently harmful, for it denies agency and opportunities to provide alternative explanations for that which has been investigated and documented. Thus, covert research is highly questionable. After all, if the only person knowing the "truth" of the situation is the researcher, how can we trust the research findings that themselves cannot be verified?

Some years ago a newspaper reporter presented himself to a Sydney high school as a student. He spent some weeks at the school and then wrote an "exposé" of the student culture. Given his descriptions it was not difficult to identify the school, or indeed some of the students themselves. However, they had no right of reply, no means to redress some of the harm that was done to the reputation of their school. As a research ethics manager, Gorman (2007) points out the difficulties in research for journalists. She argues that although they do not see themselves having a duty to disclose to their sources they do have a duty to society as a whole, but that does not give them a right to use force, coercion or to engage in exploitative behaviour.

> Journalists have often justified their actions as being for the benefit of society at large. But one of the underpinning ethical principles, that of respect for persons, derives from the view that someone cannot be used as a means to an end, especially if they have no choice in the matter (Gorman, 2007, p. 15)

In conducting social research it is essential that the risks to those participating are carefully and sensitively weighed against the benefits that the research may bring.

Transparency

In decrying covert research I also wish to advocate for research practice that fully informs all who take part through a process of consent. The challenge lies with the ways in which consent is obtained. Too often the requirement is a legalistic one, couched in a language that is unnecessarily bureaucratic and alienating. Being transparent, particularly with vulnerable groups, means providing information that can be readily understood, an issue related to situated ethics.

Transparency is not only a matter of informed consent; it also relates to the ways in which the research is to be made public. How will the results be communicated? Will they be disseminated in such a way that those whose work and lives have been examined would find them inexplicable and unrecognisable? Although it may not always be possible to share a whole report, it is important that the charge of exploitation cannot be levelled.

Voice

This brings us to the matter of whose voice is heard. Does the research unintentionally seek out those who may be compliant, or articulate, or hold powerful positions? Or is it inclusive of those voices that may express dissent or difference? Much of my research has been in school-based inquiries that have involved the students as consequential stakeholders (Groundwater-Smith, 2007). I have observed how much easier it is to consult the resilient students, the ones who are seen by their schools as capable communicators, than to create opportunities to engage with those who operate at the margins of school life. When we limit the voices that are heard we are in danger of developing celebratory rather than incisive accounts of what takes place and why.

Equity

Closely linked to the matter of voice is that of equity. Problems can arise where there is an obvious power differential between the participants in the research process. Here we have something of a two-edged sword. Although in many practice-based research contexts it is more often the case that the researcher(s) has the greater control, especially in relation to those who use the service, it might also be that some participants are themselves powerful actors in the field. They may seek to mute the voices of those with lesser status. In a study conducted a number of years ago (MacDonald, Adelman, Kushner, & Walker, 1982) a group of researchers from the Centre for Applied Research in Education (CARE) at the University of East Anglia conducted an evaluation of a bilingual program in Boston, USA. The researchers interviewed the teachers in the program, which was in danger of being de-funded. But they also interviewed the powerful mayor. Although the researchers were courteous, the text of the book reveals that the latter interview was conducted in a far more confronting and abrasive manner than those with the teachers in the threatened program, the argument being that he had many more avenues for expressing and defending his policies.

Benefit

Practice-based research is first and foremost a human endeavour, with all the dilemmas and traps that can be imagined in complex social settings. "Who benefits?" can be a tricky question. If the truth be told, the principal benefit may often come the researchers' way. A well-conducted study published in a prestigious journal may contribute to academic advancement but have little impact upon the lives of those who were the subjects of the inquiry. Many indigenous people argue that their lives and the conditions of their living have been "colonised" by researchers. Tuhiwai Smith (1999, quoted in Robinson-Pant, 2005, p. 14) points out how Western research cultures privilege certain discourses and forms of communication, for example the written over the oral. Nowhere has this been more evident than in the Australian "History Wars" where the historian Keith Windschuttle (2002) claimed that much of the calamitous history of Indigenous Australians in colonial times was little more than a fabrication, in that little is documented in the official records and much relies on verbal testimony. Although this sorry story may seem somewhat remote from our central concern for researching ethically in practice-based contexts, it speaks to us of the damaging ways in which academic careers can be built upon the backs of those who have little or no power or authority in our society.

Integrity

Clearly, the maxim of benefit is closely allied to that of integrity, which requires both the individual and the institution to have a proper regard and respect for both self and others. A research practice that is based upon integrity foresees the consequences of both the underlying convictions and policies and the overt actions. Integrity requires reflection and self-assessment, with due concern for both the means and the ends of the research. Institutions that commission research should be structured in such a way as to promote integrity (Babbitt, 1997). Those engaged in practice-based research may find their personal integrity undermined if the commissioners of the research have difficulty in promoting ethical values.

Liberty

An important value to be considered in the context of practice-based qualitative research is that of liberty – being able to ask, debate and publish the difficult questions and issues. One of the challenges facing those who undertake commissioned research, as opposed to internal practitioner research, is the extent to which control is exercised over the publication of results, particularly when they are of a controversial nature. As Curtain (2000) pointed out, the bargaining power of the researcher is often low, as through the tendering process, those who commission generally have an alternative regarding to whom they can turn. Although there may be sound reasons for not releasing a given report, it should also be made clear why this is so and that it is not merely a capricious decision designed to protect powerful and entrenched interests. A specific recommendation made by Curtain is that the commissioned researcher should have the right to publish with an explicit acknowledgement that the report reflects the view of the researcher(s), and a statement as to the reservations that may be held by those commissioning the study.

Care

Clearly all the above maxims impact upon the notion of care; that is, showing consideration and respect for all who are engaged in the research process. Exhibiting care requires that all who are engaged in the research process are alert to the responses and needs of others. It is an empathic enterprise that seeks to weigh the requirements of one group against the needs of another. But there is another perspective of care that should be taken into account, and that is being careful about the research itself.

We might ask ourselves a series of questions:
- Have we been clear about the nature of the research in terms of its goals?
- Have we thought through the most appropriate methodology that will attend to the maxims outlined above?
- Have we ensured that we have engaged with the full range of stakeholders?
- Have we collected data in such a way that allows for confirmation and disconfirmation?
- Has the relationship between the researcher(s) and participants been fully considered?
- Has due attention been given to the publication and dissemination of the research?
- Has the research effort been worthwhile, contributing to the public good?

Being careful must surely be central to the work of undertaking research, whether quantitative or qualitative. It is not always easy. Too often, in response to the need to make policy-on-the-run, researchers are asked to produce "quick and dirty" research, which is generally of little real use and may indeed compromise the enterprise and impact negatively upon researcher professionalism.

ETHICAL ASPECTS OF PROFESSIONALISM

The eight maxims discussed above accord well with Bottery's (1996) articulation of the ethical aspects of professionalism which are essential in the formation of professional practice that also includes practitioner inquiry, these being: an ethic of truth; an ethic of subjectivity; an ethic of reflective integrity; an ethic of humility and an ethic associated with the duty of care. Of these I want most particularly to focus upon the notions of truth, subjectivity and reflective integrity. Can we ever know that we have rendered a "true" account of the circumstances being investigated? The answer is probably "no"; but we can, as a realisable goal, ensure that we have not dissembled, that we have recognised our subjectivity and values and the subjectivity and values of those who participate in the research. Where possible, these have been made explicit, and we as researchers have subjected ourselves to a scrutiny that involves others being able to critique and question our research practices as a result of our being open and transparent.

I have argued elsewhere (Groundwater-Smith, 2006) that knowledge about practice is gained basically through a process of mutual understanding, a so-called double hermeneutic process (Giddens, 1976). Those directly engaged in the research interpret an already interpreted world; those affected by the research may comment on that interpretation, and so on. In the process of mutual understanding the research partners and participants try to get to know and to trust each other as equals in self-knowledge about their other-ness (Ricoeur, 1991). According to Ricoeur, practical reasoning is answering the question, "Why, to what end are you doing the research?" It is ordering "the long chain of reasons" that drive inquiry (p. 193). It is knowledge gained through dialogue as a necessary condition for all who participate to learn their possibilities for self-determination.

All of these are realisable goals. They are tools for thinking when designing research in practice settings. Importantly they can also be made explicit. However, such goals themselves are mediated within different settings and contexts and take on different significance in relation to the practices conducted therein.

SITUATED ETHICS

Because the view I hold of practice-based research is one that believes that it is undertaken in the company of others, it is essential that we have an understanding, not only of who those "others" are but of the context in which they act, a context that shapes their actions, a context that has a history and social geography (Simons & Usher, 2000). In effect, it is a context that acknowledges that the physical, geographical, and historical conditions in which practices arise will play their part in shaping that context and the values that arise therein. Carr (2006, in which he cites Gadamer) reminds us that we should consider contexts within whichever epoch prevailed that conditioned the practices that arose within them. Just as the members of a group of researchers interact one with the other intersubjectively, they also do so under a range of conditions and in a variety of practice settings that give shape and substance to what they can imagine, undertake and reflect upon. In this way we can consider that practice-based research is enacted within what Kemmis and Grootenboer (2008) referred to as "practice architectures" (pp. 57–61). As they argued:

> The way these practice architectures are constructed shapes practice in its cultural-discursive, social-political and material-economic dimensions, giving substance and form to what is and can be actually said and done by, with and for whom.

Thus although the intentions and principles of practice-based research may be shared across many practice settings, the enactment must necessarily vary in accordance with the material, sociopolitical and cultural formations within which they are constructed. In effect the research is itself mediated inter alia by place, time, culture and history, as well as by the tools that it employs. To illustrate the argument I shall discuss two contexts, one that considers inquiry in multi-cultural settings, the other that employs the medium of visual imagery as a research tool which has a number of associated problematics.

Inquiry in Multi-Cultural Settings

Anna Robinson-Pant (2005) took on the challenging task of examining the issues and dilemmas faced by international students undertaking postgraduate research studies in the United Kingdom. Of course, her book is not exclusively directed to that setting and could equally apply in places such as Australasia or Canada, or the United States of America for that matter. She was concerned to uncover the ways in which the social and educational histories of the postgraduate students and their academic teachers had an impact upon the ways in which they conceptualised and evaluated educational research. In particular, she was anxious to address the matter of developing a critical orientation to research practice. Her aim was to use the opportunity to examine postgraduate research conducted by overseas students as a time when a richer and better-informed perspective can be developed regarding the ways in which postgraduate research can be conceptualised as a moral practice beyond the rituals of teaching research methods and academic writing processes.

A feature of the book is the inclusion of extended reflections written by the research students themselves. Scholastica N. Mokake's powerful piece on the inappropriate oversight of research ethics management committees (pp. 118–123) should be required reading for those institutions whose objective seems more aligned to risk management than ensuring harm minimisation – a position in contrast to that advocated for by Gorman (2007) and cited earlier in this chapter. Mokake concludes:

> A number of guidelines for ethical research have appeared recently emphasizing the notion that the researcher should respect the rights of the people they study. That is, what I am trying to say here, I respect the rights of the people I am researching. Therefore, I am suggesting that the researcher should be left to follow procedures which safeguard the people of the researched area. It may not make sense to conduct research in Africa following the research procedures of the United Kingdom. (p. 123)

Confronting people with very limited literacy skills with official, indeed officious, letters requiring "informed consent" could itself be seen as an unethical practice in that there is scant regard for the dignity of those being assailed by the bureaucratic demands. Furthermore, different cultural contexts require sensitive interpretations of what has taken place and why it is so. This is not to invoke some kind of crude social relativism, but rather to invoke the need to be alert to what is honoured and respected in a given community. It is not uncommon, in school education for example, to find an orientation that decries the practice of coaching students in preparation for taking tests for placement in selective schools or of engaging in what is to be seen as rote learning or repetitive practice. Some might argue that there is an implicit valorising of innate capabilities over effort, the latter being decried as the concern of overly ambitious parents. But a researcher willing to maintain an open mind, and able to probe those parental ambitions, may find that they are based upon much deeper beliefs than hitherto imagined. For many families with a Confucian orientation effortful learning, closely allied to hard work, is essential for academic success (Tweed & Lehman, 2002), surely a position to be honoured and respected.

Turning now to a very different matter in relation to a consideration of situated ethics I wish to discuss an issue associated with method in context, rather than culture in context i.e. the use of visual media, in particular photography.

Visual Imagery as a Qualitative Research Tool

In her powerful polemic *Regarding the Pain of Others*, Susan Sontag (2003, p. 81) reminds us that photographs objectify, "they turn an event or a person into something that can be possessed. And photographs are a species of alchemy, for all that they are prized as a transparent account of reality". She does not invoke the notion of alchemy by chance, but uses it as a metaphor that suggests a capacity to take messy, chaotic fragments of what is taking place and apparently rend them as a coherent whole. Just as alchemists seek to transform the commonplace into a valuable commodity, so can the photographer render the complex world of practice into a fixed image on a page. Transparency is a chimera; it does not exist; photography, and for that matter moving images, are seductive but opaque, for much that is not in the image is lost or remains obscured.

For this reason the use of visual imagery as a qualitative research tool, although powerful, must be tempered with caution. Prosser (2000) pointed out the ethical predicaments faced when employing visual imagery and argued that participants must be assured that they will not be misrepresented, or their image distorted or taken out of context. Even the title of an image can mislead. Captions need to reference who, what, where, when and why. But too often they implicitly editorialise: "Children enjoying a football game". How do we know that they are enjoying it? On what basis is the claim being made? Prosser also made a case for ensuring that the act of capturing images is overt and not one where the subjects of the photography are unaware of the pictures being taken.

One way to overcome some of these difficulties is for the participants themselves to be the people who take the photographs and provide their explanations of their relevance to the matter being investigated. In my work with the Australian Museum we have given young people cameras and asked them to photograph the things that helped and hindered their learning in the museum (Groundwater-Smith & Kelly, 2003). The photographs then became a touchstone for further discussion and conversation. Schratz-Hadwich, Walker and Egg (2004) presented a powerful and moving account of the ways in which young people visually evaluated the provisions made for their wellbeing in contexts where they had encountered violence and oppression, arguing that it was a step "into integrating experience and tacit knowledge which otherwise might not become visible" (p. 20). Simons and Usher (2000) have reminded us that situated research is "immune to universalization" (p. 2). The above discussion also reminds us of the complexity of qualitative research as a deeply human enterprise.

CONCLUSION - RESEARCHING AS A MORAL PRACTICE

As I have already asserted, to engage in research is to undertake an intentional activity whose purpose is to investigate knotty and challenging problems. It is an attempt to make sense of the practice setting and render it intelligible to the self and others. But it is more than just undertaking a set of specific actions, of ticking the boxes that may be a requirement of sponsoring organisations and the like. It is working the terrain as a moral practitioner. As Pring (2001, p. 421) wrote, "It is impossible to conceive of a moral life without implicit reference to a set of principles that are embodied within moral practice. But that does not mean that one can, as it were, read off from that code or those principles what exactly one should do on any one occasion."

Practice-based researchers engaged in qualitative research in any number of social enterprises not only have a technical obligation to undertake the research in a responsible manner, but also have a moral obligation to maximise the participation of all who have a stake in the work.

REFERENCES

Ahmed, P., & Machold, S. (2004). The quality and ethics connection: Towards virtuous organisations. *Total Quality Management, 15*(4), 527–545.
Babbitt, S. (1997). Personal integrity and politics in moral imagination. In S. Brennan, T. Isaacs, & M. Milde (Eds.), *A question of values: New Canadian perspectives on ethics and political philosophy* (pp. 107–131). Amsterdam & Atlanta: Rodopi.
Bottery, M. (1996). The challenge to professionals from the new public management implications for the teaching profession. *Oxford Review of Education, 22*(2), 179–197.
Carr, W. (2006). Philosophy, methodology and action research. *Journal of Philosophy of Education, 40*(4), 421–435.
Curtain, R. (2000, June). Towards greater transparency in policy making. *Canberra Bulletin of Public Administration, 96*, 1–5.
De Ruyter, D. (2003). The importance of ideals in education. *Journal of Philosophy of Education, 37*(3), 467–482.
Giddens, A. (1976). *New rules of sociological method.* London: McMillan.
Gorman, S. (2007). Managing research ethics: A head-on collision? In A. Campbell & S. Groundwater-Smith (Eds.), *An ethical approach to practitioner research* (pp. 8–23). London: Routledge.
Groundwater-Smith, S. (2006, March 17–18). *Practice based research: The dilemmas we face.* Keynote presented to the UTS Student Research Conference, University of Technology Sydney.
Groundwater-Smith, S. (2007). Student voice – Essential testimony for intelligent schools. In A. Campbell & S. Groundwater-Smith (Eds.), *An ethical approach to practitioner research* (pp. 113–128). London: Routledge.
Groundwater-Smith, S., & Kelly, L. (2003, September 11–13). *As we see it: Improving learning at the museum.* Paper presented at the annual conference of the British Educational Research Association, Edinburgh.
Groundwater-Smith, S., & Mockler, N. (2008). Ethics in practitioner research: An issue of quality. In J. Furlong & A. Oancea (Eds.), *Assessing quality in applied and practice-based research in education – continuing the debate* (pp. 79–91). London: Routledge.
Hazlett, S., McAdam, R., & Murray, L. (2007). From quality management to socially responsible organisations: The case for corporate social responsibility. *International Journal of Quality and Reliability Management, 24*(7), 669–682.
Heyting, F. (2004). Beware of ideals in education. *Journal of Philosophy of Education, 38*(2), 241–247.
Kemmis, S., & Grootenboer, P. (2008). Situating praxis in practice. In S. Kemmis & T. Smith (Eds.), *Enabling praxis: Challenges for education* (pp. 37–62). Rotterdam: Sense.
MacDonald, B., Adelman, C., Kushner, S., & Walker, R. (1982). *Bread and dreams: A case study of bilingual schooling in the USA.* Norwich: Centre for Applied Research in Education, University of East Anglia.
Pring, R. (2001). The virtues and vices of an educational researcher. *Journal of Philosophy of Education, 35*(3), 407–422.
Prosser, J. (2000). The moral maze of image ethics. In H. Simons & R. Usher (Eds.), *Situated ethics in educational research* (pp. 116–132). London: Routledge Falmer.
Ricoeur, P. (1991). *From text to action: Essays in hermeneutics, II.* Evanston, IL: Northwestern University Press.
Robinson-Pant, A. (2005). *Cross cultural perspectives on educational research.* Maidenhead: Open University Press.

Schratz-Hadwich, B., Walker, R., & Egg, P. (2004, November 28–December 2). *Photo-evaluation: A participatory tool in child care and education.* Paper presented to the annual conference of the Australian Association for Research in Education, Melbourne. Retrieved from http://www.aare.edu.au/04pap/sch04245.pdf

Simons, H., & Usher, R. (2000). *Situated ethics in educational research.* London: Routledge Falmer.

Sontag, S. (2003). *Regarding the pain of others.* New York: Farrar, Straus & Giroux.

Tweed, R., & Lehman, D. (2002). Learning considered within a cultural context: Confucian and Socratic approaches. *American Psychologist, 57*(2), 89–99.

Tuhiwai Smith, L. (1999). *Decolonising methodologies: Research and indigenous peoples.* London/Dunedin: Zed Books/University of Otago Press.

Windschuttle, K. (2002). *The fabrication of Australian history: Volume 1.* Sydney: Macleay Press.

AFFILIATION

Susan Groundwater-Smith PhD
Faculty of Education and Social Work
University of Sydney
Australia

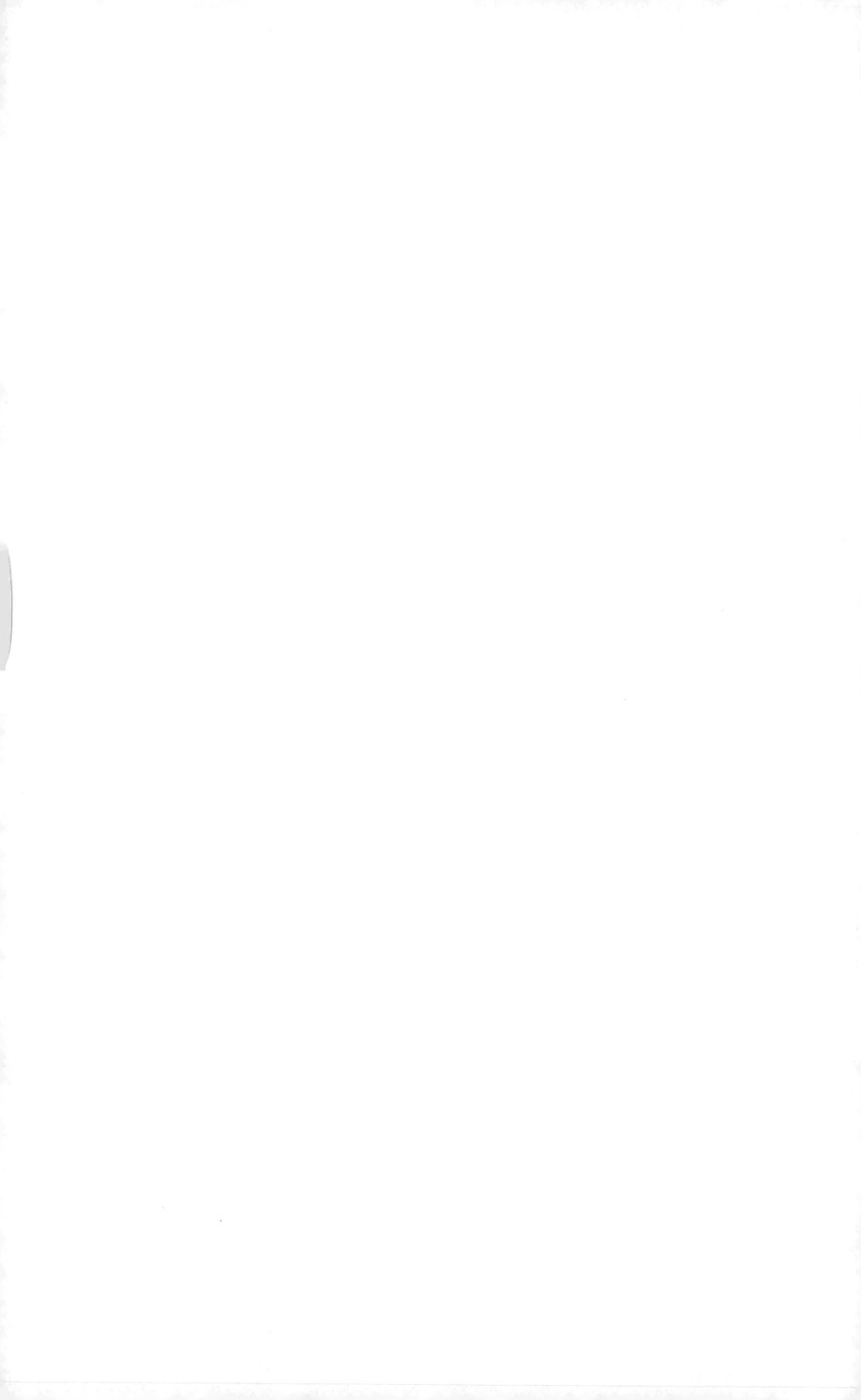

NITA CHERRY

10. RESEARCH AS PRAXIS:

Growing as a Person through Research

INTRODUCTION

Most of what is written about research, understandably, is focused either on the subject matter of the research or on the design and implementation of its methods and processes. Consideration of the researcher as a person comes into play most often from the perspective of researcher-as-designer of the research, researcher-as-creator or interpreter of data, or researcher-as-ethicist or activist. Indeed, many qualitative methodologies regard transparent inquiry into the researcher's presence and mindset in any given piece of research as critical to the rigour and richness of the methodology.

What is much less common is interest in the researcher as ongoing practitioner-of-research. I suggest that it is helpful for everyone who engages with research over a significant period of time (either directly or through the supervision of others) to think of themselves as practitioners of research and to be insightful about the ways in which they are influenced by their experiences of research. The kind of insight I have in mind goes well beyond simply a consciousness of preferred methods and techniques, to a mindfulness of how we are changed as people by our engagement with research. Indeed, I suggest that a person's research practice deserves the kind of reflexive mindfulness that would transform it into praxis. This framing draws attention to the reciprocal dynamics between the ways the researcher influences the research and the ways in which research itself changes the researcher.

WHAT PRACTICE REPRESENTS

Drawing attention to the researcher-as-practitioner-of research straight away shifts the focus from any particular piece of research – or even the outcomes of the researcher's body of work as a whole – to the distinctive ways in which the researcher engages with his or her research activity. It also draws into focus the ways in which the person can be changed by the practice of research.

Practice in any context (including research) represents a composite or amalgamation of the ways individuals have learned to engage with the phenomena and situations that recur in their life or work. So it incorporates the very complex, integrated set of behaviours – thoughts feelings, actions – through which a human being or group of people consistently engage with the tasks, problems and issues that regularly involve or confront them.

J. Higgs, N. Cherry, R. Macklin and R. Ajjawi (eds.),
Researching Practice: A Discourse on Qualitative Methodologies, 87–94.
© *2010 Sense Publishers. All rights reserved.*

Parenting is a good example of a complex phenomenon about which people get lots of advice, that is the subject of all sorts of cultural norms and expectations, and about which many books have been written. But it is not something that parents can learn or do by rote. They must develop and then keep adjusting the practices that make up their own particular way of being a parent.

In the context of vocational and professional work, practice means the range of phenomena that the person regularly deals with. Some of those phenomena will involve tasks and issues that the person regards as being routine and not particularly hard. Others will be more difficult, requiring the person to dig a bit deeper than usual for an effective outcome. Others again will be right at the edge of the person's practice expertise and might involve significant development of the person's repertoire.

The idea of practice is very familiar to us when we think about the services that people are able to provide under any process of formal trade, professional or legal accreditation. But I'd suggest that is useful to apply the notion of practice to include any body of work that a person regularly participates in that requires more than just a limited and set range of behaviours. Given that most jobs involve some kind of human interaction, there are very few jobs that are so predictable that they have no element of choice at all. So I'd suggest that most people could be said to have a practice in the sense that I'm describing. Certainly research is an activity that falls well and truly within the domain of practice.

Practice consists of many ways of "knowing" and sense-making, and many ways of linking knowledge to effective action. It implies both variety of repertoire and organisation of that repertoire into skilled enactment. It can involve both long and conscious deliberation and rapid choices that are made inside and outside of conscious awareness. As Polanyi (1967) has pointed out, many aspects of practice become tacit and we know much more than we can say.

Although many aspects of routine practice might become habitual or automatic, the implication of professional practice is that it has a repertoire from which selections need to be made in the face of novel or more complex situations. So there is an element of choice – conscious or unconscious – of the specific techniques that might be used in response to a particular situation. Sometimes those choices need to be made quickly, under pressure and in conversation with other people. At other times, the choices can take a long time or be made privately and individually. Sometimes the impacts and consequences of choices are immediately obvious and at other times the results are more subtle and take longer to appear. Whatever the situation, such choices are made by human beings, and as such are distinctive and personal, especially when viewed over time.

PRACTICE IN THE CONTEXT OF COMPLEXITY

The value of examining practice is perhaps most obvious to us when the field of practice is complex, risky, problematic and/or rich with possibility. Complexity, as I'm defining it here, consists of dilemmas, problems and opportunities located at the limits of a person or group's existing practice wisdom. Of course, complexity is a matter of degree. What is complex for one person at one time might not be complex for another. But in more absolute terms, complexity could be said to be present for individuals when they find that any response they offer is much less than complete, that what they do will probably makes things even more problematic (at least initially) or have consequences that are hard to predict or control.

To engage with such complexity implies the experience of being profoundly tested in terms of skill, knowledge and confidence and being found wanting, at least initially. Many people retreat at this point, and either acknowledge that something is "too hard" for them or else pretend that the issue is not worth bothering with. Sometimes they just try to simplify it in ways that don't do justice to the issue but make them feel as though they are doing something useful about it. To stay engaged without distorting or diminishing the situation means operating in the space of "not-knowing" for extended periods of time. This experience might be exciting, scary, or just something uncomfortable that has to be lived with.

In his book *Educating the Reflective Practitioner*, Schön (1987, p. 3) summed up very nicely the dilemma confronting practitioners in this context:

> In the varied topography of professional practice, there is a high hard ground overlooking a swamp. On the high ground, manageable problems lend themselves to solution through the application of research-based theory and technique. In the swampy lowland, messy, confusing problems defy technical solution. The irony of the situation is that the problems of the high ground tend to be relatively unimportant to individuals or society at large, however great their technical interest may be, while in the swamp lie the problems of greatest human concern.

As Schön put it, these messy, problematic situations arise when we are confronted with things that fall outside the categories of existing theory and technique, when there are serious conflicts among the values that are being brought to bear on the situation, or when there are varying multi-disciplinary perspectives available to us. These indeterminate zones of practice – characterised by uncertainty, uniqueness, conflict and confusion – sit apart from what he called the canons of technical rationality.

Arguably these are precisely the sorts of situations that become central to the continuing development of serious professional practice. Such situations will trigger either regression of practice (flight from the complexity involved) or growth of practice to a whole new level of skill. I suggest that those who try to research the issues of serious professional practice will inevitably face the same complex challenges and opportunities and the same pathways to regression or growth of their practice.

THE PERSONAL DIMENSION: FROM PRACTICE TO PRAXIS

Any serious examination of professional practice – and how it evolves – inevitably involves attention to the *being* of practitioners and not simply to their tools of trade or to the curricula and formal learning processes through which those tools are acquired. The practice of individuals and of a group or society are the embodiment, through action, of what they know, what they have learned, what they are learning and who they are becoming.

Higgs and Titchen (2001), in particular, have explicitly and exquisitely described and conceptualised the processes of knowing, doing, being and becoming that complex professional practice development entails. What they described is a continuing personal journey. In their framing, practice is not something that can be separated from the person who enacts it. The key choices made along the pathway of the practice journey are not only about the particular sets of knowledge and technique to be applied, but how they will be applied; the ethical and social dimensions that are important in those applications; and the kind of attention they pay to the wider consequences of what is done or not done. Even more fundamental choices concern what people choose to learn along the way; how much complexity they are prepared to engage with; where and with whom they will work; and what political, commercial, organisational, cultural and family pressures they will accommodate or ignore. I would add to their framing of the practice journey the idea that people make conscious or unconscious choices about whether the responses they make to practice challenges are growthful (moving forward to enhance their practice) or regressive (restricting what they do).

It is this perspective, in the context of the complex challenges and possibilities of contemporary life, that has led to the suggestion that in life and in work, we should aspire to the cultivation of praxis. It is not enough simply to do things, to apply technique or technology without mindfulness of who and where we are, what shapes our choices for better or worse, and the footprints that we leave.

Some have spoken of the need for practice artistry (Schön, 1987) and the holistic reflexivities (intellectual, aesthetic, ethical and ecological) that need to inform it (Bleakley, 1999). Others again have drawn on the possibilities of engaging multiple intelligences (Gardner, 1983), multiple modes of human experience, multi-disciplinary perspectives (Bowden & Marton, 1998) and cultural wisdoms from across the world (Houston, 2000).

Bleakley (1999) suggested that nothing less than reflexive praxis will do, formed through the integration of "what I do" (what I have learned or has become habit for me) with the surfacing and acknowledgment of "what I believe, think and feel", informed by critical and creative consciousness of the physical, aesthetic, ecological, social, moral, spiritual and cultural milieu which shapes me and upon which I, in turn, impact. All of this carries the implication that praxis is dynamic and changing.

Bleakley's requirements are daunting. The business of practice – knowing, doing, being and becoming – requires disciplined, sustained attention or mindfulness as well as the power and pleasure of being in the flow of mastery. Few of us could claim that kind of comprehensive commitment for long periods of time, whether it be in our relationships or in our work.

But that is the kind of commitment that in some form or another (even if some of the dimensions are missing) has been asked of all the professions. And increasingly, the ecological dimensions, along with the spiritual and aesthetic, are coming to claim or reclaim much of Western practice. It is the absence of these dimensions that is being blamed for many of the contemporary nightmares we have created.

RESEARCH AS PRAXIS

If researchers are in the business of crafting useful ways of knowing or engaging with the world's juicy opportunities and wicked problems, then arguably their practice requires exactly the sort of mindfulness that Bleakley had in mind.

It is in the world of complex practice that research of all kinds should have much to offer, unless we choose as researchers to remain on Schön's high ground and stay well away from his swamps. Arguably, qualitative research has developed in the ways that it has, precisely because we *do* want to work in the messy swamps. Qualitative researchers are very likely to acknowledge the complexity of their subject matter. They are very likely to eschew overly simplistic solutions in favour of long-term and sustainable engagement with issues that would otherwise remain in the too-hard-basket. At their very best, they are likely to irritate others by insisting on making things problematic which others would much prefer to keep simple. This is the fertile and dangerous territory that can be meat and drink to qualitative researchers.

Advanced qualitative research in the swampy lowlands takes research practice – and researchers themselves – right to the heart of the exciting challenges of innovation, entrepreneurship, creativity, artistry, and industry. It can involve the most poignant and painful of dilemmas, where there are no thrilling victories to be had by anyone; there is just ongoing confrontation with things like crushing poverty and endless violence, the moral dilemmas of perpetuating the gap between the "haves" and "have nots", and the remorseless exploitation and degradation of the planet… and the more prosaic but universal pleasure and pain of loving, parenting, working, aging and dying.

It is a small but logical step to suggest, then, that much qualitative research itself constitutes complex practice. To undertake research in the zone of complexity is to be confronted constantly with challenging – at times deeply troubling or extremely tempting – choices. The nature of the challenge can vary. The choices might be risky ones that involve confronting the status quo, or taking on the existing interests of research partners, funders and stakeholders.

Although researchers can often be thought of as explorers, who therefore have a license to be "lost" a lot of the time, maintaining a state of humble "not-knowing" can be as hard for researchers as for anyone else. And being ethically engaged might mean turning away from situations that are otherwise very attractive. For all of these reasons, research experiences over time not only impact upon – even confront and challenge – researchers, but inevitably change them, whether they are conscious of it or not.

TURNING POINTS IN PERSONAL DEVELOPMENT: SOME EXAMPLES

A PhD student is keen to engage with the question of how the spiritual experience and practice of business leaders is related to their business practice. Her enthusiasm and energy for this broad topic are obvious as she talks, and are reflected in the breadth of her reading and writing.

By the time she has refined her study to meet the requirements of her supervisor and the University's ethics committee, she has come to believe that the emotional and imaginative dimensions of spiritual experience are so personal, fragile and subjective that she cannot legitimately and helpfully research them at all. The co-operative inquiry that she had envisaged, mirroring the "I-thou" dynamic that had inspired her in Buber's (1937) writing, has not got off the ground. Instead, she devises questionnaires that tap into the intellectual responses that people she now thinks of as "subjects" give when she asks them about their enacted values at work. Her initial energy and passion for the research are muted, but she works her way thoroughly and meticulously through the data, creating codes and extracting themes. When she revisits the literature to help make sense of her findings, she has lost confidence in her own judgment about what is useful, and ends up relying on conceptual traditions favoured by her colleagues. She goes on to publish and to supervise others, but the imaginative and generous framing that infused her early work is no longer present and she is cautious about what she encourages her own students to attempt. She tells her classes that complex human experiences are best tackled through careful incremental studies, rather than holistically. Aesthetics and spirituality are no longer things she seeks to explore through her work, and are not part of her day-to-day discourse. And the idea that those whom she interviews might join her in deep mutual inquiry into their shared experience is not something that she would consider.

I meet her again some years later at a conference where a young student is making a presentation using alternative texts to study the role of music in spiritual practice. When she hears and sees this presentation, she is moved to tears. The confident and expressive young woman calls up her own younger self, but free to engage in a way that has been missing from her own life and practice for many years. Not only has her research been robbed of that imaginative and creative younger self, but so has she. As well, she is suddenly conscious of the ways in which she has treated her research as commodity or product, rather than as a pathway to her own profound growth.

An experienced researcher is successful in securing a competitive grant requiring linkage with an industry partner. As time goes by, the research unexpectedly draws attention to some formerly unnamed issues at the heart of practice within the organisation. The researcher has not had to deal with the sort of pressure that is now brought to bear to limit the reporting of these issues. Other members of the university research team advise that it is not ethical or helpful to pursue issues that were not identified in the initial scoping of the project. In the face of considerable pressure, the researcher becomes anxious and even contemplates withdrawing from the project. Withdrawal seems attractive, because it allows the researcher to make a powerful point and at the same time to feel at ease with himself. This might even seem like a step forward in the development of his practice, requiring courage and conviction. Indeed, for a number of days, he congratulates himself for being prepared to take such an independent step. But something nags at him. The researcher realises that if he persists, he is creating problems for himself, for his team and above all for his research partner. But making something problematic is arguably at the heart of complex research practice and he believes he must find a way through. The way he does it is to seek a pathway with the partner rather than trying to resolve it for the partner.

The voice he must find for this conversation is not one he has had to find before: a mixture of confidence ("it will be a helpful thing for all of us if we can continue to engage with this unwelcome issue"); honesty ("it will be hard"); authority and expertise ("but working on it with me gives you a different perspective than just grappling with it on your own"); empathy ("I think I understand the significance of this issue to you"); and integrity ("I can be trusted with this"). There were potentially many traps in this situation for the researcher. Withdrawing altogether could have seemed like a courageous and growthful – even ethical and proper – thing to do. However, seen from another perspective, it can be construed as a regression of practice. The really difficult issues would have been avoided or ignored, in favour of a seemingly safer option that could be justified on all sorts of grounds.

To remain engaged in a complex and threatening situation, and negotiate with others to do so, is a hard thing to do when the others are powerful stakeholders who simply want the issue to go away. In this situation, the researcher was not able to offer a neat solution to the issues involved. He was not able to offer certainty about the outcome. But he did find a way to create a space that was tolerable, to inspire confidence that something could change, that possibilities and options would be created that otherwise would not be available. The impact on the researcher himself was significant. He grew in confidence, temperament and in the breadth of his skill repertoire. Subsequently, right from the outset of projects, he was able sometimes to create spaces in which he and others could imaginatively and helpfully frame research questions worthy of the complexity involved. He was able to win mandates to design research methodologies that would develop the skills and confidence of his research partners in tandem with his own.

CONCLUSION

I have suggested here that people's research practice reflects their individual and idiosyncratic integration of knowing, doing and learning, that it is profoundly influenced by who they "are", and in turn influences who they become.

Research practice can and does evolve with varying degrees of self-consciousness and self-awareness. Ultimately it can become a set of unexamined habits. I argue that, as in life, and certainly in professional practice more generally, research practice is never left unaltered when it is significantly challenged and tested: it either regresses or grows, but it cannot stay the same. A commitment to the development of research praxis takes this change process from the incremental formation of unconscious habit to the meta-awareness of reflexive praxis.

Research praxis is what results when action is enriched by exploring the sort of wise questions suggested by Peter Reason (2001), questions such as:
- why am I doing what I'm doing? thinking what I'm thinking? feeling what I'm feeling?
- what assumptions and beliefs are shaping my perceptions? why do I think this will be appropriate or effective?

- what other possible perspectives and experiences could enrich and inform the way I and others are engaging with this situation?
- how can I access those perspectives? who could help? who am I ignoring or avoiding?
- how much am I reflecting a particular culture and time? how can I and others transcend that context to illuminate and enrich what we do and who we are?

In an age of complexity and paradox, I argue that the need to develop praxis (not just practice) is important for everyone who wishes to positively live in and influence the world, in the context of their paid or unpaid effort. That seems to me to be an imperative for researchers, seeking to contribute to our knowledge, our culture and our private and public discourse.

REFERENCES

Bleakley, A. (1999). From reflective practice to holistic reflexivity. *Studies in Higher Education, 24*(3), 315–330.
Bowden, J., & Marton, F. (1998). *The university of learning: Beyond quality and competence in higher education.* London: Kogan Page.
Buber, M. (1937). *I and thou.* London: T. & T. Clarke.
Gardner, H. (1983). *Frames of mind: The theory of multiple intelligences.* New York: Basic Books.
Higgs, J., & Titchen, A. (Eds.). (2001). Framing professional practice: Knowing and doing in context. In J. Higgs & A. Titchen (Eds.), *Professional practice in health, education and the creative arts* (pp. 3–15). Oxford: Blackwell Science.
Houston, J. (2000). *Jump time: Shaping your future in a time of radical change.* Harmondsworth, England: Viking.
Polanyi, M. (1967). *The tacit dimension.* New York: Doubleday.
Reason, P. (2001). Learning and change through action research. In J. Henry (Ed.), *Creative management* (pp. 182–194). London: Sage.
Schön, D. A. (1987). *Educating the reflective practitioner.* San Francisco: Jossey-Bass.

AFFILIATION

Nita Cherry PhD
Faculty of Business and Enterprise
Swinburne University of Technology
Australia

ROBERT MACKLIN

11. RESEARCHING IN THE FACE OF THE OTHER:

Doing Decent Research

In Chapter 8 Joy Higgs and I argued that researchers cannot view the world from an objective position. All research is conducted through multiple lenses. The downside of this is the spectre of relativism. If every lens reveals a truth, what makes one description of the world better than another? Why should we give more credence to one researcher's ideas over another's? All finding are truths and thus anything or, perhaps nothing, goes. At the end of our chapter we pointed to a way out of this conundrum. The truths that survive will be those that, if convincingly presented by the researcher, are accepted by the researcher's peers and his or her broader audience as one of the possible truths about a phenomenon. Such truths will have longevity to the extent that they remain convincing and to the extent that they are pragmatically useful.

In this chapter I expand on this idea, but do so as a way to suggest that in some situations morality must come before the pursuit of truth in any research project. That is, I argue that morality is not an external constraint on research, but an imperative that may be more important than the pursuit of truth itself. I make this claim because the perspectival nature of research, for me, suggests that every means possible is not justified by the pursuit of truth as an end in itself. I make this claim because I believe that sometimes as researchers we are called upon to go even further than required by the means–ends formula. Sometimes we must care for the other, not just respect their autonomy. In these situations morality stands before epistemology and it is to ethics[1] that we must sometimes turn for guidance on how best to conduct research.

In making this move I can be accused of simply shifting the shadow that relativism casts to questions about what counts as decent moral research conduct. I acknowledge this, but argue that the moral imperative should be seen as, if not less subjective, at least more important than the imperative to uncover a truth.

THE WORK OF AGNES HELLER AS A PHILOSOPHICAL UNDERPINNING OF QUALITATIVE RESEARCH

What follows draws on the arguments of the social and moral philosopher Agnes Heller. She argued (1990b) that when seeking to understand the social world we are seeking true knowledge. Yet in doing so we must accept that this knowledge is situated and that social researchers' understandings of the people they study will always be relative and incomplete. Despite this, social researchers cannot, without risking irrelevance, renounce all claims to true knowledge about modern society. As Heller explained, we get around this as social researchers by following sets of social conventions that point us towards "norms of verisimilitude", the quality of "seeming true", as guides for giving theories or findings weight. This can be done, Heller suggested, by drawing a distinction between "true" knowledge and (the) "Truth". Researchers can give weight to their arguments by avoiding the claim that they correspond to a transcendent "Truth". Instead our task is to argue that where our work accords with the norm of verisimilitude it should be seen as contributing to true knowledge.

As to what constitutes the norms of verisimilitude, Heller argued that pursuing true knowledge is about, *inter alia*, reconstructing, depicting, narrating, and interpreting how things happen and work, what they mean and how to understand them in a *plausible* way. She suggested that the norms of verisimilitude in social research amount to "norms of plausibility". And turning to these norms, she suggested that while social scientists must accept that there may be many equally plausible theories on an issue, a plausible piece of work will contain a core of knowledge that we would expect anyone to arrive at if they thoroughly studied the issues. Quoting Heller, if the researcher:

> studied all the available sources, thoroughly observed the relevant phenomena and entered into discussion with relevant members of the social science community familiar with the matter under scrutiny. (1990b, p. 19)

Being objective is another norm of plausibility in social research – "one must be objective to obtain true knowledge" (1990b, p. 26). But by this, Heller did not mean value free research. Instead, given that social research extracts meaning from the spoken or written, present or past testimonies of participants in events, objectivity involves giving all relevant witnesses a fair hearing. Giving a fair hearing is about obtaining testimonies in conversations on equal terms rather than through interrogation. Expanding here, Heller summarised her "fundamental criteria of objective (just) interpretation in social science":

> If someone has questioned the available and relevant witnesses and has tried hard to discover what they have really meant, irrespective of whether this testimony is reliable or unreliable; if the social scientist has given hearing to those witnesses whose testimonies are unfriendly to this scientist's initial position, value commitments, theory, and the like; if this social scientist has entered into communication in the form of symmetric reciprocity with every witness who was ready to enter into a communication of this kind – if all these things have been done, then the interpretation will have exhausted every criterion of objectivity and thus scientificity. (1990b, p. 28)

Flowing from this, "being objective" for Heller is about not using the addressees of research purely as means to achieve a researcher's goals (ends). That is, social researchers must not manipulate the people they are studying into confirming their ideas or theories by, for example, mobilising emotional responses or playing on particular interests. This does not mean that social theories must be value-free: it means that in pursuing true knowledge social researchers must not seek to exclude facts that question their theories or the values guiding their research.

Building on this argument, Heller argued that social researchers can claim a right to a "procedural-formal" consensus from peers if they play the game according to the norms. Further, researchers can achieve a substantive consensus if others agree that a theory or finding is good, right, or plausible, even though it may be one of many and even if criticised. Moreover, this consensus does not imply complete agreement but a *fair* consensus between social researchers and between the researcher and the researched. She suggested that we should regard as an *ideal* consensus, situations where both scientists and non-scientists who are familiar with a particular theory can say there is truth in its propositions.

Thus, my response to the spectre of relativism is to argue that although we study the world through a variety of lenses and can never access *the* Truth, social researchers need not give up their profession. By using norms of verisimilitude, we make judgments about whether a particular finding or theory is robust enough to count as *a* truth and is thus appropriate for dissemination. To further articulate the norm of verisimilitude, I have included in Figure 11.1 eight broad guidelines for social researchers to consider when engaged in their profession. Heller's discussion of the pursuit of truth in social research provides a philosophical justification for an approach to research that recognises the socially constructed nature of knowledge without slipping into relativism. In this figure, Heller's ideas are distilled into a set of eight broad guides for researchers. They are guides that non-positivist researchers can use to underpin their pursuit of "true knowledge" when thinking about the grounding and conduct of their research practices.

THE PLACE OF MORALITY

In adopting the principles of objectivity as defined above, researchers will not only give plausibility to their work; they will also be taking a moral orientation. Essentially, they will be acting in accord with an ethical norm that social researchers should not use their research subjects as *mere* means to achieving research goals (ends). The norm also stresses the importance of giving people a fair hearing, which flows out of the principle of non-instrumentation and points toward the idea that good research involves free dialogue between equals. From this perspective, morality and epistemology stand at the very least on an equal footing. The norm of objectivity means that being moral in research is not simply a constraint that must be met in order to pass through university ethics committees. Rather, it becomes an essential requirement to the acceptability of any piece of research. Morality and epistemology interlink because they rely on the same norms. That is, manipulative behaviour and deceit (which might be employed to avoid missing some facets of social life) are unacceptable from both an epistemological and moral perspective, and thus findings that derive from such research behaviour should be treated with suspicion.

1. The pursuit of true knowledge in research is always value-laden and cannot be grounded in an Archimedean point outside history and culture. Qualitative researchers must acknowledge this and be open about their values to the people they are researching and to their peers in the academic community.

2. The pursuit of true knowledge in research is not a precise science. Good judgment plays a vital role in any inquiry. Qualitative researchers should avoid preset inflexible strategies and opt for emergent, evolving, and flexible research designs and practices.

3. The pursuit of true knowledge in research requires objectivity, which means giving a fair hearing to all relevant witnesses in accord with good judgment and higher theories that provide frameworks for selecting witnesses and topics for conversation, and without excluding witnesses hostile to a researcher's opening position, values and theories. Therefore, qualitative researchers should, as best they can and in accord with higher theory, talk to all available and relevant people.

4. Giving people a fair hearing when pursuing true knowledge in research requires entering into relations of symmetric reciprocity with witnesses. Qualitative researchers must therefore avoid interrogating people. Instead, they should seek to converse as equals with the people being studied, and they should acknowledge that the outcomes of their inquiries will be a result of these collaborative conversations.

5. Giving people a fair hearing when pursuing true knowledge in research also means not using people purely as *means* to achieve a researcher's goals. Qualitative researchers must not manipulate respondents into confirming their theories by, for example, mobilising emotional responses or playing on particular interests.

6. The outcomes of the pursuit of true knowledge in research should emerge from a fair consensus between researchers and the people they are researching, where "fair" means the sharing of some values, a proper translation, and a mutual readiness for understanding. Qualitative researchers should translate their observations into a language that the people they study can understand and engage with.

7. The pursuit of true knowledge about a phenomenon in research will always be incomplete and will likely result in more than one equally plausible theory about the phenomenon. Therefore, qualitative researchers should avoid claims that their work is exact, final and cumulative in an absolute sense and should be open to alternative perspectives on the phenomenon they are studying.

8. Researchers can claim a right to the acceptance of their work from peers as "true knowledge" in research if they have followed the norms of social inquiry, including "objectivity", and insofar as their work is accepted by peers as plausible, even though it may be one of many such works and even if it has been criticised. Qualitative researchers should follow the norms of objectivity, discuss their work with their peers, and be open to criticism and debate.

Figure 11.1. Guidelines for social researchers – in pursuit of verisimilitude.

However, I think that this happy coincidence does not allow us to move on, blithely confident in the belief that in professional research practice ethics and epistemology will always coincide. I argue that the full range of ethical norms accepted in our societies go beyond the means–ends principle and its underpinning norm, autonomy. That it is not in itself a sufficient guide for ensuring moral research practices. A choice in some circumstances will thus have to be made on the relative priority of morality and epistemology. I suggest that given the lensed character of research and because of the morally rich nature of the relationship between researchers and the people they are researching, especially in qualitative approaches, the choice should always be to place morality before epistemology.

This claim that the choice should always be to place morality before epistemology can be asserted because the lensed and situated nature of social research means that Truth will always remain outside our grasp, and we thus have no transcendent reason or grounds to act immorally as social researchers. Quite obviously, this begs a number of questions: Why should we be decent? And if we should, how can we?

It would be great if at this point I could simply produce some universally accepted justification for why we should be decent or, better still, a wondrous discovery of the Truth that justifies decency beyond doubt. Unfortunately, however, as most readers will realise, morality is just as mired in truths as opposed to the Truth as is social research. Every explanation for why we should be decent is historically and culturally grounded. No reason can be put that transcends history and culture. Thus, I cannot reach for a transcendent "God's eye view" argument that researchers should put decency ahead of getting to a truth. I am reduced to trying to provide convincing arguments (that have verisimilitude and are robust enough to be accorded the status of a truth that social researchers should listen to) for why researchers should be decent.

TAKING A STANCE ON DECENCY

My argument is that morality is so enmeshed and integral to all human relations, including qualitative research relationships, that social researchers cannot avoid taking a stance on decency. Every research interaction we engage in is morally laden and thus, even if we make no explicit choice, we nevertheless choose to be decent or not. That is, there is no escaping the moral impact that we have as social science researchers. The following examples illustrate this contention.

In-depth interviews are perhaps the most frequent way in which qualitative researchers enter into a relationship with the people they are researching. And I suggest that when social researchers conduct interviews they are engaging in a form of interaction that is thoroughly shot-through with moral implications. For instance, the norm in qualitative interviews is two people conversing on a topic, but it may be the case that the interview is of great and/or fundamental significance to only one of these people. In some cases the interest is largely that of the interviewer. Interviewees may be interested, but face time pressures, be unsure of the relevance of the interview to their life and wellbeing, and may have not met the interviewer before and may not again. The interviewer, however, when returning behind the university gates, faces the necessity to have something to show for the time spent and, more than this, if long term employment and a career are important, must have something that is publishable. During the interview, then, the intent is to obtain rich information, new insights, deep understandings and nuanced information. To this end social researchers utilise a range of communication skills, including skills that can be used manipulatively. Facing a strong imperative to get the "right" kind of information from the interviews, but not necessarily facing a very willing witness, interviewers inevitably act in morally loaded ways when it comes to applying the tools of their craft. If they decide (explicitly or not) to use every means possible to get as much information as possible then they will likely breach ethical norms. But if they are committed to non-manipulation, they will keep their strategies on a moral leash. Regardless of the specific actions pursued, a moral position will have been taken by the researcher: it is not possible to cast the interaction in a-moral terms.

My second illustration reverses the parties' interests. It may be the case in some situations that an interview is fundamentally more significant to an interviewee than the interviewer. This could be the case if the topic being discussed is sensitive or fraught with issues that bring up painful memories for the interviewee. In such situations, whereas the interviewer may be simply looking for one more conversation that confirms emerging hunches or theories, far more may be at stake for the interviewee, who may be looking for an opportunity to speak about personal history and pain – to, in a sense, reach out and reveal this history to some "other". The interviewer thus has a decision to make, about whether to plough on regardless and keep the interview focused, professional and task-oriented, or to listen carefully to the interviewee, hear the story and thus to some degree become not just an interested observer but a short-term engaged participant in the individual's life. Regardless of what position the interviewer takes, the interaction cannot be seen in a-moral terms: he or she will be taking a moral stance regardless of what is said or left unspoken.

In-depth interviews are therefore morally loaded, as are other actions in the qualitative research craft: question development, interview analysis, etc. In bolder terms, qualitative research practices are also moral practices, and it is not possible to be an a-moral qualitative researcher: we can be decent or indecent, but we cannot avoid a stance. It is my position that researchers should choose to act morally (in both decision making and direct actions) rather than doing what is worse, from my perspective, choosing to sacrifice morality and do whatever it takes to get the information needed. In taking this position, however, I cannot provide an argument as to why being moral is to be preferred in any utilitarian or teleological terms. That is, I can't promise that doing the morally right thing will be somehow rewarded with outcomes that will shore up employability or further a career. I suggest that the history of the research profession, like the history of humanity generally, is littered with the bodies of decent people who never "made it". Doing well by doing good is a happy coincidence, not an inevitable outcome.

My suggestion is ultimately an appeal to what I hope is your moral sensibility, but I will attempt to go a little further by once again drawing on the work of Agnes Heller (1987, 1988, 1990a, 1996). According to Heller it is the existence of decent people that grounds morality. Decency survives today not because it meets teleological ends, nor because it accords with reason, nor because we all blindly accept certain norms and values. It survives due to the existence of decent people who prefer to follow moral norms rather than break them and, indeed, would prefer to suffer wrong (e.g. lack of career progression) than breach norms. It is in the existence of such decent people that Heller grounded morality: morality survives because decent people exist. And in making this claim she argued that these decent people exist because they have made an "existential choice of decency".

For Heller (1993, 1990a), people in modern societies face a historico-social contingency. Although everybody is born with genetic capacities inherited from their parents, and although the circumstances into which individuals are thrown at birth affect their ability to exploit these capacities, people born into modern societies do not face a predetermined social role marked out for them by their parents' location in society. Instead, all moderns can make choices, and indeed the modern person must choose a *telos* if he or she does not wish to lead a purely contingent life. That is, the modern person must make an existential choice.

One of the fundamental choices a person can make, according to Heller, is the existential choice of decency. Everyone, she argued, can destine themselves to be decent, and this involves committing to being decent and in so doing choosing to accept all the circumstances they face, all their bad and good luck, and all their talents, assets, and infirmities. Heller provided the following advice to people facing this choice:

> Choose yourself as a human being who is destined to be good. Destine yourself to become what you are: a decent, good person ... Be the addressee of a moral philosophy so that it can speak to you. (1990a, p. 24)

GOING BEYOND THE HAPPY COINCIDENCE?

At this point we can ask, what happened to the happy coincidence between morality and epistemology brought about by the norms of objectivity and more particularly the means–ends principle? The implication of this is that the decent social researcher may also be a successful researcher because the moral norm "never treat another person as a mere means to your ends" is also an epistemological norm that if followed helps a person's research findings or theories to be accepted as truthful (if not the Truth). Unfortunately, however, I don't think this can be sustained. I think that the decent person in being decent may be called upon to go beyond the means–ends principle.

Heller recognised that moral norms vary significantly across communities, but nevertheless suggested that there are moral universals that all decent people in modern societies use to question or reject other normative criteria. She discussed these universal norms and principles and argued that she, as a moral philosopher, had identified them in discussion with people who themselves strive to be decent.

They are not commandments, but guidelines that people who have chosen themselves to be decent are party to developing and which they and all decent people can consult. However, she also recognised that the guidelines are not a closed set to which nothing can be added or taken away (1990a). This opens the door for me to critique her structure or hierarchy of norms, and it is this critique that leads me to suggest that the means–ends principle is not always enough.

For Heller, the means–ends principle or, as it is also called, the substantive formula of the categorical imperative – *never treat another person as a mere means but also as an end in themselves* – was the "*simplest*, the most radical, the clearest and most sublime universal maxim one can dream of " (1990a, p. 105). Heller claimed that the formula can be seen as the universalisation and absolutisation of what she called the constitutive moral principle, which itself derives legitimacy from serving as the prohibitive version of several orientative principles of autonomy. The constitutive moral principle of autonomy is:

> Do not violate another person's body or soul; do not manipulate others or keep them in tutelage because of their race, sex or membership of other human groups. (1990a, p. 46)

The orientative principles of autonomy are set out in Heller's book, *A Philosophy of Morals*, along with other orientative principles that as a collection make up what she called "the universal orientative principle of care" (1990b, p. 41). The difference between *prohibitive* and *orientative* is important. An orientative principle does not stipulate exactly what to do but simply orients the decent person's behaviour in a general direction. Orientative principles are also situation-sensitive, person-specific (people care and want to be cared for in their own way), and can be waived by universal moral maxims, norms or laws and, for some concretisations, by institutional rules. According to Heller, universal moral maxims are yardsticks that can help us decide what to do when facing difficult situations. These yardsticks are higher norms that help us establish a moral priority, and for Heller the means–ends formula and the constitutive moral principle of autonomy are important prohibitive universal moral maxims.

I see nothing wrong with social researchers using these maxims and the orientative principles of care as guidelines for their professional research practices. In addition, if one accepts that the principles of care remain only orientative rather than prohibitive then the happy coincidence between ethics and epistemology probably remains intact. The contingencies of life and interpersonal politics aside, morally decent researchers *will* also be successful researchers.

Heller's stress on autonomy fits very strongly with her commitment to freedom and "life-chances" (equal opportunity), which she portrayed as being ultimate substantive values in modern societies, values upon which all other principles and maxims are grounded (1990a). I endorse this commitment: respecting someone's autonomy, especially where they are the subject of our research, is unquestionably important. However, the question I pose is, is it the case in modern society that *care* must be trumped by norms and maxims that stress the importance of the autonomy of the individual?

In other words, is it the case that while researchers should care for the people they are researching they should do so only within the constraints imposed by the need to respect someone's autonomy? Or again, is care so important a principle that it may justify breaching a person's autonomy in some circumstances? If it is, then I suggest our happy coincidence between morality and epistemology cannot be guaranteed. Moreover, it will mean that for decent researchers sometimes their morality will trump the principles that guide good research. In some cases care as an ethical principle means that decent researchers will stop short of asking some interviewees questions because to do so would be uncaring given the interviewees' life circumstances. Alternatively, in some situations they will go beyond being the task-focused researcher who sticks to the script and distance that perhaps befit the research relationship, and engage with the interviewee who is looking for real engagement and care.

I am not saying here that such scenarios are so common that Heller's implied suggestion, that good research and decent (moral) research are both underpinned by the means–ends principle, is flawed. I suggest that if one accepts Heller's discussion of social science and morality, in most situations there will be a happy coincidence between morality and epistemology. Respecting someone's autonomy means giving them a fair hearing, and this is both good moral and good research practice. However, I am saying this cannot be guaranteed. Sometimes care, as a principle of decency, will call upon the decent researcher to put morality first. No universal rule can be made of this, but it is a possibility that cannot be ignored. In some situations we will have to put morality before epistemology.

CONCLUSION

I am going to finish at this point and leave these concerns hanging, leaving decent researchers facing a potential conundrum that they potentially did not know about. But morality is never safe in this respect. All decent people face difficult decisions, and as highly educated professionals, researchers cannot expect to avoid tough judgments. Many debates rage about the relationship between care and autonomy (for a summary and major contribution, see Slote, 2007). Heller seems to come down on the side that one can care and still allow people their autonomy. I suspect this is mostly the case, but it cannot be guaranteed in every situation and it will be up to the researchers to make the call. It will never be an easy call, and every situation will be different and may demand a different leap of faith and judgment.

Being a good researcher is hard; being a decent one can be harder.

NOTES

[1] Ethics can be taken as a collective noun for the norms of right or wrong; morality is about people's relationship to the norms and the extent to which they allow themselves to be guided by the norms and rules (see Macklin, 2009).

REFERENCES

Heller, A. (1987). *Beyond justice*. Oxford: Blackwell.
Heller, A. (1988). *General ethics*. Oxford: Blackwell.
Heller, A. (1990a). *A philosophy of morals*. Oxford: Blackwell.
Heller, A. (1990b). *Can modernity survive?* Berkeley, CA: University of California Press.
Heller, A. (1993). *A philosophy of history in fragments*. Oxford: Blackwell.
Heller, A. (1996). *An ethics of personality*. Oxford: Blackwell.
Macklin, R. (2009). Moral judgement and practical reasoning in professional practice. In B. Green (Ed.), *Understanding and researching professional practice* (pp. 83–99). Rotterdam: Sense Publishers.
Slote, M. (2007). *The ethics of care and empathy*. Abingdon: Routledge.

AFFILIATION

Rob Macklin PhD
The Research Institute for Professional Practice, Learning & Education
Faculty of Business
Charles Sturt University
Australia

JOHN A. BOWDEN AND PAMELA J. GREEN

12. RELATIONALITY AND THE MYTH OF OBJECTIVITY IN RESEARCH INVOLVING HUMAN PARTICIPANTS

INTRODUCTION

In this chapter we explore fundamental aspects of research involving human participants that transcend the so-called qualitative/quantitative divide. Comparisons are made between qualitative research and quantitative survey research, with the notion of relationality as a key element in explaining the similarities and differences. Past discussion of such differences has been hijacked by contrasts made between the supposed objectivity of quantitative research methods and subjectivity of qualitative methods. Such a dichotomous distinction is simplistic. We show in this chapter that subjectivity is the natural order in all research involving human participants and that the notion of objectivity in any such research is a myth.

We argue that neither a qualitative approach nor a quantitative approach is intrinsically superior to the other and that the main criterion upon which to base the choice of research method relates to consideration of which method is most appropriate to the particular situation. In the next section, we explore the influences on such a choice of research method, whether qualitative or quantitative.

DECIDING WHICH RESEARCH METHOD(S) TO USE

Four elements need to be matched: the research questions, the research methods, the perspectives of the researchers and the nature of the target audience. These elements are not independent but rather are highly interactive; any matching process must be iterative. However, for ease of discussion, we examine separately some relationships among those elements, as shown in Figure 12.1.

Initial research questions usually focus on the interests of the researchers. In developmental research, the kinds of questions chosen are also likely to be influenced by the nature and expectations of the target audience. Altenatively, the questions or interests of the reseachers will cause the researchers to seek out such an audience, perhaps the organisation commissioning the research or those involved in the activities being researched. In curiosity-driven research, the target audience may well be fellow researchers in the same field, and the kinds of questions researched would relate to perceived gaps in the field of knowledge.

J. Higgs, N. Cherry, R. Macklin and R. Ajjawi (eds.),
Researching Practice: A Discourse on Qualitative Methodologies, 105–112.
© *2010 Sense Publishers. All rights reserved.*

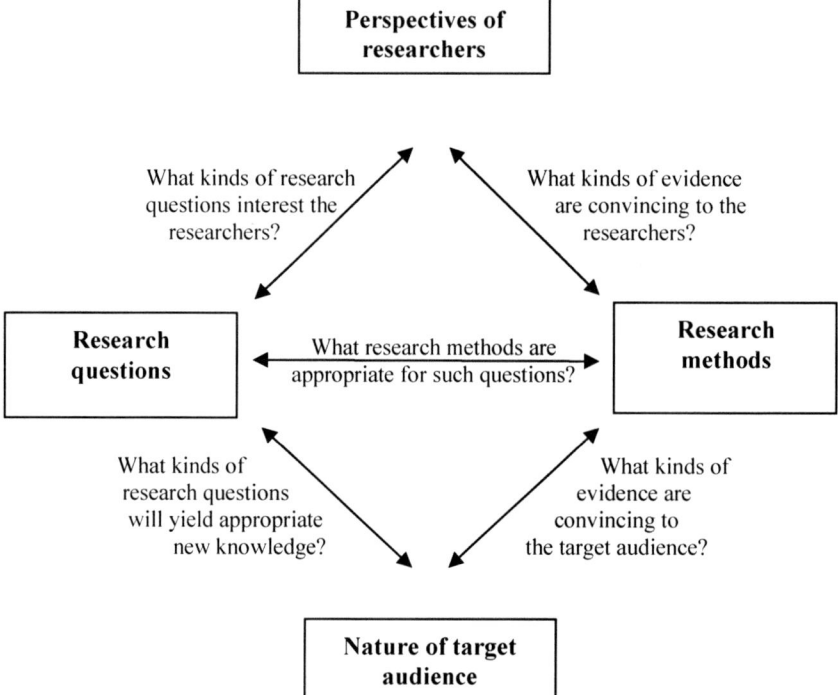

Figure 12.1. Choosing a research method – elements and relationships.

Once initial research questions have been framed, a choice must be made about methods used to address them. The primary criterion for that choice is the appropriateness of the contending methods for the kinds of questions being investigated. Does the chosen method provide the kind of evidence that can lead to resolution of the research questions?

A secondary but still important criterion is the kind of evidence that the researchers find convincing. For some researchers, only research that provides generalisable, statistical evidence is compelling. Other researchers are persuaded only by direct, qualitative evidence that illustrates what the particular phenomenon means to human participants. These differences relate primarily to the framework underpinning each researcher's way of seeing research (discussed further below).

Moreover, researchers need to be aware of the kinds of evidence that the target audience will find convincing. In curiosity-led research, what would have credibility with the target audience might be self-evident, given the mutual awareness of various members of a particular research community. Most researchers know what sort of evidence influences fellow researchers in their field. In developmental research, however, the target audience may well be practitioners or other interested parties, not researchers, and care must be taken to ensure that reports of research findings have clear and credible meaning for them. Such a developmental project is discussed in Chapter 14 in relation to a research study referred to as the "physics project" (Bowden et al., 1992).

The nature of the elements of a research project and their relationships may vary with time and context. For instance, for the authors of this chapter, research experience of recent decades has led to a personal preference for qualitative evidence that focuses on meaning rather than on generalisable, statistical evidence. That was not always so for both authors. For example, around 1980, one of us was a principal investigator in a national four-year study of university academics' attitudes and values using a comprehensive, specially designed survey instrument (see e.g. Bowden & Anwyl, 1983). At that time, the research questions, research methods and perspectives of the researchers and the target audience were all in harmony. However, given changes in the perspectives and interests of one of the authors (JAB) over the intervening period, that would not be so now. The choice between quantitative and qualitative research methods is just that – a choice made at the time and in the prevailing circumstances, which includes the philosophical and theoretical perspectives of the researcher at the particular time. One research method is not inherently better than the other, merely more or less appropriate to the particular situation; the choice is reliant on the elements and relationships depicted in Figure 12.1.

FRAMEWORKS AND RESEARCH COMMUNITIES

Quantitative survey research, in common with most science, is usually undertaken within a positivistic frame of reference. In contrast, qualitative research such as phenomenography (described in detail in Chapter 14) falls under the frame of an interpretivist perspective. This contrast may have led in the past to the distinction commonly made between scientific (quantitative) survey research and qualitative research – that the former is objective and the latter subjective (e.g., see Duffy, 1987; Judge, Thoresen, Bono & Patton, 2001. This is a false dichotomy, as both qualitative research and quantitative scientific research involving human participants are contextual. The major difference is that each scientific theory is sanctioned by the relevant scientific community and is not overturned until social processes within that community dictate the change (see discussion of scientific revolutions by Kuhn, 1970). Bowden (2008) contrasts that process with qualitative research and suggests that "within studies of human activity ... if any such social framework exists, it is merely one among many competing frameworks, each with their own different theoretical perspectives" (p. 218).

Despite the presence of many competing frameworks within qualitative research, one aspect shared by all qualitative research is its inherent subjectivity. As detailed in the next section, we argue that there is also inherent subjectivity in quantitative research involving human participants.

SUBJECTIVITY

All researchers working with human participants try to ascertain something about the human experience of particular situations. Researchers are human beings, researching into human experience and communicating outcomes to other human beings. It is impossible to take the person out of such research, and therefore impossible for such research to be objective. All research into human experience has subjective aspects. The difference is not between objective, quantitative research and subjective, qualitative research but rather variation among different kinds of subjectivity and the situations in which it arises, in both quantitative and qualitative research. Subjectivity is the natural state of all research involving human participants.

Quantitative survey research is subjective in that the ideas expressed by the researcher are central. It is focused not on what the researched think about the phenomenon but rather on what they think about the researcher's thoughts or ideas that the researcher chooses to put before them for a score. If the researcher were to ask different questions or to express the survey items using different words or to label the rating scales differently, it is almost self-evident that the research outcomes would be different. Indeed, more than half a century ago, survey researchers discussed the importance of question wording (see Moser, 1958, pp. 222–9). Decades later, Krosnick (1989) reported on a national survey of attitudes towards the U.S. civil justice system and law reform. Public reports variously claimed strong public support for and high proportions in favour of specific changes in the civil justice system, despite the fact that respondents were merely invited to register on a four-point scale how acceptable they found each reform. Krosnick investigated whether using words like "favour" or "support" rather than "acceptable" would change the result. Indeed they did – in substantial and somewhat unpredictable ways. Wording matters.

The processes by which researchers choose which items to include for scoring and which words they use to express them are subjective. Different items or forms of expression would be likely to produce different research outcomes. We take the position that "objectivity" in any such quantitative survey research is not a valid concept. A more relevant and important concept is "rigour". It is not possible to develop rigorous approaches to research involving human participants without first acknowledging its inherent subjectivity. It is important to try to understand what it is about both qualitative and quantitative research methods involving human participants that is subjective, as we have already begun to do here in relation to quantitative survey research.

Open-ended interviews often used in qualitative research enable participants to introduce the full range of issues that they deem relevant and to explain their own meanings. Where subjectivity comes in is in the way that the interview is conducted (whether respondents are encouraged to be open and forthright, whether the interviewer asks leading questions or not, and so on) and how the data are analysed. That is why we have argued elsewhere (Bowden & Green, in press) that publications reporting research involving human participants should provide details of that kind about the research methods used. Without that level of detail about the methods and the research methodologies that guide them, no reader can be confident of the findings.

There is another subjective element in quantitative research that is hidden. Even if "tight" wording is chosen for survey items, it is likely that the meaning of any item will vary from one respondent to another. Further, scores for survey items say little about the congruence between researchers' intended meanings for the items and the meanings that respondents inferred from reading them. Any score that respondents ascribe to an item is a response to the meaning that they interpret from the form of words, a meaning that may not be the same as that intended by the researchers or even that inferred by another respondent ascribing the item the same score. Most handbooks of quantitative research (such as Peat, Mellis, Williams & Wei Xuan, 2002) address these issues by developing validity protocols for survey instrument design that include elements like item wording, rating labels and rating scales. Further, the very issue of subjectivity is addressed by such means as construction of multi-item scales, along with factor analysis or some other statistical tool (see Peat et al., 2002, for example). These processes do not remove the subjectivity but they provide a way of addressing it, at least in part.

There are parallel issues for qualitative researchers, which are discussed in Chapter 14. One example given there is our "success in research" project (Bowden & Green, 2005) in which we ran pilot interviews before data collection began. When we asked interviewees to "tell me about some research that you have been engaged in that you view as being successful", interviewees struggled to come up with any authentic examples. Instead they offered little or merely gave "textbook" type responses about categories of research. When the words "in some way" were added to the question, interviewees spoke at length about their own experiences. It seems that the extra words enabled interviewees to no longer feel under pressure to claim total success for projects that might have been partially flawed. Whatever the cause, this example in qualitative research parallels those in quantitative survey research, namely different and unexpected interpretations by participants of the meaning of the researcher's question, depending on the words used. Pilot interviews are a common process used to minimise the negative impact of such varied interpretations on the quality of the research outcomes.

RELATIONALITY

Dualism and Non-Dualism

Before we can begin to understand the concept of relationality, we need to address the issue of non-dualism which is at its core. Qualitative research approaches like phenomenography are based on a non-dualist perspective (see Bowden, 2005, pp. 11–12). Dualism, or a dualistic perspective, focuses on two worlds – an inner world of the individual and an outer world that the individual observes. In non-dualism the separation of the inner and outer worlds is seen as not useful. Indeed, non-dualists would argue that such a separation is not possible – who is to say what that outer world is except another observer? – and that means you are now dealing with another inner world, but of a different individual. The inner worlds are an inescapable part of every attempt to define an outer world. Hence, non-dualists argue that separation of the two is impossible. Two human beings cannot discuss any "outer-world" except through their own inner-world interactions with it.

BOWDEN AND GREEN

Relationality in Qualitative Research

The concept of relationality is central to qualitative research. Relationality refers to the variation in meaning of a phenomenon across people, time, process and situation. Qualitative researchers, who have their own ways of seeing a particular phenomenon, are trying to discover how other people see it. This is an acknowledgement that there are different ways of seeing and that the variation is both legitimate and interesting. Qualitative researchers acknowledge that their ways of seeing are not the only ones and they need to ensure that their ways of seeing do not unduly affect data collection or analysis. Consequently, the idea of "bracketing" the researcher's ways of seeing is an important part of much qualitative research. Bracketing is addressed by privileging the ideas and words of the researched as the only acceptable evidence of the research outcomes at all stages from data collection to analysis. This is illustrated in Chapter 14 when the research practices of developmental phenomenography are discussed. Figure 12.2 illustrates a typical situation within qualitative research.

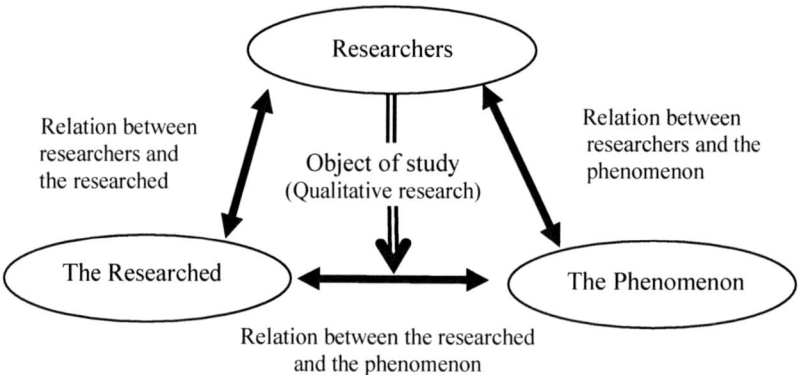

Figure 12.2. Relationality and qualitative research (Adapted from Bowden, 2005, p. 13).

The object of study is the relationship between the researched and the phenomenon. It is acknowledged that the researcher has a relationship with both the participants and the phenomenon. As mentioned above, the researcher's relationship with the phenomenon is dealt with by bracketing. The researcher's relationship with the participants is addressed by using appropriate protocols for selecting, approaching, interacting with and gathering data from participants and reporting outcomes in ways that do not harm them (discussed in Chapter 14).

Relationality in Quantitative Survey Research

Quantitative survey research can be depicted as shown in Figure 12.3. It is a fallacy to express quantitative survey results as being about the relation between the researched and the phenomenon, a fallacy that ignores the underlying subjectivity in quantitative research that was discussed above. The object of study is not the relation between the researched and the phenomenon as it is in qualitative research. Rather it is the relation between the researched and the researcher's ways of seeing the phenomenon, as evidenced by the items chosen by the researcher for inclusion in the survey and the ways in which those items are expressed.

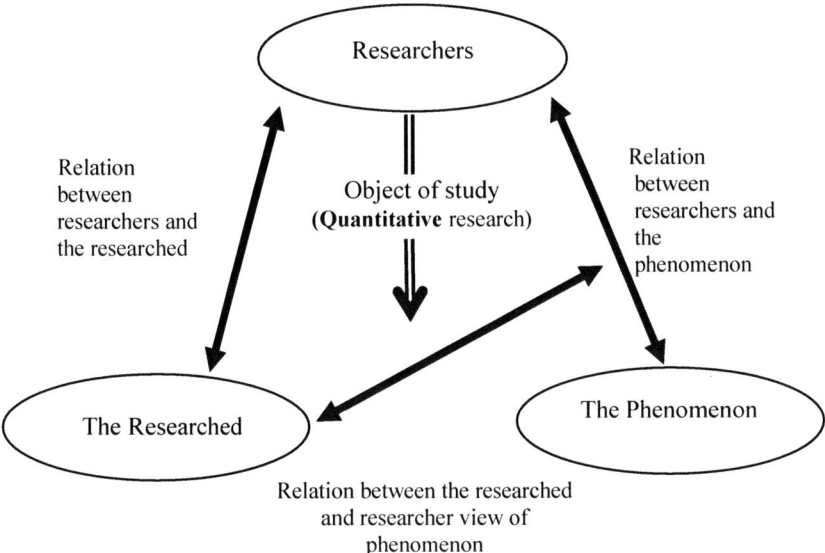

Figure 12.3. Relationality and quantitative research.

Normally the relation of the researcher to the researched in quantitative research is dealt with through random sampling and other research protocols. However, the relationship between the researcher and the phenomenon is at the centre of the research. It forms part of the object of quantitative survey research as a design feature.

CONCLUSION

The time has come to abandon the tribal conflict between quantitative and qualitative research, with its spurious claims of objectivity for one but not the other. Objectivity in relation to research involving human participants is a myth. It should be acknowledged that all such research, whether quantitative or qualitative, has subjective elements whose influence on the quality of research outcomes can be offset by rigorous research practices. Denial of that inherent subjectivity will not make it disappear. Only acknowledgement of its existence can enable researchers to deal with it appropriately.

REFERENCES

Bowden, J. A. (2005). Reflections on the phenomenographic team research process. In J. Bowden & P. Green (Eds.), *Doing developmental phenomenography* (pp. 11–31). Melbourne: RMIT University Press.

Bowden, J. A. (2008). Conceptions of universities as organisations and change in science and mathematics education. In O. Skovsmose, P. Valero, & O. Christensen (Eds.), *University science and mathematics education in transition*. New York: Springer.

Bowden, J. A., & Anwyl, J. (1983). Some characteristics and attitudes of academics in Australian universities and colleges of advanced education. *Higher Education Research & Development, 2*, 39–61.

Bowden, J. A., Dall'Alba, G., Laurillard, D., Martin, E., Marton, F., Masters, G., et al. (1992). Displacement, velocity and frames of reference: Phenomenographic studies of students' understanding and some implications for teaching. *American Journal of Physics, 60*, 262–269.

Bowden, J., & Green, P. (in press). "Qualitative methods" for ergonomics research involving human participants. In S. Hörte & M. Christmansson (Eds.), *Ergonomics research*. New York: Springer.

Bowden, J. A., & Green, P. (Eds.). (2005). *Doing developmental phenomenography*. Melbourne: RMIT University Press.

Duffy, M. E. (1987). Methodological triangulation: A vehicle for merging quantitative and qualitative research methods. *Journal of Nursing Scholarship, 19*(3), 130–133.

Judge, T., Thoresen, C., Bono, J., & Patton, G. (2001). The job satisfaction-job performance relationship: A qualitative and quantitative review. *Psychological Bulletin, 127*(3), 376–407.

Krosnick, J. A. (1989). A review: Question wording and reports of survey results. *Public Opinion Quarterly, 53*(1), 107–113.

Kuhn, T. S. (1970). *The structure of scientific revolutions* (2nd ed.). Chicago: The University of Chicago Press.

Moser, C. A. (1958). *Survey methods in social investigation*. London: Heinemann.

Peat, J., Mellis, C., Williams, K., & Wei Xuan. (2002). *Health science research: A handbook of quantitative methods*. London: Sage.

AFFILIATIONS

John A Bowden PhD
Swinburne Research, Swinburne University of Technology
Australia

Pamela J Green PhD
Swinburne Research, Swinburne University of Technology
Australia

ROSEMARY LEONARD

13. THE PLACE OF QUALITATIVE RESEARCH IN HELPING VOICES BE HEARD

When I first sat down to write about qualitative research helping voices be heard I thought "Yes it does" and then wondered what I would write for the other 3,997 words. But a moment's reflection reminded me that when I think about voices being heard, I think about that amazing collage of diverse people that makes up Australia and indeed the world, and the fascinating process of hearing all their stories. But not all researchers share this view. Table 13.1 reflects research voices.

Table 13.1. Issues in the amplifying or silencing of voices at the different stages of the research process

Amplifying	*Silencing*
Stage of the Research	
Epistemology	
Interpretive, critical, post-modern	Theory testing
Theory	
Constructivist	Determinist
Research question	
Broad / open/ participant-led/ PAR*/ memory work	Constrained
Participants	
Effort to encourage diversity/ participant-led	Most convenient or narrowly defined
Method	
creative/ flexible/ responsive/ opportunities for clarification/ participant-led	Invites passive responses/ Participants report what they think the researcher wants to hear
Interpretation	
Commonalities and differences/ contextual/ participant involved	Commonalities/ generalised/ context-free
Writing and Dissemination	
Diverse media and styles for different audiences/ participant involved	Academic style in academic journals

*PAR = participatory action research

J. Higgs, N. Cherry, R. Macklin and R. Ajjawi (eds.),
Researching Practice: A Discourse on Qualitative Methodologies, 113–121.
© 2010 Sense Publishers. All rights reserved.

One view of research is that its role is to separate the truth from the voice of the speaker. It is "true" that water boils at 100 degrees Celsius at sea level, regardless of who is speaking. This is the truth of the natural sciences and it has a certainty that many in the social sciences envy.

There are many researchers in the social sciences using both quantitative and qualitative methods who regret their dependence on the voices of their participants. They would like to be able to rely on objective evidence, such as observation that would not "distort the truth". But objective evidence could also be seen as an impoverished knowledge. Objectively, we can see the water boil but we can never know what it feels like to be boiling water or to really understand the experience of boiling. The water can have no voice in our research. Of course in scientific and objective research voices are still heard, but in most research they are the voices of the author, the scientist or some other acknowledged authority.

Further reflection reminded me that there are many stages in the life of a research project, and it is no easy task for the voices to be carried through this process and then to finally be heard. Table 13.1 gives some indication of the efforts that need to be put into helping voices to be heard at each stage of the research process.

EPISTEMOLOGY, THEORY AND THE RESEARCH QUESTION

Most voices do not get the opportunity to get past first base. Traditionally, research questions are designed to test some aspect of an existing theory. Many social science theories are deterministic. They describe causal relations between variables in ways that leave little room for diversity, agency or creativity. Indeed, if the theories were correct, it would be almost impossible for a person to create a theory. The most obvious example is Skinner's theory that behaviour is controlled by sequences of rewards and punishments. It is hard to imagine a sequence of rewards and punishments that would lead to Skinner's creation of his theory.

Even qualitative research can be designed to test a theory rather than to listen carefully to the participants' voices. Over the past 20 years, constructivist and postmodern theories (e.g. Lather, 1991) which allow for diversity have become increasingly popular with researchers, but they are still in the minority. Even within constructivist and postmodern paradigms, research questions that start with a biological event such as menopause can inadvertently give the impression that life is biologically determined. Although it is helpful to understand women's diverse experiences of menopause, if that is the main focus of research about mid-life women, an implication is that it is the most important event. The Women Coming of Age (WCA) study (Leonard & Burns, 1999) found that menopause was rarely mentioned. Such questions position women as passive, reacting to life events rather than exercising high levels of agency.

There are some methodologies that specifically focus on fostering diverse voices. In participatory action research (e.g., Hart & Bond, 1995) the research question is framed by a group or community to address a local issue. The group may invite a researcher to assist them in the process of organising and documenting the process. As the research takes place over a period of time, participants can allow the it to evolve with more research questions, actions or new data collection techniques. The knowledge created is therefore highly relevant to the group, but not necessarily for others. Memory work (Haug et al., 1999; Onyx & Small, 2001) is another participant-led method whereby members of a small group each write a memory triggered by a selected word and then discuss the written material before selecting another trigger word. Again, because it is an iterative process, there is room for development of the research question. Discussions specifically include research literature, so the findings can inform academic debate, but memory work makes great demands on the participants in terms of their level of literacy and intellectual discussion.

Although specifically participatory methods such as PAR or memory work are particularly valuable, most participant-led research follows more traditional methods, occurs when people approach researchers with a problem, and they work together to develop appropriate research questions and methods. Further, research does not have to be led by participants to allow the voices of diverse participants to be heard. Nor can it be assumed that work initiated by participants will necessarily end with their voices being heard. The following sections identify some of the issues and decision points.

THE PARTICIPANTS

A major decision point in the research process is the decision as to who will be invited to participate and thus whose voices will be heard. This decision is usually made by the researcher on the basis of the research question and practical considerations such as the size of the budget. The researcher might believe that the phenomenon of interest is universal, and thus any group of humans would be suitable participants. This has typically been the case in psychological studies of perception and personality. If this is the researcher's belief then college students are the obvious choice as a cheap and available option. In other cases, researchers desire to be inclusive and advertise the project widely. However, people from different socio-demographic groups do not respond uniformly. Factors such as language and literacy barriers, time or caring constraints, personal interest, and perhaps most importantly, the belief that they do not have anything special to say, filter the participants. Thus people who are marginalised by society because they are very young, poor, mentally or physically frail, or from non-Anglo backgrounds are under-represented in such research. Those who are highly privileged or just overworked may also choose to absent themselves.

In my experience, when people are approached directly they will often demur at first but when reassured that they are important and can make a contribution to the study they are more than happy to help. There is an ethical issue here. At what point does reassurance end and pressure start? This problem is compounded by the situation where the most vulnerable are both in greatest need of reassurance and most likely to feel pressured. Feldman, Radermacher, Browning, Bird, and Thomas (2008) discussed the difficulties of reaching people from non-English-speaking backgrounds, arguing that interpreters are not an unnecessary expense but an essential cost of research. The issue is not just a practical one; it is a matter of reassuring participants that their views are valued. She also highlighted the problems with recruitment when people feel pressured by a government body to agree to an interview but withdraw because they were not really willing.

When we do make the effort of finding ways to include those who are usually excluded, the results are often surprising. Jan Mason's (2008) work with children in care is a good example. Children are usually excluded on the basis that they are not seen as being able to participate in research and because the processes of gaining consent of the children and guardians are onerous. Children in the care of the State are seen as a particularly vulnerable group, having in many cases been removed from their parents because of fears for their safety. However, Mason found that children aged 8 to 18 were willing and able to give a sensible account of their needs. Moreover, their needs were different from those perceived by their carers or case workers. Central to the children's lives were particular personal connections and the importance of being able to have some control over their connections and the way they lived their lives. The adults were more concerned with directing the children to desirable goals for their adulthood, such as a good education.

With many marginalised groups the building of trust is essential because their experiences of officialdom put them at a disadvantage. Aboriginal people have been betrayed so often that they need considerable reassurance that any proposed research will be different. Nicholls (2009) emphasised the need for constantly reviewing and negotiating the design and process of the research through processes of reflexivity, for the researcher, her interpersonal relationships and for the group collectively.

PRAGMATICS OF DATA COLLECTION

This is the phase of the research process that is crucial for helping voices to be heard. Flexibility and creativity are often needed to find a genre with which people are comfortable. Gwyther and Possamai-Inesedy (2009) discussed the benefits of emerging methods such as auto-ethnography, performance ethnography and arts-based enquiry. However, being flexible and creative often means that methods cannot be determined in advance. When funding bodies and ethics committees require a clear statement of method before a project can start, researchers have to be prepared, if necessary, to go back to those committees and explain a change in method.

Voices can best be heard through the medium in which the participants feel most comfortable and empowered to speak, and with techniques that help them to articulate their stories. A traditional survey which collects qualitative data through the written form will be alienating for many people, but I am reminded of a student who used a survey with open-ended questions on the topic of loneliness. As might be expected she did not receive many responses. The ones she did receive, however, were almost poetic and quite moving; some, for example, had come from isolated rural women who would not have been reached easily with other methods.

Many more people are likely to feel comfortable with the interview format, but some people, particularly those who are marginalised from society, find it difficult to be articulate in English about their experiences or opinions.

One of the great advantages of qualitative research, however, is that it can include an evolutionary process whereby participants are given time and support to find their voice. In the WCA study (Burns & Leonard, 2005), for example, the interview started with a mapping of seven different life careers (occupation, voluntary work, family, relationships, social networks, financial, health). For each of these careers, past, present and future involvements were explored, with careful prompting also to elicit participants' ideas about their futures. Although the interviews were audio-recorded, the interviewer noted key events in each career on a date chart. At the end of this section of the interview the participant could see her life set out in front of her and check for any significant events that had not yet been discussed. The date chart then helped the participant to reflect on her life as a whole, describing her life in terms of chapters of a book and also identifying the important turning points in it.

Careful consideration needs to be given to the choice of interviewer. Rubin and Rubin (1995) saw interviews as guided conversations in which the rules of conversation applied. Once a relationship is identified or negotiated there will be cultural rules about appropriate ways to communicate and appropriate topics of communication. Generally people will feel they can speak more freely with people who are similar to themselves, but the basis of similarity is not always obvious. Whereas age and gender might be important to one person, religion or politics might be more important to another. For some groups it is difficult to find a similar interviewer. For a middle-aged female researcher interviewing male prisoners the first step was finding a common attitude or life experience. Although this could take some time, the interview could not progress until the point of commonality was identified. She always found one. As Nicholls (2009) argued, the Self-Other hyphen both connects and distinguishes between the researcher and participants. Even interviewers who are "fully fledged insiders" can inadvertently silence participants who want to voice views that are not considered appropriate for their shared group identity.

The Older Women and Empowerment Project (OWEP) (Leonard, 2000, 2003) had started as a PAR project with three organisations, but in the time it took to gain funding the original women had become busy with other projects so new participants were invited. The project aimed to create knowledge about how older women were silenced in their organisations and how they could have a stronger voice, and it also aimed to assist the women to organise for change. It was essential to hear from all the participants, especially the quieter ones, not just to collect data but for them to experience voicing their issues in a group setting. Workshops were planned with representatives of the organisations, with the following strategies: a familiar venue which was comfortable and informal; a warm and personal welcome to each participant; seating in small groups with others from their organisation; use of accessible language; varied program and activities; presenters who were members or had worked with the organisations; discussions centring on everyday issues and experiences.

Despite these preparations there was an uncomfortable silence at the first workshop. When asked if there was a problem the participants said "We don't know what you want us to say." Even when we explained that it was up to them, not us, there was a further long pause. The social pressure to take up a role as expert was palpable, but when we stayed silent, the women started to fill the space with their own discussions and ideas. By the follow-up workshop the women were very much partners in the process, and our expertise became a resource that the women could use to help them address their issues.

Written or spoken media are not suitable for all people or all topics. Arts-based inquiry allows people to use different media to find their voice (Higgs, Titchen, Horsfall, & Armstrong, 2007). For example, Photovoice (e.g., Booth & Booth, 2003) is a method that gives the camera to the participants and thus uses photography as a means of entry into the worlds of others. They can amplify their place in and their experience of the world, and the visual imagery is used to enable people to think critically about their social networks and relationships.

ANALYSIS AND INTERPRETATION

When a large amount of complex qualitative information is generated by any method, it probably needs to be collated into a more manageable form. One commonplace method is to identify categories. But the process of categorisation loses much of the complexity and value of the information. In her chapter "Seeking Susan", Denise Farran (1990) documented her analysis of a relatively short interview with a teenager, Susan, about her attendance at a leisure centre. Farran described the losses involved in the subsequent categorisation as follows: loss of detail, loss of variability in the length of answer or in tone, loss of order as the meaning changed with the order in which things were said, loss of answers which did not fit neatly into categories. The types of losses that Farran identified for categorisation apply to all analysis that focuses on the commonalities but ignores the differences among voices. Commonalities are important – there is power in unison – but not at the expense of presenting the diversity of responses.

Clearly, there is the risk that an academic researcher can be dismissive of some statements from participants as ill-informed or irrelevant. Usually this can be avoided by a clear decision to foreground the participants' voices. However, there may be real conflicts. For example, a feminist researcher might be uncomfortable with female participants who take the blame for their own disadvantage. Sometimes this becomes obvious immediately and can be discussed in the interview. In other cases it is possible to return to the participants with the researcher's concerns. In the OWEP project, the analysis found that the women used predominantly internal attributions for their lack of involvement in their organisations; that is, they tended to see their lack of participation in terms of their personal inadequacy (e.g. lack of confidence or skills). In contrast, they used a predominance of external attributions for positive outcomes such as their satisfaction with their involvement in the research workshops (e.g. the friendliness of the organisers, the way the workshops were set up). In the follow-up workshop the women were challenged to consider alternatives; if they could participate in the research workshops satisfactorily because of the way they were set up, surely their organisations could be re-organised to facilitate participation.

Memory work and PAR incorporate a place for participants to contribute to the interpretation, but researchers need to be aware of this as a crucial stage with other methods also: the stage where meanings are made. There are numerous ways to gain participants' input. Feedback can be obtained through focus groups, forums, draft reports in accessible language; or the first stage of the analysis can be incorporated into the interview. An example is the exchange when the women in the WCA project identified turning points and named the chapters of their lives.

In the OWEP project we found that it was our meeting with the older women that "kept us honest". Listening and seriously engaging with the world as seen by research participants takes time but the potential rewards are great. They offer the chance to see concepts and issues in totally new ways that would not be seen in conventional theory-testing models. Far from "biasing" the work, our feminist commitment helped us to engage respectfully with the voices of the older women and not to impose our own assumptions onto the data.

WRITING AND PRESENTING THE FINDINGS

Another set of decisions relates to the presentation of the findings. Academic kudos for the researcher, informing a broad cross-section of society, inciting social or political debate, reporting back to the participants, gaining feedback on the research, changing social practices or attitudes can all be legitimate aims for the dissemination of the findings, but it is unlikely that they can all be achieved by the one publication.

Academic journals give the greatest kudos, and it should be a mark of respect to the participants that their voices are heard in those respected publications. However, such publications have a word limit, and many articles go unread. Indeed, one of the practical challenges in respecting diverse voices is that there is so much information to present. It takes far fewer words to describe commonalities than differences, yet both are important. How to divide up the data is a difficult decision with no ideal solution. Of the participant-led research methods, PAR is often seen as too specific in focus and not generalisable to the wider society. Hence PAR is often difficult to publish in scholarly journals. In contrast, memory work specifically incorporates theory and is designed to make an academic contribution.

There is power in authorship. Sitting on one's own, writing up a project for publication in an academic journal, it is easy to fall back into the bad habits of researchers. For example, although the OWEP study was supposed to be about empowerment the women had kept talking about friendship and socialising. I was systematically ignoring that material and getting a little annoyed at how much of it there was, when I remembered that as a feminist researcher my job was to help the women's voices to be heard, not to use my power as author to censor them. When I then engaged with friendship and socialising, I realised how important they were in contributing to the women's engagement in their organisations.

Moreover, when I went to the literature there was no theory that allowed for a mutually enhancing relationship between socialising and empowerment. So, rather surprisingly for such a grounded project, the first article was a theoretical one.

There are many ways voices can be silenced at this final stage. In an exercise in memory work, Small, Cadman, Friend, Gannon, Ingleton, Koutroulis, et al. (2007) identified "numerous acts of powerlessness through self-doubt, anxiety, 'being good', trying hard to be seen as credible, putting burdens of nurturing and perfection on ourselves, and catching ourselves being silent/silenced in the very act of making our participants' voices, including our own, heard" (Small et al., 2007, p. 276).

Seriously engaging with the task of allowing voices to be heard requires diverse strategies such as reports, performances, websites, and public forums to allow the participants to speak directly to the public. The participants and their advocacy groups can often advise on the best strategies. In PAR, part of the action can be the dissemination of the findings, especially in ways that are useful to similar groups. Research that aims to help voices be heard must recognise dissemination as an integral part of the research process. Ollerton's (2009) Photovoice project is a delightful example. As part of the project the young people with disabilities exhibited their photos of their experiences with social barriers at a civic centre exhibition attended by local councillors and politicians, and also set up their own website. They travelled as a group to another city to present their findings about their concerns at a conference to the disability movement, and are currently contributing to the government Review of the Disability Standards for Accessible Public Transport.

The joy of qualitative research is that it can take seriously the task of listening and finding ways for people to express themselves, especially those who are often omitted from research because nobody asked, or they think nobody is interested or the participation is too difficult. But it cannot be taken for granted that a qualitative method will give voice. This chapter addresses some of the issues to be considered but no doubt there are others, and each project faces its own challenges. Holding on to the goal of helping voices be heard guides us to the decisions on the left of the table rather than those on the right.

REFERENCES

Booth, T., & Booth, W. (2003). In the frame: PhotoVoice and mothers with learning difficulties. *Disability and Society, 18*(4), 431–442.

Burns, A., & Leonard, R. (2005). Chapters of our lives: Life narratives of lower-income midlife and older women. *Sex Roles, 52*(5/6), 269–277.

Farran, D. (1990). Seeking Susan: Producing statistical information on young people's leisure. In L. Stanley (Ed.), *Feminist praxis: Research theory and epistemology in feminist sociology*. London: Routledge.

Feldman, S., Radermacher, H., Browning, C., Bird, S., & Thomas, S. (2008). Challenges of recruitment and retention of older people from culturally diverse communities in research. *Ageing & Society, 28*, 473–493.

Gwyther, G., & Possamai-Inesedy, A. (2009). Methodologies a la carte: An examination of emerging qualitative methodologies in social research. *International Journal of Social Research Methodology, 12*(2), 99–115.

Hart, E., & Bond, M. (1995). *Action research for health and social care: A guide to practice.* Buckingham; Philadelphia: Open University Press.

Haug, F., et al. (1999). *Female sexualization: A collective work of memory* (E. Carter, Trans., 2nd ed.). London: Verso.

Higgs, J., Titchen, A., Horsfall, D., & Armstrong, H. (Eds.). (2007). *Being critical and creative in qualitative research.* Sydney: Hampden Press.

Lather, P. (1991). *Feminist research in education: Within/against.* Geelong, VIC: Deakin University Press.

Leonard, R. (2000). Older women, community organisations and social capital. *Third Sector Review,* 6(1), 43–58.

Leonard, R. (2003). Doing feminist action research: Examining women's participation in third sector organisations for older people. *Third Sector Review* (Special issue: Doing third sector research), 9(2), 81–93.

Leonard, R., & Burns, A. (1999). An analysis of turning points in the lives of midlife and older women. *Australian Psychologist,* 34(2), 87–93.

Mason, J. A. (2008). Children's standpoint: Needs in out-of-home care. *Children and Society,* 22(5), 358–369.

Nicholls, R. (2009). Research and indigenous participation: Critical reflexive methods. *International Journal of Social Research Methodology,* 12(2), 117–126.

Ollerton, J. (2009). Rights, camera, action! A collaborative exploration of social barriers to self-determination for people with learning difficulties. Disability Health & Research Network Conference "Getting the Message Out", Vancouver.

Onyx, J., & Small, J. (2001). Memory-work: The method. *Qualitative Inquiry,* 7(6), 773–786.

Small, J., Cadman, K., Friend, L., Gannon, S., Ingleton, C., Koutroulis, G., et al. (2007). Unresolved power for feminist researchers employing memory-work. In I. Ateljevic, A. Pritchard, & N. Morgan (Eds.), *The critical turn in tourism studies: Innovative research methodologies* (pp. 261–278). Oxford: Elsevier.

Rubin, H. J., & Rubin, I. S. (1995). Interviews as guided conversations. In H. J. Rubin & I. S. Rubin (Eds.), *Qualitative interviewing: The art of hearing data* (pp. 122–144). Thousand Oaks, CA: Sage.

AFFILIATION

Rosemary Leonard PhD
Social Justice and Social Change Research Centre
University of Western Sydney
Australia

JOHN A. BOWDEN AND PAMELA J. GREEN

14. THE VOICE OF THE RESEARCHED IN QUALITATIVE RESEARCH:

Rigour and Research Practices

Research involving human participants (here we are referring to the *researched* rather than the researchers) is usually concerned with accessing their voices by collection of data about their experiences and perceptions, often through qualitative interviews. This chapter presents a three-part typology of the voice of the researched – individual voice, collective voice and researcher-interpreted collective voice. Phenomenography is used throughout the chapter as a concrete example of a qualitative research approach that prioritises the "voice of the researched". By reflecting and writing about the voice of the researched, we have made our own thinking known not only to readers but to ourselves. As Calkins (1985) has suggested, writing helps you to know what you think: "Through writing, we can resee, reshape and refine our thoughts (p. 191). We did not know how this chapter would turn out when we began but we were curious to find out.

WHAT IS THE VOICE OF THE RESEARCHED?

In trying to access the voice of the researched, researchers may perceive various possible meanings for that term. One meaning is the voice of the individual person from whom data are gathered (*individual voice*). Another is a combined voice developed and agreed upon by a group of people discussing a particular issue (*collective voice*). A third meaning involves individual voices being made explicit with someone (normally the researcher) interpreting from them an integrated collective account (researcher-interpreted *collective voice*).

Many political and social-change groups claim to be expressing the voice of particular groups. In politics this notion of voice has collective overtones. Individual voice may be the foundation of collective voice, but the most active meaning in terms of policy formation relates to an interpreted collective voice. Feminist movements, both past and present, have rightly been concerned that the voice of women should be heard and have equal impact on social attitudes and behaviour (see e.g. Belenky et al., 1997). Minority groups are often concerned that their voices be heard in order to prevent their cultural values being overwhelmed by the majority culture (see e.g. Rowell, 1995). Although such groups may see individual voice as the basis for their political position, they are more likely to derive policy and practice from an interpretation of the collective voice through interactions with a range of individuals and groups.

What characterises these political uses of voice is that the interpreted collective voice is used for purposes of power – to attract support and/or as a social-change tool. In most qualitative research, the notion of voice concerns not political power per se but rather an intellectual interest in accessing the meaning behind the voices. In qualitative research, the term "voice of the people" is not a political slogan but rather a descriptive research goal.

THE ISSUE OF VOICE IN QUALITATIVE RESEARCH

A fundamental characteristic of qualitative research into human experience is that its practitioners claim to be enabling those whom they are researching to make explicit their own ways of seeing. Indeed, the initial development of many qualitative research methods derived from dissatisfaction with quantitative methods that, at best, calculated the degree to which the researched supported the ideas put forward by the researcher (see Chapter 12 for details).

So qualitative researchers are interested in accessing the voice of the researched, but can any researcher validly claim to have revealed the "true" voice of the researched anyway? In an absolute sense, it is not possible. The expression of voice is idiographic, that is, located in a given time and place. Hence, voice is both dynamic and subjective. What is accessed by the researcher is always a filtered voice, as a result of the limitations of any communication process in data collection and reporting, as well as the researcher's input into data analysis. The degree of filtering that occurs is variable, depending on the methods used. Consequently, one goal of the researcher should be to maximise the opportunity for the researched to express their perspectives without constraint and to minimise the extent to which the researcher influences the nature of that expression. Then it is the researcher's task to try to represent the expressed perspectives as faithfully as possible. All of these elements comprise aspects of rigour and credibility in qualitative research.

Even transcripts of interviews cannot be claimed, per se, as the voice of the researched in any absolute sense. Readers of a transcript access the voice of the researched through their own interpretations of the text. Furthermore, the researched are asked to tell their stories about something – an input by the researcher. In addition, the researched tell their stories in a setting, usually in the presence of a researcher, following some negotiation that places them in that situation. All those aspects affect the approach adopted by the researched to their story-telling and contribute to a self-filtering of their voice. We are reminded of a cartoon (Larson, 1984) depicting some islanders sitting in their huts and being urged by their leaders to hide their television sets and radios – because the anthropologists are coming.

Another situational factor is that any voice is always changing subtly as the context shifts. Research captures a filtered interpretation of the voice of the researched in the particular time and space in which the data are collected. Although all research with human participants has contextual limitations, the negative effects of these limitations can be minimised by appropriate research

THE VOICE OF THE RESEARCHED

procedures but should be acknowledged when outcomes are communicated. Nevertheless, the "true" voice of the researched is never directly accessible to researchers. In a research sense, *true* (voice) is a myth.

Rigour and Voice

What counts as rigour in research is particular to the specific research approach and the activities undertaken within it. Rigour includes the researcher's commitment to making every research action a means for maximising opportunities for the researched to express their own voices and minimising the extent to which those voices are filtered. Hence, the ways of working within any given approach determine the extent to which the research is seen as rigorous. Robust research is well grounded when attention to details that count with respect to rigour is treated seriously and carefully. In phenomenography, rigour relies on key practices throughout the research processes from planning to representation of findings.

PHENOMENOGRAPHIC RESEARCH PRACTICES AND THE VOICE OF THE RESEARCHED

Marton (1992, p. 253) suggested that

> whatever phenomenon people encounter, there is a limited number of qualitatively different ways in which the phenomenon is experienced, conceptualised, or understood. [Phenomenography is] a research method designed to discover and describe such differences.

The research outcome is a set of categories of description representing a mapping of those different ways of seeing. Marton (1986) had previously defined phenolmenography as "a research method adapted for mapping the qualitatively different ways in which people experience, conceptualise, perceive, and understand various aspects of, and phenomena in, the world around them" (p. 31). In the same paper, he referred to what he called a "pure" phenomenographic interest: "describing how people conceive of various aspects of their reality" (p. 38).

Bowden (1995, p. 146) introduced the term *developmental phenomenography* to describe a particular, applied form of phenomenography that goes beyond pure phenomenography and is:

> research which, through finding out how people experience some aspect of their world, will enable them or others to change the way their world operates, normally in a formal educational setting. My perspective is developmental. My reasons for undertaking the research are concerned with how I can use the research outcomes to affect the world I live and work in. The research outcomes are not the objective per se.

Bowden illustrated how variation in intended use of the research outcomes affects the ways in which the research needs to be undertaken. The key practices of phenomenographic research relating to the ways that the voice of the researched is privileged are shown in Table 14.1.

Table 14.1. Phenomenographic research practices and the voice of the researched

Researcher questions	Research practices and their implications
1. *Focus* – What do you want to know?	*Map the variation* in ways of seeing by accessing individual voices in data collection, researcher-interpreted collective voice in analysis and combining them in publications.
2. *Sampling* – How do you select the research participants?	*Ensure access to various, relevant, individual voices* by choices that maximise the range of ways of seeing the phenomenon represented amongst the researched.
3. *Interviewing* – How can you encourage interviewees to talk about the issue of concern, without unduly influencing their responses?	*Privilege the individual voice of the researched* by maximising opportunities for its expression and minimising filtering (by neutral questions, bracketing researchers' perspectives and avoidance of judgmental statements or spontaneous introduction of new content). In developmental phenomenography, ensure that all interviewees experience similar conditions during the interviews.
4. *Preparing for analysis* – How to ensure that transcripts are accurate?	*Preserve the individual voice of the researched.* Complete transcripts are taken verbatim from audiotapes of interviews and checked against the audiotapes by the interviewers themselves.
5. *Analysis* – How can you analyse transcripts so that the voice of the researched is maximised and the voice of the researcher minimised?	*Privilege the collective voice of the researched and minimise filtering* by using the individual voices in transcripts as the only acceptable evidence, as categories of description are mapped across individual accounts in an iterative process. Phenomenographic outcomes represent a snapshot at the time and under the conditions in which data were originally collected.
6. *Representation of findings* – How can the categories of description represent the voice of the researched when they have been compiled by researchers?	*Represent both the researcher-interpreted collective voice and individual voices.* Steps 1–5 ensure that the collective voice expressed in categories comes only from the individual voices as evidenced in the transcripts and that filtering is minimised. Both the researcher-interpreted collective voice (as categories of description) and individual voices (as excerpts to enhance meaning of various aspects) are published.

Let us now examine the phenomenographic research practices and implications listed in Table 14.1 in some detail. Most are broadly relevant to other qualitative approaches as well.

Focus

In phenomenography, reasons for undertaking research vary considerably and are contextual. The central focus is on accessing individual voices and interpreting from them a collective voice for the researched. One such example (the *physics project*) is about first year university students' understandings of basic physics concepts (Bowden et al., 1992). Physics lecturers at a particular university had comprehensively tested their final year students and found that they did not adequately understand the basic concepts that they had learned in first year. When students needed to use those concepts in more complex situations in later years, their understanding of them was partial and seemingly less comprehensive than it had been in first year. The lecturers wondered why this had happened and what could be done about it.

The phenomenographic physics project investigated the range of understandings of basic concepts that students had during first year. It turned out that, despite getting good examination grades on what was largely quantitative problem-solving, first year students understood the underlying concepts in a variety of more or less powerful ways. It was not that by third year they had forgotten what they had learned. Rather the research showed that most had never understood the basic concepts in first year in the ways lecturers thought they had; this was masked by a superior ability to calculate numerical answers in exams (Bowden et al., 1992).

Sampling

The aim is to ensure that a sufficient number of relevant voices are heard. Phenomenographers normally use maximum variation sampling, a form of purposeful sampling (Patton, 2002), as it maximises the range of individual voices, thereby enriching the researcher-interpreted collective voice. It was used, for instance, in a study (the *success in research project*) of what researchers understood as success in research, which was aimed at informing research development programs in the university concerned (Bowden et al., 2005). To maximise the variation in ways of seeing research in the sample interviewed, researchers in the project

> tried to ensure that the interviewees included both men and women, researchers from a variety of fields and across a range of research experience. Further we decided, since a major reason for doing this research was to feed back the results into (X) University's research development program that the researchers interviewed should all be (X) academics (Bowden, 2005, p. 16).

The researchers in the *physics project* faced a more complex choice. They could interview current third year students and ask them to recall what they understood about key concepts studied in first year, in the hope of gaining direct access to the voice of the researched. Yet, if their lecturers' rationalisation was accurate and students had by third year forgotten what they had learned in first year, researchers had no way to access the earlier understandings. Consequently, the researchers chose to interview current first year students whose first year educational experience was similar to those whose performance triggered the research.

The voice of the researched in such circumstances is located in time and space. The voice of final year students is located in the "present" (at the time of initiation of the research) and within the context of final year study. The lecturers had uncovered convincing evidence about that voice. The voice of the same students several years earlier (in first year) is located in a different time and space, both inaccessible. The decision to interview current first year university physics students took researchers to a similar space but at a different time. The researchers were confident that, while not directly accessing the time and space that the final year students had experienced several years earlier, they were accessing a time and space combination that had similar characteristics. They still felt that they were privileging the voice of the researched, trying to make that voice explicit and maximising the opportunity to take it into account in their analysis.

Interviewing

A practical issue for developmental phenomenographic researchers is how to encourage interviewees to talk about the topic of interest and to say as much as possible, without the researcher unduly influencing what interviewees have to say. Researchers want to hear the voices of the researched in relation to a particular phenomenon and ensure that they hear as much as the researched might be able to reveal. This means that the researcher needs to inform the researched of the focus of the project. The inclusion of an opening scenario for the interview provides such information. For example, in the *success in research project* the opening scenario was framed in each interview partly as follows:

> First, I would ask you to tell me about some research that you have been engaged in that you view as being successful in some way ... Second, I will ask you to tell me about some research that you have been engaged in that you view as being unsuccessful in some way (Green, 2005, p. 38).

The consistent use of an agreed opening scenario ensures that each interviewee experiences the same set of information and requests. Interviewers need to be sure that from then on only the voice of the researched is heard. They encourage interviewees to say everything they can about the topic by using neutral questions (Bowden, 2005; Green, 2005) such as:
– What did you mean by that?
– I didn't quite understand that; could you tell it to me again using different words?
– You used the term Z; could you tell me more about that?
– You mentioned S and then said it was different from T; can you explain?

The rationale is that interviewers should ensure as far as possible that the voice of the researched is fully heard and should be respectful of that voice. Consequently, they should not comment judgmentally on what interviewees say. Nor should interviewers spontaneously add further ideas of their own to the conversation. They must bracket their own perspective during the interview. Otherwise, questions would arise about whether the data from the interview truly reflected the voice of the researched, or whether what was said was catalysed by the interviewer's comments beyond the common opening scenario.

Developmental phenomenography is focused on the voice of the researched, and the use of a consistent opening scenario followed only by neutral questions and no judgmental statements (or body language) is recommended as standard practice for interviews (Bowden, 2005; Green, 2005).

Preparation for Analysis

Given the primacy of the interview transcripts, it is vital that they be complete and accurate. The individual voices of the researched must be preserved. Interviews are audiotaped and transcribed in full. However, if the interviewer has unintentionally influenced the content of the interview late in the interview (for example, by making a judgemental comment on something the interviewee has said), thereby filtering the voice of the researched, only the data prior to that point are analysed in developmental phenomenography.

Sometimes the interviewer will transcribe the audiotapes. However, normal practice is to have the audiotapes professionally transcribed. The interviewer then reads the draft transcript while listening to the tape. Getting the transcription right – in terms of both accuracy and completeness in relation to the individual voices of the researched – is essential. At the analysis phase the only source of evidence that is acceptable in developmental phenomenography is that contained within the transcripts (Bowden, 2000, 2005; Green, 2005).

Ideally, in phenomenography, a full set of transcripts would be available prior to the commencement of data analysis. At the very least, all interviews should have been completed before analysis begins. This is to guarantee that knowledge by the researcher of early analysis results will not inadvertently influence subsequent interviews and distort the voice of the researched.

Analysis

How can transcripts be analysed so that the voice of the researched is maximised and the voice of the researcher minimised? Traditionally, phenomenographic analysis has been carried out by individual researchers and often still is. The researcher would read the transcripts and then develop a draft set of categories. The transcripts would be read again by the researcher and the draft modified. This iterative re-reading and re-drafting would be repeated until saturation occurred, that is, until the re-reading failed to produce any significant change in the categories of description.

More recently it has been argued that group analysis produces an outcome more likely to reflect the voice of the researched and is the recommended approach for developmental phenomenography (Bowden, 2000, 2005; Green, 2005). In the group process, one of the researchers acts in exactly the way the individual researcher has done traditionally. However, there are other researchers engaged in the analysis who also read the transcripts. The group meets after each version of the draft categories of description has been written and all members of the group act as devil's advocates in various ways, probing the draft and asking for justification from within the transcripts for the particular formulation. Questions might include:
– Why did you write this category in this way?
– Where in the transcripts is there evidence for this?
– Does this aspect of the category relate to other categories? If so, how and where is the evidence in the transcripts?
– What does this mean for the ongoing reconstruction of the categories?

This devil's advocacy is intended to guard against "group think" which can allow a group of researchers to come to a conclusion too early. Team members return constantly to the transcripts in order to be as faithful as possible to them (see Sandberg, 1995, on this issue). This underlines the primacy of the transcripts – the voice of the researched – in formulating the outcomes. The group process makes it less likely that the analysis will stop part-way. Given the purpose, that the categories of description should reflect the full range of voices of the researched collectively to the greatest extent possible, the group process has the best potential to achieve this goal.

As a consequence of its adversarial approach, however, group analysis of this kind demands high levels of goodwill and accumulated trust, a commitment to constructive comment, as well as a close observance of the transcripts throughout the analysis. During the process, a number of iterations of vigorous debate and analysis followed by re-analysis continue until a researcher-interpreted collective voice is agreed upon. Although success in the process is dependent on trust among the group, the continual involvement in devil's advocacy and changed thinking that follows can, by its nature, itself contribute to building up of mutual trust (Bowden, 2005; Bowden and Green, 2005, Green, 2005).

A second relevant aspect of the analysis is the "whole of transcript" versus the "pool of excerpts" approach. The latter involves collecting together excerpts from different transcripts that appear to be similar and then deriving each category of description from one of those pools of similar utterances. The whole of transcript approach (Bowden, 2005) involves the researcher in seeking meaning of any utterance by moving backwards and forwards in the transcript so as to comprehend the meaning of the utterance in context. At all times the whole transcript is available to the researcher but it is usually not read in full each time. This approach does not involve separate analysis of each individual transcript. The analysis remains focused on interpretation of the collective voice derived from the contextualised individual voices.

We regard the whole of transcript approach as superior to the pool of meanings approach because it focuses more on the voice of the researched. It assumes that the voice of the researched is best represented by the meaning of any utterance made rather than by separating the utterance from the context that provides its meaning and relegating it to be one example of a set of words held in common in a pool. The pool of excerpts approach is more likely to result in a researcher-created set of categories, catalysed by the words within the pool of excerpts, but not necessarily influenced sufficiently by their contextual meanings (that derive from the individual voices in the transcripts).

Representation of Findings

The collective voice of the researched within phenomenography is accessed through the interpretive lens of the researcher and represented as categories of description. Such categories are derived from the individual interviews taken together, and in any published work (e.g. Bowden et al., 1992, 2005) phenomenographers commonly include quotations from individual interviews to illustrate further the meaning of one or more aspects of a category of description and to expose the individual voices of the researched.

It should be emphasised that both the *success in research project* and the *physics project* led to changes in the universities concerned by those responsible for the areas investigated. However, how this change aspect of developmental phenomenography occurs should be reflected upon because such research does not produce generalisations. Rather it produces categories of description that relate to the particular set of interviewees and the context in which the data were collected. Such categories of description are then reported in any publication of the research as the outcome of the phenomenographic study, the voices of the particular researched. Of course, the research is undertaken in a way that makes results relevant to the issue that was its origin. Those concerned with the original issue, the primary audience, can use the research outcomes as data when analysing their own situation in their own way. However, they have to take responsibility themselves for exploring any relation between the research outcomes and more generalised implications.

CONCLUSION

This chapter has focused on the voice of the researched. It has suggested a broad typology of three kinds of voice relevant to qualitative research – individual voice, collective voice and researcher-interpreted collective voice. Developmental phenomenography produces a researcher-interpreted collective voice from a group analysis of representations of relevant individual voices. This approach to research is based on a relational perspective (elaborated earlier in Chapter 12) that leads to the conclusion that any phenomenon may be seen in a variety of ways by different people and in different contexts. It is acknowledged that the researcher can influence both the nature of data collected and the nature of the analysis. The intention is for the research outcomes to be as faithful as possible to the voices of those interviewed. This requires research rigour which is ensured by particular approaches to data collection and analysis. For example, the use of research practices directed at minimising the influence of the interviewer on the expression of individual voices helps to ensure that the research is rigorous. During the analysis phase, maintaining the interview transcripts as the only input to development of categories of descriptions and the use of devil's advocacy in a group process are two examples of such rigour. Throughout the chapter, the full range of research processes and practices in developmental phenomenography have been described and analysed in relation to rigour in developing outcomes faithful to the voice of the researched.

REFERENCES

Belenky, M. F., Clinchy, B. M., Goldberger, N. R., & Tarule, J. M. (1997). *Women's ways of knowing: The development of self, voice and mind* (Tenth anniversary ed.). New York: Basic Books.
Bowden, J. A. (1995). Phenomenographic research: Some methodological issues. *Nordisk Pedagogik, 15*(3), 144–155.

Bowden, J. A. (2000). Experience of phenomenographic research: A personal account. In J. Bowden & P. Walsh (Eds.), *Phenomenography* (pp. 47–61). Melbourne: RMIT University Press.

Bowden, J. A. (2005). Reflections on the phenomenographic team research process. In J. Bowden & P. Green (Eds.), *Doing developmental phenomenography* (pp. 11–31). Melbourne: RMIT University Press.

Bowden, J. A., Dall'Alba, G., Laurillard, D., Martin, E., Marton, F., Masters, G., et al. (1992). Displacement, velocity and frames of reference: Phenomenographic studies of students' understanding and some implications for teaching. *American Journal of Physics, 60,* 262–269.

Bowden, J. A., & Green, P. (Eds.). (2005). *Doing developmental phenomenography.* Melbourne: RMIT University Press.

Bowden, J., Green, P., Barnacle, R., Cherry, N., & Usher, R. (2005). Academics' ways of understanding success in research activities. In J. Bowden & P. Green (Eds.), *Doing developmental phenomenography* (pp. 128–144). Melbourne: RMIT University Press.

Calkins, L. (1985). Learning to think through writing. In A. Jaggar & M. T. Smith-Burke (Eds.), *Observing the language learner* (pp. 190–198). Newark, NJ; Delaware, DE: International Reading Association.

Green, P. (2005). A rigorous journey into phenomenography: From a naturalistic inquirer viewpoint. In J. Bowden & P. Green (Eds.), *Doing developmental phenomenography* (pp. 32–46). Melbourne: RMIT University Press.

Larson, G. (1984). *Anthropologists! Anthropologists!* The Far Side FarWorks Inc, one-panel syndicated comic. Retrieved from July 19, 2009, from http://books.google.com/books?id=vbu2gis26C0C&pg=PA85&dq=references+larson +anthropologist+1984+far+side

Marton, F. (1986). Phenomenography – A research approach to investigating different understandings of reality. *Journal of Thought, 21*(3), 28–49.

Marton, F. (1992). Phenomenography and "the art of teaching all things to all men". *International Journal of Qualitative Studies in Education, 5*(3), 253–267.

Patton, M. (2002). *Qualitative research and evaluation methods* (3rd ed.). Newbury Park, CA: Sage.

Rowell, J. (1995). The politics of cultural appropriation. *The Journal of Value Inquiry, 29*(1), 137–142.

Sandberg, J. (1995). Are phenomenographic results reliable? *Nordisk Pedagogik, 15*(3), 156–164.

AFFILIATIONS

John A Bowden PhD
Swinburne Research, Swinburne University of Technology
Australia

Pamela J Green PhD
Swinburne Research, Swinburne University of Technology
Australia

JOY HIGGS AND DEBBIE HORSFALL

15. BEING CRITICAL AND CREATIVE IN QUALITATIVE RESEARCH

FOUNDATIONS

Being and becoming critical and creative in qualitative research requires us to grow as people and researchers through a lifetime journey. Before taking the first steps, sustained and deep preparation of the ground is necessary. (Higgs & Titchen, 2007, p. 1)

The notions of criticality and creativity in qualitative research are tantalising, exciting and powerful. Before we launch into this space of excitement and stretching of our imaginations, strategies and talents, however, we take a moment to ask: Why? Why are we doing research at all? What do we hope to achieve? How will we know we have succeeded?

Without addressing these questions it is easy to become lost in the excitement, besotted with the creativity, perhaps for its own sake, and immersed in being creative. So first we reflect on the foundation questions before addressing the apparent topic of the chapter. In the end, we found (in writing the chapter) that this section is both critical and creative, but at a foundation level. (Note the deliberate switching of tenses – the circularity of this process and argument is a nicely intriguing one.)

Why are we doing Research at all? What do we Hope to Achieve? How will we know we have Succeeded?

The core goal of research is to produce knowledge, but beyond that, research enables us to understand and to change. Research can be a fascinating pursuit of wisdom and understanding. Some forms of research (e.g. action research) can also be a deliberate means of changing circumstances, people and influences, as opposed to reporting findings and leaving others (or ourselves) the task of changing the practice or phenomenon we have researched subsequently. As practitioners, educators and researchers, we also grow through doing research; we become more able to make a meaningful contribution to each of these roles and pursuits. And, like throwing a pebble into a seemingly still pool, we can create ripples of questions, challenges, awareness and insights that provoke others to take a new direction of practice, learning or research.

We can seek to understand richly, deeply, unexpectedly and at times shockingly, the nature of being in the human worlds of the people we work with in our research. We enter these worlds to gain a sense of being (*Dasein*). In using the term *Dasein*, Heidegger (1926/1990) was illuminating the basic nature of human existence and emphasising the essential importance that *being* has for the way we understand and interpret the world. Such *being* is being-in-the-world; it is the coherence of a being or human entity situated and engaged in the world in the context of the time and place of that being, experience and existence. When we engage with people during research we are seeking to make clearer or more explicit the nature of their being.

Through understanding we produce knowledge that enters the discourse of the relevant field of literature and research. From such contributions, new research and practice development lead to changes in practice, in systems, and potentially, indirectly, in people's lives. Critical paradigm research in particular engages with change directly; it seeks change to the way lives, circumstances and systems have been socioculturally or historically constructed, and challenges the taken-for-granted or entrenched realities of these situations. The purpose of research in this paradigm is to develop knowledge or understandings in order to effect change, hopefully for the better. Infused with a Politics of Hope (see Macy 1983, 1991, 2000), researchers seeking change often have an ecological world view – that change can and does occur at many levels: for the researcher and the participants, in all types of social practices, services, systems, society and structures of thinking. Often, as in the case of all types of action research, change is built into the research process rather than something hoped for once the research is concluded (Horsfall, 2005).

Beyond the achievement of understanding, knowledge and change, a key aspiration of researchers – here we speak for ourselves, but find resonance in the work of many colleagues – is to produce findings which are credible and transferable and useful. We hope that what we find of value, others do too. So we know we have succeeded if we find the research illuminating, if others value it, if it makes a difference to the way people think and to the way things (systems, lives, well-beings) are in the human world.

BEING CRITICAL AND CREATIVE

In 2007, building on previous decades of research, a group of us (Higgs, Titchen, Horsfall, & Armstrong, 2007) set out to make "the processes and experiences of ... [qualitative] research more transparent and explicate the research craft knowledge embedded and embodied within it ... [to invite] readers to explore ways of transforming and illuminating the processes of qualitative research to draw on the seemingly contradictory but liberating synergy of research that is both critical and creative" (Higgs & Titchen, 2007, p. 1). In this collection of research works and frameworks we pursued nine themes around being critical and creative in qualitative research:

1. Authentically Pursuing One's Philosophical Stance

Being critical (in the midst of creativity) in qualitative research involves recognising, understanding and explicating the researcher's philosophical stance and striving towards epistemological and ontological authenticity throughout the research endeavour (see Chapter 4).

2. Examining Complementary Research Strategies

This theme pertains to pursuing a blend of complementary research strategies based upon an understanding of the phenomenon we are seeking to explore as a reality amenable to different ways of knowing. Through these ontological and epistemological explorations we can choose research strategies that are appropriate to the phenomenon and recognise which strategies can be seen as complementary. Part of this decision making involves looking at the methodological preferences, strengths and experiences of the researchers.

3. Pursuing Social Action and Change

Research can be a space for social change, liberatory action and politics (see Horsfall, 2001). Such research actively and self-consciously seeks to make a difference in the world at personal, community, organisation or social levels.

4. Valuing Creative Imagination and Creative Arts in Qualitative Research

This theme involved recognising the place of creative epistemologies and arts within the research processes and products. The entire research process, from the initial idea or question to its publication, requires researchers to create ways of engaging that are unique to their research questions, participants and contexts.

5. Engaging in Critical and Creative Conversations

Critical and creative conversations can be used to pursue research that entails meaning construction with multiple perspectives (see Higgs, 2006).

6. Engaging in a Reflexive Journey

Through reflexivity (i.e. self reflection leading to development), researchers learn from experience and from conversations with critical companions (see McCormack & Titchen, 2006) to reshape the type of researchers they are becoming.

7. Recognising the Importance of Research to Serve Practice

Research is one way of knowing that informs practice. Of particular importance, we contend, is the need to research and articulate practice epistemologies and ontologies to inform professional practice and education (see Higgs, Andresen, & Fish, 2004).

8. Appreciating Multiple Effects of Research

In this theme we recognised the value of appreciating and celebrating the multiple and sometimes unexpected effects of the research process and product on people, organisations, communities and societies (see Titchen, 2004).

9. Embracing and Exploring Ethics, Moral Discourse and the Sacred as the Ethos for Researching

Research that embraces moral and sacred issues is situated in what Lincoln and Denzin (2000) have called the age of spirituality in qualitative research. There are exciting new areas of research that pursue the spiritual aspects of life and practice (see Campbell's (1984) moderated or professional love).

PURSUING 7TH AND 8TH MOMENT RESEARCH

Critical and creative research provides a way of pursuing what Lincoln and Denzin (2000) described as the 7th and 8th moments in qualitative research. The term 7th moment research refers to research with an explicit intention to nurture human flourishing for those within the research and for its beneficiaries. 8th moment research highlights multivoiced texts, cultural criticism, and research that is messy, uncertain and reflexive.

With Angie Titchen (Titchen, Higgs, & Horsfall, 2007) we identified seven key signposts for these 7th and 8th moments, seven indicators of what it means to immerse ourselves in critical and creative research in these moments:
- the need for transformational research leaders who value diverse ways of being in research, support holistic knowledges and facilitate research cultures that support critical-creative research and push at the boundaries of research
- the importance of an inherent, lived reflexivity for creating and enacting innovative research strategies
- the need for paying far more attention to everyday lived ethics in research education and practice (beyond the dictates of ethics committees)
- the importance of blending creative research strategies and boundary riding (between different research approaches) with credibility and authenticity in research and scholarship
- the promotion of human flourishing and particularly spiritual wellbeing in research spaces
- the inclusion of *critical creativity* as a paradigm or research framework alongside other more established research frameworks, by researchers who wish to engage in 7th and 8th moment research in ways that are epistemologically and ontologically congruent with human flourishing
- the need for rigorous philosophical, theoretical and methodological critique of research that blends artistic with cognitive critique.

EXPLORING CRITICAL AND CREATIVE RESEARCH

So what does critical and creative research look and feel like from the inside out? The following approaches and ideas are drawn from the authors' experiences and align with the nine themes above.

Having or Creating a Starting Point

Unless you have been specifically employed to work on a research project, the likelihood is that you will create your own place to start. The impetus or desire to begin, to do something, is probably different for all of us. What we have in common, as researchers, is that we notice things in the world around us, we have curious, creative, questioning minds and, perhaps contentiously, we have enough audacity to believe we can contribute in some way.

> I notice peoples and their way of being in the world
> And ask – Does it have to be this way?

Often the starting point for research is noticing (seeing, feeling or intuiting) that something is not quite right: for example, in relationships, in a theoretical model, in practices, in a service provision, in society. The researchers' desire urges them to understand what is not quite right, why, and work out how it could be otherwise. Consider the following real life example. This is a comment made by a practitioner:

> *"Do you know most people want to die at home?*
> *Yet most people actually die in an institution."*

The researcher's mind asks:

> Has it always been like this? Why don't people die at home?
>   Who, or what, is stopping them?
>   Whose interests are being served here?
>   What would it take to make it happen?
> What about people who do die at home? How does that happen?
>   Why and how do they make that choice? What works for them?
>   Who else is asking these questions?
> Why does this make me feel angry?
>   What would I want for me? For those I love?
>   Do I have what it takes to support someone to die at home?
> Do I want to talk to dying people? Am I able to?
>   Who do I need to talk to? What can I do?
>   How can I put my skills and talents and desires to work here?

> Questions
> Bursting through flesh
> Unable to be held
> Minds imploding.
>
> Don't just stand there
> Do something!

Creating a research framework or model

> Let us move then
> from a passion,
> a thirs
> a compulsion
> to know,
> to know more – deeply
> and more explicitly
> some ... *phantome*
> of human existence
> someone's being-in-the-world
> to create a frame
> for this knowing journey
> a means of pursuing
> the ephemeral
> of transforming inchoate knowing
> to choate
> and thus to touch
> this Being
> with mind and spirit.

The task and means of creating this framework or model for the knowing journey are examined in Chapters 4 (philosophical frameworks), 8 (research lenses), and the numerous methodological chapters in Section 3 of this book.

Transformational Leadership and Cultures

Research team leaders and supervisors with aspirations to foster critical and creative research face the demanding task of guiding colleagues, novices and students in a way that acknowledges the at times harsh realities of judgment norms at the same time as creating a liberating structure and climate for research adventures. The leader guides as well as opens doors, communicates expectations as well as listens to new ideas, and transforms as well as remains open to transformation. Transformational research leaders live inspirational and facilitative roles and encourage transformative learning that is a blending of reflexivity, re-creation and critical self-evaluation. And they foster transformational cultures that facilitate mutual journeys with students, practitioners and participants; journeys that challenge practice, understandings and research values and enable critical, creative and spiritual becoming of these travelling companions.

Research is embedded in a cultural context, and being a researcher within the qualitative tradition means embracing the influence of different cultural contexts on the knowledge generated. Living research in such contexts requires researchers to be aware of and explicitly address the expectations and opportunities for meaning making and knowledge shaping that these cultures provide. Learning to live research authentically in consideration of cultural issues is critical for research that seeks to be people-centred, illuminative and transformative.

Authentic Collaboration

To pursue and accomplish authentic collaboration between researchers and participants involves critically valuing participants' voices in their telling of their experiences of the phenomenon being studied. Genuine collaboration requires creative spaces for expressing ideas and values and receptive spaces for listening to shared experiences as well as discordant visions and for negotiating ways of honouring the differences and diversity that individuals bring to the research endeavour. Being ethical in research interactions requires a sensibility to situations and cultures and to other participants in terms of feelings, respect, social and power relationships, conventions and interests.

Reflexivity and Critique

In pursuing research adventures which seek transformation and human flourishing, the process is as vital as the outcome of the research. By this we mean that the actual doing of the research, the working with others (co-researchers, participants, colleagues, and stakeholders) must be deeply grounded in creative, democratic, enlivening and transformative ways of doing and being. This does not imply pursuing an agenda of benevolence or one where everything and anything is acceptable and valuable. Rather, our role as critical, creative researchers is to facilitate research processes which are deeply respectful, inclusive, accessible and sometimes challenging (see Horsfall & Titchen, 2009, for concrete examples). This facilitation can only be achieved if we know ourselves, our biases and our socially constructed positions in the world; if we are aware of relations of power and how they may play out in research relationships; if we state our agendas while at the same time being flexible; if we are as transparent as we possibly can be; and if we communicate all of this clearly. This level of reflexivity and clarity, or standing strongly in your own shoes, provides the space for transformative critique. Critique is possible when we are clear about who we are, what we want and where we think we are going – in terms of the research – while at the same time holding these things lightly, being able to change our minds in the light of creative critique. Although seemingly paradoxical, we are able to do these things when we accept that all knowledge is partial, contingent and socio-historically created.

Metaphors and Images

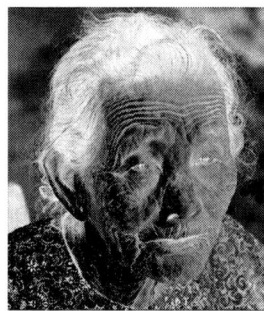

To the scholar
the task of capturing
the elusive essence
the feelings
tantalisingly out of reach

of words

and lines of words

in grammatical exactitude
across the page.

Enter imagery

like a shower of light

gems

like a torrent
of grey pain

and pictures

that
bring the record
of living
to life.

CONCLUSION

Being critical and creative in research is doing, knowing, being and becoming one with research that is transformative and illuminating. We hope that we have explained and shown what we mean by this, and in so doing have whetted your appetite for embarking on this exciting endeavour. Being a critical and creative researcher opens possibilities throughout the process of research: possibilities to ask questions differently – or to ask different questions; to work with others in deeply collaborative and enriching ways; to explore, analyse and present our enriched understandings about phenomena differently; to contribute to knowledge production and to the reality of peoples lives in ways which enliven, enlarge and challenge the way things have been done before; to do, know, be and become more than we were before. Working this way can creatively challenge whose and what types of knowledge count, and whose and what types of knowledge are worthy of pursuit, as well as illuminating the "says who?" and "so what?" questions in research. In this way, critical and creative research practices transform the epistemological foundations of research practice, and that is certainly worth doing in this moment of time.

REFERENCES

Campbell, A. V. (1984). *Moderated love*. London: SPCK.

Heidegger, M. (1926/1990). *Being and time* (J. Macquarrie & E. Robinson, Trans. from the German *Sein und Zeit*). Oxford: Basil Blackwell.

Higgs, J. (2006). *Realising hermeneutic dialogues: Creating spaces for critical, creative conversations in learning, research, clinical decision making and practice advancement*. CPEA Occasional Paper 5. Collaborations in Practice and Education Advancement, The University of Sydney, Australia.

Higgs, J., Andresen, L., & Fish, D. (2004). Practice knowledge – its nature, sources, and contexts. In J. Higgs, B. Richardson, & M. Abrandt Dahlgren (Eds.), *Developing practice knowledge for health professionals* (pp. 51–69). Oxford: Butterworth-Heinemann.

Higgs, J., & Titchen, A. (2007). Becoming critical and creative in qualitative research. In J. Higgs, A. Titchen, D. Horsfall, & H. Armstrong (Eds.), *Being critical and creative in qualitative research* (pp. 1–10). Sydney: Hampden Press.

Higgs, J., Titchen, A., Horsfall, D., & Armstrong, H. (2007). *Being critical and creative in qualitative research*. Sydney: Hampden Press.

Higgs, J., & Titchen, A. (2007). Becoming critical and creative in qualitative research. In J. Higgs, A. Titchen, D. Horsfall, & H. Armstrong (Eds.), *Being critical and creative in qualitative research* (pp. 1–10). Sydney: Hampden Press.

Horsfall, D. (2001). Black holes in the writing process: Narratives of speech and silence. In H. Byrne-Armstrong, J. Higgs, & D. Horsfall (Eds.), *Critical moments in qualitative research* (pp. 81–91). Oxford: Butterworth-Heinemann.

Horsfall, D. (2005). Creative practices of hope. In D. Gardiner & K. Scott (Eds.), *Proceedings of international conference on engaging communities*. United Nations, Queensland State Government and Queensland Department of Main Roads, Brisbane, Queensland. Retrieved October 14, 2009, from http://www.engagingcommunities2005.org/abstracts/Horsfall-Debbie-final.pdf

Horsfall, D., & Titchen, A. (2009). Disrupting edges – opening spaces: Pursuing democracy and human flourishing through creative methodologies. *International Journal of Social Research Methodology*, *12*(2), 147–160.

Lincoln, Y. S., & Denzin, N. (2000). Paradigmatic controversies, contradictions, and emerging confluences. In N. K. Denzin & Y. S. Lincoln (Eds.), *Handbook of qualitative research* (2nd ed., pp. 163–188). London: Sage.

Macy, J. (1983). *Despair and personal power in the nuclear age.* Gabriola Island, Canada: New Society.

Macy, J. (1991). *Mutual causality in Buddhism and general systems theory.* New York: SUNY.

Macy, J. (2000). *Widening circles.* Gabriola Island, Canada: New Society.

McCormack, B., & Titchen, A. (2006). Critical creativity: Melding, exploding, blending. *Educational Action Research: An International Journal, 14*(2), 239–266.

Titchen, A. (2004). Helping relationships for practice development: Critical companionship. In B. McCormack, K. Manley, & R. Garbett (Eds.), *Practice development in nursing* (pp. 148–174). Oxford: Blackwell.

Titchen, A., Higgs, J., & Horsfall, D. (2007). Research artistry: Dancing the praxis spiral in critical creative qualitative research. In J. Higgs, A. Titchen, D. Horsfall, & H. Armstrong (Eds.), *Being critical and creative in qualitative research* (pp. 282–297). Sydney: Hampden Press.

AFFILIATIONS

Joy Higgs AM PhD
The Research Institute for Professional Practice, Learning & Education
The Education For Practice Institute
Charles Sturt University
Australia

Debbie Horsfall PhD
Social Justice and Social Change Research
University of Western Sydney
Australia

STACY M. CARTER

16. ENACTING INTERNAL COHERENCE:

As a Path to Quality in Qualitative Inquiry

*In which we get thoughtfully messy,
and refuse to clean up afterwards*

In this chapter, I am going to make an argument.[1] It's an argument about how to *judge* quality and *do* quality in qualitative research. I'm a little trepidatious taking this on: it's an old subject, and many great authors have written on it elegantly (just a few examples: Angen, 2000; Barbour, 2001; Flick, 2007; Mason, 2002; Seale, 1999). People come to blows over the quality of qualitative research, perhaps because it goes to the question of whether it's worth doing research at all. Questions about quality are a big deal.

THE ARGUMENT STARTS HERE

Before I can talk about research quality, I need to define some central concepts, which I've expounded elsewhere (Carter & Little, 2007). A basic framework for research involves three key elements: methods, methodology and epistemology. Epistemology is a justification for the knowledge created in research. Methods are the actions taken by a researcher, including creating, engaging with and writing about data. Methods are what researchers do to create knowledge. Methodologies are justifications for research actions: they evaluate, formulate, or analyse methods. Methodologies reflect methods, can guide methods, and critically, also idealise methods (Kaplan, 1964). To illustrate this idealisation: think about the last research report you wrote, particularly the methodology section. Now think about the research activities on which it was based. Were these identical? Of course not. Was your published methodology a lie? I hope not! Methodology, our attempt to evaluate, formulate or analyse our methods, is always, whether done concurrently or retrospectively, a somewhat idealising sense-making process. It cannot be any other way.

This leads to my basic argument about quality. I am going to argue against mere procedure, whether that procedure is a well-known qualitative methodology or an instrumental checklist, as a path to research quality. I am going to argue instead for internal coherence between epistemology, methodology and method as the more difficult but necessary and ultimately more satisfying path to quality. I will make a critical distinction between claiming and enacting. I will conclude with what I see as the implications for the way we write.

But we are going to start with a mess.

CLEANING UP THE MESS

In fact, all research is a mess, but qualitative research is especially messy: so much so that it's an acknowledged part of our tradition. When we make motherhood statements about qualitative research, we often describe it as iterative and circular, feeding back on itself in an ever-tightening spiral, moving back and forth between analysis and data creation, remaining open to surprise (Lincoln & Guba, 1985).

Given that embracing mess is part of our collective identity, it's amusing to notice what happens when we articulate our methodologies. The fertile complexity that we are so happy to claim at a general level disappears when we make specific justifications for actual projects. Like children whose allowance depends on the state of their bedroom floor, we push the evidence of what we have really been up to into the cupboard, and stand nervously against the door. Often (now I'm stretching the metaphor to breaking point) we slap a label like "grounded theory" on the door to try to stop people looking inside.[2] Worse still, we sometimes use these methodological labels to stop ourselves from thinking about the process of research at all, which seems likely to be the opposite of what the authors of those methodologies intended us to do with them. We use idealised extant methodologies as armour, to protect us from the terrifying prospect of having to understand what it is that we are doing, to continuously think out our methods, to make our own internally consistent decisions, to defend ourselves against criticism.

But I'm getting ahead of myself.

WHY CHECKLISTS WON'T GET YOU TO HEAVEN

Lately, at least in health and medical research, several checklists for evaluating qualitative research reports have been produced (Tong, Sainsbury, & Craig, 2007 refer to, and consolidate, a large number of these checklists). Commentaries on the place of checklists have also been written (e.g., Barbour, 2001; Flick, 2007). We're all familiar with checklists for quality improvement. When a hospital manager sets a maximum time that patients will be allowed to wait in the emergency room; when a professional organisation measures the "competencies" of its members; when a process worker systematically examines every tenth widget coming off the production line, we see checklists in action. In some situations, checklists are the best path to quality (they're especially useful for the widget-checker, who has to look at exactly the same features of exactly the same widgets over and over again). In contrast, along with some other authors, I think that checklists are often the opposite of quality assurance for qualitative research.

What is my reasoning? Checklists institutionalise the abdication of individual researchers' responsibility to think about what they are doing as they are doing it and to ensure that the logic of their study remains internally coherent. A checklist is not about logic, it is about procedure. A checklist says: don't think too hard, just tick these boxes! A checklist turns methods into magic.

Checklists are used as though they are neutral, but they are not neutral: they come with epistemology built in. Every checklist says something about the nature of knowledge. If you tick off "member checking of transcripts" on a list, you are accepting the idea that every informant has a truth inside their head, which they might have expressed incorrectly the first time but will be able to "correct" when they see it on paper. If you tick off "high agreement between coders" on a list, you are acting as though the only "true" things in your data are those which you and your colleagues can agree on, thus denying your own ability to make a creative, unique, useful argument with your data. These are enormous assumptions, and it is crude and ridiculous to elide such enormous philosophical issues into a set of tiny checkboxes.

EXTANT QUALITATIVE METHODOLOGIES ARE IDEALISED RESOURCES, NOT ABSOLUTE RECIPES

At the outset I said that I was going to argue against both instrumental checklists and slavish adherence to extant methodologies as paths to research quality. You'll also remember that methodologies, whether developed concurrently with research action or constructed retrospectively, are idealised. When you articulate a methodology, in your own head or for an audience, you are finding a way of justifying your research actions. A methodology cannot be a blow-by-blow account, it's not a massive concrete description of every step you took. It's reconstructed logic: an explanation, a justification. It's an attempt to make sense of things.

Now – think about the traditions we call methodologies in qualitative enquiry. Some of the basics are grounded theory, phenomenography and phenomenology, ethnography, case studies and narrative enquiry, but the list gets longer all the time. These methodologies, these clearly and not-so-clearly articulated traditions, are terrific resources. But they are reconstructed, idealised. They can never be realised in an absolutely "pure" form in method, because they are not methods, they are methodologies; they are not actions, they are justifications. Methods only exist in the time and place in which they are practised, and that time and place will subtly or not-so-subtly shape them.

I have written previously about what extant methodologies can do for you (Carter & Little, 2007). In short, methodologies should interact iteratively with your objectives, research questions and study design; they should connect you to the theories and disciplines which they come from and contain; and, if you think about them while you're doing your research rather than trying to tack them on at the end, they will shape the methods that you use. They can only do this for you, however, if you approach them intelligently as a resource. You should ask not "how to do" grounded theory, but what it will do for you and prevent you from doing, whether it's the best solution, and whether there's another methodology that would allow you to do more of what you want to do. You should think about the theoretical perspectives that are inherent in grounded theory (most versions have symbolic interactionism, at the very least, at their heart), and what assumptions are inherent in that way of viewing the world. And if you're going to use grounded theory thoughtfully, you will, as best you can in the situation, take advantage of the set of methods it suggests, particularly the step-by-step thinking discipline of theoretical sampling plus constant comparison.

Extant methodologies are not there to tell you what to do. They are resources that you can use to help you to think.

THE ALTERNATIVE TO CHECKLISTS AND METHODOLOGICAL "PURITY": CLAIMING AND ENACTING INTERNAL COHERENCE

So if you can't check things off on a list to ensure quality in your work, and if following a methodological formula won't guarantee quality in your work, what will? Internal coherence is the key. What do I mean by internal coherence? I mean having an epistemology, a methodology and a set of methods that each make sense in themselves, and that go together.

To achieve this, it is critical to realise the difference between claiming and enacting. Tell people that they must do something, and they will often start nervously claiming that they have done it, even if they don't know where to start. This became painfully obvious to me early in my supervisory career, during a day of student presentations. These students had all attended seminars where I had talked about different extant methodologies. Clearly I had done a woeful job, because at some point in each student's presentation, they said "and so I think I am doing ... [very small voice] *grounded theory?*" Each student who joined this "*grounded theory?*" queue made me sink a little further into my seat. My attempts to open up a world of possibilities had instead generated the contagious perception that studies needed labels. These students were claiming rather than enacting: they were using methodologies as armour, not resources. Because they didn't really understand the methodologies they were claiming, they were in fact making themselves more vulnerable. (This can be less true in journal articles, where editors and reviewers often let authors use such labels when there is little evidence that the authors have enacted them.) This moment crystallised for me the difference between claiming and enacting, albeit uncomfortably.

INTERNAL COHERENCE AND REFLEXIVITY

Because enacting internal coherence is the antithesis of a checklist or procedural dogma, it is more difficult to assess and practise. This is because enacted internal coherence depends on researchers really understanding what they're doing, and being consistently thoughtful about it. In fact, enacted internal coherence is a product of *reflexivity*, a concept to which we now turn. Schwandt highlighted several possible meanings of reflexivity: critical self-reflection, often recorded in a field journal; an awareness of one's role as researcher; or an ideological position producing "messy", "experimental", "incomplete" or "open-ended" texts, in which the writer is fully present (2007, pp. 260–261). In my experience reflexivity, at least for novices, most commonly translates into "self-awareness-plus-confession". If you can't be a blank slate, the thinking goes, an objective conduit for the unsullied truth, then you should let people know exactly what kind of slate you are. This is closest to Schwandt's first kind of reflexivity, but it puts the self-inspection not just in the field journal, but also in the monograph or article or book chapter.

I am no champion of false objectivity or the myth of the detached researcher: these are delusions of grandeur. At the same time, I increasingly think that vomiting up your darkest secrets is not reflexivity.[3] Confession can just be catharsis; worse, it can be self-indulgent catharsis; worst of all, it can be self-indulgent catharsis that bears no relation to the empirical work. Confession is no good at all if it doesn't illuminate anything for the reader. Of course I'm not the first to claim this. Jennifer Mason's (2002) excellent introductory text, for example, has this idea woven through. Bourdieu made a similar point in his 2002 Huxley Memorial Lecture, arguing for reflexivity as an unswerving anthropological analysis of anthropologists and the field of anthropology, contrasting this with:

> what Clifford Geertz ... calls, after Roland Barthes, "the diary disease", an explosion of narcissism sometimes verging on exhibitionism, which came on the wake of, and in reaction to, long years of positivist repression (2003, p. 282).

So: reflexivity is something more troubling than confession. Reflexivity is paying attention to every step of the research process, particularly to the fact that you yourself are doing it (whether you are asking questions or identifying a code or building an argument or crafting a sentence) and then making an account of what you actually did, all of the careful chaos and your role in it. Reflexivity is taking responsibility for your research. Reflexivity enables you to enact internal coherence, and this enacted coherence can rescue reflexivity from the quicksand of narcissism.

ILLUSTRATING COHERENCE (OR INCOHERENCE)

To be able to judge whether both claimed and enacted epistemology, methodology and methods are coherent, we need to know where to look for them. This section gives some examples of where to look.

Let's start with epistemology, as it commonly trips people up. As I have argued elsewhere, methods make epistemology visible (Carter & Little, 2007). If you can see the data creation, analysis and writing strategies of a researcher – the methods – you can see the epistemology (of course, this relies on clear reporting). If you want to be coherent, you need to ensure that your enacted epistemology is the same as your claimed epistemology.

It is common to hear a PhD scholar, towards the end of the project, claiming one epistemology and enacting another (or in fact, just generally getting in a muddle.) So, for example, Sam might claim that her analysis expresses the objective truth about the process she is studying. "I have found out what it's absolutely like", she says, "I really know the truth about these peoples' experience now". But nothing follows to substantiate that very big statement. She does not claim to have been able to "bracket" herself and simply report the participants' knowledge (I personally find this logic unsupportable, but it would be consistent with her claimed epistemology), she has done nothing to minimise her impact on her informants, there were not multiple analysts or measures of agreement between them, she has not verified her work with her participants. Her claim of objectivity is empty. On the other hand, John claims to have conducted a constructivist analysis. However, he says, he has a problem. His committee think his informants were telling him what he wanted to hear. His findings are not reliable, they say – how can you trust clinicians to tell the truth about a subject as delicate as his? He did not ask consistent questions, he had different conversations with each informant. His results are meaningless. John is terribly shaken by this. He doesn't understand his claimed epistemology, so he cannot argue convincingly against his committee. A constructivist researcher would never assume that there is a single, stable, accessible truth inside the heads of his informants. He would believe that the world is the way that we make it in our talk and our actions, and that the talk of participants reveals a great deal about this process. He may not find a universal truth, but he can develop a complex picture of how people construct an issue in a particular context – in this case, clinicians with relevant experience in conversation with him.

What about the idealised sense-making exercise that is methodology? What might an incoherent methodology look like? Imagine researchers claiming grounded theory as their methodology and studying diet and eating. We developed questions, they say, about knowledge, attitudes and behaviours around food and eating. We drew a quota sample, making sure we had even numbers of men and women, of parents and non-parents, and of high-income and low-income people, and ran focus groups with the folks we had recruited. We developed a list of key themes before the interviewing started, coded the data with these themes, and made constant comparisons between groups according to demographics and their knowledge, attitudes and behaviours.

This is not a coherent methodology. Why not? You could argue this simply as a matter of taxonomic precision. A grounded theory study needs a few key features (including, minimally, theoretical sampling, and inductive development of "open" or "line by line" codes from the data, informed by one's theoretical sensitivity (Charmaz, 2006; Glaser, 1978; Glaser & Strauss, 1967). If we call everything grounded theory, the term becomes meaningless. But there's a more important objection that is more relevant to coherence. Grounded theory arises from a particular theoretical base, symbolic interactionism. Symbolic interactionism was posited in direct opposition to the kind of individualistic behaviourism that brought us KAB (knowledge-attitude-behaviour) research (Becker, 1998). Interactionism posits that active people are constantly constructing the meaning of things together, and changing those meanings in interaction. It does not conceptualise things like "attitudes" as static: it is interested in change and agency and dynamism. The lack of coherence between the methodology claimed and the evident theoretical commitment in this situation suggests a lack of understanding of the theoretical ideas inherent in the methodology, and thus a lack of coherence.

IN WHICH WE MAKE A THOUGHTFUL MESS, AND REFUSE TO CLEAN UP AFTERWARDS

A good methodology leads to, and demonstrates, a thoughtful mess because a good methodology is one that is constantly being revised, always open to new leads. A qualitative research question is a puzzle that can be solved in an infinite variety of ways, so we need to spell out the ways in which each puzzle was solved. Although I don't always agree with their solutions, the people who have created checklists for reporting qualitative research are onto something in this regard: we need to improve the quality of our reporting. At the moment, particularly in practice disciplines like health and medicine where word lengths are short and quantitative techniques dominate, there is a tendency to simply list methods, and provide no methodological reasoning at all.

> METHODS: We interviewed 50 people. Their demographics are in the table. We used analytic tricks from grounded theory. We generated seven themes. RESULTS: Theme One…

(I'm exaggerating, but you see my meaning.) A label is claimed as armour, and the inappropriate implicit reasoning that accompanies it (the provision of demographics, for example – on this see Morse, 2008) demonstrates that it was not used in any meaningful way. This is not a methodology, it is not a justification.

A good methodological argument will tell the messy story of method, and will do it in a way that explains method in the context of theory, and of the objectives and questions that a study addressed, and will show the way that epistemic questions shaped methodological choices. A methodology must be a story, because it needs to justify something that people did in a place over time. If it is really going to reflect the mess of research, it is going to have to talk about how things shifted and changed. Contrast the impoverished text above, for example, with Becker and colleagues' classic interactionist ethnography, *Boys in White*. Although not everyone will agree with the methods or theoretical commitments of the authors, I commend the first chapter to you as an example of transparent methodologising. Some four pages in, just for example, the authors write:

> In explaining our further theoretical specification of the problem, we are tempted to make our decisions seem more purposeful and conscious than in fact they were. We did not have a well-worked-out rationale for these choices. Rather, we went into the field and found ourselves concentrating on certain kinds of phenomena; as we proceeded, we began to make explicit to ourselves the rationale for this concentration of our interest. The areas we found ourselves concentrating on were consistent with our general theoretical assumptions, but did not flow logically and inevitably from them (Becker, Geer, Hughes, & Strauss, 1961, p. 20).

They go on to explain how they chose what to attend to in the field. Setting aside the obvious problem of monograph writing versus paper-length writing, this fragment is a far cry from "We interviewed 50 people". So: if a researcher who had enacted internal coherence wrote a great methodology, what might it look like? It might tell the reader, for example:
– What theoretical or political commitments guided the choice of topic;
– What extant methodologies were selected/combined and why, and how these resonated with theoretical commitments;
– The reasoning behind the initial site or sample selection;

- How the sampling evolved over the course of the study, and why;
- How the researchers related to the participants, consistent with their epistemological commitments;
- How the researchers' interpretation of the data compared with the "first order" accounts of the participants;
- What each investigator's role was in the analysis;
- How the theories brought into the analysis changed the analysis over time;
- How the researchers ensured the quality of the study, consistent with their epistemological commitments;
- How the ethical aspects of the study evolved, not just that ethics "approval" was gained (Guillemin & Gillam (2004) have shown how ethics and reflexivity are intertwined).

All these elements should be in agreement, and all should be couched in the language of the researcher's theory of knowledge. This may be the present, fractured voice of the poststructural analyst, or the distant, ordered voice of the "social scientist". This is matter for personal conviction, as long as it is done consistently.

You may have noticed something in the list above. There's a lot of talk about theory. That's because theory is central and necessary to this process. The understanding required to enact internal coherence is likely to require the work of others. Thousands of researchers and theorists have gone before you and have wrestled with the issues you are confronting. You need their writing. It can inspire you, it can feed creative abduction from your data, it can create a context for your original work. Enacting internal coherence is much easier when you have a bigger picture to relate it to, whether this comes from your own explorations or from your knowledgeable colleagues.

Qualitative research is untidy. We have been saying so for decades. It's time we learned (or perhaps remembered) how to write articles that show it, to make an argument for the consistent thinking and acting that holds a messy research venture together. It's time editors and reviewers demanded and made space for it.

Get out there. Read a lot. Make a thoughtful mess. Refuse to clean it up. Explain how you made it. Be proud of the originality of your insights.

That's qualitative enquiry.

NOTES

[1] Some of these ideas were presented at the International Institute for Qualitative Methodologies Conference entitled "Advanced Qualitative Methods" in October 2008, and I very much appreciate the support and feedback I received from the folks in the audience. Rose Barbour's infectious enthusiasm, in particular, encouraged me to write down and extend my ideas, and for this I'm very grateful.

[2] You will see that I often use grounded theory as an example in this chapter. This is for two main reasons: because I use grounded theory myself so it's easy for me to talk about, and because it seems to be the methodology most offended against. I'm sure similar complaints could be made by those working in other traditions.

³ I am indebted to Jennifer Mason for this bit of my argument. She gave an excellent workshop after the aforementioned conference, in which she talked about the experience of reading theses with confessional preambles that bore no relation to their other content. Her comment planted the seed for this section of my chapter.

REFERENCES

Angen, M. J. (2000). Evaluating interpretive inquiry: Reviewing the validity debate and opening the dialogue. *Qualitative Health Research, 10*(3), 378–395.
Barbour, R. (2001). Checklists for improving rigour in qualitative research: A case of the tail wagging the dog? *British Medical Journal, 322*(7294), 1115–1117.
Becker, H. S. (1998). *Tricks of the trade: How to think about your research while you're doing it.* Chicago: University of Chicago Press.
Becker, H. S., Geer, B., Hughes, E. C., & Strauss, A. L. (1961). *Boys in white: Student culture in medical school.* Chicago: University of Chicago Press.
Bourdieu, P. (2003). Participant objectivation. *The Journal of the Royal Anthropological Institute, 9*(2), 281–294.
Carter, S. M., & Little, M. (2007). Justifying knowledge, justifying method, taking action: Epistemologies, methodologies and methods in qualitative research. *Qualitative Health Research, 17*(10), 1316–1328.
Charmaz, K. (2006). *Constructing grounded theory: A practical guide through qualitative analysis.* London: Sage.
Flick, U. (2007). *Managing quality in qualitative research.* London: Sage.
Glaser, B. (1978). *Theoretical sensitivity: Advances in the methodology of grounded theory.* Mill Valley, CA: Sociology Press.
Glaser, B., & Strauss, A. (1967). *The discovery of grounded theory.* Chicago: Aldine.
Guillemin, M., & Gillam, L. (2004). Ethics, reflexivity, and "ethically important moments" in research. *Qualitative Inquiry, 10*(2), 261–280.
Kaplan, A. (1964). *The conduct of inquiry: Methodology for behavioral science.* San Francisco: Chandler.
Lincoln, Y., & Guba, E. (1985). *Naturalistic inquiry.* New York: Sage.
Mason, J. (2002). *Qualitative researching* (2nd ed.). London: Sage.
Morse, J. M. (2008). "What's your favorite color?" Reporting irrelevant demographics in qualitative research. *Qualitative Health Research, 18*(3), 299–300.
Schwandt, T. A. (2007). *Dictionary of qualitative inquiry* (3rd ed.). Thousand Oaks, CA: Sage.
Seale, C. (1999). *The quality of qualitative research.* London: Sage.
Tong, A., Sainsbury, P., & Craig, J. (2007). Consolidated criteria for reporting qualitative research (COREQ): A 32-item checklist for interviews and focus groups. *International Journal for Quality in Health Care, 19*(6), 349–357.

AFFILIATION

Stacy M Carter PhD
Centre for Values, Ethics and the Law in Medicine and the School of Public Health
The University of Sydney
Sydney
Australia

CAROL GRBICH

17. INTERPRETING QUALITY IN QUALITATIVE RESEARCH

This chapter explores the issue of quality in qualitative research: how different approaches to qualitative research approach that issue, and the generic parameters of quality that are generally common to all. The chapter will be of assistance to researchers who are designing and presenting their research as well as to readers who seek to establish the quality of what they are reading.

THE ISSUE OF QUALITY

There are many different approaches to undertaking qualitative research, each with its own purposes, protocols, ways of doing things and, in some cases, expectations of how the final product will look and what it will achieve. Table 17.1 provides an indication of the current diversity of approaches grouped on the basis of the level of researcher involvement.

Table 17.1. Various approaches in qualitative research

Minimally involved Researcher	*Participant researcher*	*Highly involved researcher*
Grounded theory Straussian	Glaserian	postmodern
Ethnography classical	critical	auto/cyber/ethno drama
Phenomenology Husserlian	existential/hermeneutic	postmodern
Feminist research traditional forms	memory work	postmodern
Evaluation summative	formative	postmodern
Action research interventionist	participatory action research	postmodern

J. Higgs, N. Cherry, R. Macklin and R. Ajjawi (eds.),
Researching Practice: A Discourse on Qualitative Methodologies, 153–163.
© *2010 Sense Publishers. All rights reserved.*

To add further to this complexity, these approaches continue to change as creative researchers mix and match for different purposes; for example, within a classical ethnography a smaller data set from a Glaserian or postmodern form of grounded theory may be used to capture the minutiae of interaction of the particular group under study.

So how can you as a novice researcher evaluate the quality of the particular articles and reports you come across in your literature searches and about which you need to develop some critical overview? And what do you need to be careful of when you write your own articles for publication? As a starting point you could accept that if an article is published in a peer reviewed journal then at least the quality has been acceptable to the reviewers and the editor. Unfortunately, reviewers and editors are not always at the cutting edge of the quality debate and may well accept or reject articles on the basis of standards that are not applicable.

Although there have been many attempts to define quality there is currently no accepted overall gold standard for assessing qualitative studies. Moreover, the increasing popularity of qualitative approaches in health, management, indigenous research, architecture and the built environment has further complicated the development of any general guidelines. For example, the word "trustworthiness", which is often used for assessing participant researcher approaches, may well be open to completely different interpretations depending on whether it is being used by a doctor, an architect, a manager, a sociologist, a psychologist or a social worker – so you can see that the notion of quality may mean different things when diverse disciplines as well as ontological and epistemological orientations are involved.

Bearing these issues in mind, this chapter attempts to broadly define how you as reader might seek to determine the quality of a journal article or research report and also to indicate where you as researcher need to ensure that you have provided adequate information so it can be seen that you have carefully attempted to address areas of potential contention in documents you hope to publish.

So what has been the problem with developing and using tick-box checklists? In spite of concerns regarding different ontological and epistemological approaches, there has been a proliferation of checklists, the sheer number of which can prove overwhelming and confusing to new researchers. A recent review of criteria for assessing interview and focus group studies revealed more than 22 checklists (Tong, Sainsbury & Craig, 2006) but none in widespread usage. The diversity between and within approaches for collecting, creating, analysing and interpreting qualitative data makes the appropriateness of transferring checklists from one style to another problematic. Furthermore, the idiosyncratic nature of qualitative methods means that checklists which have been developed have tended to service individual or particular research styles and cannot easily be more broadly applied.

Mixed Methods

Apart from the diverse nature of qualitative research, another complicating factor in attempting to assess quality in qualitative research lies in the recent trend towards mixing qualitative and quantitative methods within one study. This has the

advantage of providing more in-depth and robust analyses of policy and practice issues by triangulating and integrating several different types of data. The three most usual mixes are:
1. *Integrated* – involving the inclusion of qualitative (open-ended) questions within a dominant quantitative data set
2. *Triangulated* – involving different but complementary data sets relating to one question
3. *Sequenced* – where a qualitative data set explores an issue in depth in order to provide insight and to facilitate the development of the right questions for a larger quantitative study; or vice versa where a qualitative study tries to find detail on the whys and wherefores of quantitative findings.

Despite the obvious advantages in mixing methods, researchers face several dangers in attempting to do so. The first involves the putting together of two fundamentally different research approaches, where there is always the risk of doing neither properly – that is, failing to conform to the different philosophical tenets involved by not collecting, analysing and presenting multiple forms of data so that both are appropriately represented. There is also the tendency to gloss over the analysis of both data sets in favour of quicker, more shallow approaches and oversimplified results. This may well "homogenise" the data and fail to alert both researcher and readers to the diversity of outcomes which might otherwise have been exposed.

From the assessor's perspective and taking a very long view, the use of mixed methods should seek to fulfil at least the following agendas in order to achieve the minimum level of quality:

– There should be some overt and clarified outcome to be gained in mixing the methods.
– Once this is established, each approach should enhance the other. For example, the quantitative data should seek to uncover the overall aspects of a phenomenon, whereas while the qualitative approach should move beyond description and validation of approximate "fixed" truths identified in quantitative survey work to uncover the qualitative complexity of the phenomenon under examination.
– Each approach should be treated as separate in terms of data collection, creation and analysis, and the approaches should be combined in a balanced way.

Qualitative Approaches

To return to qualitative research methods used alone, let us first tackle one of the oldest approaches so that we can begin to understand the issues involved. Following Table 17.1, ethnography can be classical in the tradition of the exploration of the ways of living of particular tribal or other groups, critical in the use of an a priori framework of a critical theorist such as Karl Marx to examine a particular context for issues of the location of power, auto in the study of the self in particular contexts, such as one's own experience of love, divorce, childbirth, etc., or cyber in the exploration of location and the definitions and parameters of virtual realities and cyberspace together with one's individual capacity to inhabit these.

Data collection ranges from meticulous techniques of interviewing, observation and the collation of existing documents by a distant, minimally involved researcher to the researcher becoming highly involved and stepping into created situations and using the self and own experience to provide the data. Results then range from traditional display (typical or extreme quotes and case studies) and interpretation using particular conceptual or theoretical frameworks to large amounts of creative display (pastiche, dynamic visuals, poetry, drama and short stories), leaving any interpretation to the reader.

The other approaches listed in Table 17.1 are equally complex. Phenomenology may be allied in terms of design and interpretation to either Husserl or Merleau Ponty, and furthermore may have a classical, a hermeneutic, an existential or a postmodern orientation. Grounded theory can take a Straussian, Glaserian or postmodern orientation; Action and evaluation research can be researcher- or participant-controlled or even postmodern, and feminist research can be added to any of the above to provide a particular ideological interpretation that favours an acceptance of the exploitation of women in society.

To these multiple design options may be added mixed approaches (quantitative + qualitative, qualitative + qualitative), and a diversity of analytic regimes from enumerative through to iterative approaches with their various versions of thematic analysis, but also including the option of investigative approaches for existing documentation (structuralist, poststructuralist, discourse, narrative and conversational analysis) or the minimal/no-analysis approaches of phenomenological, auto-ethnographic and other postmodern styles. All these serve to complicate the task of providing a generic tool to assess any qualitative study.

Where then does this leave us as readers and researchers attempting to assess the variety of approaches listed above? Over time it can be seen that qualitative approaches have shifted from the meticulous, distant approach of minimally involved, researcher-controlled studies where rigour and justification dominate, through notions of clarity, trustworthiness and dependability of the involved but professional participatory researcher, to the multiple perspective, voice dominated, subjective accounts of the highly involved researcher. Separating these out in this way is contentious, as there is overlap on the boundaries and in some studies aspects of one approach slide in to aspects of another. Although the boundaries are clearer between participatory and highly involved groupings, the innovative displays of the highly involved approaches can already be seen appearing in the results sections of participatory research.

From Table 17.1, the three groupings can be seen to reflect both researcher position and time sequences: minimally involved describes a pseudo-objective approach most used prior to the 1960s but still in use; participatory approaches entail recognition of both researcher and participant input, and became popular from the 1960s; and highly involved approaches emerged in the mid-1980s, with a strong emphasis on subjectivity. Despite the multiplicity of options available and the new trends which emerge annually, it is possible to use these groupings, artificial although they are, to develop generic sets of criteria. In themselves such criteria cannot critique the detail of individually named methodological approaches but they can provide an overall assessment framework for the reader/researcher to utilise for presenting qualitative research and assessing its quality. With an arbitrary line drawn between "participatory" and "highly involved", Table 17.2 provides an overview of aspects which it is suggested are important to take into consideration in the assessment of qualitative approaches which fit into minimally-involved and participatory approaches, whereas Table 17.3 attempts the more difficult ask of doing the same thing for highly involved approaches.

Table 17.2. Criteria for assessing quality in minimally-involved and participatory research (adapted from Kitto, Chesters & Grbich, 2008)

Clarification

- What were the research question/s?
- What were the aims of the research?
- What did the researcher seek to investigate?

Justification

- Why was a qualitative approach the best option to answer this question?
- Why was the particular qualitative research design chosen?

Process

- Was ethics approval been obtained?
- Were the techniques of data collection clearly documented?
- How were participants/settings accessed?
- What sampling techniques were used to answer the research question?
- Who was interviewed/observed? how often? and for how long?
- What interview questions were asked?
- What was the purpose of any observation/s?
- Which existing documents were accessed? How were they assessed?
- How was collected data managed?
- Were the forms of data analysis completely transparent?
- What were the major outcomes of the analytical process in terms of findings?

Representativeness

- Were all the results reported? If any data was discarded why did this occur?
- Was a holistic view achieved?

Interpretation

- Was a more conceptual discussion of the results and linkage to existing theory/ new theory/models of practice developed to explain the relevance of findings to a targeted audience or discipline?

Reflexivity

- Was a clear statement included about the impact of the researcher's views upon the data and the methods chosen ?

Table 17.2. (Continued)

Transferability
- Was a critical evaluation undertaken of the application of findings to other similar contexts?
- How do the results match/contradict others on this topic?
- Was the relevance of these findings to current knowledge, policy, and practice or to current research discussed?

Taking in turn the seven aspects in Table 17.2, let's see what this means for you as a researcher/reader:

1. Clarification

The research question is the key to the project. Does it actually reflect what has been investigated? "Simple and succinct" is useful in designing research questions. Don't try to blind the reader with complicated language which only you and a few colleagues can to translate without a glossary. Are the aims reflected in the design or has the researcher undertaken to do one thing but been sidetracked into different territory so that the question no longer matches anything, except in passing? If there was more than one aim, consider how these have been incorporated in the study design.

2. Justification

This is crucial. Why did you undertake this study in the way you did? When considering a number of other possible approaches, why did you decide that this question and the design used would produce the best data? Show that your question, the aims of your study and the design are a perfect match. Justify your design. Did you use any forms of data triangulation, such as multiple sources, i.e., documents, interviews, survey data, observation; or multiple methods? Perhaps ethnography and phenomenology together, or multiple theories? (multiple theoretical and conceptual frames applied to the research to enhance insights into phenomena).

3. Process

This segment is an exposé of what you actually did and needs to be very explicit. It is presumed that you have ethics permission to undertake research, so clarify where this was obtained (make sure all relevant authorities have given permission) and when (in case permission ran out before you undertook your data collection). Then detail the research process: how did you access your participants? What processes of permission seeking and gaining were undertaken? How did you develop rapport? How did you deal with refusals, vulnerable people or those who wished to withdraw from the study or refused to answer particular questions? Who were these participants of yours? A profile table (usually with pseudonyms) giving important information such as numbers, ages, gender, years of experience in a particular situation, educational levels, etc. is useful in longer articles and reports but may be too bulky or unnecessary in shorter articles where general characteristics may be summarised.

Indicate which sampling techniques were used. As you know, the most commonly available non-probability sampling approaches are: maximum variation (where representativeness of all aspects of the topic are sought), homogeneous (a group fitting particular inclusion criteria which you have specifies), snowball (networking from one difficult-to-access type of participant to others), and convenience (easily accessed individuals/groups, such as your own workplace – which of course presents its own ethical dilemmas of the "insider" type).

Describe your data collection techniques. How did you interview? Face to face? Telephone? Focus group? Teleconference? Videoconference? Email? Explain why you chose these techniques and indicate the question areas explored and the type of interview: guided, structured or unstructured? Who did you observe? When? How often? For how long? For what purpose? Were any interview transcripts sent back to the participants for checking and if so what was the outcome? What existing sets of documentation did you collect? What did you do with them? How was your data collected and managed?

What forms of data analysis were undertaken? If more than one analyser was involved, how did you resolve any differences in findings and perspective? It is insufficient to say that you undertook thematic analysis… readers need to know exactly how you did this – transparency of process is essential. And to finish up, overall, how did your design enhance the trustworthiness and dependability of your findings so that readers are convinced that you have done everything humanly possible to answer the research question/s?

4. Representativeness

Does your data include all that was collected? "Binning" that which doesn't fit is unacceptable. Diversity of results is welcomed in qualitative research, rather than conformity and homogeneity. If you found your results all heading in the same direction, what did you do to check that your sampling strategy had been inclusive of a variety of opinions and experiences? Did you resample? If so, when and why? Did you pursue or further seek out any negative cases – that is, those which don't appear to fit the majority view? If so, explain. An audit trail – monitoring changes and decisions taken in the project, should be recorded in the researcher's diary.

5. Interpretation

Display of results is one aspect of interpretation. It is suggested that you use visual displays strategically (i.e., charts, quotes, visual images and tables). Quotes also permit the participants to speak with their own voices rather than through your summaries or your out-of-context interpretations. It is possible also to hypertext to your original data set so the reader can see where your quotes have come from. The other aspect of interpretation involves the process of taking your results and elevating them from the "she said", "they said" level to a more abstract form of analysis which situates your results within the wider framework of the context, be it other literature, a workplace, a government department or private entity, or a specific economic culture, in order to expose current policies or ideas which are impacting on the experiences of those within the setting and to develop better models of practice or recommendations for change.

6. Reflexivity

This is difficult as it involves developing a critical awareness of yourself as a researcher and an evaluation of your impact on the data collection together with the impact of your data collection techniques on your results. So who are you really?... are you researching domestic violence in families because you have been involved as a recipient or a perpetrator of such violence? And if so, how have your position and your perspectives skewed your vision, slanted your design and questions and impacted on the interpretation of your results? How has being the researcher in this study changed your previous views on this topic?

7. Transferability

To what extent can your findings be applicable to other similar settings, situations and experiences? If you have studied a situation in one part of the country, are your findings relevant to another part where resources, policies and individuals in key positions may have created different outcomes? If you have studied 12 families in a particular situation, to what degree can you assume that your findings will mirror the experiences of other families in similar situations? Clearly, logical generalisations are appropriate sometimes but the limitations of a direct transfer of findings mean that that this transfer must often be carefully qualified. Finally, to what extent has this study successfully contributed to knowledge?

Now let us attempt the development of assessment criteria for non-traditional, highly involved approaches.

Table 17.3. Criteria for assessing quality in highly involved research (Adapted from Grbich, 2004)

Researcher position
- Was the researcher highly involved as a participant in his/her own right, or did the researcher take a decentred focus on others' perspectives?

Process
- Did the design involve small scale mini-narratives where reality was seen as multiply constructed?

Truth
- Was truth viewed as a complex constructed entity, which is multi-faceted?

Reflexivity
- Did the researcher provide a self-critique in the research process?

The reader
- Were readers allowed to interpret data rather than have it interpreted for them by the researcher?

We now examine the five aspects in Table 17.3 in more detail.

1. Researcher position

Subjectivity is crucial here. The study either examines the experiences of the researcher in particular situations or it seeks out the individual views of many participants and displays them to the reader with minimal comment. In either aspect, exposure of who the author actually is (past influences, beliefs, values and experiences, as well as the author's responses in all situations) need to be provided.

2. Process

Small-scale mini-narratives are looked at in depth, but multiple methods (both qualitative and quantitative) are often needed to present a holistic view of any situation or experience. Juxtaposition is often be called upon to identify voices/perspectives which have previously been marginalised or silenced by powerful discourses. The emphasis is on the complexity of both situations and language – in particular identifying aspects of double coding, irony, paradox, the longevity of particular discourses and discursive practices. Seeking multifaceted realities is essential, as is the exposure of complex individuals with past lives as well as current issues and experiences. There is no assumption of universality, generalisability or even transferability of any findings, which are seen as transitory entities.

3. Truth

Truth does not lie in interpretations provided by the grand narratives and theories of the past. Truth is multifaceted and multi-constructed, such that many voices and many approaches may be required to expose it at any moment. Language, discourse and discursive practices obscure truth and need tracking to enable new but transitory re-presentations to emerge. But as truth is a constructed entity it is subject to negotiation and is situated with individuals, groups and cultures and will experience continuous challenge, change and reconstruction.

4. Reflexivity

Reflexivity is essential given the highly involved role of the researcher. Reflexivity needs to be addressed in the form of self-critique, involving the researcher's history, culture, class, experiences and level of empathy. It also needs to be addressed in terms of diversity of process, capacity to connect, and intertextuality (connections with other relevant sources of influence), as well as the researcher's epistemological positioning and ongoing response to research outcomes.

5. The reader

The role of the researcher is to take the reader as close as possible to the experiences under observation, with minimal or no researcher interpretation, so that

the reader can share the experiences as much as possible. Readers also have the power to decide:
- whether the researcher has presented an accurate account of own/others' experiences
- whether and to what extent the researcher/participants have been changed by the research experience
- whether as readers they have had the opportunity to be exposed to experiences similar to those they have had – or have never had – in order to enrich their knowledge base (Morrow, 2005).

REFLECTIONS

Putting this all together, what should you expect from a journal article in order to fit the guidelines above and indicate the quality of a piece of qualitative research? If the article falls into the groupings in Table 17.1 as minimally-involved or participatory research or some combination of the two, it should provide a brief but clear indication in the *abstract* as to what the research questions were, how they were investigated (e.g. 22 female students aged between 22 and 24, accessed through an advertisement in the monthly student newsletter, interviewed once for 2 hours regarding their views on diet), what was found, and what the implications of these findings are, all within 200 words. This is the "What, who, how and so what?" segment.

The *introductory* section should pick up on the "what" aspect by providing a brief but critical review of the relevant literature, indicating the importance of the research undertaken, both to the general community and to the academic world. The *methods* section should follow the checklist in Table 17.1 under "process". It should also provide clear justifications for the approach used (e.g. ethnographic, or a collation of various options) and why this approach was the best way of answering the research question. There should be precise description of how the participants were accessed, how they were sampled, how data collection was undertaken, how the data was managed and analysed (in detail) and how any ethical issues were dealt with.

The *results* should then incorporate all findings and the discussion should demonstrate that the researcher not only understands the findings but can knowledgeably interpret them in a more abstract manner and link this discussion with the articles reviewed in the introduction. The *implications*, any new models of practice, and recommendations should then flow neatly from this, leaving the reader with a sense that the research is not only valuable but has achieved a high level of quality.

At the other end of the scale, in the highly involved forms of qualitative research, the article might provide only a brief introductory paragraph which indicates which experience/investigation was involved and how creation, construction or collection of data occurred. Then, re-presentation of this data forms the bulk of the article. Innovative forms used include poetic representation of an interview; a short story to expose an experience; pastiches of many voices on particular aspects of the research; juxtaposition of data, theory, and visuals to contrast one set of information or interpretation against another; layering of stories to contrast different viewpoints or experiences; visual and/or aural documentation inserted at key points to bring researcher experiences to the reader.

Interpretation may also be included amongst the data, weaving the researcher's views with those of a number of theorists but in an open-ended manner, inviting reader opinion. Finally, a segment documenting the researcher's critical reflectivity is either interwoven or placed at the end. Generalisation and transferability are not expected here. Active data experience dominates.

You can see from the above that although the development of assessment guidelines for particular groupings of qualitative research approaches is feasible and useful, it will always be contentious with regard to boundary control and the different epistemologies and ontologies involved.

REFERENCES

Grbich, C. (2004). *New approaches in social research*. London: Sage.

Kitto, S., Chesters, J., & Grbich, C. (2008). Quality in qualitative research: Criteria for authors and assessors in the submission and assessment of qualitative research articles for the Medical Journal of Australia. *Medical Journal of Australia, 188*(4), 243–246.

Morrow, S. (2005). Quality and trustworthiness in qualitative research in counseling psychology. *Journal of Counseling Psychology, 52*(2), 250–260.

Tong, A., Sainsbury, P., & Craig, J. (2006, July 10–11). *Critical appraisal criteria for interviews and focus groups*. Conference presentation at Qualitative research in evidence-based healthcare — an exploration of scope and methods, Adelaide, South Australia.

AFFILIATION

Carol Grbich
School of Medicine
Flinders University
Australia

JOY HIGGS

18. DEMYSTIFYING DATA ANALYSIS:

A Kaleidoscope of Decision Making, Congruence and Evolution

INTRODUCTION

Data analysis is an interesting idea. On face value it supposes that the data is already collected and that you are analysing it using a planned and appropriate strategy to address the research goals and questions. However, there are numerous deficiencies in this view. In this chapter I reflect on the complexities and challenges of data analysis and also reflect on its essential features.

The core metaphor I am using to make sense of data analysis is a *kaleidoscope*, a device for bringing a set of lenses, in the environment of a pair of rotating tubes, to the task of producing patterns from a number of individual pieces of coloured glass. *Data analysis* is a process for bringing a set of interpretive lenses, framed in a research paradigm and strategy, to the task of producing a group of themes or interpretations from a set of individual pieces of data. The number of twists the user (or different users) makes to the kaleidoscope is a matter of taste, and probably time; in the end, the picture(s) formed are pleasing to the user's eyes and the patterns formed may evoke familiar or unfamiliar images. Researchers bring their own research frames of reference, viewpoints and strategies to the task of interpretation of data, and these influence the extent and depth of data processing, the images formed (e.g. narratives, analysed themes, models) and the meaning making (e.g. knowledge, themes, theories) derived.

DATA – IT STARTS WITH ...

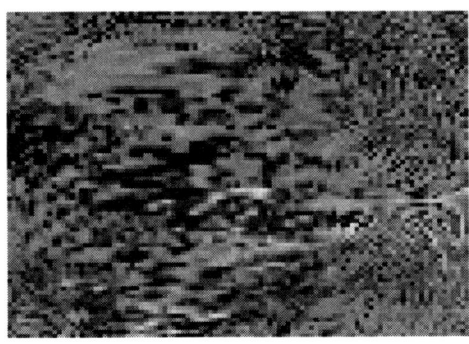

Data analysis in qualitative research is a journey rather than a task. It starts with the first data collected or created and co-exists with this data creation/collection and the entire meaning making journey. This image portrays the messiness and complexity of data. Consider yourself being immersed in this moving array of multi-hued pieces of data.

Data analysis is iterative and evolving rather than sequential and contained within a schedule or process. The analytical, or more inherently, the data interpretation process, addresses many *process* questions:
- Is the data creation/collection process producing the form, amount, quality of data I need to address my research questions and goals?
- If not,
    - what changes should be made – to the process, the continuation of the process (volume of data), source of data, etc?
    - are the data creation/collection strategies (e.g. interview questions) inadequate?
    - do the research questions need changing to better represent the emerging research findings/themes?
- Is the analysis process sufficient to the task and doing justice to the data, questions, and research goals?
- If not,
    - what other analysis options could I use?
    - what other frames of reference could I adopt?
    - what other strategies could I use to obtain additional perspectives (e.g. reference groups)?

COMPLEXITIES – DATA ANALYSIS DEPENDS ON …

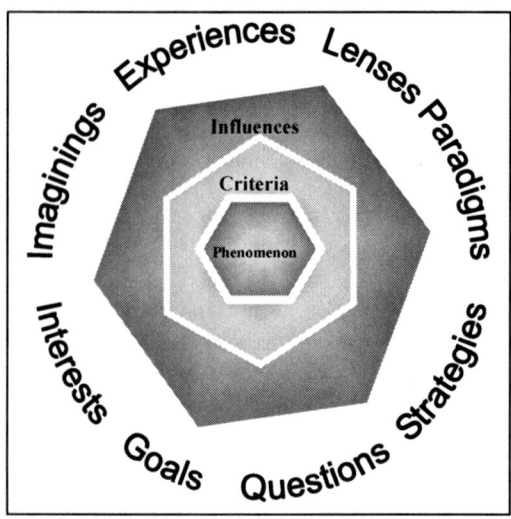

In turning the kaleidoscope of data analysis there are multiple factors that influence the frame of reference of the researcher and create the research space (the vision field). Frequently the qualitative research context is framed by a complex set of circumstances that reflect the complexities of being human (the researcher/s) and conducting research about being human (the participants).

Influences include:
- the motivations or interests of the research paradigm and the researcher
- the lenses or perspectives that the researcher brings to bear (either from acculturation or choice) to the design and interpretation of the project

- the focus and intent of the research as reflected in the stated goals and questions of the project
- the strategies adopted by the researcher
- the experiences of the researcher/s and participant/s embedded in the research design, conduct, reflections, interpretations and data
- the researcher's capacity for interpretation and imagination.

Data analysis approaches vary across different research strategies. This is represented in Table 18.1 and is discussed in various chapters in this book.

Table 18.1. Data analysis and research strategies

Research strategy	*Descriptor*	**Key dimensions**	*References*
Ethnography	Describing a culture and its operation plus underpinning belief strategies, etc.	Cultural domain analysis Taxonomies Typologies Frame analysis Social network analysis Event analysis	Grbich, 2007
Grounded theory	Generating theory from real life situations where the focus is on "the microcosm of interaction" (Grbich, 2007, p. 70)	(Glaser's approach) Emergent directions Constant comparison coding Theory generation (Strauss' approach) Coding and hypothesis testing Data fracturing coding Meticulous axial coding Theory verification	Glaser, 1992 Strauss, 1987 Grbich, 2007
Phenomen-ology	Describing and making meaning from lived experiences: portraying the essence of the experience	Phenomenological reduction Bracketing of own experience (or alternatively, recognising own lenses) Immersion in the data Identification of themes Creative interpretation Thick rich description	Moran, 2000 Grbich, 2007 Giorgi, 1985 Colaizzi, 1978 Holloway, 2008
Hermeneutic phenomen-ology	Interpreting lived experiences	Immersion Understanding Abstraction Synthesis + themes Illumination and illustration of the phenomena Integration	Higgs et al., 2007 Moustakas, 1990 van Manen, 1990

STRATEGIES – DATA ANALYSIS ENTAILS …

In essence data analysis involves:
- *managing the data* to organise, access and transform it into forms (e.g. electronic text or images) that are safely stored, tagged (e.g. with source, date, sequence information) and readily available in both original and processed forms for repeated engagement.
- *critically appraising* the quality and sufficiency of the data.
- *processing the data* according to the chosen research strategy. This commonly involves *coding* and *reducing* the volume of data to a more manageable and *grouped* set of data.
- *identifying, describing and interpreting core themes* or messages in the data by searching for relationships within the data.
- *developing* a whole or gestalt to identify the relationship among the themes and make sense of them.
- *reporting on the themes and/or gestalt* (at conferences, to reference groups, to supervisors and thesis examiners, to readers of journal papers) to communicate the research findings and critiquing these findings through a critical analysis of the research and comparisons with other research findings,
- *utilising feedback from the reporting* to continue the data analysis, critique of the method/analysis process and identification of further research implications.

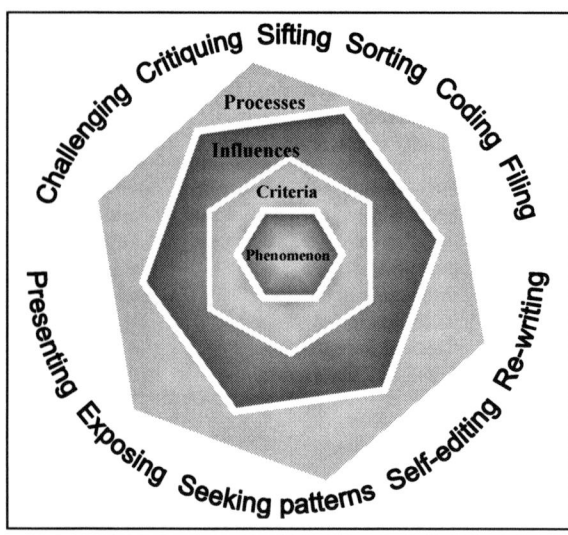

At a "meta" level each of these stages involves interpretation of the data, critique of the methods of analysis and critical self-appraisal, to ensure that the strategies and findings address the relevant analysis criteria, research goals and research questions. In these activities (see circle of words) the researcher acts at an advanced level of reflection and self-critique.

CRITERIA – DATA ANALYSIS NEEDS TO ADDRESS …

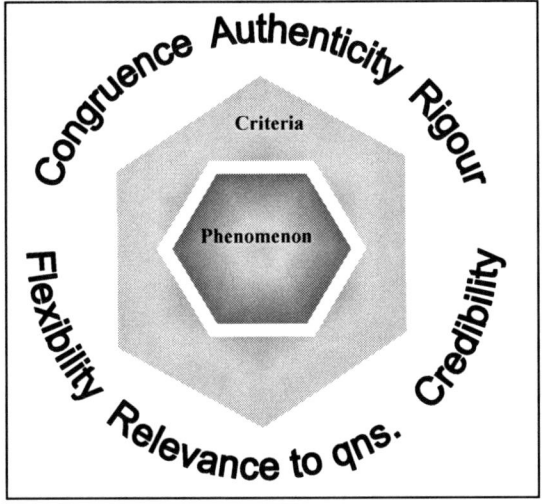

Throughout data analysis the matter of ensuring and judging the quality of the process should guide the researcher's actions.

Criteria to judge the quality of the data analysis process and product include:
- Congruence of the data analysis process with the overall research strategy
- Authenticity of the researcher's behaviour to the research strategy, paradigm and philosophy
- Rigour or demonstrated pursuit of an appropriate research strategy
- Flexibility in implementing data analysis to match the research journey, emerging findings and data quality, while pursuing each of the above criteria
- Relevance of the analysis strategy to the research questions
- Credibility of the process and the subsequent findings.

Importantly, these criteria overlap in effect and consequent behaviour of the researcher. They are all important activities in the pursuit of quality data analysis and research products.

REVIEW – THE DATA ANALYSIS WORKED OUT???

In the end, how did the data analysis process succeed?

Were the emergent themes meaningful and relevant to the research questions?
Was the phenomenon under investigation illuminated?
Did the process crystallise a new understanding of the phenomenon?
Was the researcher's perspective transformed?
Were there changes to the entry point (people's lives, situations, status quo, practices?

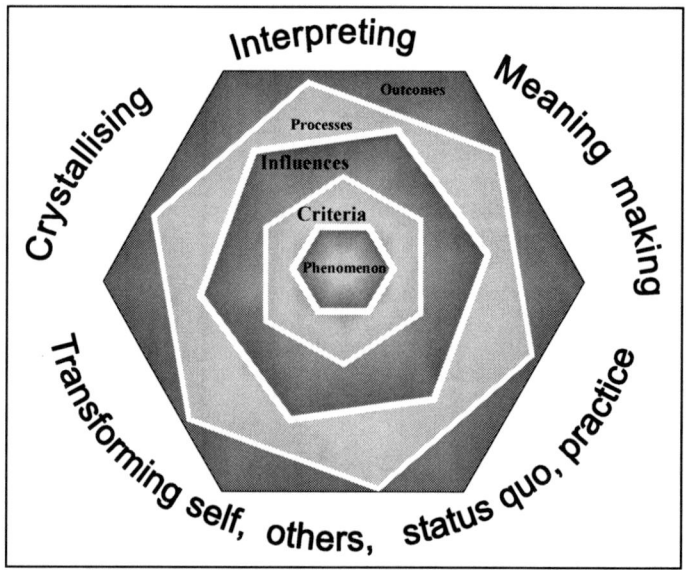

In each of these questions – and their answers – we see the kaleidoscoping action of data analysis at work within the frame of reference and quality criteria used to judge the research.

In essence, data analysis re-images a phenomenon through selected lenses, bringing particular features of the phenomenon into prominence through the way that our lenses focus on them. Moreover it is part of the reverse focus of the research findings back onto the researcher and the processes (particularly the interpretations of data analysis) used in the research. This reflexivity embodies research praxis.

META-ANALYSIS

In this section I address the "big picture" issues of data analysis. In using the term meta-analysis I am not referring to a review of multiple research findings. Rather, I am focusing on the matter of how the research utilises metacognition (or critical self-awareness) throughout the research process in order to be self-aware of actions and how they impact on the research, and of lenses used deliberately or unavoidably in interpretations. Also there is the matter of looking from above or beyond after the analysis is seemingly done. Whether the research product is a set of themes, a narrative imbued with thick rich description, a theory, a model, or some other form, there is a critical set of interpretive questions to ask.

> Is this product a good, true, meaningful representation of the core knowledge I have realised about my phenomenon?
>
> Is the product a valuable contribution to the knowledge of the field?

Have I identified flaws or limitations to the research process or product that should be reported to reflect these limits to scope or value or simply to point to further research needed?

Are there important implications and further matters to address in research, practice, education, policy, systems, and so on?

Each of these questions is part of the "meta" view and process of analysis.

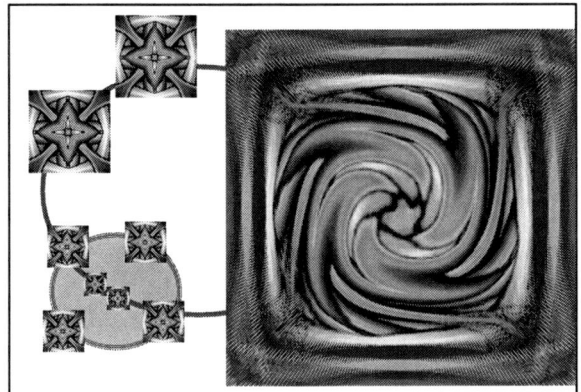

Consider this "model" product of a research project. From the data analysis turns of the kaleidoscope, various emergent themes and connections have been identified. The gestalt interpretation is one of a major dynamic phenomenon with a set of subsidiary interactive dimensions and two points of review.

It reflects the experience of a "rite of passage"
with a trialling phase with peers
and two public declamations;
the individual cycles through several rites
eventually becoming guide instead of initiate.

CONCLUSION

In data analysis we are interpreting, we are seeking truth and knowledge; but we are also asking whose truth? (Armstrong & Higgs, 2007). In this chapter, through the imagery of a kaleidoscope, the goal has been to focus on the images, processes, essences and nature of data analysis, with some brief reference to specific approaches. The core message is that data analysis needs to be an authentic, relevant process that pervades the research and is shaped to fit the particular research process.

REFERENCES

Armstrong, H., & Higgs, J. (2007). Transforming data: Whose truth? In J. Higgs, A. Titchen, D. Horsfall, & H. Armstrong (Eds.), *Being critical and creative in qualitative research* (pp. 178–189). Sydney: Hampden Press.

Colaizzi, P. F. (1978). Psychological research as the phenomenologist views it. In R. S. Vailé & M. King (Eds.), *Existential phenomenological alternatives for psychology* (pp. 48–71). New York: Oxford University Press.

Giorgi, A. (1985). *Phenomenology and psychological research*. Pittsburgh: Duquesne University Press.
Glaser, B. (1992). *Basics of grounded theory analysis*. Mill Valley, CA: Sociology Press.
Grbich, C. (2007). *Qualitative data analysis: An introduction*. London: Sage Publications.
Higgs, J., Trede, F., Ajjawi, R., Loftus, S., Smith, M., & Paterson, M. (2007). Journeys from philosophy and theory to action and back again: Being critical and creative in research design and action. In J. Higgs, A. Titchen, D. Horsfall, & H. Armstrong (Eds.), *Being critical and creative in qualitative research* (pp. 202–214). Sydney: Hampden Press.
Holloway, I. (2008). *A-Z of qualitative research in healthcare* (2nd ed.). Oxford: Blackwell.
Moran, D. (2000). *Introduction to phenomenology*. New York: Routledge.
Moustakas, C. (1990). *Heuristic research: Design, methodology, and applications*. Newbury Park, CA: Sage Publications.
Strauss, A. (1987). *Qualitative analysis for social scientists*. Cambridge: Cambridge University Press.
van Manen, M. (1990). *Researching lived experience: Human science for an action sensitive pedagogy*. New York: State University of New York Press.

AFFILIATION

Joy Higgs AM PhD
The Research Institute for Professional Practice, Learning & Education
The Education For Practice Institute
Charles Sturt University
Australia

CAROL GRBICH

19. QUALITATIVE DATA ANALYSIS

INTRODUCTION

The purpose of data analysis is to help the researcher manage large amounts of messy, unstructured data through the use of meticulous processes which systematically organise it. The final goal of analysis is not to force or homogenise data into one neat box so that a single truth emerges, but to seek diversity and to illuminate the many truths inherent in the answers to the research questions posed. Qualitative research encompasses many distinctive cultures of inquiry and a number of different approaches and protocols for data creation, collection and analysis. These protocols are often specific and particular to the relevant culture of inquiry, and represent the ways in which each form of inquiry grapples with (and attempts to resolve) some much larger issues: issues concerned with what rigour in analysis means from different ontological and epistemological perspectives.

However, some cultures have been less helpful in defining the processes of analysis which should be used, with some even challenging the necessity for definitive guidelines, arguing that approaches to analysis should emerge from readers' engagement with the work, as co-creators of meaning. In the light of these variations, it is useful to consider two fundamental questions underpinning the design of any qualitative research inquiry:
– What types of data do you plan to collect?
– What generic steps can you take to analyse your data and to help you answer your research question?

For some cultures of inquiry, a third question might be relevant: What role can computer programs play in helping you to manage and analyse your qualitative data? This chapter explores two ways in which the various cultures of qualitative inquiry could be expected to deal with these questions.

DATA TYPES AND THEIR PREPARATION AND MANAGEMENT

The most common form of data is that gained from spoken texts, usually in the form of transcribed interviews. This is closely followed by existing written texts in the form of policy documents, case histories, historical photos, and existing spoken and visual radio and television interviews. Finally, observational records collected and written by the researcher, together with the researcher's diary records and visual data collected by the researcher or the participants complete the main sources.

Wherever possible, data is spatially organised so there is room for analysis and comment. But the emphasis and management of data collection varies considerably depending on the qualitative culture within which you are working. Let us say, for example, that you are attempting a classical ethnography of the lifestyle of young people living on the street.

The data you collect may include observation, formal and informal interviews and any other documentation (both written and visual) to which you might have access, such as diaries or photos. In this situation, the traditional expectations are that you will take a formal approach to data management; your recorded interviews will be transcribed in full, including coughs and silences, with a spare column on the right hand side for analysis (see Table 19.1). Your researcher observations, visuals and existing documentation will also be copied and set out so that there is a clear working space for researcher comment.

But should you undertake an auto-ethnography the focus would then change from you as an observer and recorder to you as a member of the group. You would put yourself onto the street, sleep where others sleep, learn their survival methods, their values and loyalties, and you would document these (probably with a tape recorder when you have a quiet moment) with minimal interpretation. Later, when you have left the group, you would turn these recordings into a more creative form of presentation (poetry, stories, plays, visual documentaries) in order to share your experiences more closely with future readers. Thus the overall process would be quite different.

From these examples you can see that in one approach meticulous documentation and analytic management of data are involved; the researcher spends considerable energy in accounting for all his/her data and justifying design and analytic approaches. In the other approach meticulous documentation persists but the researcher's involvement is recognised in the creative but reflective process of minimally-analysed, creatively produced displays of data. The reader is then the judge and jury, and the emphasis is on the impact that this data display produces as readers reflect on their own similar experiences or learn new knowledge.

Taking these two ethnographies as key examples of different analytic possibilities, we now examine each in more detail, as "more traditional" and "less traditional" approaches.

ANALYTIC STEPS: MORE TRADITIONAL APPROACHES

The underpinning structure for generic data analysis in qualitative research is the *iterative* approach. This means that one set of information feeds into another set, creating adaptation and change as you communicate intensely with your data in order to maximise outcomes. Here every single piece of data you collect is used as a check against the whole study. This approach should lead you to see better ways of investigating your questions as you continue with data collection; it may also alert you to the need to re-sample, to include groups you originally did not think to involve, in order to answer your research questions more completely. This constant interaction will also alert you to the fact that after a certain period of time no new information is emerging, and this indicates that you have achieved saturation and data collection can now cease.

Data Reduction

Once you have sorted, transcribed or copied your interview, observational or existing documentation data into manageable formats there are two major steps to be undertaken: *preliminary data analysis* (PDA) and thematic analysis and coding. PDA occurs during data collection every time you collect, transcribe or copy data.

a) Preliminary data analysis

Table 19.1 demonstrates this process used on a segment of a face-to-face interview:

*Table 19.1. Transcript of one interview response to the question.
"Now that you have been a male primary for a year
how do you think others view the home role?"*

Interview response	*Preliminary data analysis*
It's the perception of the division between male and female roles that I find a key to most of the injustice I've encountered during this past year. When it comes to the crunch, most males prefer to be breadwinners; they see this as the more important role. This has also to do with money and title and status.	Injustice – what injustices has he experienced? *I need to check this aspect with him and with other participants.
I remember when my wife graduated from medical school, amongst the group she was part of, what struck me as odd even then was that the men all looked forward to their futures as doctors and that's natural enough, but there was never any question that they wouldn't work full-time. Several were in stable relationships and their partners had started careers of their own. But none of the graduates, male or female, ever questioned who would stay home should they start a family. There was no question of whose career was expendable. As soon as they had children both the wives of doctors and the female medical gradates would all give up work and retire to the house.	Do all men prefer to be breadwinners? *I need to check this with the group and with others.

This fits in with the societal view of the nurturing role of women. It also matches with Talcott Parsons' (1955) views, but perhaps a radical feminist interpretation might be interesting here. Did he have different earlier socialisation experiences than the others in order to want to be a father at home? *I need to re-interview him and the others in my study on this. |
| | * Note to self |

PDA involves an ongoing process of summary and critique which helps you to become familiar with your data, enables you to keep tabs on it and avoids the situation you would otherwise find at the end of data collection, being faced with a room full of data and having absolutely no idea where to begin to make sense of it.

It also allows you to follow up leads as they arise and to become alert to information which you need to pursue further. Each transcript or data segment can then be summarised with a face sheet. This is a sheet of paper which is attached to the front of each data segment, be it interview, observation, or document, providing a quick summary checklist of basic demographic data and a set of bullet points, as shown in Table 19.2.

Table 19.2. Example of a face sheet for interview, documentation or observational data

Research question	**How do men act and survive in the role of primary caregiver?**
Participant profile: age, status, etc.	Tony[1], aged 42
Interview/ observation/ document no.	Interview no. 2
Date	24/04/09
Time	10am – 12.45am
Place of interview	His home
Comments	Daughter aged 18 months present some of the time before being put to bed.
Issues emerging from the interview/observation/document	Men in the home role experience perceptions of injustice?
	Men prefer to be breadwinners? (status, money, role)
Issues to be followed up by the researcher	– Is "injustice" a common experience for these men? Does the experience differ if the male caregiver works part-time?
	– Do some men in this situation prefer to stay home full-time rather than be full- or part-time breadwinners?
	– The early socialisation of men who stay home needs investigating
	– Are male breadwinners implementing part of the radical feminist view that the reproductive role (and in this case its associated responsibilities) should be taken from women/shared equally?

From this you can see that PDA and face sheet management provide a working commentary which helps you keep track of your data, helps to identify gaps both within the data and within your own knowledge base, and allows you to identify potential interpretive frames to start to make sense of your findings. Having identified these you now have an opportunity to adjust your design to fill any perceived omissions before they become gaping holes.

As you go through the process of PDA you may find it helpful to summarise what is emerging after every three to five pieces of data. This will help you to consolidate information into manageable groupings which can then provide a basis for the establishment of themes or groupings of like information. Here is an example of a data summary.

Public perceptions of the role of male primary caregiver (after 5 interviews)

> There appears to be a general consensus that there is a continuum of possibilities from a direct and often almost antagonistic response from other men who are not in this role to an over-effusive but positive response from other female caregivers.
>
> Tony mentioned that he was accosted by a parking attendant male who commented "At least I've got a *real* job" when Tony indicated he was a father at home, and Peter said his mates had said to him "What a great job [the home role], I guess you sit at home watching television all day?" At the other extreme, John noted that when he attended a mixed playgroup with his daughter one of the women commented regarding his decision to stay home, "Aren't you marvellous!" while Mike in a similar environment was asked, "Did you really make that cake?
>
> My husband would never be able to do that!" All felt that these comments indicated a lack of real acceptance of men in the caregiving role. Closer to home, Peter indicated that his parents were not keen on his movement from workforce to home and that his mother had said, "Well that's fine and we love for you to visit during the day but it really is a woman's job, they are better at dealing with children's issues".
>
> Joe's parents indicated they assumed it would only be a temporary arrangement which would reverse when the couple had had their fill of change – he of the home role and she of her career. The status of the home role was often seen to be a lowly one. David commented, "I have spoken to a number of women and they indicated that they didn't really enjoy the long-term mother-at-home role and thought they were viewed by the general community as 'mindless minders' so they couldn't really see why a man would want to do it unless he had no choice".

Be careful to stay with the data at this stage and avoid the temptation to move into over-interpretation. Let the data speak for itself, rather than forcing it (through highlighting selectively) and exposing only the things you think are important. These critiquing, commenting and early summarising processes are repeated until all the information you have collected has been dealt with, all the missing data has been chased up. You will then be in a strong position to claim that you have done all that is possible to provide complete answers to your research questions.

If you decide, however, that you need to pursue more detailed analytical approaches, it is suggested that once all your data is complete and transcribed and preliminarily analysed, you take a break for a couple of weeks to clear your head. During this time you might pass over a clean copy of your database (without your preliminary analytical comments and summaries) to see what a friend, partner or colleague would make of what it contains.

This way other gaps may be brought to light and other perspectives trained on your transcripts, allowing aspects your biases may not have permitted you to see to be brought into the light. Further data collection can then occur even at this late stage.

b) Thematic data analysis and coding

Here the focus is on developing groupings of data. PDA can be seen as a vertical process, building the data base from bottom to top, whereas thematic analysis can be viewed as a horizontal process, cutting across the data base to link like areas into more meaningful segments to facilitate analysis, display and interpretation.

With your data now complete and the decision to move to thematic analysis taken, the next decision concerns the degree to which you will segment your data. Do you wish to leave it largely intact and stay with broad groupings, or do you want to pull the data apart line by line or even word by word? This decision is linked to the qualitative approach you have chosen. For example, ethnographic, phenomenological and narrative approaches tend to leave the data as intact as possible in order to retain the context, whereas grounded theory – (the Straussian (1987) version) favours a much more deconstructive approach, as does discourse analysis.

In other approaches the degree of segmentation is up to the researcher and her or his justification of the approach. The next example, the block and file approach, tries to keep the data as intact as possible:

Block and File Approach

Step 1.   Identify relevant data and list.

Step 2.   Group these responses into labelled columns or summarise their essence on a conceptual map (although this can provide a good overview it has the tendency to contain only abbreviated data and to oversimplify, as it becomes cumbersome very easily).

Step 3.   Display and interpret results. This can be undertaken separately as display (results) then interpretation (discussion), or it can occur concurrently as you weave your display of results and interpretations together.

Step 1. Identify relevant data and list.

Five (of a total of 25) interview responses to the question posed to male primary caregivers, "Why did you decide to stay home?" were identified, then cut and pasted into one file headed by the question, then separated into groupings with headings reflecting the different response orientations.

QUALITATIVE DATA ANALYSIS

Step 2. Group these responses into columns or conceptual maps and label them.

Table 19.3 shows the labelled columns of thematic analysis.

Table 19.3. Thematic analysis – developing labelled columns

Progression of sharing	**Pre-planned sharing**	**Workforce change**	**Desire for change**
I've always worked from home and initially we just shared our baby's care while my wife attended university part-time. In the second year she went full-time studying elsewhere at night and weekends because our baby was so wakeful. Because of these factors we decided to put our daughter into day care from 9am to 2pm weekdays so we could both get some work done and I took over the rest of the day and at night. For the first year we survived on unemployment benefit and we both stayed home with Paul, then we decided to job share. We both work on a blueberry farm. My wife works 3 days a week and I work 2 days.	We had always planned that my wife would look after our first child during the first 12 months then she would go back to work and I would take over until the next child arrived. But I had trouble using my qualifications and had to take up taxi driving working 12–13 hours a day for 4 years, no holiday or sick pay and even working those hours I couldn't make as much as my wife so our original decision made sense when the second child came along and here I am.	Well my wife had been at home for 12 years over four children, then I was retrenched and she found full-time work so I decided to stay home with our one-year-old and start to set up a second-hand book business from home.	We didn't plan to share parenting. I worked full-time and helped out when I was around and got up during the night. After 3 months my wife went crazy and said she was sick of being home. My job was giving me migraines and my wife was offered a good job so we rapidly reversed roles. We both see this as a permanent change

These labelled columns are not set in concrete – they are working options to be changed and renamed as other data is inserted. The worst outcome would be to create headings early and try to force all responses into them instead of letting them develop in a fluid manner.

Coding

This is the more meticulous process of identifying categories and subcategories and tagging them with words, phrases or numbers (see Table 19.4 for an example). Again, the degree of segmentation depends on the researcher and the qualitative approach taken. Some researchers use coding prior to or as a part of developing themes; others do it later as an organising technique for data entry into computer management programs; yet others don't use coding at all. Some codes are generated from the data; others are applied by the researcher. The idiosyncratic nature of qualitative data analysis allows these variations and insists only on transparency of process and justification of style by the researcher in the writing-up process.

Table 19.4. Coding

Interview segment 101*	*Numerical Codes*
We didn't plan to share parenting.	1
I worked full time and helped out when I was around and got up during the night.	5
After 3 months my wife went crazy and said she was sick of being home.	6
My job was giving me migraines and my wife was offered a good job so we rapidly reversed roles.	6, 7, 10
We both see this as a permanent change	10
*101 refers to the pseudonym given to this participant (10) and to the fact that it is his first interview (1)	**Key to codes** 1. unplanned arrangement 5. initial arrangement 6. wife change 7. husband change 10. current arrangement

Some segments will have overlap and will require more than one code. This again is an evolving process, with codes being expanded and amalgamated and new sub-codes being developed all the time. The writing up and interpretation then develops from these codings. How many codes or themes should you aim for? Beyond half a dozen is considered unwieldy, but it is assumed that each code will have a number of sub-codes.

Step 3. Display and interpret results

The processes of data reduction in PDA and thematic analysis and coding serve the major purpose of identifying patterns in the data you have collected. As noted earlier, PDA is often seen as sufficient analysis for display of quotes and development of interpretive theoretical or conceptual frames or models. Thematic analysis ensures that your themes are solid and that you have explored all patterns

QUALITATIVE DATA ANALYSIS

in a careful manner. Display then occurs using quotes, tables, graphs and visual images, or any of the more innovative forms of display from less traditional approaches (see the following section). In data interpretation the researcher attempts to make sense of these patterns in terms of previous research (comparative), conceptual frameworks (power, class, exploitation, etc.) or theory (theory of planned behaviour, theory of reasoned action, etc.). Interpretation is used to shed light on the data and to raise the discussion to a more abstract level.

ANALYTIC STEPS: LESS TRADITIONAL APPROACHES

As noted earlier, much looser approaches exist, usually applied to autoethnography, phenomenology and to postmodern studies, but they can be used more widely if the researcher prefers. Here too you need to get your data into a transcribed/copied format so you can view, read and re-read it. You may set it out with spare columns as in PDA but your management can be totally idiosyncratic, so long as you have some created space in which to write and to put different blocks of data together. Try the following suggestions:
- Play around with the data, noting ideas
- Go over the transcripts and try to create names for chunks of data
- List topic names and group them meaningfully, note exceptions, brainstorm
- Write analytic memos about each group (use previous brainstorming)
- Play with metaphors, analysis of specific words, flip-flop techniques, what if ?
- Write segments into poems, vignettes, plays, short stories, documentaries, pastiche.

(Adapted from Bellavita, cited in Ely, Vinz, Downing, & Anzul, 1997)

This is a truncated version of PDA and thematic analysis, but one that recognises the role of the researcher as data maker and places the emphasis on an outcome of creative interpretative display to bring the reader close to the experiences viewed and shared by the author. The putting together of data segments is essential, be it in vignettes (short researcher-created narratives from compressed data), poems derived from edited existing or interview texts, or pastiche displaying many perspectives (voices) around a particular theme, person or views. Where conceptual and/or theoretical interpretation is used, many rather than a few are desirable.

COMPUTER PROGRAM MANAGEMENT

Computer-assisted qualitative data analysis systems (CAQDAS) are useful if you have a large database or feel that word-processed files are inadequate. Small simple databases such as one off interviews with 20 or 30 people can be managed without computer programs, which can be time-consuming to learn. Computer programs cannot analyse your data – you have to do this – but they are designed to help you manage your data more effectively. There are many software packages to choose from. The main clearing house is at http://caqdas.soc.surrey.ac.uk where links and demonstration segments are provided.

There are 3 types of CAQDAS
- Code and retrieve programs
- Theory generation programs
- Content analysis programs

Code and retrieve programs, such as Ethnograph, are single file systems involving the attachment of codes to a text segment. This process follows PDA and thematic analysis, which are better undertaken off-screen as there is a considerable error rate reading on screen. The coded passages are then filed and stored with some form of identification tag. Some programs also allow the attachment of memos, diary records and your observational notes. In some cases frequency output can be exported to statistical packages such as SPSS.

Theory generation programs, such as NVivo, MAX/QDA, ATAS/TI, are generally two-file systems: one for your data and one for your literature, theory, memos and so on. They are often underpinned by the grounded theory approach where the researcher moves between the two systems using the Boolean logic "and", "or" and "not" and linking data with conceptual and theoretical frameworks in order to interpret it. Most have an SPSS interface and some have content analysis options as well.

Content analysis programs, such as TEXTPAK, have the capacity to undertake *word frequency* counts (how often a word appears in a document), *key word in context* searches (which contextualise individual words by displaying 8–10 words on either side), *category frequency* counts (where synonyms are grouped into categories and the number of categories occurring in the document is shown), *cluster analysis* (where groups of words that are used in similar situations are displayed) and identification of *co-occurrence* of pairs of words.

Although they can be useful, these computer packages do tend to fragment and force the rich and complex qualitative data into decontextualised coded formats. The mathematical logic which underpins these programs separates you from your data, leading you toward counting and frequency statistics rather than facilitating in-depth subjective examination and challenging of theoretical frameworks with your data.

REFLECTIONS

From this chapter you can see the importance of undertaking qualitative data analysis with care. You must never lose track of your research question/s which you have so carefully translated into your chosen methods of data collection and now into your data analytic approaches. Within traditional approaches, careful preliminary data analysis, thematic analysis, coding, and the use of computer management, where necessary, should enable you to group and manage your data with ease, dependability and trustworthiness. Less traditional approaches recognise researcher involvement, allowing researchers considerable flexibility to develop idiosyncratic forms of management in the creative interpretive process.

NOTES

[1] All participants' names in this chapter are pseudonyms.

REFERENCES

CAQDAS Networking Project. Retrieved May 7, 2009, from http://caqdas.soc.surrey.ac.uk
Ely, M., Vinz, R., Downing, M., & Anzul, M. (1997). *On writing qualitative research: Living by words.* London: Falmer.
Grbich, C. (2007). *Qualitative data analysis: An introduction.* London: Sage.
Parsons, T. (1955). *Family socialisation and interaction processes.* Glencoe, IL: The Free Press.
Strauss, A. (1987). *Qualitative analysis for social scientists.* Cambridge: Cambridge University Press.

AFFILIATION

Carol Grbich PhD
School of Medicine
Flinders University
Australia

FRANZISKA TREDE AND STEPHEN LOFTUS

20. HERMENEUTIC RESEARCH:

Exploring Human Understanding

INTRODUCTION

Modern hermeneutic research is a well-recognised approach to qualitative research in which there is a strong emphasis on dialoguing with texts (or text analogues, which can be as diverse as artworks, people or professional practices). By comparison, other qualitative methods adopt a position in which the researcher's analysis is more one-way. Hermeneutics is concerned with researchers perceiving, making meaning from, and interpreting the text being studied. Modern hermeneutic research is based on the assumption that understanding is grounded in a context, the social world. The interpreter and the text being studied are each embedded within and emerge from a context comprising history and culture, which is often referred to as a tradition. The tradition that grounds the interpreter may be quite different from the tradition that gave rise to the text. Hermeneutics "is the art of bringing what is said or written to speech again" (Gadamer, 1996, p. 119) by exploring the interrelationships between the interpreter, the text, and the context. A hermeneutic approach requires reflection and dialogue, and an important part of this reflection and dialogue requires researchers to test their own thinking, to expose the assumptions of their own traditions as well as those of the text, and to integrate diverse perspectives or pre-understandings into a deeper meaning.

HISTORY

Hermeneutics is derived from the Greek word *hermēneuein* meaning to interpret and to reveal. The name of the Greek god, Hermes, is derived from this verb. Hermes was the messenger of the gods and his task was to convey messages from the gods to mortals, interpreting the messages so that mortals would understand them. The term hermeneutics was first known to be used in the seventeenth century in connection with biblical exegesis or commentary. For Protestants the source of divine authority became the Bible rather than the hierarchy of the Catholic Church, and there was therefore a need to develop a rigorous means of interpreting scripture. There is a strong tradition of scriptural hermeneutics to this day. Modern hermeneutics that extends beyond religious text interpretation can be traced as far back as the 18th century. Its key thinkers have been Schleiermacher, Dilthey, Heidegger and Gadamer.

Palmer (1969) described a number of branches of hermeneutics, as diverse as biblical exegesis and psychotherapy, that have developed over the last three centuries, although he also took pains to emphasise that there are also branches within those branches, and that the history of hermeneutics is complex. Palmer noted that each main branch has taken a different focus to the issues around interpretation. For example, in the early 19th century Schleiermacher (1805–1829/1977) developed hermeneutics into the art and study of understanding all human texts or tools of communication, not just religious texts. He claimed that readers cannot immediately understand the text author and therefore need to consider the context and intentions within which the author is making her/his argument. Schleiermacher related text interpretation to interpersonal communication, and through his work hermeneutics became the study of understanding not only of texts but also of the self. Schleiermacher coined the term "the hermeneutic circle". From this viewpoint, the act of interpretation involves a recurring "movement" (or sense making and comparison) between the parts and the whole of a text to reveal the meaning expressed in the text.

In the latter part of the 19th century Dilthey (1883/1988) developed and broadened Schleiermacher's ideas, advocating hermeneutics as an approach to interpretation within the human sciences (which at the time were considered to be subjects like law, literary criticism and history). Dilthey made the distinction that whereas the natural sciences sought to explain the natural world, the human sciences sought to understand the world of human meaning, and contended that this understanding should be in terms of the relationship between parts and wholes of the texts.

In the 20th century Heidegger (1923/1962) developed hermeneutic phenolmenology, because he recognised a close relationship between the philosophy of phenomenology and hermeneutics. One of Heidegger's great insights was that the ways in which we interpret the world and gain knowledge of it arise from the ways we exist in the world. This is often summarised by saying that our epistemology arises from our ontology. Our "being-in-the-world" profoundly shapes the way we interpret everything around us.

Gadamer, Heidegger's student, developed this notion further, arguing that we need to pay explicit attention to the ways in which our previous experience shapes our (current) interpretations. Gadamer's (1976) philosophical hermeneutics approach places great emphasis on seeing our interactions with the world around us and with each other as a form of dialogue, in which language (or linguisticality) plays a fundamental role. This insight has profound implications for how we think about modern hermeneutics, together with the writing, and other work, that emerges from it. For example, Shotter (2008) argued that this more interactive and linguistic approach links hermeneutics with the work of scholars such as Wittgenstein (1953/1958) and Bakhtin (1986). From this new viewpoint, the hermeneutic construction of meaning then becomes a joint project between those engaged in the activity of interpretation, be they biblical scholars and the original authors of scriptural texts, separated in time by many centuries, or a psychotherapist sitting face to face with a patient and helping the patient to come to a new understanding of his or her situation in life.

Within the Anglo-American context philosophical hermeneutics was further developed by others such as Rorty (1980) and Taylor (1995). Rorty, for example, realised that interpretations and descriptions of the world are always tools for a particular purpose. It is impossible to give a complete account of the world as it "really" is, that is, how it exists, without interpreting it in some way.

> We can only make sense of accounting for [the world] in terms useful for this or that human purpose, but we cannot make sense of describing it "in its own terms" (Rorty, 1980, p. 40).

Interpretations are always made through the filter of previous knowing and language, and rather than asking whether an interpretation corresponds with reality it is better to ask whether an interpretation is coherent and useful.

Within the European context philosophical hermeneutics was further developed by Habermas (1990a, 1990b), Ricoeur (1990), and Derrida (1967/1978). Each of these thinkers and philosophers brought a unique focus and purpose to interpretations of texts. Derrida, for example, challenged Gadamer's philosophical hermeneutics by asking questions about the possibilities of understanding. He contended that not all communication partners try to understand and not all speakers make themselves understood. Derrida problematised consensual understanding by arguing that it should not be taken for granted that communication partners are willing to engage in dialogue in order to find common ground. He challenged the assumptions that people communicate with each other with the aim of reaching shared understanding. People may have very different intentions, such as simply being heard, informing others or asserting their own positions.

For the rest of this chapter we focus on Gadamer's philosophical hermeneutics, as his work has had the most profound effect in shaping modern hermeneutics. We have written previously about understanding and using other modes of hermeneutics (particularly Habermas' critical hermeneutics) and refer readers to this work (Loftus & Trede, 2009).

KEY IDEAS IN GADAMER'S PHILOSOPHICAL HERMENEUTICS

In the second half of the 20th century Gadamer (1976/1996) saw a danger in the unquestioning way that the methods of the natural sciences were coming to dominate much scholarly inquiry. He maintained that the preoccupation with scientific method as a guaranteed means of finding "the truth" was misleading. One of the dangers in this position is that a large number of the philosophical assumptions that underpin the scientific method are simply taken for granted and largely invisible. For example, Francis Crick, one of the co-discoverers of the structure of DNA, later studied consciousness, once declaring that consciousness was now essentially a neuroscientific problem and that philosophical debates about consciousness could now be abandoned (Crick, 1995). This position ignores the fact that consciousness is still very much an issue for philosophical debate. Further, Crick's conclusion simplistically takes for granted – without justification or explication – that the particular philosophical assumptions of neuroscience are "true"; in effect making these assumptions invisible and therefore unquestioned and seemingly unquestionable. Crick's position highlights a perspective (or tradition) that philosophical hermeneutics aims to transcend. A hermeneutic approach pays particular attention to articulating and questioning the underlying assumptions of different traditions, and frees us so that we can understand phenomena such as consciousness from different traditions. Thus Gadamer's philosophical hermeneutics is a liberating approach to inquiry.

Tradition

The assumptions, beliefs and practices we learn from others can be collectively referred to as *tradition*. The neuroscientific approach to researching consciousness, referred to above, is an example of a tradition. Neuroscientists share particular beliefs about what they do when they undertake research, how that research can be done, what makes a research question valid and what a valid answer might look like. There is also a distinctive neuroscience discourse that insiders must use in order to be accepted. Any texts produced by neuroscientists are expected to fit within this discourse. Tradition is an umbrella term for all these various features that form a large part of the context of any community of practice, such as the one that is made up of neuroscientists. Gadamer's tradition has much in common with Kuhn's (1996) notion of a paradigms, which is the set of ideas and assumptions that a community of practice, like neuroscientists, uses to perceive and conceptualise the world.

Language

Another important aspect of Gadamer's hermeneutics is the prominence given to linguisticality (Gadamer, 1960/1992). According to this view, it is not possible for human beings to have direct and unmediated encounters with the things of experience. Our tradition provides us with the interpretive repertoire to make sense of the world. This interpretive repertoire has its foundation in language. The importance of language in this view cannot be emphasised enough. As Gadamer wrote:

> Language is not just one of man's possessions in the world; rather, on it depends the fact that man has a world at all. (Gadamer, 1960/1992, p. 443)

When people enter a health profession, for example, they are gradually shaped by their education to gain skills in understanding their patients and interpreting their patients' health problems in particular ways that are infused with the language of their profession. These interpretations cannot exist without the language of the profession.

Fusion of Horizons

Elsewhere we have written of a hermeneutic approach as aiming for consensus (Loftus & Trede, 2009). Rather than being complete agreement and having one agreed position, this is the idea of consensus in its broadest sense of reaching an understanding rather than having the same (final) viewpoint. Hermeneutic researchers do not have to agree with the ideas in a text. However, to be successful they need to develop an understanding of the position taken by an author of a text, and understand how and why an author might have adopted a particular position, even if they completely disagree with the ideas expressed or implied in the text. This kind of consensus is what is meant by the term *fusion of horizons*. It is based on the metaphor that each person stands within a *horizon of understanding*. Our traditions/paradigms provide us with this horizon of understanding. In writing a hermeneutic research report, researchers are writing both about the author's position and their own interpretation; fusion of horizons is not a subsuming of the researcher's interpretation.

Dialogue and the Hermeneutic Circle

When we encounter others and engage in dialogue our horizons may merge, meaning that our understanding is expanded. The dialogue required for this to happen generally requires a to-and-fro of questions and answers between all concerned. That is what is meant by the *hermeneutic circle*. This concept can also include the idea of *part-whole* understanding. To understand the whole we need to understand the individual component parts, and to understand the component parts we need to understand the whole. Some writers also discuss the *hermeneutic spiral* (Paterson & Higgs, 2005). This variation on the circle metaphor suggests the growth of understanding that occurs during dialogue, resulting in the research questions and answers gradually transforming each other. It is often the case in a major hermeneutic research project that as a researcher's understanding deepens the original research questions evolve, and the project ends up answering different questions to those originally posed. Whereas this might be seen as a problem in quantitative research, in hermeneutic research it can be taken as a demonstration of the hermeneutic process in action. The research questions that are finally answered will normally be deeper and more meaningful than those originally asked.

USING A HERMENEUTIC STRATEGY

There is a problem with trying to use Gadamer's philosophical hermeneutics directly as a basis for research work, since Gadamer steered away from offering a method for researchers to follow. However, it is possible for researchers to formulate a research strategy based on Gadamer's philosophy, building on the ideas and assumptions above.

Most writers on philosophical hermeneutics discuss its philosophical perspective and tradition (e.g. Ormiston & Schrift, 1990; Figal, 2007) or use the philosophical hermeneutic concept of human understanding to explore phenomena (e.g. Alejandro, 1993; Kögler, 1999). This literature offers philosophical musings about the phenomenon of human understanding. It provides signposts but no definitive method for hermeneutic researchers. A prescriptive method might undermine the nature of exploring human understanding and reduce hermeneutics to a detached, objectified approach to interpretations.

Gadamer (1976/1996) stressed that hermeneutics should not be seen as a research technique but as a disposition towards deeper understanding informed by a hermeneutic philosophical perspective. However, hermeneutic researchers do face the very real and practical problem of deciding how to conduct their research. There is a need to develop a research strategy that suits the particular phenomenon of interest. We use the term *strategy* as opposed to *method* to emphasise the importance of keeping an open attitude to the research process and to avoid closing down inquiry in ways that can sometimes occur with a rigid adherence to a particular (more prescribed) method. The task for hermeneutic researchers is to operationalise the hermeneutic circle, fusion of horizons and dialogues with texts into a tailor-made research strategy for their project. Moreover, like all qualitative inquiry, the strategy also needs to show congruence between philosophical underpinnings, the phenomenon under study, the research questions and goals, and the overall research design (Paterson & Higgs, 2005). Developing a research strategy begins with formulating the original research questions.

Research Questions

Formulating and refining research questions is a central activity in any research project. Questions are an indicator of what is going to be explored, and they inform the intention of the inquiry (Trede & Higgs, 2009). Research questions in philosophical hermeneutics pose questions about possibilities for understanding a phenomenon X. Typical hermeneutic questions are open questions that invite descriptions and interpretations; for example: *What is the participants' perception and understanding of X? What does this text say about X?* Posing questions is itself a creative and interpretive exercise. Gadamer (1960/1992) stressed the hermeneutic implications of posing questions. Questions point towards a specific direction of understanding. Questions need to have an openness and transparency about them, to enable responders to speak freely from their pre-understanding and create opportunities for providing thoughtful and reflective responses (Elm, 2007).

The process of identifying questions can be seen as a hermeneutic task in itself, because thinking about what questions to ask will make apparent what insights researchers want to gain from their inquiry. Careful wording of the research question requires reflection on what questions have already been posed in the literature and what new insights could be gained from the chosen line of questioning. The research questions set the scene for subsequent question-and-answer dialogues in the text construction and interpretation phases.

Constructing Texts: The Role of Researchers and their Participants

In contemporary hermeneutic research, texts comprise the primary research "data". Constructing texts (e.g. from interviews) or collating existing texts (e.g. from publications) to produce a "text set" in hermeneutic research replaces the data collection phase of other research strategies. The goal of producing texts or text sets is to gather manifestations of existing understandings of the phenomenon being studied.

HERMENEUTIC RESEARCH

Texts can be collected in written, artistic or oral forms (Willis & Smith, 2000). Text constructions can include the pertinent literature and other written artefacts such as policy documents or Web-based texts. Texts can also consist of transcripts from interviews and/or focus groups with research participants, field notes and reflective journals maintained by the researcher. Beyond written artefacts, texts can include other modes of human expression such as music, poems, sculptures, film, dance or paintings that are produced during a research project (Higgs, Cherry, & Trede, 2009). There is no limit to the creativity that can be used in constructing texts. The researcher's disposition is to be curious, to capture pre-understandings, and to learn and explore in order to gain greater understanding. It was important to Gadamer that, where appropriate, researchers connect with the historical literature that forms part of the tradition of the phenomenon being studied. The task of text construction is then to create bridges between the existing tradition and current understanding and at the same time to highlight the tensions that exist.

Text constructions can focus on phenomenological expressions of lived experiences, arts-based data, or collections of narratives in order to draw out pre-understanding within the wider context. Descriptive expressions are rich sources for interpretation. The purpose of such text construction is to have a starting point for interpretations. In fact, the collection of texts is a question-and-answer dialogue and has inbuilt reflective and hermeneutic components.

In the text construction phase, research participants and collected artefacts come to the foreground. Research participants are typically asked to reflect on how they make sense of the phenomenon under investigation, how they understand it and what aspects are important for them. The aim of hermeneutic interviews is to gain deeper understanding of the participants' perceptions and experiences. It is not a question of the researcher agreeing with and sharing these perceptions. The aim for the researcher during the text construction phase is to understand the interpretations and perceptions of the participants. The researchers' task is to enable participants to offer their perspectives and interpretations of the phenomenon being studied. This seemingly simple task of eliciting participants' perceptions may indeed be complex, because a hermeneutic perspective resists a completely detached, objective stance towards texts. Researchers bring their pre-knowing, their assumptions and biases to the text construction and interpretation.

Researchers need to establish a relationship between their own tradition and that of the participants. This is achieved through a question-and-answer dialogue with participants where researchers can test their own thinking by constantly checking that they have understood what participants are trying to convey. When participants are encouraged to articulate their interpretations they may be prompted to reach a deeper understanding of the phenomenon. Hermeneutic interviews are not monologues but dialogues, where both dialogue partners can ask questions and respond to questions. The interviews operationalise a question-and-answer dialogue and the fusion of horizons in spoken language. Hermeneutic researchers are *involved* researchers (Habermas, 1990b). The text construction phase therefore has elements of text interpretation built in. During this phase a sense of anticipation and key questions for text interpretation arise.

Table 20.1 provides sample questions of text construction and text interpretation. The questions are taken from a study that explored the perceptions and interpretations of physiotherapists who assessed physiotherapy students in their workplace.

Table 20.1. Hermeneutic questions

Text construction questions	Text interpretation questions
How did you learn to assess students? (descriptive)	What does the interview say about scholarly practice and professional development of assessment?
What are your perceived strengths and weaknesses in assessing students? (interpretive)	Are interviewees aware of personal, cultural, gender and other aspects that influence their assessments?
What do you think are criteria for good assessment practices? (descriptive)	Is there evidence of self-criticality?
Have you failed a student on placement? Tell me more. (descriptive-narrative)	What do the interviews say about universities' engagement with and support for clinical educators?
Can you reflect on an assessment incident where you learned a great deal about assessment? (interpretive-narrative)	

There are many possibilities for generating texts and interpreting them. For example, the following techniques might be employed. The researchers first interview physiotherapists posing the questions listed above, then listen to the recorded dialogue and summarise each interview for key messages. These summaries are returned to participants to check for shared understanding. The dialogues and shared summaries can then be interpreted by the researchers. New insights gained from this analysis can again be shared with participants as a group or individually, to collect further texts on the previous texts. Deeper understanding from this process of hermeneutic circles can then be trialled and further interpreted. Researchers can send raw transcripts to their participants and invite them to edit and add to them. In other projects the participants might give only one interview, and all further interpretation will be done by the researcher (e.g. Loftus, 2009). The cycle of dialogues can be endless, but is usually restricted by resources, time, and the requirements of the project (Fleming, Gaidys, & Robb, 2003).

If artistic artefacts are part of the text construction, participants can be invited to interpret them. In many research projects participants are asked to tell stories of their experience. It is then possible to borrow insights from narrative inquiry to inform the research (e.g. Webster & Mertova, 2007; Riessman, 2008). There are countless possibilities for text construction strategies and preliminary interpretations. Di Cesare (2007) discussed this infinite conversation in philosophical hermeneutics. He asserted that the key attitudes that make ongoing conversations possible are curiosity, transparency, openness, and a critical perspective to self and otherness.

Despite the infinite possibilities for ongoing dialogue, for the purpose of a confined project researchers need to take responsibility for final interpretations and bring the conversation to a close, or at least a preliminary close.

Interpreting Texts: The Role and Nature of Dialogues

To ensure quality in research it is important that interpretations of texts are rigorous, transparent and structured. A key feature of quality in hermeneutic research is understanding and gaining insights into the "whole" phenomenon (context and phenomenon), its "parts" (particular aspects of the phenomenon, individual participants or texts), and through this movement between the two, illuminating their interrelationship and mutual integration. This movement from parts to the whole and back again needs to be present in all phases of text interpretation and is a trademark of hermeneutic research.

Over the centuries hermeneutic research has evolved from rigidly using a formulaic method, to understanding a text from only the author's perspective, to interpreting texts from within the interpreter's context. In hermeneutic research the researcher's voice and interpretation come to the foreground in the text interpretation phase. The disposition of hermeneutic researchers is empathic in order to fuse horizons, and it is critical in order to ascertain different horizons.

During the text interpretation phase the researchers conduct dialogues with the written texts. Although Gadamer (1960/1992) stressed the power of oral conversations, the reality of most research projects means that the majority of such dialogue is with written texts. Texts, of course, cannot literally ask questions. However, by the researcher's close reading and deep immersion in the text, it is possible for the ideas expressed or implied in the text to challenge or confront the researcher's assumptions, and so a dialogue begins. These questions and answers are a means to achieve a fusion of horizons between the researchers and their texts.

Questions focus on parts of the phenomenon, and answers provide insights into these parts while simultaneously offering deeper understanding of the whole. This phase of dialoguing with texts requires researchers to engage with the possibilities of how texts can be understood. Reflecting on possible interpretations of texts under study has the potential to facilitate new, creative, and liberating insights into them. Such a reflective, self-critical attitude towards texts and the self enables researchers to find their own voice and develop new insights. It is the researchers' task to bring out the voices of the texts as well as their own voices, and allowing both to speak to each other so that text interpretations are dialogues between researchers and texts. In all phases of the research, researchers are in close relationship with their texts, their chosen phenomenon and associated questions and goals. There are guides for newcomers to hermeneutic research who feel the need for more systematic procedures for engaging with research texts (e.g. Dahlberg, Drew, & Nyström, 2001; Cohen, Kahn, & Steeves, 2000). However, it must be emphasised that these should not be used as recipe books. There can be no escape from deep engagement and dialogue with the texts.

The hermeneutic circle lends itself to a systematic approach. The circle is only complete when there is movement between the whole and its parts. It includes reading the entire constructed texts, then scrutinising details of aspects of the texts and relating them back to the whole texts. The hermeneutic circle can have many variations and cycles. Although what is presented in formal reports might not include the entire detailed dialogue journey, findings from interpreting the whole and its parts that give rise to deeper understanding are foregrounded.

FINAL REMARKS

Meaning cannot be completely grasped. Exploring human understanding is infinite, dynamic and dependent on contexts. "There can be neither a first nor a last meaning" (Bakhtin, 1986, p. ix). By understanding others researchers understand themselves better, but never completely. The hermeneutic mission is to advance practical wisdom and help others appreciate new insights into the studied phenomenon. Philosophical hermeneutics is the pursuit of searching for agreement and identifying shared directions for the future. It is an appropriate research inquiry for addressing current global challenges such as sustainability, human rights and environmental literacy.

REFERENCES

Alejandro, R. (1993). *Hermeneutics, citizenship, and the public sphere*. Albany, NY: State University of New York Press.
Bakhtin, M. (1986). *Speech genres and other late essays*. Austin, TX: University of Texas Press.
Cohen, M., Kahn, D., & Steeves, R. (2000). *Hermeneutic phenomenological research: A practical guide for nurse researchers*. London: Sage.
Crick, F. (1995). *The astonishing hypothesis: The scientific search for the soul*. New York: Scribner.
Dahlberg, K., Drew, N., & Nyström, M. (2001). *Reflective lifeworld research*. Lund: Studentlitteratur.
Derrida, J. (1967/1978). *Writing and difference* (A. Bass, Trans.). London: Routledge & Kegan Paul.
Dilthey, W. (1883/1988). *Introduction to the human science: An attempt to lay a foundation for the study of society and history* (R. J. Betzanos, Trans.). Detroit, MI: Wayne State University Press.
Di Cesare, D. (2007). Das unendliche Gespräch. Sprache als Medium der hermeneutischen Erfahrung. In G. Figal (Ed.), *Wahrheit und Methode* (pp. 177–198). Berlin: Akademie Verlag GmbH.
Elm, R. (2007). Schenkung, Entzug und die Kunst des schöpferischen Fragens, Zum Phänomen der Geschitlichkeit des Verstehens in Gadamers "Analyse des wirkungsgeschichtlichen Bewußtseins". In G. Figal (Ed.), *Wahrheit und Methode*. Berlin: Akademie Verlag GmbH.
Figal, G. (2007). *Wahrheit und Methode*. Berlin: Akademie Verlag GmbH.
Fleming, V., Gaidys, U., & Robb, Y. (2003). Hermeneutic research in nursing: Developing a Gadamerian-based research method. *Nursing Inquiry, 10*(2), 113–120.
Gadamer, H.-G. (1976). *Philosophical hermeneutics* (D. E. Linge, Trans.). Berkeley, CA: University of California Press.
Gadamer, H.-G. (1960/1992). *Truth and method* (J. Weinsheimer & D. G. Marshall, Trans.). New York: Crossroad.
Gadamer, H.-G. (1976/1996). *Reason in the age of science* (F. G. Lawrence, Trans.). Cambridge: The MIT Press.
Kuhn, T. (1996). *The structure of scientific revolutions* (3rd ed.). Chicago: University of Chicago Press.
Habermas, J. (1990a). A review of Gadamer's truth and method. In G. L. Ormiston & A. D. Schrift (Eds.), *The hermeneutic tradition: From Ast to Ricoeur* (pp. 213–244). Albany, NY: State University of New York Press.

Habermas, J. (1990b). The hermeneutic claim to universality. In G. L. Ormiston & A. D. Schrift (Eds.), *The hermeneutic tradition: From Ast to Ricoeur* (pp. 245–273). Albany, NY: State University of New York Press.

Heidegger, M. (1923/1962). *Being and time* (J. Macquarrie & E. Robinson, Trans.). New York: Harper and Row.

Higgs, J., Cherry, N., & Trede, F. (2009). Rethinking texts in qualitative research. In J. Higgs, D. Horsfall, & S. Grace (Eds.), *Writing qualitative research in practice* (pp. 37–50). Rotterdam: Sense Publishers.

Kögler, H. H. (1999). *The power of dialogue: Critical hermeneutics after Gadamer and Foucault.* London: The MIT Press.

Loftus, S. (2009). *Language in clinical reasoning: Towards a new understanding.* Saarbrücken, Germany: Vdm Verlag Dr. Müller.

Loftus, S., & Trede, F. (2009). Hermeneutic writing. In J. Higgs, D. Horsfall, & S. Grace (Eds.), *Writing qualitative research in practice* (pp. 61–72). Rotterdam: Sense Publishers.

Ormiston, G. L., & Schrift, A. D. (1990). *The hermeneutic tradition: From Ast to Ricoeur.* Albany, NY: State University of New York Press.

Palmer, R. E. (1969). *Hermeneutics: Interpretation theory in Schleiermacher, Dilthey, Heidegger, and Gadamer.* Evanston, IL: Northwestern University Press.

Paterson, M., & Higgs, J. (2005). Using hermeneutics as a qualitative research approach in professional practice. *The Qualitative Research Report, 10*(2), 339–357.

Ricoeur, P. (1990). Hermeneutics and the critique of ideology. In G. L. Ormiston & A. D. Schrift (Eds.), *The hermeneutic tradition: From Ast to Ricoeur* (pp. 298–334). Albany, NY: State University of New York Press.

Riessman, C. K. (2008). *Narrative methods for the human sciences.* London: Sage.

Rorty, R. (1980). *Philosophy and the mirror of nature.* Princeton, NJ: Princeton University Press.

Schleiermacher, F. (1805–1829/1977). *Hermeneutics: The handwritten manuscripts* (H. Kimmerle & J. Duke, Ed., & J. Forstman, Trans.). Atlanta, GA: Scholars Press.

Shotter, J. (2008). *Conversational realities revisited: Life, language, body and world.* Chagrin Falls, OH: Taos Institute Publications.

Taylor, C. (1995). *Philosophical arguments.* Cambridge, MA: Harvard University Press.

Trede, F., & Higgs, J. (2009). Framing research questions and writing philosophically. In J. Higgs, D. Horsfall, & S. Grace (Eds.), *Writing qualitative research in practice* (pp. 13–26). Rotterdam: Sense Publishers.

Webster, L., & Mertova, P. (2007). *Using narrative inquiry as a research method.* London: Routledge.

Willis, P., & Smith, T. (2000). Coming to being, seeking and telling. In P. Willis, T. Smith, & E. Collins (Eds.), *Being, seeking, telling: Expressive approaches to qualitative adult education research* (pp. 1–20). Adelaide: Post Pressed.

Wittgenstein, L. (1953/1958). *Philosophical investigations* (G. E. M. Anscombe, Trans., 3rd ed.). Upper Saddle River, NJ: Prentice Hall.

AFFILIATIONS

Franziska Trede PhD
The Education for Practice Institute
Charles Sturt University
Australia

Stephen Loftus PhD
The Education for Practice Institute
Charles Sturt University
Australia

SANDRA GRACE AND ROLA AJJAWI

21. PHENOMENOLOGICAL RESEARCH:

Understanding Human Phenomena

Phenomenology is a historical movement and tradition that has been used extensively to research practice. It explores and describes human phenomena as they present themselves in the lived world, and is particularly suited to studying real life and complex aspects of practice. Other research methodologies can also be used to portray human phenomena, and novice researchers sometimes have difficulty choosing the most appropriate approach for their research. However, this is made easier when they have an understanding of the philosophical assumptions of research approaches, their ontologies and epistemologies (see Trede & Higgs, 2009). Advanced researchers may also face the challenge of choosing different research approaches; their choices may well be based on preference and nuances as well as philosophical and personal positions. Research questions arise from philosophical underpinnings and shape all aspects of the research, including research design, data collection and analysis strategies, and ways of reporting. The methodology chosen needs to be inherently congruent with the research questions and underlying philosophical and theoretical frameworks (Carter & Little, 2007).

Phenomenological research seeks to reveal and richly portray the nature of human phenomena and the experiences of those who live through them, taking into account the contexts in which these experiences occur and the subjective meanings participants give to particular situations. Despite the evolution of several major branches of phenomenology, phenomenologists generally agree that the central concern of this approach is to return to embodied, experiential meanings of aspects of people's lives (Finlay, 2009). An underlying premise of phenomenology is that experiences and their significance to individuals are valid sources of knowledge. The aim of this chapter is to provide a guide for phenomenological research, with the caveat that the phenomenological tradition (intentionally) does not offer rules and procedures for inquiry, rather presents *a way of seeing* (Moran, 2002). The chapter explores what it means to be a phenomenological researcher:

– locating phenomenological research in a research tradition, drawing on its historical development
– identifying key elements of phenomenological research
– suggesting strategies for doing phenomenological research.

POSITIONING PHENOMENOLOGICAL RESEARCH: MAJOR ORIENTATIONS OF PHENOMENOLOGY

Phenomenology cannot be understood simply as a method or a set of tasks. It is best described as a historical movement exemplified by a range of diverse thinkers and philosophers. Phenomenology originated from the work of German philosopher Edmund Husserl, who sought to overcome the perceived limitations of positivism, which holds that the world is operated by laws of cause and effect that can be uncovered through the use of the scientific method. Phenomenology expanded into several branches, including the transcendental phenomenology of Husserl (1859–1938), the existential phenomenology of Maurice Merleau-Ponty (1908–1961) and Jean-Paul Sartre (1905–1980), the hermeneutic phenomenology of Martin Heidegger (1889–1976), Hans-Georg Gadamer (1900–2002) and Paul Ricoeur (1913–2005), and experiential phenomenology of Max van Manen (1942–). Each tradition has its distinctive focus, as briefly described below and summarised in Table 21.1.

Table 21.1. Orientations in phenomenology (adapted from van Manen, 2002)

Types of phenomenology	Main proponents	Main focus	Basic themes
Transcendental	Husserl	Concsciousness and the essence of a phenomenon	Intentionality, eidetic reduction (bracketing), constitution of meaning
Existential	Heidegger Merleau-Ponty Sartre	Pre-reflective lifeworld of everyday experiences	Lived experience, modes of being, ontology, lifeworld
Hermeneutic	Heidegger Gadamer Ricoeur	Interpretation	Interpretation, textual meaning, dialogue, pre-understanding, tradition, language
Experiential (or Phenomenology of practice)	van Manen	Contexts of practical concerns of everyday living, practice and application	Practical, applied

Transcendental Phenomenology

Transcendental phenomenology refers primarily to the work of Husserl, who was concerned with reality as it presents itself to human consciousness. For Husserl, phenomenology was a rigorous human science, precisely because it investigates the way that knowledge comes into being and clarifies the assumptions upon which all human understandings are grounded. Understandings are not simply of objects themselves; they are understandings of objects in relation to subjects. Husserl advocated a return *to the things themselves* in order to illuminate and describe the essence of the phenomenon of interest. Phenomenology "focuses on the structure and qualities of objects and situations as they are experienced by the subject" (Moran, 2002, p. 2). Eidetic reduction (the process of reflecting on what makes a phenomenon uniquely different from all other phenomena) may be viewed as the key to transcendental phenomenology.

A contemporary exponent of Husserl's transcendental phenomenology was Giorgi, who views phenomenology as a rigorous science and is critical of interpretive approaches to phenomenology. According to Giorgi, phenomen-ological inquiry should be a descriptive method, since it is through analysis and description of how things are constituted in and by consciousness that we can grasp the phenomena of our world (Giorgi, 1970). Giorgi (1997) described phenomenological method as three interlocking steps: (1) the phenomenological reduction, (2) description, and (3) the search for essences.

Existential Phenomenology

In contrast to Husserl's description of a disembodied consciousness that constitutes the meaning of things, Merleau-Ponty described consciousness as embodied awareness of primordial experience (van Manen, 2002). Consciousness is existence in and toward the world through the body. Whereas Husserl's phenomenology is oriented towards transcendental essences, Merleau-Ponty's phenomenology is existential, oriented towards lived experience, the embodied human being in the concrete world. The lifeworld is a world that is already there or pre-given, that is, it is the world experienced before the individual has consciously thought about it (Merleau-Ponty, 1962). In existential phenomenology the focus is on individuals' experiences of being-in-the-world, therefore research questions in this tradition tend to be oriented towards ontological rather than epistemological phenomena (see Chapter 6).

Hermeneutic Phenomenology

The fusion of phenomenology with hermeneutics began with Heidegger, who drew on the hermeneutic tradition of Schleiermacher (1768–1834) and Dilthey (1833–1911), and continued with contemporary philosophers Gadamer and Ricoeur. Hermeneutics is the interpretation of texts of many forms, including artwork (Bullock & Trombley, 2000). Van Manen's work (1997) represents a contemporary and valuable way of adopting hermeneutic phenomenology as a methodology by combining a descriptive and interpretive approach to studying lived experience.

Hermeneutic phenomenology is a "research methodology aimed at producing rich textual descriptions (and interpretations) of the experiencing of selected phenomena in the *lifeworld* of individuals, that are able to connect with the experience of all of us collectively" (italics added; Smith, 1997, p. 80). Whereas Husserl's phenomenology focused on consciousness as the medium through which we know objects, Heidegger's focus was on language and time as the media for experiencing the world or being in the world (Thompson, 1990). Hermeneutic phenomenology brings with it a concern for researchers to move their research gaze beyond appearances to the underlying significance of the events being investigated (Sharkey, 2001).

Phenomenology and hermeneutics share the assumption that questions of meaning are primary. Three main points of departure between these two approaches concern the importance of prejudices (or pre-judgments) in shaping understanding, lived experience as a source of meaning, and language as a medium for understanding. Contrary to Husserl's position, Heidegger and Gadamer rejected the notion of reduction and bracketing in favour of recognition that tradition shapes and constrains the meanings we encounter in the world. By assigning words or language to any experience or phenomenon, the person choosing the words or using them in a particular context has already made an interpretation. Consistent with the philosophical roots of hermeneutics, in hermeneutic phenomenology there is no single interpretation of any phenomenon, only (re-)interpretations of interpretations, that potentially offer deeper or richer layers of meaning (van Manen, 1997).

Phenomenology of Practice

Phenomenology of practice is a phenomenological research approach that seeks to answer questions about how people act in everyday situations and about matters of practical and ethical concern (van Manen, 2007). Van Manen's vision for phenomenology of practice is that it can be applied to researching practice rather than exploring the philosophy of phenomenology itself, a preoccupation of the founding philosophers. Practitioners often adopt this research approach, and the products of their research tend primarily to have pedagogical value for practice. Phenomenology of practice makes accessible the non-cognitive (pre-reflective) dimensions of practice so they may be communicated, internalised and reflected upon. Accessing these dimensions through research requires an orientation that is sensitive to the experiential, moral, emotional and personal dimensions of professional life (van Manen, 2007).

> The pathic dimensions of practice are pathic precisely because they reside or resonate in the body, in our relations with others, in the things of our world, and in our very actions. These are the corporeal, relational, temporal, situational, and actional kinds of knowledge that cannot necessarily be translated back or captured in conceptualizations and theoretical representations. In other words, there are modes of knowing that inhere so immediately in our lived practices—in our body, in our relations, and in the things around us—that they seem invisible. (van Manen, 2007, p. 22)

KEY ELEMENTS OF PHENOMENOLOGICAL RESEARCH

Several key research elements are fundamental to an understanding of phenomenology, including the focus on the lifeworld, intentionality and essence, subjectivity and bracketing (see Table 21.2).

Table 21.2. Key elements of phenomenological research (adapted from van Manen, 2002)

Lifeworld	the everyday world as it is immediately experienced, that is, before it has been transmuted by abstract thought processes
Intentionality	this refers to directedness or relatedness. This means that all thinking (imagining, perceiving, remembering, etc.) is always thinking *about* something.
Essence	the core meanings or fundamental elements that uniquely determine the nature of a phenomenon
Bracketing	the act of suspending our beliefs, preconceptions and prejudices in order to be open to the essential nature of lived experiences

Lifeworld

Phenomenology, the study of human phenomena, focuses on subjective experiences and personal meanings constructed from the experiences of the lifeworld, "the world of commonsense knowledge of everyday life ... constituted by the thoughts and acts of individuals and the social expressions of those thoughts and acts" (Schwandt, 1997, p. 83). The term lifeworld (*Lebenswelt*) was first used by Husserl in *Ideas 1* (1983) to describe the concept of the ordinary world we associate with all our possible experiences. By 1928 Husserl had further developed this concept to mean the world as it is experienced before it has been conceptualised theoretically (Moran, 2000). Van Manen (1997) described phenomenology as "different from almost every other science in that it attempts to gain insightful descriptions of the way we experience the world pre-reflexively, without taxonomizing, classifying, or abstracting it" (p. 9). It is the world as it is immediately experienced in a given time and space.

In phenomenology there is a conceptual and temporal distance between the object (the lifeworld) and the act of thinking about it. Without conscious thought the presence of the lifeworld is not acknowledged (Giorgi, 1970). "A lived experience does not confront me as something perceived or represented; it is not given to me, but the reality of lived experience is there-for-me because I have reflexive awareness of it, because I possess it immediately as belonging to me in some sense. "Only in thought does it become objective" (Dilthey, 1985, p. 223). Conscious thought not only brings objects into existence but helps us make sense of our world. Phenomenologists focus on what people experience and, to varying degrees, how they interpret their experiences (Patton, 2002). In transcendental phenomenology, for example, researchers lay people's theorised interpretations aside and use observation and questioning techniques that try to reach people's immediate experiences. In other traditions (e.g. hermeneutic phenomenology), researchers relish the rich layers of meaning provided by all levels of interpretation, including researchers' *reading between the lines* of participants' narratives to interpret what is taken for granted.

Intentionality and Essence

Phenomenology recognises that all consciousness is consciousness *of* something. Intentionality is the term used to refer to this notion of the essential relation between conscious subjects and objects (Crotty, 1998). It is used to describe the process whereby thinkers direct thoughts towards what is being thought about, a going back to the *essence* of the phenomenon, *back to the things themselves* (Husserl, 1970). According to Husserl, essence refers to the essential meaning of the phenomenon after its various social and cultural meanings have been peeled away. Transcendental phenomenologists endeavour to remove successive layers of a priori judgment and to transcend all preconceptions in order to arrive at a consciousness of pure essences. Phenomenologists look to uncover essential meanings, meanings that are invisible in the data but that become apparent to the researcher through the research process. Essences appear only after reflection, a process which van Manen (1997) called the *inseparable connectedness* between human being and the world.

Bracketing

In phenomenology the subjectivity of both participants and researchers is valued and the outcome of phenomenological inquiry depends on the researcher's ability to engage with the informants' reality (Swanson-Kauffman & Schonwald, 1988). An important dimension of Husserl's phenomenology is bracketing, which involves suspending researchers' preconceived notions so that the experience of the phenomenon itself can be revealed (Crotty, 1996). According to Husserl (1970), an individual's natural attitude is formed by unquestioned assumptions about the world that are handed down by previous generations. Laying aside our natural attitude leaves us open to others' experiences. Researchers become "experiencing interpreters" of the phenomenon (Crabtree & Miller, 1992, p. 24).

Husserl's view of bracketing of prejudices in order to illuminate the pure essence of a phenomenon is distinct from Gadamer's (1989) view. Gadamer regarded prejudices and traditions as essential for understanding because they form our vantage points or horizons and thus cannot be eliminated. Gadamer asserted that the point is not to free ourselves from all prejudices but to examine our historically inherited and unreflectively held preconceptions and alter those that disable understanding (Moran & Mooney, 2002). According to Gadamer, the important thing is to be aware of one's biases so that texts can be presented in all their *otherness* and thus assert their own truths against the researcher's fore-meanings (entry understandings) (Moran & Mooney, 2002). In hermeneutic phenomenology researchers' prejudices and traditions are regarded as important for understanding and, rather than bracketing them, they are made obvious to allow comparison with those of the research participants. Therefore, researchers try to recognise and make explicit understandings, beliefs, biases, assumptions, presuppositions and theories that are brought to the research (van Manen, 1997) and to achieve "freedom from *undisclosed* prejudices" (Moran, 2002, p. 2).

DOING PHENOMENOLOGICAL RESEARCH

In this final section we present strategies for conceptualising and conducting phenomenological research. The ways in which key elements of phenomenology are used in research depend on the research phenomenon, and the chosen research approach and phenomenological tradition which inform decisions throughout the research journey. The following strategies are presented as a guide to researchers pursuing a phenomenological approach and do not presume to be prescriptive of how phenomenology *should* be done.

1. Philosophical Stance

First ensure that phenomenology is an appropriate methodology for your research. If you hold that:
- human beings are best understood from the reality of their own situated life experiences (Crabtree & Miller, 1992),
- every participant's interpretation of the world is unique, culturally derived and historically situated (Crabtree & Miller, 1992),
- human experience is the cornerstone of knowledge about human phenomena (Morrissey & Higgs, 2006),
- the everyday world is a valuable and productive source of knowledge (Becker, 1992),
 then the philosophical propositions of phenomenology fit with your standpoint.

2. Research Questions

Phenomenologists ask questions about the lifeworld of phenomena, events and relations as experienced by individuals (Smith, 1997). According to Moustakas (1994, p. 59):

> The research question that is the focus of and guides an investigation must be carefully constructed, every word deliberately chosen and ordered in such a way that the primary words appear immediately, capture my attention, and guide and direct me in the phenomenological process of seeing, reflecting, and knowing. Every method relates back to the question, is developed solely to illuminate the question, and provides a portrayal of the phenomenon that is vital, rich, and layered in its textures and meanings.

When choosing a particular approach you may want to consider, for example, the extent to which your research aims to describe experience in general (i.e. shared by many) or to explicate individual embodied experience (existential phenomenology). Is it the hidden meanings in pre-reflective practice experiences that you are interested in (experiential phenomenology)? Do you want to interpret meaning beyond the participants' lived experiences with a focus on language, culture and tradition (hermeneutic phenomenology)? Some examples of research using various phenomenological traditions are provided in Table 21.3.

Table 21.3. *Phenomenological traditions/orientations: Examples of research*

Phenomenological tradition	Examples of research
Transcendental	Moerer-Urdahl and Creswell (2004) used transcendental phenomenology to study reinvestment or the *ripple effect* for nine individuals who participated in a youth leadership mentoring program. Transcendental phenomenology worked well for this study as this methodology provides logical, systematic, and coherent design elements that lead to an essential description of the experience. According to the researchers, the essence of the experience of being a mentor was *giving*, and giving had the potential to be a multiplier of relationships that culminated into a ripple effect.
Existential	Thompson and colleagues (1990) conducted an existential phenomenological exploration of everyday consumer experiences of contemporary married women with children. A central dilemma of human existence – dealing with the anxiety and uncertainty of freedom – was evident in this research. According to the researchers, the research revealed the existential significance of making everyday decisions as meaningful and caring in nature.
Hermeneutic (interpretive)	Ajjawi (see Ajjawi & Higgs, 2007) used hermeneutic phenomenology to investigate how experienced practitioners learned to communicate their clinical reasoning. She demonstrated how hermeneutical interpretation can devise a model of learning to communicate clinical reasoning, along with a phenomenological description of participants' lived experience of learning to reason derived from the participants' lived experience.
Experiential (phenomenology of practice)	Langeveld (1983a, b) explored the secret place of the child allowing the reader to appreciate the *felt meaning* of that special place that young children seek out at times. The *secret place* is the place where the child withdraws from the presence of others. From Langeveld's pedagogical interest in children and focus on common events, a phenomenology of practice facilitates a pedagogical sensitivity which can be seen in tactfulness on the part of the adult.

3. Attitude of Researcher

According to Husserl, in order to go behind and beneath descriptions given by individuals to discover the true nature of a phenomenon, researchers put aside or bracket their preconceptions and expectations. To Husserl (1970) this was the process by which consciousness is *purged*, the laying aside of our natural attitude, our unquestioned assumptions, so that we could uncover something invisible in the data, the true essence of the phenomenon. In transcendental phenomenology this attitude is maintained through all stages of the research.

Finlay (2009) argued that bracketing involves looking at the data with the attitude of relative openness. This involves a process of critical self-awareness on the researcher's behalf, or reflexivity, where the researcher shifts back and forth from personal assumptions to looking at participants' experiences in a fresh way (or moving beyond the partiality of previous understanding). Therefore, the researcher "engages in a dialectic movement between bracketing pre-understandings and exploiting them reflexively as a source of insight" (p. 7).

As researchers we favour Gadamer's approach. We have found attempts to remove our own perspectives and assumptions to be unrealistic and unachievable, but have benefited from the recognition of our pre-judgements to maintain a focus on the participants' lived experiences. Maintaining an openness and curiosity towards data is facilitated through a reflexive attitude.

4. Data Collection

Phenomenologists try to understand what another person is experiencing as directly as possible (Patton, 2002). This is why such data collection strategies as interviewing, focus groups, and observation are important. Other data collection methods that can be used to explore the subjective experiences of participants include blogging, participants' verbal diaries, photographs, paintings, storybooks and films. Interviews are typically unstructured, semi-structured or open-ended, and allow time for participants to talk at some length about their experiences. Phenomenological questions like *What was it like (for you)?* or *What does it mean to you?* elicit descriptions of subjective experiences, including thoughts, perceptions and feelings (Crotty, 1996).

The exact sample size for phenomenological research cannot be predetermined. Data collection desirably continues until redundancy of information (theoretical saturation) occurs and the phenomenon under study has been deeply explored.

5. Data Analysis

Data analysis is best (and indeed inevitably) conducted concurrently with data collection, so that questioning, interviewing, observation or other data collection methods can be progressively guided by the data. A key feature of the process of data analysis in phenomenology is constant comparison "to discern conceptual similarities, to refine the discriminative power of the categories, and to discover patterns" (Tesch, 1995, p. 96). The process requires long engagement with the data; it takes considerable time and mindfulness on the part of researchers to be aware of their preconceptions and to be alert to themes emerging from the data. Emerging themes can be refined, expanded, and discarded throughout the data analysis process. Ultimately a set of themes emerges which represents answers to the research questions.

Researchers need to be careful not to introduce predetermined or premature categories (based on prior understanding and early data analysis respectively) into the data analysis, which could compromise the findings. This is not to be confused with the lens or theoretical framework through which you view your research (see Chapters 7 and 8). For example, taking a feminist perspective illuminates phenomena from a particular perspective but does not predetermine data analysis categories. Whatever the perspective adopted, it must be explicitly acknowledged. Data analysis still requires (a) reflexivity on the part of researchers to acknowledge their preconceptions and prejudices, (b) long engagement with the data, and (c) constant comparison to derive themes which coalesce to form a rich description of the phenomenon.

Other strategies to minimise the risk of misinterpretation or systematic bias in data analysis include the use of several reviewers and member checks (e.g. returning transcripts and/or interpretations to participants for comment or framing interview questions to explore themes arising from preliminary data analysis). It is necessary that researchers "employ every reasonable and appropriate measure to present the lived world of people in everyday life with clarity and authenticity" (Barnacle, 2001, p. vii).

6. Writing Phenomenological Research

Phenomenological text should present the lived quality and significance of the experience in a full and deeply meaningful way (van Manen, 1997). Phenomenological writing seeks verisimilitude, where the written report "rings true" in language, style, mood and content to the phenomenon under study.

Therefore, the aim of phenomenologists is to construct an evocative description (text) of human actions, behaviours, intentions, and experiences as we meet them in the lifeworld. Devices such as evocative stories, rich descriptive passages, participant quotations, extracts of field notes, vignettes and models (pictorial representations of the whole data set) can be used provided they are consistent with the research approach and true to the nature of participants' real experiences. In phenomenological writing, such devices illustrate research findings and stand as evidence for them (Grace, Higgs & Ajjawi, 2009). Phenomenological descriptions invoke *the phenomenological nod* in readers, in recognition of a phenomenon so richly and evocatively described that readers too may experience or recognise it from their experience it (van Manen, 1997). Consequently, readers can analyse their own experience in terms of identified themes (Swanson-Kauffman & Schonwald, 1988).

CONCLUSION

With its focus on people's experiences of the everyday world, phenomenology is an important methodology for studying real-life and complex aspects of practice. We have presented an overview of phenomenological research. Researchers using phenomenology need to be well informed about its traditions and the philosophical assumptions, ontologies and epistemologies associated with them. Four recognised traditions of phenomenology are (1) transcendental phenomenology, which focuses on consciousness of the external world and its inevitable relationality (we are always conscious of some part of the external world); (2) existential phenomenology, which emphasises embodied, individual experience; (3) hermeneutic phenomenology, which recognises the importance of our preconceptions in shaping understanding, and focuses on language to explore meaning in lived experiences; and (4) experiential phenomenology, with its focus on understanding experiences in the practical and applied world of practice.

Despite its evolution into several main branches, some question the usefulness of phenomenology for researching a modern "messy" world. Husserl's focus on essence may be seen as reductionist, and assertions of authentic selves and universal truths as out of step with a post-post-modern world (Finlay, 2009). The challenge then for researchers adopting phenomenology is first to understand the traditions of phenomenology and its key thinkers, then to be critical and thoughtful about how these traditions are used to inform research practices, and finally to represent the multidimensionality and multiple voices of contemporary practice.

REFERENCES

Ajjawi, R., & Higgs, J. (2007). Using hermeneutic phenomenology to investigate how experienced practitioners learn to communicate clinical reasoning. *The Qualitative Report, 12*(4), 612–638.

Barnacle, R. (2001). Introduction. In R. Barnacle (Ed.), *Phenomenology* (monograph) (pp. i–x). Melbourne: RMIT University Press.

Becker, C. (1992). *Living and relating: An introduction to phenomenology*. Thousand Oaks, CA: Sage.

Bullock, A., & Trombley, S. (Eds.). (2000). *The new Fontana dictionary of modern thought* (3rd ed.). London: Harper Collins.

Carter, S. M., & Little, M. (2007). Justifying knowledge, justifying method, taking action: Epistemologies, methodologies and methods in qualitative research. *Qualitative Health Research, 17*(10), 1316–1328.

Crabtree, B., & Miller, W. (Eds.). (1992). *Doing qualitative research: Research methods for primary care* (Vol. 3). Newbury Park, CA: Sage.

Crotty, M. (1996). *Phenomenology and nursing research*. South Melbourne: Churchill Livingstone.

Crotty, M. (1998). *The foundations of social research: Meaning and perspective in the research process*. Sydney: Allen & Unwin.

Dilthey, W. (1985). *Poetry and experience: Selected works* (Vol. V). Princeton, NJ: Princeton University Press.

Finlay, L. (2009). *Debating phenomenological research methods, Phenomenology and practice*. Retrieved May 21, 2009, from http://www.lindafinlay.co.uk/

Gadamer, H.-G. (1989). *Truth and method* (J. Weinsheimer & D. Marshall, Trans., 2nd ed.). London: Sheed & Ward.

Giorgi, A. (1970). *Psychology as a human science: A phenomenologically based approach*. New York: Harper & Row.

Giorgi, A. (1997). The theory, practice, and evaluation of the phenomenological method as a qualitative research procedure. *Journal of Phenomenological Psychology, 28*(2), 235–260.

Grace, S., Higgs, J., & Ajjawi, R. (2009). Writing phenomenologically. In J. Higgs, D. Horsfall, & S. Grace (Eds.), *Writing qualitative research on practice* (pp. 115–126). Rotterdam: Sense.

Husserl, E. (1970). *Logical investigations* (Vol. I–II). London: Routledge & Kegan Paul.

Husserl, E. (1983). *Ideas pertaining to a pure phenomenology and to a phenomenological philosophy: First Book* (F. Kersten, Trans.). The Hague: Nijhoff.

Langeveld, M. J. (1983a). The stillness of the secret place. *Phenomenology and pedagogy, 1*(1), 11–17.
Langeveld, M. J. (1983b). The "secret place" in the life of the child. *Phenomenology and pedagogy, 1*(2), 181–194.
Merleau-Ponty, M. (1962). *Phenomenology of perception* (C. Smith, Trans.). London: Routledge.
Moerer-Urdahl, T., & Creswell, J. (2004). Using transcendental phenomenology to explore the "ripple effect" in a leadership mentoring program. *International Journal of Qualitative Methods, 3*(2). Article 2. Retrieved November 2, 2009, from http://www.ualberta.ca/~iiqm/backissues/3_2/pdf/moerercreswell.pdf
Moran, D. (2000). *Introduction to phenomenology*. London: Routledge.
Moran, D. (2002). Editor's introduction. In D. Moran & T. Mooney (Eds.), *The phenomenology reader* (pp. 1–26). London: Routledge.
Moran, D., & Mooney, T. (Eds.). (2002). *The phenomenology reader*. Abingdon: Routledge.
Morrissey, G., & Higgs, J. (2006). Phenomenological research and adolescent female sexuality: Discoveries and applications. *The Qualitative Report, 11*(1), 161–181.
Moustakas, C. (1994). *Phenomenological research methods*. Thousand Oaks, CA: Sage.
Patton, M. Q. (2002). *Qualitative research and evaluation methods* (3rd ed.). Thousand Oaks, CA: Sage.
Schwandt, T. A. (1997). *Qualitative inquiry: A dictionary of terms*. Thousand Oaks, CA: Sage.
Sharkey, P. (2001). Hermeneutic phenomenology. In R. Barnacle (Ed.), *Phenomenology* (monograph) (pp. 16–37). Melbourne: RMIT University Press.
Smith, D. (1997). Phenomenology: Methodology and method. In J. Higgs (Ed.), *Qualitative research: Discourse on methodologies* (pp. 75–80). Sydney, NSW: Hampden Press.
Swanson-Kauffman, K., & Schonwald, E. (1988). Phenomenology. In B. Sarter (Ed.), *Paths to knowledge: Innovative research methods for nurses* (pp. 97–105). New York: National League for Nurses.
Tesch, R. (1995). *Qualitative research: Analysis types and software tools*. New York: Falmer.
Thompson, C. J., Locander, W. B., & Pollio, H. R. (1990). The lived meaning of free choice: An existential-phenomenological description of everyday consumer experiences of contemporary married women. *Journal of Consumer Research, 17*(3), 346–361.
Thompson, J. L. (1990). Hermeneutic inquiry. In L. Moody (Ed.), *Advancing nursing sciences through research* (Vol. 2, pp. 223–280). Newbury Park, CA: Sage.
Trede, F., & Higgs, J. (2009). Framing research questions and writing philosophically: The role of framing research questions. In J. Higgs, D. Horsfall, & S. Grace (Eds.), *Writing qualitative research on practice* (pp. 13–25). Rotterdam: Sense.
van Manen, M. (1997). *Researching lived experience: Human science for an action sensitive pedagogy*. (2nd ed.). London: The Althouse Press.
van Manen, M. (2002). *Orientations in phenomenology*. Retrieved August 27, 2009, from http://www.phenomenologyonline.com
van Manen, M. (2007). Phenomenology of practice. *Phenomenology & Practice, 1*(1), 11–30.

AFFILIATIONS

Sandra Grace PhD
The Education for Practice Institute
Charles Sturt University
Australia

Rola Ajjawi PhD
The Education for Practice Institute
Charles Sturt University
Australia

INGER MEWBURN AND ROBYN BARNACLE

22. MAKING A THESIS TEXT IN CREATIVE PRACTICE-BASED RESEARCH:

Razzle Dazzle

Writing an exegesis or thesis can be a struggle for many creative practice based researchers, such as those undertaking design-led or art-based investigations. A key challenge is how to move beyond treating the text in merely descriptive or explanatory terms, as an extended didactic on the work done – that of the creative project. This difficulty is only intensified if the researcher does not normally work with ideas through the medium of text.

Our aim in this chapter is to emphasise that thesis writing does more than merely convey something about the creative work. When employed well, it not only has the potential to inform creative projects but can also provide a site of artful scholarly performance. This is because writing, like creative investigations, is a meaning-making activity, or is a site in which meaning is performed and brought into being. Moreover, thesis writing provides a site in which scholarly identity work is done, or where scholarly identity is performed into being through the rhetorical and other moves of the text.

This chapter maps out a way of thinking about doctoral writing for creative practice based researchers as a creative problem. Writing is positioned as a set of material–semiotic practices, or as a process of *making – the making of scholar and scholarship*. But this is not to deny that the thesis and creative artefact do different things. Our key point is that the researcher, the text and the project work have qualitatively different kinds of agency, and that in order to work well with text, the researcher can benefit from recognising these differences. A written word is not the same as a spoken one, yet text "speaks" to us so directly that it can be easy to forget that it is a representation – and therein lie both its power and its difficulty. A thesis can never accurately represent the project work, and nor should it try. A thesis tells a story (of scholarship). To illustrate this point we begin with a story about the covert power of representation, but since book chapters are a serious business, it is rhetorically shifted into the third person.

A WORLD CREATED BY REPRESENTATION?

Some 15 years ago, as a recently graduated architect, Inger went to work in a busy architectural practice specialising in institutional work. As a junior member of staff Inger was immediately put to work on routine drawing tasks on the computer.

J. Higgs, N. Cherry, R. Macklin and R. Ajjawi (eds.),
Researching Practice: A Discourse on Qualitative Methodologies, 209–216.
© 2010 Sense Publishers. All rights reserved.

There was endless "busy work" associated with managing the computer-aided (CAD) documentation of these large buildings: making small changes in details, drawing sinks, toilets and stairs. Day after day she stared at and manipulated these drawings which floated in the darkness of her computer screen. Slowly, without even realising it, Inger lost sight of the vital difference between drawings and buildings: materiality.

This became particularly apparent after a week of working on some bathroom renovations for a large military base. Cosily enmeshed in her world of CAD representation and distant from the messy reality of the building site, Inger became quietly obsessed with drawing the individual tile grout lines so that they matched up perfectly with the location of the basins below. The resulting drawings deeply appealed to her sense of architectural order. Perhaps, she mused, this orderliness would subliminally impress itself on the soldier answering the call of nature and speak to his or her own sense of military order. However, when given the drawings, the project manager laughed and told her kindly that she had wasted her time with all these tile lines. To demonstrate why, he ran his ruler over the space where the basin would be installed. The ruler showed her that the actual room was 100mm longer than the room she had drawn; the grout lines on the drawing could never be reproduced in actuality. The project manager, noticing the horrified look on her face, said kindly, "The drawings don't matter as much as you think, luv — the builders make most of it up".

MAKING TEXTS / MAKING REALITIES

Beginner architects may find out the hard way that a representation is never the same as the real thing by forgetting that, as Robin Evans once remarked, architects don't make buildings, they draw them (Evans, 1997). Inger was unconsciously treating the drawing like some sort of mirror showing the reflection of the yet-to-be-built, rather than a set of instructions for what a building might eventually become. An architectural representation is a rather unfaithful mirror, if it can be said to be one at all. Builders may have other ideas about what the drawing instructions mean – and more power to bring them into being; or a building might resist the architect's intentions with its stubborn materiality. *A drawing is never the same as the building that is made from it because the translation process is never perfect.*

Sometimes it's easy to forget that representations *are* representations, because we tend to "make sense" of them almost automatically. Movies are a good example of the interpretative process we undertake to make sense from representations. In film-literate cultures we often follow action which is cut between multiple camera points of view and jumps around in time and place. Yet we have become so accustomed to this form of viewing that we can barely notice the artifice and effort that is necessary to maintain it. This is why a TV series like "24", where the action takes place in real time, can come to be seen as novel: it makes us suddenly aware of the existence of "TV time" as distinct from our experience of bodily time. Although the action in a TV drama might be jumping between places and times, we develop practices of watching that smooth over these inconsistencies and make a coherent story out of what is presented to us.

In a thesis text, the author provides a representation that tells a story about the research and the audience make sense of it through their own practices of interpretation. Laurel Richardson (2000) pointed out that it is surprisingly easy for researchers, like novice architects, to lose sight that writing is a practice of representation, not a kind of mirror or reflection of what happened during the research process. Kamler and Thomson (2006) echoed Richardson's point, stating that in a thesis text "what we write is not what actually happened, but a written approximation" (p. 11). For Kamler and Thomson, however, the key issue is how the writer's identity is performed in that writing. According to them, a thesis text performs identity work at the same time that it tells us what the researcher did and what they learned. In other words, a thesis text should evoke the authority of "scholar" such that it can effectively do the identity work that in turn will allow the candidate to demonstrate his or her ability as scholar.

Of course, a thesis text needs a reader to make this scholarly performance come alive. Just as we happily make sense of jumps between people, place and time in film or in fiction, thesis readers may not be consciously aware of the process of interpretation that is going on when they encounter a text. Kamler and Thomson urged scholars to make texts that speak with appropriate scholarly authority: respectful, yet critical (what they call a "hands on hips" stance). However, the act of reading makes a certain kind of reality out of the text. If the text fails to exude the appropriate scholarly authority to the examiner, like the grout lines in the soldier's bathrooms, the reality created by the examiner and text in the performance of reading might not be the one that the writer imagined.

THE DAZZLE

Thus far we have emphasised how the thesis text is a representation that is never perfect or complete. We have also stressed the importance of recognising that the thesis text is doing scholarly identity work at the same time as telling a story of scholarship. These observations put us in a position to address two key issues that creative researchers face. The first is the difficulty of writing the sheer amount and variety of creative work that many researchers produce into a coherent story. The problem of making sense of the research done is complicated by the second, related problem, wherein researchers may find it difficult to write about their projects with appropriate scholarly authority: the problem of tone and style. Let's begin by looking into the problem of coherency. As the artist or designer knows, creative works can seem to have a life of their own. The architect practitioner and researcher Pia Ednie-Brown (2008, p. 18) expressed it this way:

> The projects discussed in this thesis were like living creatures that I was responsible for, but were never utterly in my control. They provided me with legs with which vaguely forming ideas could learn to walk and take unplanned excursions to return with unexpected surprises. They frustrated my progress, always seemed to be diverting me from focussed paths, confusing

me with their immensity, fatiguing me with their demands and unpredictability. But then, they would turn around and help me realise something that I didn't see coming at all.

One knee-jerk response to this quote is to think about knowledge produced in and through projects as actively resisting the discursive mode of the text. But this obstinacy is a characteristic of research writing practice common to many fields because most research involves working materials of some sort. A chemist can struggle to turn colours in test tubes into text; a physicist may struggle to translate numbers in a print out to a written theory. All researchers struggle with the fact that, as Richardson (2000, p. 760) put it, words can never fully capture the studied world, "however much we might persist in trying". That is why writers like Richardson warn of thinking of writing as a way of "telling" the reader about what was found out and insists that writing should be understood as a way of knowing.

One way of approaching the problem of knowing and telling with respect to both the project and text is to see each as performing different work. In case of creative practice based doctorates, the text performs two distinct types of work: formative work (contributing to the author's understanding of his or her practice) and academic identity work (performing the scholar to the examiner). The problem for the researcher is not one of "forcing" the knowledge-in-project into the "alien" world of the text, but a matter of translating the knowledge produced in and through the project work into — and out of — the medium of the text. To translate is to make two words equivalent but not the same; as John Law (2008, p. 144) put it, "since no two words are equivalent, translation also implies betrayal... a translation is both making equivalent and about shifting." As projects are written about, ideas are moved between material forms. With this translation they change; knowledge materialised as project or as text will always be different and can be thought and worked in different ways, as Ednie-Brown's quote also reflects. Yet translation is not necessarily a one-way deal; rather, is a precarious and ongoing process that is easily undone. If the researcher does not work to hold the thesis together the translation will become so garbled that it fails to make a coherent story. Researchers who work text and project work at the same time can use this precariousness to their advantage to move ideas forward, but they must also learn to live with the uncertainty that this movement produces.

Creative researchers may be able to learn something about this mode of writing from the practices of writing in ethnography. Law (2004) described the problem of data overload and making sense of it as "the dazzle". This is illustrated through a story about time he spent as a researcher exploring the everyday life within a large commercial laboratory in England. Law told of how, initially at least, there was just too much going on for him to be able to make sense of:

> Meetings, activities, experiments, disasters, triumphs, comings, goings, arguments, friendships, documents, policies, programmes, aspirations, promotions, conferences, memos, cups of coffee — all of these and much more were included in the daily round of laboratory work...To misquote TS Eliot, there was too much reality to bear. (Law, 2004, p. 108)

To make sense of what Law experienced as dazzle, he became more attuned to the practices of data-taking he was using and how, in turn, these practices acted to shape what he saw. Specifically, he described how shifting to note-taking rather than tape-recording worked to selectively focus his attention. The act of taking notes by hand, as well as reducing the amount of information he could take from what was happening in front of him, productively "othered" certain dimensions of experience, such as the spaces in which the action was taking place and the nonverbal behaviours of the participants. He reported that these notes acted as a "condensate of traces" in which certain patterns started to emerge, as well as certain silences. He described the patterns emerging from his note taking as "modes of ordering" through which he made sense of the buzzing activity around him.

Law's point is that the omissions in his note-taking method were useful. Rather than attempting to mirror or capture all of reality in his notes, he used the coupling of himself with his notepad as an instrument for "tuning into" the parts of reality that were of most interest to the task at hand. The practice of note taking had "artful effects", allowing him as a researcher to selectively amplify, attend to, and magnify the patterns he was interested in, to create a story. That is not how we might usually think about a content or discourse analysis, where we work to capture as much as possible in order to shape the mass of material through sorting and ordering. Here the practice of representation itself acted as a winnowing process within the very act of observing. By becoming aware of note-taking as a practice of representation and using it productively to guide his research, Law was able to see forms emerging in the dazzle.

TEXT DOES WORK

If writing is itself a form of meaning making, ideally writing acts as a material aid to creative thinking so that new understandings of the project work can emerge. However, here a tension arises because a creative practice based researchers are also making a document which speaks of their skill in research to an audience of their peers. Besides using writing as a tool of thought to make sense of their creative work, researchers must pay attention to the accepted practices of textural representation within their discipline and how they align themselves, or not, with these practices. Kamler and Thompson warned that these practices must be consciously attended to so that an appropriate scholarly voice emerges which "speaks" to the examiner. The main struggle for the candidate, according to Kamler and Thomson, is that the data (or creative work) can easily be privileged over the making of a new kind of self through text. By becoming more conscious of the textural practices of representation in their discipline, they argue, candidates can start to adopt this new identity and use it to craft their work (also see Barnacle & Mewburn, 2010).

The notion of text work as identity work is clearly useful, but the idea of identity work in creative disciplines like art and design needs to be approached with care. In the sciences, for example, the practices of writing as a way of representing data have been developed in tandem with, and are entangled within, the established practices of "doing science". The techniques of experimentation and the techniques of writing have been jointly developed over time and are based in epistemological and ontological understandings that go relatively unquestioned. In effect, the empirical scientific method offers the scientist thesis writer both a style of writing and a method for doing the research.

For the artist or designer, however, the matter of knowledge and identity is less clear-cut. Creative research projects do not "embody" knowledge in a straightforward way. A good example is painting. The knowledge of a painter may be required to make a painting, but its status as a knowledge object within a research project is less clear. Is the knowledge embodied in the painting about the painter's technique or the culture within which it was produced? Alternatively, is the knowledge embodied in the painting found in the intentions of the painter or the expressive affects that are provoked in the viewer? The architect researcher Peter Downton (2003) pointed out that the problem for creative researchers is that scientific methods (such as observation, measurement and the construction of predictive theories) have been widely adopted outside of science and this has resulted in the practices of representation in science being reified as the activity of research per se, which makes trouble for those working with other ways of knowing.

Perhaps the most obvious point of differentiation between a science thesis and a creative practice based thesis, as has been argued elsewhere (Allpress & Barnacle, 2009), is in the way the thesis is conveyed. To have a thesis means taking a position: putting something forward. Whereas the thesis is conveyed largely theoretically in a conventional, written research thesis, it is conveyed largely empirically in research conducted through the production of creative works. A science thesis represents or stands-in-for the evidence obtained through scientific methods. In creative research, however, a position is put forward empirically through the creation of some kind of empirical artefact which itself embodies and could be said to "perform" the research.

With the potential for competing "knowledge claims", creative researchers can struggle to articulate a contribution to knowledge in their thesis text and the requisite identity work that this implies. It is no wonder that they are sometimes, as Paul Carter (2005) put it, "tongue tied" when called upon to explain their work. Carter criticised artists for falling back into the "worn out trope" of letting the work speak for itself. He encouraged them to try to find ways to work with text such that the separation between object and text is a gap that can be exploited. He pointed out that works that are produced with no accompanying language from the artist are either over-interpreted or under-interpreted by others so that the meaning is "detached from the matrix of its production" (Carter, 2005, p. xii). The problem with this state of affairs, according to Carter, is the perpetuation of the Romantic myth of the creative process as outside the process of rational inquiry.

So, where does this leave the creative practice based researcher needing to translate between project and text? The standard conception of the doctoral thesis, as it is often represented in books on thesis writing, tends to be of limited value because it assumes a scientific practice with all that entails about knowledge and knowing: a clear link between method and knowledge, a subject apart from the object, and theory intended to predict and explain the data gathered. Alternatively, we encourage creative practitioners to think about the text as a knowledge artefact in its own right, one which works with the projects but is other to them.

According to Steven Scrivener, a supervisor who has worked with creative practice based candidates over some 20 years, creative practice based research tends to fall into two main types, which he has labelled "creative production projects" and "creative problem solving projects" (2000). The main difference between the two, he argued, is in the way that the knowledge in and of the artefact can be understood. In creative problem based projects, objects are created for a reason and can be tested on the basis of their performance. This implies a process of testing which produces evidence that can be used in a scholarly argument. In a creative production project, on the other hand, artefact design is more speculative than purposeful, with the aim of being suggestive and open-ended. In creative production based projects, according to Scrivener:

> Problems seem to arise when the candidates' primary interest is in producing artefacts, i.e., in creative production, and when their practice is closely associated with their self-identification as creators. For these candidates, the artifacts arising from the research cannot simply be conceived as by-products or exemplification of "know-how". Instead, they are objects of value in their own right.

Scrivener stressed that creative production projects tend to evolve and change as the interests of the maker develop. This makes any search for a definitive account of the research not only difficult, but more importantly, perhaps, misguided. The standard (scientific) thesis structure, comprising method, literature review, results and discussion sections, assumes the possibility of singularity and closure: a single definitive account of the research. Instead, if both written text and project are treated as knowledge artefacts the two can be put into productive dialogue where neither is intended to faithfully represent or instantiate the other. The thesis tells a research story, rather than portrays a reflection, and the story-telling in this instance is the craft of the scholar.

FINDING A WAY OUT OF THE MIRROR MAZE

In this chapter we have argued that conceiving of a thesis text as a faithful mirror is a trap against which creative practitioners must struggle. Just as Inger struggled against reifying drawing and building, or Law struggled as ethnographer to understand and translate the dazzle, creative practice based thesis writers must struggle against merely describing the work and the processes by which it is made. They must strive to make knowledge in two media simultaneously: in their creative practice and through writing. The knowledge(s) in writing and in the artefacts will be different because the translation process is never perfect, but creative practitioners can use this to their advantage.

We have suggested that one way to proceed is to cast aside the notion of the creative practice based thesis as a recounting of the intellectual and creative work that has been done in the project work. This frees authors to think about the thesis 'text as another kind of artefact, which is part of a thesis-project-assemblage. The thesis text, unlike the project work, is an artefact crafted in the mode of scholar. This is a performative account of knowledge making, where meaning emerges from the artefacts acting together with readers and their processes of interpretation. The question then becomes not How should I write about what I have done? but What sort of textural representation might I make? What kind of scholarship do I want to perform into being?

ACKNOWLEDGEMENTS

The authors wish to thank Dr Pia Ednie Brown, Colleen Boyle, Ailsa Haxwell and Dean Perides for their insightful commentary on earlier drafts of this chapter.

REFERENCES

Allpress, B., & Barnacle, R. (2009). Projecting the PhD: Architectural design research by and through projects. In D. Boud & A. Lee (Eds.), *Changing practices of doctoral education*. London: Routledge.
Barnacle, R., & Mewburn, I. (2010). Learning networks and the journey of becoming doctor. *Studies in Higher Education, 35*(4), forthcoming.
Carter, P. (2005). *Material thinking*. Melbourne: Melbourne University Press.
Downton, P. (2003). *Design research*. Melbourne: RMIT Press.
Ednie-Brown, P. (2008). *The aesthetics of emergence*. Melbourne: RMIT University.
Evans, R. (1997). *Translations from drawing to building and other essays*. London: Architectural Association.
Kamler, B., & Thomson, P. (2006). *Helping doctoral students to write*. London: Routledge.
Law, J. (2004). *After method: Mess in social science research*. London: Routledge.
Law, J. (2008). Pinboards and books: Juxtaposing, learning and materiality. In D. W. Kritt & L. T. Winegar (Eds.), *Education and technology: Critical perspectives, possible futures*. New York: Rowman & Littlefield.
Richardson, L. (2000). Writing: A method of inquiry. In N. K. Denzin & Y. S. Lincoln (Eds.), *Handbook of qualitative research*. Thousand Oaks, CA: Sage.
Scrivener, S. (2000). Reflection in and on action and practice in creative-production doctoral projects in art and design [Electronic version]. *Working Papers in Art and Design, 1*. Retrieved September 10, 2009, from http://sitem.herts.ac.uk/artdes_research/papers/wpades/vol1/index.html

AFFILIATIONS

Inger Mewburn PhD
School of Graduate Research
RMIT University
Australia

Robyn Barnacle PhD
School of Graduate Research
RMIT University
Australia

JILL FRANZ

23. ARTS-BASED RESEARCH FOR TEACHERS, RESEARCHERS AND SUPERVISORS

Arts-based research is central to my role as an academic. I use arts-based approaches in my research and teaching, and supervise postgraduate and higher degree students using an arts-based approach in their research. Much of this chapter is based on this experience and the experiences of my students, on what we have learned individually and collectively by way of criteria and strategies for undertaking quality qualitative research using an arts-based approach. As background information, I should also declare that I am a design academic. My teaching, research and supervision are situated largely within and across architecture, interior design, landscape architecture and, more recently, urban development and engineering in the context of work-integrated learning. Despite the discipline-specificity of these experiences, I trust you will find something relevant for your teaching, supervision or higher degree research, just as my students and I have in reading arts-based research literature from outside the design disciplines, in disciplines such as education, medicine, social science, visual arts, to mention but a few.

When I started using arts-based approaches in the early 1990s there was very little in the way of monographs or refereed journal publications – on qualitative research let alone arts-based research. Now there is a plethora of material; so much that it is difficult to know where to start to gain a basic appreciation of the field. This is made more confusing by the use of several labels and terms in place of or in association with the term arts-based research. In the next section I identify several of these terms while providing an overview of the evolution of arts-based research over the last 20 years and its relationship to qualitative research. This is followed by examples of application in teaching, research and practice. In the process I highlight issues related not only to research rigour and quality but also to the researcher's ontology and personal qualities and attitudes. The chapter concludes with a work-in-progress summary of criteria and strategies for designing, undertaking and supervising quality arts-based research, and with an invitation to extend and consolidate these through your own practice.

WHAT IS ARTS-BASED RESEARCH?

Rather than "arts-based research", Cole and Knowles (2008) have used the term "arts-informed research", which they describe broadly as a mode and form of qualitative research influenced by the arts. Using the term "arts-informed research" minimises the chance of it being misconstrued as situated exclusively in the arts.

Note that the term *arts* encompasses a range of performative and literary as well as visual modes of artistry. Arts-informed research or arts-based research is undertaken in these areas, but it is also a research approach adopted by other discipline areas. Indeed, it was in education in the U.S. and Canada that the groundwork was laid for the development and emergence of arts-based research. Central to this was a speculative paper presented by Elliot Eisner in 1993 to the American Educational Research Association, leading soon afterwards to the formation of the Arts-Based Educational Research Special Interest Group, and in 2000 the Centre for Arts-Informed Research (Cole & Knowles, 2008, pp. 58–59).

Arts-Based Research as Qualitative Research

With respect to the three paradigms illustrated in Figure 23.1, arts-based research appears to sit comfortably anywhere between the interpretivist and critical theorist continuum, accommodating aims of description, re-creation, and moral purpose.

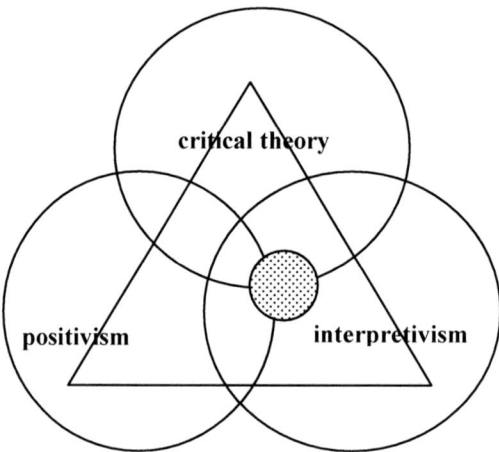

Figure 23.1. Philosophical paradigms informed by Candy (1989), highlighting where I position myself ontologically depending on the aim of the project.

Arts-Based Research: from Description to Re-Creation to Moral Purpose

Why is arts-based research different from other forms of qualitative research? What is it about the arts that opens up opportunities not afforded by other activities? In a recent publication, Eisner (2008) described his understanding of art as a form of knowledge which has a unique role in enlarging human understanding through its direct use of a range of senses to engage people emotionally and experientially. According to Eisner, the "arts provide access to qualities of life that literal language has no great power to disclose" (p. 7). Correspondingly, it also provides various means of representation and expression, opening up the possibility of vicarious participation, connection to diverse audiences, and dissemination at a deeply metaphoric level. "Science states meaning, art expresses it" (Eisner, 2008, p. 6). It is this ability to evoke meaning that lies at the heart of the creative potency of arts-based research and positions it uniquely "as a methodology for radical, ethical, and revolutionary research that is futuristic, socially responsible, and useful in addressing social inequities" (Finley, 2008, p. 71). For researchers such as Susan Finley, arts-based research challenges the traditional notion of knowledge creation, extending sites of research beyond academia to the community where everyday people participate in processes of discovery, invention, and social transformation. In this respect, arts-based research (or community-based activist art, as it is sometimes termed (Knowles & Cole, 2008, p. xii), is located at the critical theory end of the interpretive continuum, with the work of Finley and her colleagues providing highly descriptive and evocative examples of this form of arts-based research.

Art as Craft, Research as Art, Art as Research

The notion of arts-based research as craft helps to draw out additional qualities as well as disclosing how research in general, like artistic practice, relies on the creativity and intuition of the researcher, something that is not usually admitted or legitimised in the conduct and reporting of more conventional research (Leavy, 2008, p. 347). Using theatre and dance as examples, Leavy speculated that the improvisational techniques used by performers "may implicitly be a part of what qualitative researchers already do" (p. 348). According to Denzin, analysis in conventional research involves improvisation; that perception has led him to the corollary understanding that improvisation is a rudimentary research act (Denzin, 2006, in Leavy, 2008, p. 348).

The notion of craft also leads one to think about the concept of skill and its place in one's practice, be that an arts related activity like dance or painting, or be it undertaking research. Exploring the relationship between poetry and qualitative research, Cahnmann-Taylor (2008), highlighted several devices that poets and researchers use and develop as part of their practice repertoire. These include rhythm and form, and image and metaphor. In terms of the former, Cahnmann-Taylor wrote that "it is in paying attention to the rhythms of speech in communities where we carry out our research and in learning how to adapt that speech to the page that we learn to ask new questions and use poetic structure to represent and interpret complexity" (p. 31). Like other art forms, poetry utilises and celebrates the emotive aspect of life and living. Image and its metaphorical quality and capacity are integral to this. According to Weber (2007), "images [visual and mental] are essential to human sense-making" (p. 2). For many arts-based researchers, images play a significant role in their research, creating an associated area of arts-based research, "image-based research". In such research, images can be used in different ways, for example as data; to elicit data; as documentation; and as a mode of interpretation or representation (Weber, 2007, pp. 3–4).

A craft approach to one's practice involves iterative cycles of imaging (or imagining), representing and testing (terms used by Zeisel, 1981, to describe the design process), as part of a process of critical reflection. Given a presence and status through the seminal work of Schön (1983), reflection-in-action-on-action is considered central in developing and enhancing practitioner expertise. As illustrated in the examples that follow, reflective diaries and notebooks are basic tools and resources for arts-based researchers. Not only does the practice of externalisation and reflection through journalling or note-taking support research in a substantive way, it also helps achieve methodological quality and rigour. A piece of writing that I find invaluable as a qualitative researcher and supervisor of qualitative research is by Kvale (1995). In Kvale's view, rigour and quality are craftsmanship characterised by ongoing phases of checking, questioning and theorising. Rather than apply traditional research measures of generalisability, reliability and validity, Kvale and others such as Smith (2003) advocate consideration in terms of resonance, integrity, and verisimilitude.

Research as craft reminds us that it takes time to develop the skills of doing quality qualitative research, and that the best way of learning is through continuous doing and critical reflection. As well as skill, it also involves particular attributes. Many researchers undertaking qualitative research for the first time find it a daunting, frustrating and uncertain process. Along with the development of certain skills I also advocate the inculcation of attributes such as diligence; persistence; consistency; thoroughness; constructive scepticism; and a willingness to imagine, represent, and test in a detailed, extensive and critical way, to question underlying values and to understand how elements are connected to each other. As with any research, ethical considerations are paramount. In terms of my research and that of my students, I demand integrity, humility, empathy and sensitivity to the rights of others, honesty, procedural transparency and accessibility, and recognition of intellectual property and moral rights (Franz, 2007).

EXAMPLES OF ARTS-BASED RESEARCH AND ARTS-INFORMED INQUIRY IN TEACHING, RESEARCH, AND PRACTICE: A PERSONAL PERSPECTIVE

There are many dimensions to arts-based research, not least because, as noted by Cole and Knowles (2008), there are various art genres, such as writing, performance, music, painting, photography, collage, multimedia, sculpture, film and video, folk arts, and installation art, to mention but a few. As further explained by Cole and Knowles and illustrated in the following examples from my experience, each of these genres can be used as a method, a structural element, a technical element, a communication element, an aesthetic element, and a procedural element. In arts-based research the art form can be used as a stand-alone methodology or in conjunction with other methodologies as part of one's teaching, research, and practice.

Arts-Based Research/Arts-Informed Inquiry in Teaching

I have used art as part of my teaching (where art is a pedagogical tool and informs inquiry to do with learning and teaching) and as part of my research in teaching (where the outcomes of discipline research provide content for teaching – as described in a following section), of teaching (where I undertake research projects to do with teaching and learning – see Lawson, Franz, & Adkins, 2005), and through teaching (where teaching is the site and medium for research).

Art as a Pedagogical Tool – Arts-Informed Inquiry

The process I developed to reveal students' conceptions of research at the commencement of a research methods unit is an example of art used as a pedagogical tool. In this case, I invite students to draw as well as describe in words their understanding or conception of research (see e.g. Figure 22.2(a), (b)). The drawings are then used as a resource for discussing the different ways in which research is understood, comparing them with the conception underpinning the unit curriculum, and the context of learning as involving conceptual change. Because these students are design students in their fourth year they are at ease with expressing ideas visually. The predisposition and, to a lesser degree, the ability of participants are important considerations in involving others in an art activity. Participants must be assured that the activity is not about producing exact representations or works of art. In this context, art is used as a (teaching) method, a communication element, and an aesthetic element. Through the aesthetics of the image so much more is conveyed about the content and its qualities than can be expressed in words alone.

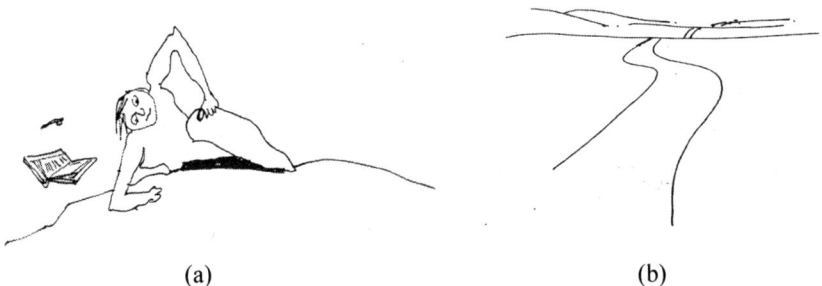

(a) (b)

Figure 23.2. (a) Research as observing and recording; (b) Research as a journey.

Art as a Vehicle and Site for Learning (and Teaching)

In the same research methods unit, I use art as a site for facilitating student learning procedurally and substantively. The main aims of the unit are to introduce students to research involving the bringing together of creative practice and systematic inquiry. In the unit project, students were asked to use installation art as the medium for exploring the conceptual notion of *edge*, in responding to the question: What is edge? "Edge" was chosen because of its significance as a spatial concept in design. Installation art was chosen as the art form because of its close link to architecture. Like architecture, it is three-dimensional, and through this quality it explicitly invites viewer/user participation; as art, it seeks to inform, to provoke, to produce an aesthetic, perhaps even transcendental response. Installation art was also viewed as an effective way of students conceiving building in more temporal, dynamic and tenuous terms; in other words, to regard a built environment as a hypothesis rather than a solution. As an additional requirement consideration had to be given to how the installation would engage people, as a way of further extending the potential for new meaning (see Figure 23.3).

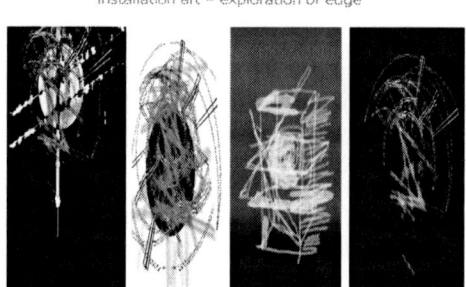

Figure 23.3. Exploring the notion of edge: drawings for an installation (Trusler, 2002)

As previously highlighted (and detailed in Franz, 2007), students were required to undertake the process in a creative as well as systematic, rigorous and ethical way. In this context, "creative" was defined as reconstructing the meaning of edge through a dialogic process with the materials of the installation and with the installation itself. More specifically, the activity entailed exploration from different perspectives and points of reference; action that provided for serendipitous occurrences; exploitation of idiosyncratic features; flexibility and adaptability; heuristic interaction; critical reflection. For the project, systematic action was described in relation to how the project was organised to open up the possibility of understanding edge in new ways. In part, this demanded that students tentatively map out an approach, recognising that down the track they should be prepared to change it in the response to issues that arose from the course of their action and from evaluation of the extent to which the plan constrained productive action. Students were also required to be ethical and rigorous in the way they organised and managed the process.

In recent years this project has evolved more fully as research employing a combination of art media and research methodologies such as phenomenology, phenomenography and grounded theory. It has also been extended to involve students in gathering empirical data through photo-elicitation. Here, photo-elicitation involves students in photographing representations of their understanding of the phenomenon under investigation, such as aspects of the built environment that for them convey or contribute to how they understand "home". These photographs then form the basis of interviews involving the students, with the photographs contributing to the data for the study. As part of the dissemination students are required to write up their findings as a journal or conference paper with the process of writing providing an additional creative space for exploration, critique and refinement.

ARTS-BASED RESEARCH

Arts-Based Approaches in Discipline Research

As a designer in and researcher of the built environment I have a vested interest in developing my understanding of related phenomena such as home and interiority. Not only does the research contribute to the knowledge base of architecture and interior design, it also provides a rich resource for teaching and higher degree supervision. Several years ago I led a group of colleagues in a collaborative research project whereby we used drawing, painting and photography to individually explore and externalise our understanding of *home*. Following this process we each selected a specified number of images which we arranged on large boards to produce a collective visual collage and narrative of home, this latter process adding another dimension and level of meaning to the work produced. These boards were exhibited in the university art museum (Franz, Hedley, Molloy, & Smith, 2002) (Figure 23.4) as part of a university-wide forum on home. During the exhibition, visitors were invited to draw their conceptions of home and pin them up on blank boards, producing data for further research. In that study, the images not only constituted data; they were also used to elicit data as well as act as vehicles for interpretation and representation (Weber, 2007).

(a)

(b)

Figure 23.4. (a) Opening night: Calling Home exhibition;
(b) Example of an image produced through and as part of my exploration

The process then informed another project, this time an independent study where I used drawing and painting to explore the phenomenon of *interiority*. In that project, conventional interpretations of interior architectural space were challenged using a combination of philosophical discourse and arts-informed inquiry. In fact, two aspects of arts-informed inquiry were incorporated; one was the use of art to help clarify and crystallise the complexities of philosophical discourse; the other was the use of art practice as research; that is, as a formalised means of generating new ideas and questions. Figure 23.5 illustrates this process (Franz, 2003).

One of the paintings produced was "Encounter with other (self)" (Figure 23.6), conveying how this and other images helped link an understanding of interiority to intersubjectivity to flesh. To date, this process of arts-informed inquiry has led me to an interpretation of interior architectural space, particularly domestic space, as a phantom limb or body prosthesis. The findings of the study were disseminated through refereed publication (Franz, 2004) and the paintings were exhibited in the university art museum (Franz, 2005a) as a way of making the visual outcome available to a wider, more public audience.

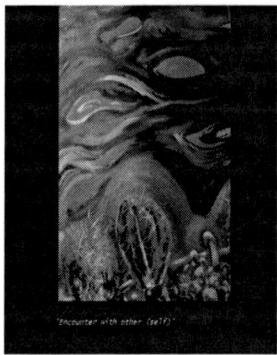

Figure 23.5. Arts-informed inquiry for the "interiority" project.

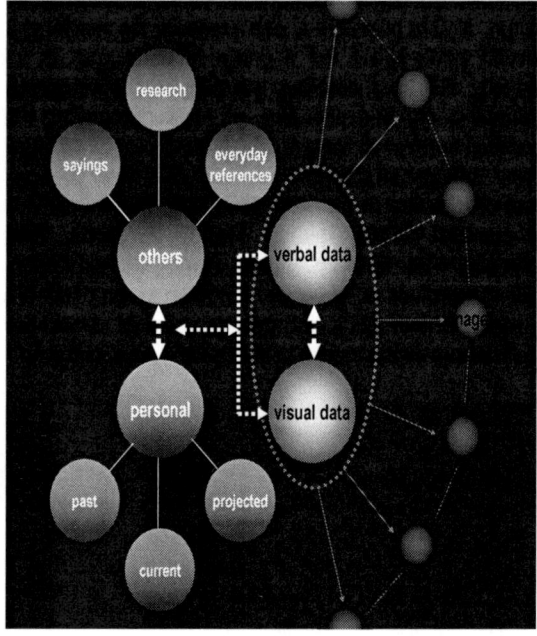

F
Figure 23.6. Encounter with other (self) (Franz, 2005a).

Arts-Based/Practice-Led Research

Another term used in connection with arts-based research is practice-led research. In general, practice-led research is used to describe research (or inquiry) generated by issues and questions arising in and through practice. This practice may be personal and artistic, such as that of a sculptor, dancer and so on; or it may be the practice of an organisation. In a paper I presented at a university speculation and innovation conference (Franz, 2005b), I extended the concept of practice-generated-research to include the notion of architecture practice as research: a situation where process and practice are integrally connected to and underpinned by a research ethos and criteria normally associated with conventional research.

CRITERIA AND STRATEGIES FOR DESIGNING, UNDERTAKING AND SUPERVISING ARTS-BASED RESEARCH

As mentioned previously, arts-based research is growing in acceptance and application and developing in turn a richer understanding of its qualities and potential. One of my

aims in writing this chapter has been to highlight through selected examples this richness and uniqueness. The picture emerging is one of an activity that:
- Embodies lived experience through the first-person narrative
- Provides for an open-ended steam of consciousness and spontaneity
- Invites serendipity and innovation
- Operates at symbolic, metaphoric levels, the ambiguity of which provides for multiple potential readings
- Is a form of making involving imaging, representing and testing
- Links mind and body, conception and emotion, the actual and the virtual
- Orientates the researcher and participant in different ways to the object of awareness and vice versa
- Is a space for describing, exploring, interpreting, awakening, challenging, confronting.... (Franz, informed in part by David Smith's presentation, AQR Conference, Sydney, 2003).

I argue, however, that capitalising on these qualities demands explicit attention at fundamental philosophical, theoretical and emotive levels, and recommend consideration of the following in designing, undertaking and supervising arts-based research:
- Understanding and making explicit one's philosophical relationship with the world (ontologically and epistemologically)
- Ensuring that the research question/topic is philosophically and methodologically compatible with arts-based research and its interpretive and critical sensibilities
- Ensuring that issues of rigour and ethics are explicitly addressed and that they reflect the nature of arts-based research in the qualitative research context
- Recognising and capitalising on emotive as well as cognitive dimensions and corresponding implications for the participant as well as the researcher
- Being emotionally and cognitively prepared to defend and substantiate a case for arts-based research.

Despite these challenges and demands, arts-based research remains an exhilarating and inspiring activity, reaching audiences and producing outcomes not possible through traditional forms of research. However, "as with science, the validity of art-based knowing and inquiry is ultimately determined by the community of believers who experience first-hand what the arts can do to further human understanding" (McNiff, 2008, p. 38). Here, then, is an invitation for you to become a member of this community and to contribute to its discourse and ongoing development through your teaching, research or supervision.

REFERENCES

Cahnmann-Taylor, M. (2008). Arts-based research: Histories and new directions. In M. Cahnmann-Taylor & R. Siegesmund (Eds.), *Arts-based research in education: Foundations for practice*. New York: Routledge.

Candy, P. (1989). Alternative paradigms in educational research. *Australian Educational Researcher*, *16*(3), 1–11.

Cole, A., & Knowles, J. G. (2008). Arts-informed research. In J. G. Knowles & A. Cole (Eds.), *Handbook of the arts in qualitative research: Perspectives, methodologies, examples, and issues* (pp. 55–70). Thousand Oaks, CA: Sage.

Eisner, E. (2008). Art and knowledge. In J. G. Knowles & A. Cole (Eds.), *Handbook of the arts in qualitative research: Perspectives, methodologies, examples, and issues* (pp. 3–12). Thousand Oaks, CA: Sage.

Finley, S. (2008). Arts-based research. In J. G. Knowles & A. Cole (Eds.), *Handbook of the arts in qualitative research: Perspectives, methodologies, examples, and issues* (pp. 71–82). Thousand Oaks, CA: Sage.

Franz, J. (2003, July). *Creative practice as a space for understanding.* Paper presented at the AQR Conference, Sydney.

Franz, J. (2004). At the in-side of the limit: Redefining the architecture, interior design relationship. In *LIMITS*: Proceedings from the 21st annual conference of the Society of Architectural Historians Australia & New Zealand, Melbourne, 2004, pp. 166–171.

Franz, J. (2005a, April 5–May 1). *At-the-edge-of-the-forest.* QUT Art Museum.

Franz, J. (2005b). *Practice-led research in architecture and design: The potential for something unique.* Paper presented at Speculation and Innovation Conference, Creative Industries, Queensland University of Technology.

Franz, J. (2007). Arts-based research in design education. *Qualitative Research Journal*, 7(2), 22–35.

Franz, J., Hedley, P., Molloy, M., & Smith, D. (2002, October 3–November 3). *Calling home.* QUT Art Museum.

Knowles, J. G., & Cole, A. (2008). Preface. In J. G. Knowles & A. Cole (Eds.), *Handbook of the arts in qualitative research: Perspectives, methodologies, examples, and issues* (pp. xi–xiv). Thousand Oaks, CA: Sage.

Kvale, S. (1995). The social construction of validity. *Qualitative Inquiry*, 1(1), 19–40.

Lawson, G., Franz, J., & Adkins, B. (2005). Rhetoric of landscape architecture and interior design discourses: Preparation for cross-disciplinary practice. *IDEA Journal*, 41–49.

Leavy, P. (2008). *Method meets art: Arts-based research practice.* New York: Guilford Press.

McNiff, S. (2008). Art-based research. In J. G. Knowles & A. Cole (Eds.), *Handbook of the arts in qualitative research: Perspectives, methodologies, examples, and issues* (pp. 29–40). Thousand Oaks, CA: Sage.

Schön, D. (1983). *The reflective practitioner.* San Francisco: Jossey-Bass.

Smith, D. (2003, July). *Arts informed inquiry.* Keynote presentation, AQR Conference, Sydney.

Trusler, A. (2002). Edge. QUT student project submission.

Weber, S. (2007). *About image-based research.* The Image and Identity Research Collective. Retrieved August 30, 2009, from http://www.iirc.mcgill.ca/txp/?s=Methodology&c=About%20image%20based%20research

Zeisel, J. (1981). *Inquiry by design: Tools for environment-behaviour research.* Cambridge: Cambridge University Press.

AFFILIATIONS

Jill Franz PhD
School of Design
Queensland University of Technology
Australia

NATASHA WARDMAN AND SUE SALTMARSH

24. ETHNOMETHODOLOGY:

The Situated Study of Professional Practice

HISTORICAL AND THEORETICAL ORIENTATION

Ethnomethodology emerged in the 1960s with the work of Harold Garfinkel, who coined the term in reference to the study of everyday methods, practices and processes through which people come to make sense of the social world (Garfinkel, 1967, p. 710). As a radical critique of predominant sociological research approaches and their underlying assumptions, Garfinkel's work was highly controversial. In particular, ethnomethodology presented an interpretation of the methods, processes and practices through which social actors produce meanings as a primary object of inquiry. Researching the social order, in other words, required investigating not only large scale events, broad trends, policy reforms and the like, but it also necessitated attending to the situated and continually changing landscapes of everyday meaning-making. Other leading early advocates of ethnomethodology were Aaron Cicourel and Harvey Sacks. Sacks in particular focused on "how, in ordinary conversation, in reporting some event, people report what we might see to be not what happened, but the ordinariness of what happened" (1995[1970], p. 216), as "it is in the communicative acts that social norms are maintained" (Rapport & Overing, 2007, p. 149). Sacks was the forerunner of conversation analysis. Unlike conventional sociological orientations, ethnomethodology "looks for order properties rather than culture, beliefs, or symbolic meaning" (Rawls, 2008, p. 710), an approach that challenged the orthodoxies of social research. Ethnomethodology required a shift in emphasis, suggesting that sociological enquiry and its processes of describing and interpreting social phenomena are productive of that which it purports to objectively observe and describe. For ethnomethodology, the social is continually being made and re-made through the meaning-making practices of both social participants *as well as* social researchers themselves (ten Have, 2007 p. 142). According to Rawls (2008):

> Only by treating objects, identities, and orders as social "things" made on the spot, by persons using shared methods or practices for doing so, can the essential social phenomenon of sensemaking, and the complex cooperative configurations of contingency and uncertainty that comprise social organization, be understood. (p. 723)

According to this view, social life is constructed through the socially situated use of language, texts and meaning-making practices in everyday life. It is contended that methods of sense-making sequentially build upon shared understandings and practices, in what Rawls (2008, p. 709) referred to as "the lived problem of order" through which workplace practices are both made stable and rendered unstable. Although it has undergone numerous transformations since the 1960s, ethnomethodology and the research approaches to which it has given rise offer a particularly productive resource for researchers interested in situated studies of professional practice. In particular, "ethnomethodological studies have provided a radical respecification of foundational matters across the human sciences" (Button, 1991, p. xi). In this chapter, we consider two important aspects of ethnomethodological approaches to professional practice research. Firstly, we offer a brief account of the professional practice of conducting ethnomethodological research and its commonly utilised techniques. Secondly, we consider ethnomethodological approaches to researching professional practice, and their usefulness in generating insights into the ways of seeing, saying and doing that characterise a given profession. We argue that ethnomethodological approaches make visible the politics of the everyday and the taken-for-granted, which we see as crucial to transformative research and professional practice.

THE PROFESSIONAL PRACTICE OF ETHNOMETHODOLOGICAL RESEARCH

The professional practice of ethnomethodological research involves attending to the ways that meaning and order are socially produced. Thus language – whether in documentary or conversational form – and social practice are primary objects of investigation. Garfinkel "rejected the idea of a single abstract theory being able to account for the diversity of human action, and called instead for concentrated empirical investigations of concrete contexts and settings" (Smith & Riley, 2009, p. 64). Along with a focus on interpretive practices (Miller & Fox, 2004) this renders observational analysis, documentary analysis, and conversation analysis particularly suitable approaches for ethnomethodological research.

Observational Analysis

Observation of "naturally occurring situations as closely as possible" (ten Have, 2007, p. 140) is one of the most widely used techniques in ethnomethodological research. Paradoxically, the ethnomethodologist must maintain familiarity with and distance from the world being studied, in order to both identify and deconstruct the processes of its constitution (ten Have, 2007). Familiarity is achievable only in the immediate and context-specific situatedness of action, otherwise known as *indexical expression* (Garfinkel, 1967, pp. 4–5). Observation analysis focuses on interactions, practices and organisation of "setting members"; and the researcher's familiarity with a given setting or professional practice field informs observation of "how setting members continually assemble and use the interactional and interpretive resources 'provided' by social settings to construct, defend, repair, and change social realities" (Miller & Fox, 2004, p. 38). Importantly, situations in which everyday sense-making practices are disrupted are likely to yield rich data (ten Have, 2007), but may also present particular challenges for the participant observer, because familiarity with the orthodoxies of the setting may form part of the researcher's own taken-for-granted sense-making practices.

Data for observational analysis are usually collected through participant observation (Pollner & Emerson, 2001), although non-participant or "hidden" observation may also be applied (Miller & Fox, 2004). The collection of observational data often involves audio/video recordings (ten Have, 2007), but taking field-notes is particularly recommended as "a crucial activity in any ethnographic endeavour, an essential step in the process of moving from the informal and intuitive knowledge that comes with experience and observation on to an analytic grasp of the forms of life being studied" (ten Have, 2004, p. 119).

Observational methods "include contextual information that is not always present in conversation analytic studies based only on mechanical recordings" (Miller & Fox, 2004, p. 45). Field notes may describe the setting, personal histories, gestures and facial expressions, and researcher reflections, in ways that are not necessarily applicable in audio recording. As ten Have (2004, p. 88) noted, "smiles and facial expressions, body movements and informal practices generally escape documentation". Thus field observations are particularly valuable for recording embodied interactions. However, observation is often not appropriate as a stand-alone strategy and is usually utilised in conjunction with other qualitative methods such as interviews (Miller & Fox, 2004) and documentary analysis.

Documentary Analysis

Garfinkel drew on Mannheim's conceptualisation of "the documentary method of interpretation" (Garfinkel, 1967) to describe how particular examples of texts or "natural documents" (i.e. not "researcher-provoked" – see ten Have, 2004, p. 88), written or otherwise, are treated as documentary evidence or clues of an underlying pattern/frame (Garfinkel, 1967; Pollner & Emerson, 2001; Smith & Riley, 2009). This presupposed underlying pattern simultaneously influences the interpretation or sense that is made from these particular examples (Garfinkel, 1967; Pollner & Emerson, 2001). Thus, "each is used to elaborate the other" (Garfinkel, 1967, p. 78), to continuously reaffirm (Coulon, 1995) a "common culture" (Garfinkel, 1967, p. 76). Documentary analysis may consider annual reports, prospectuses, financial accounts, websites, promotional videos, medical records, case notes in social work, and school records (Atkinson & Coffey, 2004, p. 57), many of which offer evidence of institutional and professional order and sense-making over time.

Documentary analysis therefore involves the analysis of documents in order to better understand *how* (Atkinson & Coffey, 2004) as well as why people or organisations document, represent and construct themselves in their setting – or in other words, it is "the study of practices of documentation" (ten Have, 2004, p. 104). This involves a focus on language or rhetorical devices used, including specialised jargon; shared meanings and cultural assumptions; intertextuality or relationships between documents; and actual or implied authorship and readership (Atkinson & Coffey, 2004, pp. 65, 66, 70). As documents are constructed and interpreted in many different ways and according to the particular backgrounds, knowledge and experience of the persons involved (Atkinson & Coffey, 2004), a documentary account is understood as a contextually situated construction of reality and should therefore be analysed as a text (Atkinson & Coffey, 2004; ten Have, 2004). Documents or texts cannot be solely relied upon for learning about the everyday operations and interactions of an organization, and records cannot be treated as unproblematic evidence (Atkinson & Coffey, 2004). However, because documents exist as "social facts" or constructions, they remain "an important part of ethnographic studies of everyday organisational life and work" (Atkinson & Coffey, 2004, p. 58).

Conversation Analysis

Some scholars (e.g. Goodwin, 2000; Miller & Fox, 2004) refer to ethnomethodology and conversation analysis as methodological domains in their own right. Others (e.g. Coulon, 1995; ten Have, 2007) may see them as more closely related (though still separate), with conversation analysis emerging (Silverman, 2006) or offshooting (Cuff, Sharrock, & Francis, 2006) from ethnomethodology. Still others depict conversation analysis as one of the most developed and influential forms (Maynard & Clayman, 1991) or fields (Coulon, 1995) of ethnomethodology. However, we refer to conversation analysis here as a useful analytic technique for ethnomethodological research, as

> The motivations for developing conversation analysis were those ethnomethodology proposed for the study of action... Conversation is an interactional activity in which participants fit their conduct – in this case their talk – to one another as the activity proceeds. (Cuff et al., 2006, p. 159)

Field research and participant observation frequently derive data from naturally occurring talk (Pollner & Emerson, 2001), or as Sacks termed it "natural language" (Rapport & Overing, 2007). For Garfinkel, "to recognize *what* is said *means* to recognize how a person is speaking" (1967, p. 30). Thus, "talk-in-interaction" (Sacks, Schegloff, & Jefferson, 1974) is sequentially (Heritage, 2004; Miller & Fox, 2004) or structurally (Peräkylä, 2004) organised, so that speakers and listeners display "appropriate" (Miller & Fox, 2004) or normative (Heritage, 2004) ways of interaction in order to demonstrate their social competence (ten Have, 2007).

Data for conversation analysis is usually generated through audio or visual recordings and then transcribed (ten Have, 2007) in order to study in detail the sequential organisation of interactions (Cuff et al., 2006). Elements of audio and/or visual transcripts of social interactions typically analysed include length and placement of pauses; simultaneous talk; speakers' intonation; stressed or elongated words; direction of gazes (Miller & Fox, 2004); turn-taking (Heritage, 2004; Cuff et al., 2006); negotiating overlaps and interruptions; how failures of interaction are dealt with; body posture in relation to talk; the organisation of laughter (Heritage, 2004); and Sacks' *membership categorization devices* (Sacks, 1995[1966], p. 238). All these practices make meaning-making and reality construction and re-construction possible (Heritage, 2004; Miller & Fox, 2004). However, ethnomethodologists rarely use formal interviews as a major data source, as they prefer to avoid data that is provoked by the researcher (ten Have, 2007). Thus, if "interviews are used at all, they tend to be 'situated' ones, that is, as ongoing talk in an observational situation, used as support for understanding what is going on" (ten Have, 2007, p. 149)

Critics argue that the mechanical, almost positivist emphasis placed on the rigorous collection and engagement with the details of conversation/interaction (Silverman, 2006; Smith & Riley, 2009) is at the expense of attending to their placement in the larger social context (Cuff et al., 2006). However, proponents argue that context is actually taken most seriously in conversation analysis (Silverman, 2006), and that researchers should not disregard the operational structure of common understandings, which in turn impact on the researcher's own sense-making (Garfinkel, 1967). The methods of observational, documentary and conversation analysis may be effectively applied to most settings, including workplace settings, for researchers interested in understanding *how* people get their job done (Goodwin, 2000; Atkinson & Coffey, 2004; Smith & Riley, 2009). In the following section, then, we turn to consideration of ethnomethodological research in professional practice.

ETHNOMETHODOLOGICAL RESEARCH IN PROFESSIONAL PRACTICE

Ethnomethodological research approaches, including ethnomethodological ethnography, have a well-established history in the sociology of workplace studies (Edwards & Belanger, 2008; Rawls, 2008). Perhaps not surprisingly, ethnomethodology has been taken up by researchers with a specific interest in its usefulness for understanding a wide range of issues in professional practice fields, notably in nursing and other healthcare professions (Wakefield, 2000; Harper, Ersser, & Gobbi, 2008; Jegede, 2009), social work (Montigny, 2007; Taylor, 2008) and education (Verkuyten, 2000; Roulston, 2001; Robinson & Cottrell, 2005). Such studies take a particular interest in the collaborative practices through which professional sense-making is accomplished, sustained, and at times reconfigured. These interests place emphasis on how professional practitioners constitute social order by both building upon prior practices *and* continually re-making them. This orientation is attractive to many researchers interested in the detail of professional practice, and the ways in which the recognisable orders associated with a given profession are established, maintained, and continually evolving.

Among the orthodoxies challenged by ethnomethodology is the distinction between "insider" and "outsider" research, insofar as researchers in this tradition tend to take up a position as participant observer with prior knowledge of and competence within the setting under observation. According to Wakefield (2000, p. 49), "ethnostudies draw on 'insider' knowledge of the setting, a fact of the account that puts the investigator in a 'uniquely adequate' position to impart knowledge or give an account of what is going on in the field". This approach reflects the view of specialised settings "as self-organising ensembles of local practices whose ways and workings are only accessible through a competent practitioner's in-depth experience and familiarity" (Pollner & Emerson, 2001, p. 123). Despite such experience and familiarity with the professional practice field, the ethnomethodologist ideally expects to exercise what Garfinkel and Sacks (1986) referred to as "ethnomethodological indifference", a term that implies unbiased and impartial recording of data, and a non-judgmental reporting of findings. However, as Wakefield's study of surgical nursing in the UK highlighted, the objective impartiality suggested by "ethnomethodological indifference" can be difficult to achieve in some situations. According to Wakefield, differing philosophies of professional practice between the researcher and members may contribute to "negatively oriented personal opinions and feelings" (2000, p. 52) that in turn distort the analytical process. Importantly to all work-based studies employing ethnographic methods, there is a need for both "constant attention to the phenomena to which one is exposed, as well as constant evaluation and re-evaluation of one's frames of reference and the influence of one's role on the social and cultural nature of the organizational and social practices that take place within the worlds of work we seek to (re-)present" (Brannan, Pearson, & Worthington, 2007, p. 400).

Attention to one's own methodological and epistemological frames of reference may be difficult when observing professional practices whose "knowledge and assumptions ... are so ingrained that [members] do not have to consciously think about them but which influence their attitudes and beliefs" (Harper et al., 2008, p. 321). Everyday practices being observed, in other words, may be guided by influences that are not readily apparent to practitioners. For the ethnomethodologist who has considerable knowledge and experience of the professional field under examination, there is an additional challenge in maintaining sufficient objectivity to render the familiar strange for the purposes of recognising that which is taken for granted. In turn, practitioners themselves are best placed to make decisions about developments in their professional work when offered opportunities to consider accepted practices from new vantage points:

> If we are to develop the capacity of practitioners to evaluate whether they want to make changes to tacit aspects of their practice, we need techniques to help them make what is familiar strange. By attending to how work gets done, rather than to how it should be done, we believe that work of the kind illustrated in this special issue can facilitate fruitful dialogue between research and practice. (Hall & White, 2005, p. 389)

This raises important questions pertaining to "the politics that lie at the heart of conducting research" (Brannan et al., 2007, p. 399). In particular, we argue that practitioner research focused on making the everyday visible is crucial to both transformative research and professional practice.

Like many other field-based qualitative inquiries, ethnomethodological studies are often situated at the nexus of professional and political change, simultaneously speaking to both accepted and contested knowledges, practices and power relations within a given field (Allen & Lyne, 2006; Cochran-Smith, 2006; Saltmarsh, in press). This is particularly the case with research that takes as its focus individual, disciplinary and organisational dimensions of professional practice. As one of us has argued elsewhere,

> Whether writing into and about expressly political issues, or addressing epistemological frameworks, bureaucratic processes, professional values and identities, or those mundane practices that represent "taken-for-granted" discursive norms, writing into or about contested spaces is itself a political act. (Saltmarsh, in press)

Although ethnomethodology is not generally seen as a politically motivated research orientation, as Denzin and Lincoln (2005, p. 6) have pointed out, "all research findings have political implications". Hence the view taken here is that even research that does not set out with expressly political aims and orientations is nonetheless political in its capacity to imply, suggest and/or initiate change. The usefulness of ethnomethodology in professional practice research lies in its attention to lived practicalities and complexities of the everyday, and its commitment to observing in close detail those ways of seeing, saying, knowing and doing that might be productively transformed.

CONCLUSION

In this chapter we have considered both the commonly utilised techniques for conducting ethnomethodological research and their usefulness for researching professional practice fields. The complexity and institutionally situated nature of most professional practice fields can offer considerable challenges for researchers interested in human activity. Ethnomethodology's orientation toward drawing on the researcher's informed knowledge and experience of a given setting or field is therefore particularly suited to practitioner researchers. For reflexive researchers, the role of participant observer also offers opportunities to explore the everyday taken-for-granted assumptions, methods, practices and processes that may influence their own sense-making, including that involved in data collection and analysis. Such approaches are well placed for generating new, setting-specific knowledge about how everyday professional practice is organised, as well as for contributing insights into how it might be re-made to achieve different outcomes and improvements. Ethnomethodological approaches, we argue, are particularly useful for making visible the knowledge, practice and politics of the everyday and the taken-for-granted, which we see as crucial to transformative research and professional practice.

REFERENCES

Allen, D., & Lyne, P. (2006). *The reality of nursing research: Politics, practices and processes.* New York: Routledge.

Atkinson, P., & Coffey, A. (2004). Analysing documentary realities. In D. Silverman (Ed.), *Qualitative research: Theory, method and practice* (2nd ed., pp. 56–75). London: Sage.

Brannan, M., Pearson, G., & Worthington, F. (2007). Ethnographies of work and the work of ethnography. *Ethnography, 8*(4), 395–402.
Button, G. (Ed.). (1991). *Ethnomethodology and the human sciences.* Cambridge: University of Cambridge.
Cochran-Smith, M. (2006). *Policy, practice and politics in teacher education: Editorials from the Journal of Teacher Education.* Thousand Oaks, CA: Corwin Press.
Coulon, A. (1995). *Ethnomethodology.* Thousand Oaks, CA: Sage.
Cuff, E. C., Sharrock, W. W., & Francis, D. W. (2006). *Perspectives in sociology* (5th ed.). Oxford: Routledge.
Denzin, N. K., & Lincoln, Y. S. (2005). Introduction: The discipline and practice of qualitative research. In N. K. Denzin & Y. S. Lincoln (Eds.), *The SAGE handbook of qualitative research* (pp. 1–32). Thousand Oaks, CA: Sage.
Edwards, P., & Belanger, J. (2008). Generalizing from workplace ethnographies: From induction to theory. *Journal of Contemporary Ethnography, 37*(3), 291–313.
Garfinkel, H. (1967). *Studies in ethnomethodology.* London: Sage.
Garfinkel, H., & Sacks, H. (1986). On formal structures of practical actions. In H. Garfinkel (Ed.), *Ethnomethodological studies of work.* London: Kegan Paul.
Goodwin, C. (2000). Practices of seeing: Visual analysis: An ethnomethodological approach. In T. van Leeuwen & C. Jewitt (Eds.), *Handbook of visual analysis* (pp. 157–182). London: Sage.
Hall, C., & White, S. (2005). Looking inside professional practice: Discourse, narrative and ethnographic approaches to social work and counselling. *Qualitative Social Work, 4*(3), 379–390.
Harper, P., Ersser, S., & Gobbi, M. (2008). Ethnomethodological ethnography and its application in nursing. *Journal of Research in Nursing, 13*(4), 311–323.
Heritage, J. (2004). Conversation analysis and institutional talk. In D. Silverman (Ed.), *Qualitative research: Theory, method and practice* (2nd ed., pp. 222–245). London: Sage.
Jegede, S. (2009). African ethics, health care research and community and individual participation. *Journal of Asian and African Studies, 44*(2), 239–253.
Maynard, D. W., & Clayman, S. E. (1991). The diversity of ethnomethodology. *Annual Review of Sociology, 17,* 385–418.
Miller, G., & Fox, K. J. (2004). Building bridges: The possibility of analytic dialogue between ethnography, conversation analysis and Foucault. In D. Silverman (Ed.), *Qualitative research: Theory, method and practice* (2nd ed., pp. 35–55). London: Sage.
Montigny, G. d. (2007). Ethnomethodology for social work. *Qualitative Social Work, 6*(1), 95–120.
Peräkylä, A. (2004). Conversation analysis. In C. Seale, G. Gobo, J. F. Gubrium, & D. Silverman (Eds.), *Qualitative research practice* (pp. 153–167 in 2007 paperback ed.). London: Sage.
Pollner, M., & Emerson, R. M. (2001). Ethnomethodology and ethnography. In P. Atkinson, A. Coffey, S. Delamont, J. Lofland, & L. Lofland (Eds.), *Handbook of ethnography* (pp. 118–135). London: Sage.
Rapport, N., & Overing, J. (2007). *Social and cultural anthropology: The key concepts.* Oxford: Routledge.
Rawls, A. W. (2008). Harold Garfinkel, ethnomethodology and workplace studies. *Organization Studies, 29*(5), 701–732.
Robinson, M., & Cottrell, D. (2005). Health professionals in multi-disciplinary and multi-agency teams: Changing professional practice. *Journal of Interprofessional Care, 19*(6), 547–560.
Roulston, K. (2001). Introducing ethnomethodological analysis to the field of music education. *Music Education Research, 3*(2), 121–142.
Sacks, H. (1995[1966]). Lecture 1: "The baby cried. The mommy picked it up". In G. Jefferson (Ed.), *Harvey Sacks: Lectures on conversation* (paperback ed., pp. 236–242). Oxford: Blackwell.
Sacks, H. (1995[1970]). Lecture 1: Doing "being" ordinary. In G. Jefferson (Ed.), *Harvey Sacks: Lectures on conversation* (paperback ed., pp. 215–221). Oxford: Blackwell.
Sacks, H., Schegloff, E. A., & Jefferson, G. (1974). A simplest systematics for the organization of turn-taking for conversation. *Language, 50,* 696–735.

Saltmarsh, S. (2009). Writing politically. In J. Higgs, D. Horsfall, & S. Grace (Eds.), *Writing qualitative research on practice* (pp. 139–149). Rotterdam: Sense.

Silverman, D. (2006). *Interpreting qualitative data: Methods for analyzing talk, text and interaction* (3rd ed.). London: Sage.

Smith, P., & Riley, A. (2009). *Cultural theory: An introduction* (2nd ed.). Malden, MA: Blackwell.

Taylor, C. (2008). Trafficking in facts: Writing practices in social work. *Qualitative Social Work*, 7(1), 25–42.

ten Have, P. (2004). *Understanding qualitative research and ethnomethodology*. London: Sage.

ten Have, P. (2007). Ethnomethodology. In C. Seale, G. Gobo, J. F. Gubrium, & D. Silverman (Eds.), *Qualitative research practice* (paperback ed., pp. 139–152). London: Sage. (Originally published 2004)

Verkuyten, M. (2000). School marks and teachers' accountability to colleagues. *Discourse Studies*, 2(4), 252–472.

Wakefield, A. (2000). Ethnomethodology: The problems of unique adequacy. *Nursing Times Research*, 5(1), 46–53.

AFFILIATIONS

Natasha Wardman
School of Teacher Education
Charles Sturt University
Australia

Sue Saltmarsh PhD
School of Teacher Education
Charles Sturt University
Australia

NITA L. CHERRY

25. ACTION RESEARCH

THE PURPOSE OF THIS CHAPTER

This chapter outlines the defining characteristics of action research and what has been expected of it as a culture of inquiry both in the past and in more contemporary times. Some of the opportunities it offers us for usefully engaging with complex issues of professional practice and life are explored, together with the challenges it poses. Suggestions for maximising its value while holding its rigour are offered.

SOME BACKGROUND

Action research has a long and interesting history. According to McTaggart (1992), the term was first used by J.L. Moreno, who is also famous for the introduction of the concepts of sociometry, psychodrama and role play. The name most frequently linked to the early development of action research, however, is that of Kurt Lewin (1946), who was concerned that traditional positivistic research methods had not been adequate to engage usefully with the social and economic dynamics of poverty and alienation that give rise to ethnic and class-based hatred.

Rapoport's (1970) definition was one of the most widely quoted when action research again started to attract serious attention from those both inside and outside the academy some decades later:

> Action research aims to contribute both to the practical concerns of people in an immediate problematic situation and to the goals of social science by joint collaboration within a mutually acceptable ethical framework. (Rapoport, 1970, p. 499)

Certainly the 1970s saw sociologists, educators and anthropologists become "increasingly preoccupied with life conditions which appeared unbearable in communities around us" (Fals Borda, 2001, p. 27) in places like India, Colombia, Mexico and Brazil.

So from the beginning, action research was positioned as a serious form of grass-roots engagement with fundamental community and social issues. Over the years, these ambitions for action research have not changed. In The Sage Handbook of Qualitative Research (Denzin & Lincoln, 2005a), it is described in this way:

> Action researchers are committed to a set of disciplined, material practices that produce radical, democratizing transformations in the civic sphere. These

practices involve collaborative dialogue, participatory decision making, inclusive democratic deliberation, and the maximal participation and representation of all relevant parties (Ryan & Destefano, 2000, p. 1). Action researchers literally help transform inquiry into praxis, or action. Research subjects become co participants and stakeholders in the process of inquiry. Research becomes praxis – practical, reflexive, pragmatic action – directed to solving problems in the world. (Denzin & Lincoln, 2005b, p. 34)

When claimed by the academy, action research was seen to have three aims: to helpfully contribute to the practical concerns of people facing problematic situations, to contribute to the goals of social science through increasing knowledge, and to help people learn so that their capacity to help themselves is enhanced and they become more self-sufficient in the future. Adding all this to ambitions of emancipation and consciousness raising (Freire, 1972), it is easy to understand how action research has come to be a container for many research practices and approaches. Indeed, Chandler and Torbert (2003) identified 27 different "flavours" of action research, ranging from an individual inquiring into his or her own practice through to large groups of people tackling issues of significance to whole communities. The time focus of these inquiries ranges from the here and now to the invention of the future. For a real appreciation of the diversity and range of research practices that have grown within the broad action research culture of inquiry, Chandler and Torbert's (2003) work and The Handbook of Action Research (Reason & Bradbury, 2001a) are excellent references that also provide helpful frameworks for navigating through this potentially bewildering territory.

The very richness of the possibilities for action research has also created some challenges for those who undertake it. In essence, these arise because issues that really matter to people create a range of divergent perspectives, interests and power dynamics. They also arise because some of the broad goals of action research already mentioned can come into conflict with each other during the research, simply because different goals matter differently to different stakeholders.

And challenges arise because the processes of action research themselves create tensions. One example is the tension between respect for the wishes of individuals and the desire for transparency in decision-making. Another is the reliance of action research on responsiveness and resourcefulness in working with whatever is at hand or comes up in the moment ("bricoleurship") when coupled with demands for research rigour and working within pre-approved ethics guidelines. These tensions are not insurmountable, but their management requires considerable skill and commitment from those who take responsibility for holding the research dimension of the work.

WHEN IT IS USEFUL

Action research is a helpful way to engage with complex issues of real-life practice that challenge existing knowledge and skills. The practice issues might be seen as problems or as opportunities; and they might affect individuals or groups, organisations or communities. Typically, these sorts of practice issues have some or all of the following characteristics:

- The questions or issues are broad or fuzzy; there might be considerable disagreement as to what the issues actually are, let alone how do deal with them.
- A wide range of factors is at play in the context, including messy dynamics and imbalances of power and authority between the actors and stakeholders involved.
- It will take time to engage with the issues, and the "end of the journey" is unknown in terms of time and effort; in fact under some circumstances the central issues or tasks carry dilemmas that can never be resolved, only "lived with" more effectively.
- There is the likelihood that a wide range of data can be created, including the significance of the lived experience of all those involved, whether they think of themselves as researchers or some other kind of participant.
- There is an opportunity for significant learning through acting and reflecting on the data that the research creates, even though some of that data will be unexpected and unwelcome, and will challenge existing mindsets; in other words, there are opportunities for exploring the strengths and the limits of existing practice.
- There is the chance to generate knowledge that includes both practice wisdom and theory that can be shared with others.

These are possibilities that are enticing, challenging, risky and fertile all at the same time, and it is not surprising that as action research became accepted as a legitimate tool for engagement with businesses and other organisations, some of the possibilities became difficult for graduate students and insider-researchers to sustain. Most notably, the original arm-in-arm, collaborative characteristics of action research in communities, and the transparency and no-holds-barred quality of its inquiry, became problematic in corporations and other organisations with secret competitive strategies and high levels of investment in not challenging hierarchies of vested authority. As an academic supervisor of many action research projects over a long period of time, much of my own effort has been focused on helping action researchers to stay in the action and not retreat to the margins where they write intense, anguished reflective pieces about their difficulties but accomplish little.

This retreat to the margins has been noted by major contributors to the action research literature. McTaggart (1992) suggested that the original values of action research are in danger of being corrupted:

> When we see modern technicist versions of action research and action learning which are oriented, for example, towards "quality control" or "staff development" with both being very narrowly understood, we understand how an emphasis on "learning" denies the fundamental liberatory aspirations of [action research] … "Workplace learning" too often means applying routines

invented by others, believing reasons invented by others, servicing aspirations invented by others, and giving expression to values advocated by others. In contrast, work place knowledge production means participation in the praxis of intervention and construction of new ways of working, in the justification of new ways of working and new working goals, and in the formulation of more complex and sophisticated ways of valuing work, work culture and its place in people's lifeworlds. (McTaggart, 1992, pp. 4, 6)

Zuber-Skerritt (1991) and Kemmis (1992) raised the same issue. For them, one of the values of action research is that it has the potential to liberate or emancipate individuals from socially conditioned mindsets and possibly even states of consciousness. This is consistent with what Freire (1972, p. 27) described as "conscientisation... The process by which people, not as recipients, but as knowing subjects, achieve a deepening awareness both of the socio-historical reality which shapes their lives and of their capacity to transform that reality."

In more recent times, the commitment to genuine participation in and with the world of human activity has been revisited and very clearly articulated by Reason and Bradbury (2001b). Their notion of participation goes well beyond simply taking action, and is quite different from sitting on the sidelines and wondering at the complexity of it all! Their description of participation as a world view is illuminating:

Our world does not consist of separate things but of relationships which we co-author ... At the centre of a participatory worldview is a participatory understanding of the underlying nature of the cosmos we inhabit and which we co-create. (Reason & Bradbury, 2001b, pp. 6–7)

From this perspective, every action and non-action has a consequence, and sitting on the sidelines is actually impossible. Action research involves heightened sensitivity to and deep inquiry into one's own intentions and impacts, intended and unintended, and one's complicity and collusion with the social dynamic in which one feels at home.

This perspective firmly locates the development of individual and collective praxis (practice informed by theory and reflection on experience) at the heart of the action research project. It also calls for the sort of reflexive practices articulated by Bleakley (1999), practices that are not only socially and culturally self-aware, but ecological, aesthetic and ethical, drawing on global as well as local dimensions.

SOME CORE FEATURES

Although variations in the form taken by action research are many, arguably these have a common heart: a commitment to sustained cycles of action, review of action, reflection and knowledge creation. One way to think of action research is that it involves three essential strands – the strands of doing, learning and knowing – that weave together in unique ways in each individual research project.

The Three Strands

The *action strand* is about doing things, not just thinking about them. The action might be planned and deliberate, driven by the insights of current practice wisdom as well as intentions and aspirations about how things should be. It might be informed by formalised theories, which can be tested in deliberate, planned action. Or it might be accidental or serendipitous action, stuff that just happens because the world of practice is not controlled or influenced only by the researcher or by the others involved. However it happens, action is the petrol in the tank of the action learning cycle. Without it, we are going nowhere. The fundamental intent of action research is not just to find out things but to take action that has the potential to make useful and noticeable differences in the world and, as action research was originally conceived, in ethical and sustainable ways.

The *learning strand* is about developing individual and collective practice, enhancing our ability and confidence to do different – possibly harder – things in the future. This second strand opens up the possibility of learning journeys that involve both the unconscious acquisition of skills and, on the other hand, highly self-conscious and self-reflective processes for gaining wisdom about ourselves in the context of practice (praxis).

Although much learning can occur unconsciously, in action research learning is deliberately enhanced by systematically reflecting on the outcomes of action, including the experiences it creates. Elsewhere (Cherry, 1999) I have listed some of the questions that are useful as triggers for reflection: "What exactly happened?", "What did I do?", "What did I say?", "What did others do or say?", "How did I feel about what was happening?", "Do I have any idea of how they felt?", "What was the impact of what I – and they – did?", "Did I do what I really wanted or intended to do?", "Do I know what I really intended?", "What would I do differently next time?" Peter Reason (2001) has given us many superb questions for creating learning from the perspectives of first person (I), second person (you and me) and third person (all of us). To arrange things so that those questions are raised again and again is central to the action research methodology. As a culture of inquiry it demands that a plan, an idea or a theory be checked against action and experience, and that action be informed and enriched by theory, planning and ideas.

Reflection takes us back into action of some kind, and action is followed by reflection of some kind, creating the conditions for the possibility that applied learning will take place. Systematic reflection about the action can create new or deeper insight and, equipped with this insight, we can slightly modify our interventions, or actively experiment with something quite different. Reflection can bring to bear a completely different perspective and lead to a reframing of what we are trying to do and actually need to do. Morgan (1983) suggested that in research, as in life, we meet ourselves:

> Both [conversation and research] are forms of social interaction in which our choices of words and action return to confront us because of the kinds of discourse, knowledge or action that we help to generate ... When we engage

in research action, thought and interpretation, we are not simply involved in instrumental processes of acquiring knowledge, but in processes through which we actually make and re-make ourselves as human beings. (Morgan, 1983, p. 373)

Practitioners and researchers both contribute to the nature of the professional experiences they have, alone and with others. Those experiences can create surprises for us, so that we experience what Argyris and Schön (1978) called dilemmas of effectiveness. This happens when our "theories" (whether or not we have articulated them to ourselves and others) fail because they have failed to effectively predict or influence the people and situations with which we are engaged. While it is sometimes possible – and tempting – to rationalise these away, it is also possible that the experience of these limits to our effectiveness will lead to a fundamental reframing of our understanding and theories of practice.

When this reframing leads to a significant shift in the way we and others view the world and in the way we act in the world, we tap the full potential of the action research process. The knowledge and wisdom of whole practice communities might be changed.

The *knowledge strand* entails enriching our collective wisdom about how and why things and people work; at its best, it creates new levels of insight – including theory – that can help in many different situations where people are grappling with complex challenges and opportunities. However, one of the most contentious aspects of action research has been the status of the knowledge it creates. Although it has not been alone in attracting criticism from the positivist and postpositivist perspectives, it has been an easy target over the years because it has not backed away from the importance of creating practice wisdom as well as contributing to the scholarly canon, or from the significance of the local as well as the elusive universal knowledge.

The debate about what counts as knowledge could be the subject of a chapter in its own right. In essence, this debate arises because there is a range of ontological and epistemological positions that can be taken about the nature of physical and social realities and the relationship of human consciousness to creating and being created by them. Reason and Bradbury (2001b) offered an elegant summary of the way in which contemporary action researchers might usefully position their knowledge claims:

> A participatory view competes with both the positivism of modern times and with the deconstructive postmodern alternative – and we would hold it to be a more adequate and creative paradigm for our times. However, we can also say that it also draws and integrates both paradigms: it follows positivism in arguing that there is a "real" reality, a primeval givenness of being (of which we partake) and draws on the constructionist perspective in acknowledging that as soon as we attempt to articulate this we enter a world of human language and cultural expression. Any account of the given cosmos in the spoken or written world is culturally framed, yet if we approach our inquiry with appropriate critical skills and discipline, our

account may provide some perspective on what is universal, and on the knowledge-creating process which frames this account. (Reason & Bradbury, 2001b, p. 7)

One of the strengths of action research is that it can utilise many research tools to gather or create data that guide the decisions about practice (what we will do next in this situation) and create useful knowledge (what are we learning that adds to what is already known by others). Action researchers and their collaborators might use tools that range from statistical analyses to procedures associated with the full range of qualitative research cultures. In this sense, action research can claim to be a culture of inquiry that provides a meta-container for many others. What it asks is that the procedures used to create or gather data or analyse and make sense of that data are used collaboratively, respectfully, transparently and with a commitment to take action and learn from that action as a core part of the research, not just subsequent to it.

WORKING WITH THE CHALLENGES AND KEEPING OPEN THE POSSIBILITIES OF ACTION RESEARCH

It is characteristic of action research that if it is "working", the knowledge and skills of both researcher and "other" will be significantly challenged and hopefully enriched by the process. This should not be surprising. Given the three strands that are woven together in action research and the nature of the issues that it tackles, it follows that the dynamics and issues that it generates are varied and at times contradictory or paradoxical. "The *action* involved is experimental – at times planned and guided and at other times spontaneous and 'free-wheeling'. The creation of *meaning or knowledge* is both systematic and creative – both about discovery or deeper understanding of what is 'out there' waiting to be known, and invention of something new and 'frame breaking'. When it comes to the *learning* strand, we both invent ourselves as well as discovering or finding ourselves" (Cherry, 1999, p. xv). It is important that the researchers involved understand when the different kinds of work are in play, and recognise the tensions and opportunities which arise as the different strands mix and at times even collide with one another. Using a range of reflective practices – like journals, "no blame" debriefs, appreciative and critical inquiry methods – can be very useful in surfacing these tensions, helping all those involved figure out how they will hold those tensions.

Action research is also challenging and useful because of its engagement with issues that are important and unfolding in real time. The sort of changes that the originators of action research had in mind went well beyond marginal shifts in the practice of individuals or small groups. They were concerned with challenging the mindsets of organisations and whole societies. Whatever its scale, this is not work for the faint-hearted.

Action research is challenging because it asks the researcher to be both rigorous in and responsive to an unfolding journey of practice in action. Rigour here means defining in advance the research protocols that both define the ethical practice of the research and define its claims to generating knowledge; and then sticking to them through the whole process.

As noted earlier, the knowledge claims of action research have been clearly located in terms of epistemology and ontology; and action researchers can co-opt a wide range of specific tools to guide, inform and make sense of the work during the life of the project. With each of these tools comes a set of protocols designed to ensure rigour in scholarly terms as well as guide their application. But I would argue that action research comes with its own guiding principles that inform researchers engaging with all the challenges and opportunities just described.

As originally framed, researchers work "arm-in-arm" with others (Prideaux, 1990), in a collaborative relationship on issues that matter to practice, to the actions and behaviour of those concerned. "Others" might be clients, colleagues, staff, customers or any other individual or group with an interest (declared or otherwise) in the action and its outcomes. In reality, collaboration might be sustained for only some phases of the action research cycle. For example, either the other(s) or the researchers might undertake a lot of the action; one or the other might lead the way in times of reflection and theory building; and patterns of involvement might change as further cycles of the process take their course. Whatever the level and focus of involvement, action research was originally developed around the core premise that people are to be engaged with, not acted upon or made the objects of research.

The nature of the others' interests can be volatile, political and conflicting, and those interests can therefore be complex in their own right. Thus one of the features of action research is the necessity for researchers to articulate how they will engage with these complexities of interest. The "rules of engagement" require care in their initial crafting as well as constant revisiting through their application, because they might themselves contain unintended imbalances of power, and unexamined marginalisation of voices and data, that replicate and further embed existing mindsets and practices. In the process of crafting rules and processes for engagement with the issues and others involved, participants become self-conscious, invited to tune in to assumptions and intentions that might otherwise remain influential, but outside awareness. This kind of reflective self-consciousness could be said to be one of the hallmarks of action research, no matter what its flavour.

Action research also calls for the examination and declaration of the value sets that are brought to the work. Whatever the particular ethical frameworks that might be agreed for a research project, transparency is usually a feature of action research. This means transparency about the intentions that are brought to the work, transparency about the ways decisions are made, how resources are acquired and used, how problems are tackled, and how communications and relationships play out.

The feature of transparency reflects and carries a number of the other features of action research. Transparency becomes the vehicle for deliberately making practice issues more problematic (why are we so sure this is the right thing to do?); challenging power dynamics (who is left out of this decision?); raising ethical issues (who is unintentionally affected by what we do?); triggering learning (what are our unacknowledged intentions, mindsets and blind spots?) and creating knowledge (what entrenched and authorised paradigms are we afraid to question?). Seen in these terms, transparency is arguably a defining feature of action research.

CONCLUSION

Action research has attracted the attention and energy of researchers over seven decades and has developed many forms. However, its fundamental commitment to the goals of shared human learning, enriched practice, ethical research and better ways of doing things that matter has not changed, Indeed, in the face of the challenges facing humanity and the ecosystems that contain it, it is arguable that the demand for robust action research practices is just as great as it was in the face of fascism and endemic poverty all those years ago. I believe that finding the confidence and skill to undertake action research remains one of the great responsibilities of the research community.

REFERENCES

Argyris, C., & Schön, D. A. (1978). *A theory of action perspective.* Reading, MA: Addison-Wesley.
Bleakley, A. (1999). From reflective practice to holistic reflexivity. *Studies in Higher Education, 24*(3), 315–330.
Chandler, D., & Torbert, W. (2003). Transforming inquiry and action: Interweaving 27 flavours of action research. *Action Research, 1*(2), 133–152.
Cherry, N. (1999). *Action research: A pathway to action, knowledge and learning.* Melbourne: RMIT University Press.
Denzin, N. K., & Lincoln, Y. S. (Eds.). (2005a). *The Sage handbook of qualitative research.* Thousand Oaks, CA: Sage.
Denzin, N. K., & Lincoln, Y. S. (2005b). Introduction: The discipline and practice of qualitative research. In N. K. Denzin & Y. S. Lincoln (Eds.), *The Sage handbook of qualitative research* (pp. 1–32). Thousand Oaks, CA: Sage.
Fals Borda, O. (2001). Participatory (action) research in social theory: Origins and challenges. In P. Reason & H. Bradbury (Eds.), *Handbook of action research: Participative inquiry and practice* (pp. 27–37). London: Sage.
Freire, P. (1972). *Cultural action for freedom.* Cambridge, MA: Center for the Study of Change.
Kemmis, S. (1992). Improving education through action research. In O. Zuber-Skerritt (Ed.), *Action research for change and development* (pp. 57–75). Aldershot, Hants: Avebury.
Lewin, K. (1946). Action research and minority problems. *Journal of Social Issues, 2,* 34–36.
McTaggart, R. (1992, November). *Action research: Issues in theory and practice.* Keynote address to the Methodological Issues in Qualitative Health Research Conference, Geelong, Deakin University.
Morgan, G. (Ed.). (1983). *Beyond method: Strategies for social research.* Beverley Hills, CA: Sage.
Prideaux, G. (1990). Action research, organisation change and management development. *Australian Health Review, 13*(1), 3–14.
Rapoport, R. N. (1970). Three dilemmas of action research. *Human Relations, 23,* 499–513.
Reason, P. (2001). Learning and change through action research. In J. Henry (Ed.), *Creative management* (pp. 182–194). London: Sage.
Reason, P., & Bradbury, H. (2001a). *Handbook of action research: Participative inquiry and practice.* London: Sage.
Reason, P., & Bradbury, H. (2001b). Introduction: Inquiry and participation in search of a world worthy of human aspiration. In P. Reason & H. Bradbury (Eds.), *Handbook of action research* (pp. 1–14). London: Sage.

Ryan, K., & Destefano, L. (2000). Introduction. In K. Ryan & L. Destefano (Eds.), *Evaluation in a democratic society: Deliberations, dialogue and inclusion* (p. 1). San Francisco: Jossey-Bass.

Zuber-Skerritt, O. (1991). Action research as a model of professional development. In O. Zuber-Skerritt (Ed.), *Action research for change and development* (pp. 112–135). Aldershot, Hants: Avebury.

AFFILIATION

Nita Cherry PhD
Faculty of Business and Enterprise
Swinburne University of Technology
Australia

FRANZISKA TREDE AND JOY HIGGS

26. CRITICAL INQUIRY

FRAMING CRITICAL INQUIRY

The term *critical inquiry* indicates that this type of research into practice is associated with the critical research paradigm. A critical inquiry is an exploration of the relationships between power, knowledge and ideology (Foley, 2000). Such an inquiry is based on a framework of critical consciousness, praxis and new possibilities, and therefore avoids alienating, objectifying, marginalising and generalising knowledge or other social constructs. Critical consciousness describes the notion of multidimensional awareness, which includes coming to understand the socio-discursive, structural–pragmatic, moral and technical–economic perspectives that shape current situations (Freire, 1973). Praxis is a term that describes action that is informed by such critical consciousness (Kemmis & Smith, 2008). Searching for new possibilities indicates that critical inquiry is an action-oriented and solution-focused approach.

Critical theorists conduct research as a response to issues such as reductionism, inequality, marginalisation, access inequity, social injustice, barriers to self-actualisation, or deterioration in human rights. Critical theorists are driven by the need to understand the reasons and interests behind hierarchical structures and the policies and practices that constrain democracy, social justice and human flourishing (Foley, 2000). They pursue the task of (1) explaining, portraying and describing a phenomenon, (2) understanding it from within traditions, social contexts, and perceived experiences, (3) questioning and problematising these interpretations, and (4) transforming the phenomenon. The aim of a critical inquiry is to transform people from being unaware or passive observers who lack control to participatory shapers of their own work and life.

Historically, critical theory can be traced back to the Frankfurt School, which was a social research institute established in Frankfurt in 1923 (Agger, 1998). It was purposefully established to develop critical theory as a response to modernism in the 19th century. Critical theory emerged first as a response to Nazism and totalitarian political systems in the 20th century (Newman, 2006), and it continues today as a response to economic rationalism, globalism, and climate change (Welton, 2005). Historically, critical theorists have responded to social and political issues of their time.

The first generation of critical theorists challenged the domination of knowledge generation by positivism and instrumental reason, and they critiqued the popular culture industry. The second generation of critical theorists critiqued scientism

(Habermas, 1972) and communication practices, especially in the public sphere (Habermas 1987a, 1987b; Kellner, 1989). The third generation of critical theorists critiqued relativism, postmodernism (Honneth, 1993) and oppressive positions on culture and gender (hooks, 1994). Currently critical theorists are responding to the oppressions of globalisation and to environmental and moral issues (Newman, 2009).

Because of their critique and resistance to dominant cultures and practices, advocates of critical theory have at times found themselves placed in unfavourable conditions. For example, Horkheimer, Adorno and Marcus, the leading thinkers of the Frankfurt School, had to flee Nazi Germany; Nelson Mandela was incarcerated in Apartheid South Africa; Paulo Freire had to live in exile from Fascist Brazil. These prominent people fought social injustice and for the good of society. Typically, critical inquiry focuses on important issues that affect not only individuals but society at large, and it acts on shared decisions for the good of all.

KEY FEATURES OF CRITICAL INQUIRY

The key features of critical inquiry are critique and transformation. Critique focuses on rethinking knowledge, power and practice and their interrelationships, as well as on awareness raising about current situations. Transformation is concerned with change, reconstruction and emancipation.

The Role of Knowledge, Assumptions and Interests

In his seminal book *Knowledge and human interest*, Habermas (1972) stated that knowledge is constituted through interests. Rather than starting with a question and searching for answers, a critical perspective starts with musing why this question rather than a different one was posed in the first place. Without questions and curiosity there would be no new knowledge and insights. Habermas argued that these questions are informed by biases, assumptions and interests that drive people to learn, think, explore, experiment, test current knowledge and discover or collectively generate new knowledge.

Questions emerge from assumptions and interests. The way we learn and practise is influenced by what we are interested in, what we want to listen to, and what we want to engage with. What we don't want to hear we tend to exclude. Further, Habermas contended that different types of questions are underpinned by different interests and generate different types of knowledge, which can be categorised as technical, practical and critical knowledge.

Technical interest is located in the empirico-analytical paradigm. It claims that there is objective, context-free, value-neutral knowledge. The intentions of conducting empirico-analytical inquiries are to control, replicate and predict events and actions. This perspective resonates with the goals of generating facts, establishing certainty, predicting future outcomes, and determining best practice. Technical interest is concerned with discovering one-way cause and effect mechanisms and applies empirico-analytical approaches to knowledge generation.

Practical interest is located in the interpretive paradigm. It accepts that knowledge is grounded in the social world, based on interpretations, and that a phenomenon can be experienced, perceived and interpreted in different ways. It is concerned with finding common ground among diverse groups of people. The aim is to reach consensus and agreement through dialogue and engagement with otherness (Gadamer, 1996).

Critical interest is located in the critical paradigm and is concerned with emancipation from unreflected, one-dimensional thinking and with unnecessary policies and practices that cause suffering, power imbalance and injustice. The aim is to liberate, transform and improve current situations.

Habermas (1972) contended that each knowledge type has its place and is important. For example, technical knowledge and skills are mostly required for technical tasks such as building bridges or operating on a brain tumour. Practical knowledge and skills are mostly required to negotiate decisions and solutions such as the type of bridge that is to be built, or informing patients about surgical and medical options so that they can make informed choices. Critical knowledge and skills are mostly required to think and act consciously in an increasingly more complex and diverse world. These skills include thinking for oneself, contesting ideas, and exposing different interests. Critical skills can focus inwardly on the self as well as outwardly on the wider community. Looking inward includes critically appraising one's impact on others; this can be an individual or collective activity. Looking outward includes critically evaluating forces that impact on current ways of thinking external to oneself. The emphasis of these skills is on the potential for doing things differently and acting in a chosen informed way on current situations. Critiquing with the moral intention to improve has been termed reflexive action.

A critical stance rejects the notion that technical knowledge is unconditionally superior to practical and critical knowledge. A critical inquiry embraces science, culture and politics and tries to overcome their divisions. Figure 26.1 illustrates the various influences that shape practice and highlights the importance of reflection and dialogue for transcending these forces of influence.

Horkheimer (1937/1972) argued that the shortcomings of quantitative (empirico-analytical) representations or knowledge can be found in their arbitrarily constructed reality. If we ask what is *best* practice, the answers automatically repress or hide other ways of practising. Such linear, closed questions conveniently ignore complexity and contradiction and instead claim rational logic and truth, and potentially close down further dialogue. Horkheimer saw a need to represent all of reality and he was convinced that such a reality had to embrace more than logic and facts. To provide an example of what is meant by all of reality, imagine the opposite of "straight". The answer could be round, wavy, zigzag, etc. The point is that there is not one correct answer but several possible answers.

Rather than thinking in dualistic terms such as straight and curvy, right and wrong, best and worst, critical theorists look beyond opposites towards higher order principles that transcend these opposites. In short, a critical inquiry searches to find new possibilities. The subject–object, knowledge–value, truth–myth dualities need to be seen in a reciprocal relationship. According to critical theory

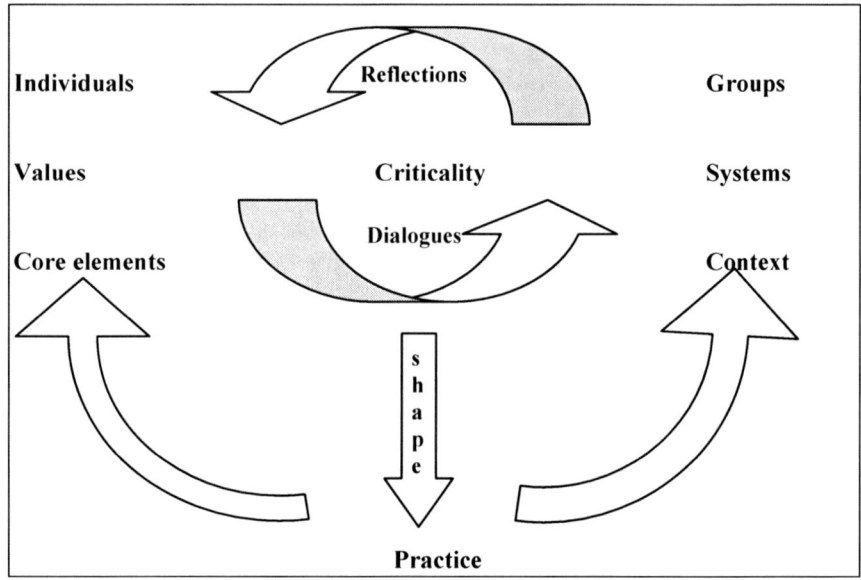

Figure 26.1. Influences that shape practice.

values and facts have a strong interdependence and cannot be separated. By relating opposites to one another, considering all the conditions and circumstances, and debating underlying interests, a critical inquiry approach offers critique with the purpose of overcoming opposites, contradictions and paradoxes (Carr, 2000). This type of reasoning is dialectical, whereas listing opposite views and taking sides is not. Listing opposites creates a divide and invites people to choose between the opposites, whereas overcoming opposites unites people.

A critical perspective presents the whole of reality as it is, without arbitrarily constructing an abstract reality with controlled variables. It is a matter of consciously including and considering different ways of knowing, rigorously discussing them collectively and appreciating their interdependence in order to explain, understand and then see the need for change. This process of critique helps people to reach shared decisions based on sound contextualised reasons for the given situation.

Power

Power plays in an important role in critical inquiry. Power implies control, responsibility, and the potential to distort or enlighten knowledge and social relations. Power can be repressive or emancipatory. Foucault (1982), one of the clearest thinkers of power analysis, claimed that power cannot be possessed but rather is exercised. Power exists only in action. It is played out in relationships where some people have more and others have less power. It manifests itself in what dictates our behaviour and what is seen as the norm. Power is closely related to traditions and cultures. Foucault argued that power can be experienced as repressive even when the intentions might be emancipatory. He stated that professional practice is littered with disciplinary, bureaucratic and authoritarian power dimensions.

Although critical theorists take a self-critical view of power and study how power relations are reproduced, Foucault challenged critical power analysis. He claimed that every power analysis is conducted from an ideology perspective and that the ideology of critical theory should be careful not to claim a stance superior to other ideologies. Foucault argued that a critique of power would simply shift power elsewhere but would not result in eliminating power imbalances. Rather than providing proof for his power analysis Foucault problematised power. His writing illuminates the complexity of power and serves as an invitation for debate (Brookfield, 2005).

Against Foucault's rather pessimistic theorising about power relations, a critical perspective on power relations appeals to humanity's ultimate aim of striving towards common social good. It rejects apologetic, purely relative and at times negative postmodern perspectives which potentially result in pluralistic paralysis and maintaining the status quo. At the same time, a critical perspective rejects determinist and predictive aspirations to social structures and relations (Trede, 2008). Horkheimer had a deep conviction "that thought was linked to social justice. ... and it was critical theory that was to distinguish itself [from phenomenology, existentialism and positivism] by addressing the political oppression of the day" (Rasmussen, 1996, p. 21).

Thus, a key feature of critical theory is to take a political, moral and rational stance on power relations, for grass roots democracy, social justice, and human rights. "Political" implies analysing and critically understanding power relations in their wider context. The critical perspective locates the personal as political. It makes an interdependent connection between the self (including professional work and personal life) and the wider social community, as illustrated in Figure 26.1.

Criticality

Criticality is philosophically grounded in the Frankfurt School, embracing ethical, moral, dialectical, social and self-aware dimensions of thinking, acting and being.

> It [critical thinking] meant analysing human activity in terms of power, and refusing to take the words, ideas, injunctions and orders of others at face value. It meant not letting other make up our minds for us. It meant abandoning the search for some fixed set of principles, and adopting a stance of informed and continual critique. Critical thinking was not a neutral activity. Like the critical theory from which it sprang, critical thinking was associated with the pursuit of social justice (Newman, 2006, p. 14).

Critical thinking opposes one-dimensional thinking and requires a distance from self, engagement with otherness, and becoming aware of unreflected, taken-for-granted practices. Marcuse (1964, p. 24) described critical thinking as:

> the ability of individuals to disengage themselves from the tacit assumptions of discursive practices and power relations in order to exert more conscious control over their everyday lives.

Critical thinking enables people to understand how current practices are reproduced and how injustices are upheld, and provides ideas and tools to overcome inequities. Critical thinkers are aware and sensitised to complexity, diversity and uncertainty, and they strive for critical knowledge and purposeful practices that improve current situations. Critical practice appreciates technical, practical and critical knowing and aspires to generate "really useful knowledge" (Thompson, 2000). Thompson explained that useful knowledge monitors current situations, whereas really useful knowledge is generated through sharing rich experiences and learning from actions. She emphasised the action aspect, the doing and learning, in critical inquiry. In a related term, critical pedagogy, the importance of critique of the status quo comes to the fore in teaching and learning, and the goal of emancipation of the individual through the empowerment of learning and knowledge is central.

OPERATIONALISING CRITICAL INQUIRY

Activities in critical inquiry can be roughly summarised as:
- critically questioning current practice
- exploring how practice could be different
- transforming practice, reflecting on transformed practice
- making further transformations.

There are diverse ways of operationalising critical inquiry. Well-known approaches of critical inquiry include action research (Zuber-Skerritt, 2006), participatory action research (Kemmis & McTaggart, 2005), and critical pedagogy (Freire, 1973; Mezirow, 1990; Brookfield, 2005). The two key features of a critical inquiry are critique and transformation, and the key elements of those processes are participatory, critical, dialogical, cyclical and relational principles and strategies. A critical inquiry generates rich contextual accounts of current practices; it scrutinises these descriptions for contradictions, injustices, inequities and oppression; through collective debates it creates possibilities to liberate current practices; and its purpose is to emancipate practices from unnecessary and unwanted constraints to inclusion, access and social justice.

Throughout the lifespan of a critical inquiry project, participants need to be aware of power relations and to make decisions on the following critical questions:
- What are the roles of researchers and participants or co-researchers?
- Are there real opportunities for cooperation and collaboration between researcher and practitioner and is participation enabling?
- How are technical, practical and critical ways of knowing blended and included?
- Is the nature of data collection monologic or dialogic?

- How is given voice to silences?
- Where are the boundaries of the topic under scrutiny: what is in and what is out?
- Who gets to make decisions? Are participants involved in data analysis?

Critical inquiry processes occur across three phases: listening, dialoguing and acting. Each phase revolves around thinking and doing, where one activity informs the other. Within each phase there are micro-cycles of all three phases.

Listening

Listening is about noticing, assessing, describing, reflecting and observing. The aim of the listening phase is to critically understand situations. A critical inquiry first establishes the context and the history that shaped the phenomenon under study. It avoids critique in a vacuum that disregards context.

First, descriptions and portrayals of current situation are collected. This phase is also described as awareness raising or *conscientisation*, a term coined by Freire (1973) to denote becoming aware of previously unreflected and taken-for-granted practices and situations. In this phase the researcher comes to understand the language that participants use and are familiar with, the dominant and marginalised ways of reasoning, and what the key concerns, challenges and interests are. Artefacts such as stories, paintings, policy documents, field visits and observations are collected, and participants are encouraged to give voice to their experiences, perceptions and interpretations.

The phenomenon under study needs to be grounded in perceptions and experiences. Activities in this phase might include mapping the current terrain, scoping, identifying current boundaries, systematically reviewing available materials and artefacts, portraying the theoretical discourse, describing key influential forces that shape the current situation, raising awareness, and helping others to develop insights into current situation. Characteristics of the listening phase may be located in phenomenological, ethnographic, grounded theory or hermeneutic approaches. The important distinctive feature in this phase is authenticity. Critical listening will shed light on implied intentions and values as well as contextual, organisational and professional authority issues that underpin current perspectives of the phenomenon under study. The purpose and the analysis of the artefacts collected in the listening phase will come alive in the next two phases.

Dialoguing

Dialoguing is about naming, articulating and critiquing. The aim of the dialoguing phase is to negotiate shared understanding. Processes used to reach agreement include exposing which aspects and perspectives in the situation are silenced or marginalised, exploring underlying values and interests, and challenging possible ways forward. Key questions to ask in this phase include: What factors create barriers to participation, inclusion, learning or self-actualisation? What should be and what ought to be (happening)? Such questions are intended to provoke critical thinking that leads to understanding the need for change.

By generating critical questions understanding is enhanced. A critical dialogue on these questions has the intention of articulating new meaning based on collective understanding.

Acting

Acting is about reframing, emancipating, testing and doing; action comprises an important part of the concept of critical inquiry. Describing and understanding current situations critically is done with the aim of designing action plans for change. Action is guided by critical consciousness, which means that there is a clear understanding of why the changes are desirable. Transformation is not simply about doing things differently, but doing things differently to improve the situation. Examples of aims of action are to enhance student participation, to undertake shared decision making with patients, or to arrange better access for underrepresented groups to community facilities. These transformations are not only changes that individual people make in their professional practice; they also influence wise and collective action. The action phase enables people to operationalise their once tacit values purposefully in their practice. It brings clarity and chosen purpose to their practice and skills to deal collectively with complexity, uncertainty and diversity.

CRITICAL FINAL COMMENT

Critical inquiry as described above is the ideal version. It is meant to unsettle readers and stimulate critical approaches to their current ways of conducting research. In reality, it is difficult to establish conditions for coercion-free discussion, for considering all perspectives and for being inclusive and critical. Researchers in critical inquiry are not immune to constraints such as time pressures. However, a critical perspective reminds us all to not stop challenging and dialoguing and pursuing a better shared world. Critical inquiry strives for critical understanding of current practices which can help to recognise the need for disobedience, alternative knowledge, creativity, action, or pursuit of social justice, citizenship and social transformation. In troubled times like these where learning and teaching are bureaucratised, caring is taken out of health outcome measures, and the environment is sacrificed for economic gain, not only a critical stance to the status quo but critical action is needed.

REFERENCES

Agger, B. (1998). *Critical social theory: An introduction.* Oxford: Westview Press.
Brookfield, S. D. (2005). *The power of critical theory for adult learning and teaching.* Maidenhead, Berkshire: Open University Press.
Carr, A. (2000). Critical theory and the management of change in organizations. *Journal of Organizational Change, 13*(3), 208–220.
Foley, G. (2000). *Understadning adult education and training.* Crows Nest, NSW: Allen & Unwin.

Foucault, M. (1982). The subject and power. In H. L. Dreyfus & P. Rabinow (Eds.), *Michel Foucault: Beyond structuralism and hermeneutics* (pp. 208–226). Chicago: University of Chicago Press.
Freire, P. (1973). *Education for critical consciousness.* New York: Seabury Press.
Gadamer, H.-G. (1996). *Reason in the age of science* (F. G. Lawrence, Trans.). Cambridge: The MIT Press.
Habermas, J. (1972). *Knowledge and human interest* (J. J. Shapiro, Trans.). London: Heinemann.
Habermas, J. (1987a). *The theory of communicative action (Vol. 1): Reason and the rationalization of society* (T. McCarthy, Trans.). Oxford: Polity Press.
Habermas, J. (1987b). *The theory of communicative action (Vol. 2): The critique of functionalist reason* (T. McCarthy, Trans.). Oxford: Polity Press.
Honneth, A. (1993). *The critique of power: Reflective stages in a critical social theory.* Cambridge, MA: MIT Press.
hooks, b. (1994). *Teaching to transgress: Education as the practice of freedom.* London: Routledge.
Horkheimer, M. (1937/1972). *Critical theory* (M. J. O'Connell et al., Trans.). New York: Herder and Herder.
Kellner, D. (1989). *Critical theory, Marxism and modernity.* Oxford: Polity Press.
Kemmis, S., & McTaggart, R. (2005). Participatory action research: Communicative action and the public sphere. In N. Denzin & Y. Lincoln (Eds.), *The Sage handbook of qualitative research* (3rd ed., pp. 559–603). Thousand Oaks, CA: Sage.
Kemmis, S., & Smith, T. (Eds.). (2008). *Enabling praxis: Challenges for education.* Rotterdam: Sense Publishers.
Marcuse, H. (1964). *The one dimensional man.* Boston: Beacon.
Mezirow, J., & Associates. (1990). *Fostering critical reflection in adulthood.* San Francisco: Jossey-Bass.
Newman, M. (2006). *Teaching defiance: Adult education in action, a book written in wartime.* San Francisco: Jossey-Bass.
Newman, M. (2009). Educating for a sustainable democracy. In P. Willis, S. McKenzie, & R. Harris (Eds.), *Rethinking work and learning: Adult and vocational education for social sustainability* (pp. 83–92). USA: Springer Science and Business Media.
Rasmussen, D. M. (1996). Critical theory and philosophy. In M. Rasmussen (Ed.), *The handbook of critical theory* (pp. 11–39). Oxford: Blackwell.
Thompson, J. (2000). *Emancipatory learning.* Retrieved October 13, 2008, from http://www.niace.org.uk/information/briefing_sheets/Emancipatorylearningmar00.html
Trede, F. (2008). *A critical practice model for physiotherapy practice: Developing practice through critical transformative dialogues.* Saarbrücken, Germany: Vdm Verlag Dr. Müller.
Welton, M. (2005). *Designing the just learning society: A critical inquiry.* Leicester: NIACE.
Zuber-Skerritt, O. (Ed.). (2006). *New directions in action research.* London: Falmer Press.

AFFILIATIONS

Franziska Trede PhD
The Education for Practice Institute
Charles Sturt University
Australia

Joy Higgs AM PhD
The Research Institute for Professional Practice, Learning & Education
The Education for Practice Institute
Charles Sturt University
Australia

DONNA BRIDGES AND SHARYN MCGEE

27. COLLABORATIVE INQUIRY:

Process, Theory and Ethics

Collaborative inquiry (CI) is an umbrella term used in new paradigm research (Reason & Rowan, 1981) to describe a participatory, democratic, reflective method of inquiry that emphasises the need for research to operate as a vehicle for social change. Collaboration in research has been highlighted by governments, research funding bodies, and human service organisations as a way forward. However, CI has epistemological and ontological roots and social political goals that are different from (simply) collaboration in research. In this chapter we discuss the usage of the term *collaboration*, demonstrating how CI is embedded in and centred around critical discourses in research that focus on creating meaningful social change and shared decision making between researchers and research participants.

The meaning of CI as a critical alternative to standard research approaches is examined and the conceptual perimeters, underlying principles, and motivations of CI are explored. We show how genres of research incorporate CI into their methodologies and explain how CI underpins these approaches to participatory research. The four phases integral to conducting a CI are outlined, accompanied by CIs that were conducted by each author. Although set in two distinct research environments, both inquiries were influenced by feminist principles and emerging critiques of social theory and social research models.

WHEN IS COLLABORATIVE RESEARCH NOT A COLLABORATIVE INQUIRY?

Collaboration is a term used widely in research communities to describe the process of working with research partners in all or part of a research inquiry. This method of research is embraced within a variety of disciplines and across a broad range of fields and methodological genres. For example, in the physical sciences collaboration is used in large scale research projects that form cooperative alliances between universities, industry and governments. The scientific community views collaboration as an exchange of ideas, resources, and information that allows the scope of research to reach into otherwise unavailable regional and global terrains (McGuinn, 2004). Collaborative research is also common in small and large-scale projects in education and in business and management research. Such models are characterised by "relationships involving exchanges of ideas and practices" (McGuinn, 2004, p. 4). Strategies of cooperation between partners can be politically advantageous and can improve academic rigour through the joint process of increasing conceptual and analytical aspects of research (Lingard, Schryer, Spafford, & Campbell, 2007). However, although collaborations have become more frequent they often occur without challenge to the epistemological orthodoxies of positivist research or to the hierarchies that exist in the world of research. On the other hand, CI is a paradigm that has traditionally challenged the central premises of positivist research and power relationships in academic research (Bray, Lee, Smith, & Yorks, 2000; Heron & Reason, 2001).

DISTINQUISHING COLLABORATIVE INQUIRY

CI is inherently challenging to the epistemological position of standard research approaches in several ways. It is research that involves participants as co-inquirers who have a role in informing and shaping the research aims, processes and outcomes. Consequently, power differentials are circumvented by the process of shared control by co-researchers in horizontal research groups where the research ultimately becomes a "joint enterprise" (Riger, 1999). The notion of being an expert about one's own life and experience is a fundamental keystone of CI. In standard research approaches, structured hierarchies too often contrast researchers as experts with informant as objects of the research. This diametrical opposition between the researched and researcher, positions the researched as incapable of giving meaning to their own experience (Reason, 1994). CI researchers aim to demystify research and to empower people to research their lived experience within the context of wider sociopolitical environments. The aim of CI is to involve all co-inquirers in cycles of reflection where understanding can be gained, knowledge produced, and change enacted (Torbert, 1983).

The epistemological position of collaborative research is that democratic participation in research opens channels of communication and engages all participants in a dynamic and cyclical process of meaning making. CI focuses upon imparting know-how about research methods so that individuals and communities can be empowered to understand and produce knowledge about their own lives. The premise of this position is that "knowledge is power" and that where knowledge is produced and located is vitally important to the emancipation of socially and politically disadvantaged individuals and groups (Lather, 1991).

Some social groups equate (externally managed) research with the stigmatising of their communities (Riecken, Strong-Wilson, Conibear, Michel, & Riecken, 2005). Researchers are viewed as passive consumers of information, ill-equipped to challenge the oppressive social and political situations they encounter. Research used for understanding without social change is perceived as irrelevant. CI methods have the potential to restore faith to communities who have come to view research as a bureaucratic way of avoiding social change. The participatory and action focus of CI is inclusive of participants, deliberately targeting issues that require social justice and social change interventions.

Participatory and democratic methods of research are inclusive and potentially emancipatory. They provide a richness of understanding that cannot be accessed by more standard interview methods. The "drive-by" method of data collection

(Riger, 1999, p. 1011) collects information from informants of research in brief, one-off interviews, a frequent approach in qualitative research. Riger (1999) and Bray et al. (2000) argue that interviews that are one-off or brief will not adequately capture the rich lived experience of people. They lack the potential to capture a true understanding of the meaning of experience or to access the deeper meaning of experience and people's interpretations of their experiences. By sharing power and establishing a framework for democratic participation, research becomes accessible, diminishing hierarchies and challenging the elitist position of researchers over participants (Treleaven, 1994; Riger, 1999).

COLLABORATIVE INQUIRY: GENRES OF THEORY AND PRACTICE

A number of research genres draw on the methods of CI to achieve the goals of participation and democracy in the research process (Bray et al., 2000). In this section we outline and discuss the most prominent of these: action research, participatory research, feminist methods, and cooperative inquiry.

Action Research

Action research (AR) is arguably the most influential of the CI approaches and is responsible for providing guiding principles in the development and emergence of many other models of CI, including participatory research, critical action research, classroom action research, action learning and action science (Kemmis & McTaggart, 2005). AR emphases the need for researchers (from outside a community or organisation) to work closely with clients/stakeholders (from inside the community or organisation) in a collective and collaborative inquiry to define a problem, seek a solution to it and act upon that solution in an integrated cycle of reflection and action (see Chapter 25). At all stages of a research inquiry AR is epistemologically concerned with collaborative processes that place all partners in roles that maximise their expert strengths, and ultimately the contributions of both researcher and client are honoured and utilised (Carr & Kemmis, 1986).

Participatory Research

Participatory research (PR) is defined as research where individuals and groups can work with researcher facilitators to produce knowledge about issues and to work toward resolving problems through action (Clover, 2007). PR is commonly used synonymously with CI, as they embrace identical principles. Both seek to reduce instances where researchers have complete control of processes and outcomes and where research as a knowledge industry contributes to furthering inequality. PR emphasises that people are at the locus of research and that social transformation should be the goal (Joyappa & Martin, 1996). It aims to empower community members through engaging them in CIs that increase members' power and voice, ultimately working toward overcoming oppressive sociopolitical conditions.

Although PR and participatory action research (PAR) are sometimes used interchangeably, subtle differences exist. They can be distinguished by the focus of PR on increasing citizen voice and power (liberation) and the focus of PAR on the cooperative aspects of research (Joyappa & Martin, 1996). Participatory inquiries seek to build, within communities, the capacity to do research, to interpret the findings and to use the results to create change, while supporting people in self-determination and in overcoming inequity (Clover, 2007).

Feminist Methods

Both participatory and action research models have been influenced by the specific goals and principles of the women's movement and by feminist critiques of traditional positivist research and social theory. There is no one feminist position: feminist methods are diverse. Nevertheless, some guiding principles exist. Feminist research methods start from the standpoint of women, challenge gender bias, and question androcentric assumptions in research that privilege the world view of educated, white, male researchers (Lather, 1991; Reinharz, 1992). Feminist methods are deeply committed to the principles of CI. CI provides feminist researchers with a framework to raise consciousness about oppressive conditions. Feminist PR identifies underlying power imbalances and seeks to change them. Relationships, responsibilities and action are at the heart of feminist PR. It is "an epistemology that assumes knowledge is rooted in social relations and most powerful when produced collaboratively through action" (Fine et al., 2004, p. 95).

Cooperative Inquiry

Cooperative inquiry (or human inquiry) is a research genre that emerged from the work of John Heron (e.g. 1981) and Peter Reason (1988). Cooperative inquiry aims to do "research *with* people, not *on* people". This principle involves certain aspects of researching that cannot be separated from the notion of CI. Firstly, a basic tent of cooperative inquiry is that human experience cannot be understood through experiments or through simply collecting data from people. To properly explore and understand human experience the researcher must come from inside the experience. Secondly, it is acknowledged that people are active agents, capable of understanding and interpreting their own experience. Further to this, accurate social research can only be conducted when engaged participants are self-directing. Therefore, everyone participating in the research becomes a co-researcher, equally engaged and responsible for the planning and processes involved. Like all methods within the framework of CI, cooperative inquiry is an active method; it seeks practical solutions to problems and applies strategies of creative action (Heron & Reason, 2001) to transform them. Cooperative inquiry uses cycles of reflection and action to understand, make sense of, and see new creative ways to view a situation. It then focuses on how change may be implemented to improve people's lives.

THE FOUR PHASES OF COLLABORATIVE INQUIRY

There is no dogma about how to conduct CI, but there are some guiding principles to be followed. We propose a four-phase approach that involves the phases: initiation, cohesion, immersion, and consolidation (see Figure 27.1). The phases can be incorporated cyclically and all phases may be repeated as needed. The subsequent sections, "Practice, process, and reflection: the collaborative inquiry experience" by Donna and "The collaborative inquiry cycle: reflections and experience" by Sharyn, illustrate how the phases were used by the authors in CI research.

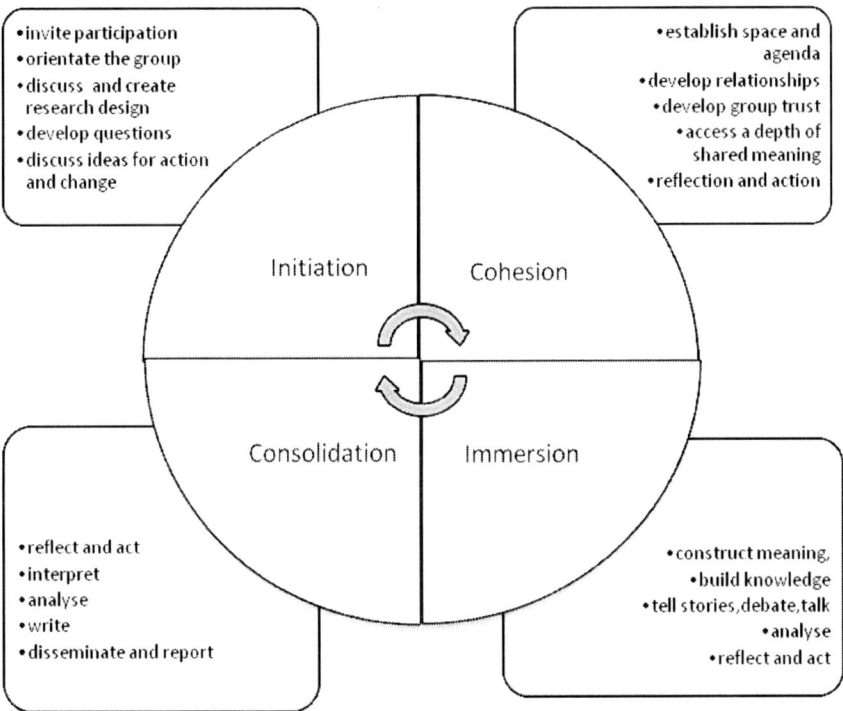

Figure 27.1. The Four Phases of Collaborative Inquiry.

PRACTICE, PROCESS, AND REFLECTION:
THE COLLABORATIVE INQUIRY EXPERIENCE, BY DONNA BRIDGES

My decision to form a CI group was born from the desire to do research for my honours degree that was ethical as well as rigorous. My feminist standpoint was that the paradigm of traditional positivist research was problematic. I wanted to do collaborative research that would offer participants something of value, seeking reciprocity as a way of ensuring that the research was not exploitative. The aims of the research were to understand and contribute to knowledge about women's roles in the community and non-government sectors in New South Wales (NSW) in terms of the nexus between women's personal agency (potential empowerment) and the professional capacity of workers to contribute to social justice and change.

Phase One: Initiation

I initiated a CI through existing networks in community management and within my local community. The six women who joined the group were all employed in the community and non-government sectors in NSW. Their roles included women's health counsellor, social worker, and community development worker. The women also described their roles based on political motivations, and these included community activist, change agent, and advocate. Members met in my home, to discuss the research and have dinner afterwards.

In initiating the inquiry I followed Treleaven's (1994) premise that participation is generated and shaped by two formative dimensions: the creation of space (a framework of enabling structures) and the development of a context. The initiation phase of the inquiry included a welcoming that immediately and intuitively began to create space for the group to become co-creators of a research inquiry. The women told stories about their backgrounds, brainstormed ideas of their own and debated those put before them by me. The epistemological assumption I made as a feminist researcher was that individuals in the group were empowered to exercise agency through their political and personal choices as they participated and played a role in co-design. Equal participation and cooperation are essential at this stage of the inquiry. This phase can also transform the researcher's role from academic researcher to co-researcher.

Phase Two: Cohesion

The second phase solidified details such as times to meet, tape-recording the sessions, and how emergent themes would be detailed and recorded. I was concerned about communicating the idea that research could be co-created as well as facilitating the development of an environment that would support participatory interaction. In this phase the group explored the research agenda. Issues such as domestic violence, suicide, refugee migration, and the stigmatisation of mental illness were identified as crucial in the work roles of the women, but further to this, they identified the need to understand the wider context where these issues reside. They explored their roles and the impact they had on community structures as they worked toward achieving social change. The group sought frameworks for creative reflective processes to analyse the social world they worked in and how they could act to make change within these contexts.

Phase Three: Immersion

The third phase was one of a deepening commitment (see Reason, 1994) to the process and within group relationships. New topics emerged as more questions were posed and the complexity of the field was understood and scrutinised. The group was eager to engage and as they warmed to the process they argued and debated, told stories and gave advice. Within a space that was growing in empathy and intimacy, they reflected about their roles as advocates and workers. I saw my role as encouraging reflective processes, recapping prior discussions and reminding the group of their goals. Reason (1994) suggested that the depth of this phase results in the cycling and recycling of all of the first three phases, and the phase operates as a "critical and risk-taking exploration" (p. 45). I found that reflective processes led to trust, which in turn supported members to challenge themselves and each other, ultimately avoiding a superficial process.

In this inquiry the cyclic dimension of reflection and change was dependent upon what each person chose to reflect upon, and in their own workplaces, chose to act upon. As they were a dispersed group with no one organisation or project as a change focus I did not encourage group members to make change in their practice or in their organisations. Each group member had a abiding sense of being a "change agent" and I did not want to force or manipulate action from them solely for the purposes of the research. Rather, I wanted to capture how they reflected on their action, their experience of who they were as community workers, and their personal agency at work. The group reflected on thought and action through the process of storytelling where members conveyed experiences and shared the process of interpreting professional encounters (see Treleaven, 1994), which in turn led to the collection of rich and meaningful data and knowledge.

Phase Four: Consolidation

I had positioned the co-creation of knowledge during group interaction as central, but my experience of writing about the project meant that I was thinking and learning as I wrote. I was creating knowledge without equal input from the participants. I worried about how I was representing participants, whether I was furthering interpretations, and ultimately about the consequences of my lone writing endeavour.

In keeping with CI, I was transparent about data analysis methods and offered the transcripts and the final draft of my writing for comments and potential contributions. My process of writing and theorising had sometimes changed the meaning from that constructed jointly by the group. When I envisioned the CI group I had not anticipated the need to write collaboratively. Writing together would have required too great a commitment from the group in time, energy and theoretical input. The balancing act that was required to manage the group's editorial rights and my academic demands was time-consuming and awkward, but the process resulted in deeper reflection and more intricate constructions of meaning. In the long run my voice as researcher was privileged over the voices of participants and not the other way around, as is sometimes said to occur in CI (see Hoskins & Stoltz, 2005). This power differential left me feeling uncomfortable and at a loss to restore the earlier ideals of participation and co-creation. I questioned what the research had left the group with. However, my faith in the reciprocity of the method was restored through reflective pieces written by participants about their experience of the CI, which conveyed how valuable the group had been to all involved.

THE COLLABORATIVE INQUIRY CYCLE: REFLECTIONS AND EXPERIENCE, BY SHARYN MCGEE

My experience of collaborative inquiry was a project developed between older women, academics and health professionals. This project was embedded in an AR approach (based on Carr & Kemmis, 1986), with a feminist lens, and was explicitly concerned with engaging older women as co-researchers in individual and collective discussions around their participation in community organisations and government consultations (see Power, Hudson, Leonard, McGee, & O'Beirne, 1994).

The project was designed to investigate the process of empowerment as it manifested itself in three community organisations operated by and for older people. These three organizations were chosen because they represented a diverse set of interests and issues for older women and were readily accessible through our existing networks. As a group we were interested in the role of older women[1] in organisations and within wider society.

Phase One: Initiation

The momentum for this project arose from a conference about challenging the myths of aging, which had a specific focus on women. It was embedded in a dialogue between the Women's Research Centre at the University of Western Sydney, community organisations, and professionals working in Greater Western Sydney (GWS). The conference provided a forum for older women to speak out about the way their voices went largely unheard in the development of government policies and programs. The participants strongly called for continuing the dialogue and developing collaborative research *with older women as subjects, not on older women as objects* of research, firmly embedding the inquiry in traditions of feminist research (see Reinharz, 1992). A mixed group of women, who were concerned with issues of aging and who lived or worked in GWS, came together after the conference. We chose to use an AR methodology because the framework it provided combined democratic collaboration with a clearly articulated methodology. The focusing and shaping of the research was an ongoing process, incorporating cycles of observation, reflection, planning, action and evaluation (based on Carr & Kemmis, 1986). Thus the group met regularly throughout the project. There was a strong collaborative process in the design and planning of the project and in terms of managing and leading the workshops.

Phase Two: Cohesion

In the early stages of the project a great deal of energy was generated among the group. No one member dominated or influenced the lively debates. Generally we looked forward to seeing each other, and trusting relationships came into being without much effort on our parts. Cohesion of the group arose quite quickly.

An issue that arose in this phase was associated with attempts to fund the research. Organisational requirements and the processes of proposal writing and submissions for funding didn't support inclusive approaches to research. Factors such as tight deadlines, the need to convince funding bodies of the importance of research questions, and the associated need to use well-established research methodologies, impinge on and militate against the use of time-consuming processes that emphasise discussion and reflection. It took several attempts and 12 months before the project was funded. Thus at the commencement of the first workshops, the project was less inclusive than originally intended. We had begun to divide into a small team of co-researchers who took responsibility for the conduct of the research and the participants of the workshops who were becoming the subjects of the research.

Phase Three: Immersion

Women from three organisations were invited to participate in workshops in different locations across GWS.[2] In the workshops, women talked about their experiences of membership and participation in decision-making in their organisations. They were encouraged to plan their ideal organisation and think about what things worked well and what things they would like to see changed in their real organisation. The workshops were highly successful in stimulating the enthusiasm of participants and initiated debate about the purpose of the research. Twelve women also agreed to be interviewed about these topics. At this stage, the role of the academic members began to dominate. The gap between the goals of the research (empowerment of older women) and the needs of rigorous documentation developed as a tension between stakeholders.

Phase Four: Consolidation

This phase split the group across the academic/non-academic fault-line, as the focus on reporting and publications was not valued in the same way by all participants. As Lingard et al. (2007, p. 512) have pointed out, "all participants are motivated by the forms of symbolic and cultural capital that count within their fields, particularly since capital is limited and field members must compete for it to attain security and prominence". Our feminist lens motivated us to reflect on whether the research process was equitable and whether it mirrored the goals of women's empowerment. We fostered equal status by sending transcripts of the butcher's paper[3] records to all co-inquirers in the first round of workshops. Everyone was invited back for two more workshops where all co-inquirers made suggestions for the way the day should be conducted and what topics should be covered. In the final workshop all were involved in appraising the views expressed in the workshops, commenting on the analysis of the information and contributing to the final report. It was at this final session that we began to see the extent of what the project had achieved. The co-inquirers were very involved in the process of the sessions and in developing tangible outcomes from the research that were accessible to others in language and presentation. One of the recommendations was to develop a brochure highlighting findings from the study and to distribute it widely. Another idea was to hold workshops for older women, focusing on skill development and promotion of community participation. Overall, the women were enthusiastic and looked for ways to build on the momentum that had been created.

Following the final workshop, the project was written up. At this stage the academic members realised that we had not considered how to end the process. Structural realities constrained further collaborative work such as holding more workshops. A brochure was written and distributed as suggested and there was a "ripple effect" of positive action that resulted from the collaboration, such as co-inquirers going on to further study and others co-editing a book.

CONCLUDING THOUGHTS: DILEMMAS AND RESOLUTIONS

The above accounts illustrate some of the tensions and strengths within the CI methodology. Tensions arose for both authors during the final analysis and writing-up stages of the inquiries in which we were involved. The act of writing and analysing can create a conflict in what was intended to be an inclusive, cohesive group, detracting from the emancipatory and transformative potential that the group has endeavoured to create and separating the academic researchers from the larger group.

Moreover, differences existed between all stakeholders in the two projects in terms of their motivations and reasons for involvement, knowledge of research, and expectations of the process and outcomes. The most obvious beneficiaries of the project were those in full-time academic positions, and this difference can add a problematic dimension to relationships.

A significant issue concerned the competing roles of "stakeholder–researcher" and "academic–researcher". As Byrne-Armstrong (2001) has pointed out, traces of positivist research models remain firmly embedded in CI genres. This is illustrated in the debates that occurred in Sharyn's research about rigour and documentation. Academic researchers are subject to the demands and discourses of the academy whereas other stakeholders are not. The demands of the university and of funding bodies competing with those of the CI paradigm, which can result in excluding rather than including stakeholders as co-researchers.

A further tension can arise from the loss of academic rigour when non-academic co-inquirers contribute to the analytical and writing phases (Hoskins & Stoltz, 2005). Resolving these issues can be challenging for the academic collaborative inquirer when a certain standard of academic writing is expected to emerge from the project. Yet reporting by the academic inquirers alone risks changing or interfering with the original meaning of received information. The discomfort involved in taking responsibility for analysis and writing can also separate the academic researchers from the group.

We agree that CI is an inclusive, emancipatory and transformative methodology. However, we also argue that it is difficult to maintain the ideals inherent in the theoretical frameworks that underpin CI during the final phases of research. The tensions described above are all aspects of CI and may indeed be the *essence* of this inquiry method. Without the human messiness of true collaboration, the method might not produce the benefits which are outlined here and in other literature. We argue that CI can make valuable contributions to the understanding and amelioration of complex social problems through the emphasis on equality between co-researchers and on influencing social action and everyday practice. CI can be a particularly useful method for practitioner researchers. But in itself, it does not resolve the complex debates and criticisms of standard research models that brought it into being in the first place.

NOTES

[1] The term "older women" refers to women who were retired or over the age of retirement, even if working, at the time of the research.
[2] The workshops were based on the Pathways to Action courses conducted by the Combined Pensioners' and Superannuants' Association (CPSA).
[3] Large sheets of newsprint paper for note-taking in groups.

REFERENCES

Bray, N. J., Lee, J., Smith, L., & Yorks, L. (2000). *Collaborative inquiry in practice: Action, reflection, and making meaning.* Thousand Oaks, CA: Sage.

Byrne-Armstrong, H. (2001). Whose show is it? The contradictions of collaboration. In H. Byrne-Armstrong, J. Higgs, & D. Horsfall (Eds.), *Critical moments in qualitative research* (pp. 106–114). Oxford: Butterworth Heinemann.

Carr, W., & Kemmis, S. (1986). *Becoming critical: Education, knowledge and action research.* London: Falmer.

Clover, D. E. (2007). From sea to cyberspace: Women's leadership and learning around information and communication technologies in Coastal Newfoundland. *International Journal of Lifelong Education, 26*(1), 75–88.

Fine, M., Torre, M. E., Boudin, K., Bowen, I., Clark, J., Hylton, D., et al. (2004). Participatory action research: From within and beyond prison bars. In L. Weis & M. Fine (Eds.), *Working method: Research and social justice* (pp. 95–119). New York: Routledge.

Heron, J. (1981). Philosophical basis for a new paradigm. In P. Reason & J. Rowan (Eds.), *Human inquiry: A sourcebook of new paradigm research* (pp. 19–35). Chichester: Wiley.

Heron, J., & Reason, P. (2001). The practice of cooperative inquiry: Research 'with' rather than 'on' people. In P. Reason & H. Bradbury (Eds.), *Handbook of action research* (pp. 179–199). London: Sage.

Hoskins, M., & Stoltz, J. (2005). Fear of offending: Disclosing researcher discomfort when engaging in analysis. *Qualitative Research, 5*(1), 95–111.

Joyappa, V., & Martin, D. J. (1996). Exploring alternative research epistemologies for adult education: Participatory research, feminist research and feminist participatory research. *Adult Education Quarterly, 47*(1), 1–14.

Kemmis, S., & McTaggart, R. (2005). Participatory action research: Communicative action and the public sphere. In N. K. Denzin & Y. S. Lincoln (Eds.), *The Sage handbook of qualitative research* (3rd ed., pp. 559–604). Thousand Oaks, CA: Sage.

Lather, P. (1991). *Getting smart: Feminist research and pedagogy within the postmodern.* New York: Routledge.

Lingard, L., Schryer, C. F., Spafford, M. M., & Campbell, S. L. (2007). Negotiating the politics of identity in an interdisciplinary research team. *Qualitative Research, 7*(4), 501–519.

McGuinn, N. F. (2004). *Learning through collaborative research: The six nation education research project.* New York: Routledge Farmer.

Power, A., Hudson, J., Leonard, R., McGee, S., & O'Beirne, N. (1994, January 25–27). *Empowerment through research: Tilting at windmills.* Paper presented at Social Research and the Quality of Life Conference, University of Tasmania, Launceston.

Reason, P. (1988). *Human inquiry in action: Developments in new paradigm research.* London: Sage.

Reason, P. (1994). *Participation in human inquiry.* London: Sage.

Reason, P., & Rowan, J. (Eds.). (1981). *Human inquiry: A sourcebook of new paradigm research.* Chichester: Wiley.

Reinharz, S. (1992). *Feminist methods in social research.* New York: Oxford University Press.

Riecken, T., Strong-Wilson, T., Conibear, F., Michel, C., & Riecken, J. (2005). *Connecting, speaking, listening: Toward an ethics of voice with/in participatory action research.* Retrieved October 27, 2009, from http://www.qualitative-research.net/index.php/fqs/article/view/533/1155

Riger, S. (1999). Working together: Challenges in collaborative research on violence against women. *Violence Against Women, 5*(10), 1099–1117.

Torbert, W. R. (1983). Initiating collaborative inquiry. In G. Morgan (Ed.), *Beyond method* (pp. 272–291). Newbury Park, CA: Sage.

Treleaven, L. (1994). Making a space: A collaborative inquiry with women as staff developments. In P. Reason (Ed.), *Participation in human inquiry* (pp. 138–162). London: Sage.

AFFILIATIONS

Donna Bridges PhD
The Education For Practice Institute
Charles Sturt University
Australia

Sharyn McGee
The School of Social Sciences
The University of Western Sydney
Australia

JAMES LATHAM AND ROBERT JONES

28. POSTSTRUCTURALIST RESEARCH:

Dipping into the Social Worlds of Multiplicities

DIPPING YOUR TOE IN

To engage in poststructural inquiry requires the adoption of a different mindset or alternative style of thought (Chia, 2003). Poststructuralism first came to prominence from the late 1960s as a reaction against the pretensions of structuralism to scientific objectivity and comprehensiveness. Structuralism had its origins in the linguistic theory of Ferdinand de Saussure (1857–1913) which aimed to reveal the universal structure of language as a constructed system of rules. His key idea was the relation of the "signifier" to the "signified". This concept was subsequently extended from linguistics to a wide range of cultural phenomena (social sign-systems or sign-worlds). Sign-systems act to structure the customs and conventions of our everyday behaviour. Structuralists conceived of the world as a series of interlocking sign-systems to which human beings respond in largely predictable ways (Sim & Van Loon, 2009). Under the surface of all sign-systems is an unconscious "deep structure" which dictates how cultural phenomena operate and determines their overall form. All sign-systems consist of a decipherable "grammar" of rules that operate on elements of a system by conventions. According to Sim and Van Loon, structuralism implies that meaning is present in all artefacts, waiting to be recovered by analysis. As such, structuralist analysis aims at revealing how we understand each other by such conventional rules – how we "signify" to each other.

Sim and Van Loon (2009, p. 86) argued that "structuralism went too far as an all-embracing form of analysis [in that] nothing could escape being part of a sign-system". The world was depicted as being too neat and orderly. Inevitable questions arose about the role of differences, rogue elements, and items or issues that did not fit the system. Poststructuralist analysis arose in the late 1960s in opposition to structuralism, in order to embrace rather than ignore the complexities of such differences. Poststructuralism is a perspective that denies location and structure in favour of the fluid, unpredictable nature of life. In adopting this approach we must abandon positivist methodologies of social enquiry in favour of techniques that deconstruct, disorganise and disorder our social frameworks, in order to recentre those aspects of our lives that were previously marginalised, ignored or excluded. In following a poststructural approach to research we are concerned with para-analysis (Linstead, 2004) of the social; that is, we bring forward and legitimise those forms of knowledge that are often tacit, silent, invisible and indeed unpresentable within modern epistemologies (Chia, 2003). When we do this we create richer, alternative social landscapes that generate questions about the "other".

As an approach to social research, postructualism is set apart from other approaches because of the heterogeneity of its fields, in contrast to the usual homogeneous field of a singular scientific methodology (Weedon, 1987). If we were asked to suggest one mental key that would sum up and constantly guide the poststructural way of thinking, we would say "multiplicities". These multiple theoretical positions are developed in and from the work of theorists such as Deleuze and Guattari (1983, 1987), Derrida (1973), Lacan (1977), and Foucault (1978, 1979), with more contemporary contributions from scholars such as Cooper (1990), Jones (2004), St Pierre (1997) and Chia (2003). There are many more contributors in this field, and a literature search will reveal a rich seam of heterogeneous thinkers. In this chapter we explore some of the concepts and processes within the multiple fields of this fascinating area of social research. However, as the limitations of space preclude an in-depth and detailed analysis, we present an outline framework and description of what is a rich, detailed and rewarding area of research, for you to dip your toe into.

ASSUMPTIONS

Although we argue that poststructuralist scholars pursue heterogeneous fields, their work is inevitably influenced by sharing some basic ontological assumptions about language, meaning, and subjectivity (Weedon, 1987). The basis of these shared assumptions lies in the rejection of the modernist ontology of location, distilling, and subjugation. In effect, life forces and experiences are in a constant state of flux and change (Cooper & Law, 1995; Chia, 2003). Further, human beings are not the centre of the universe as espoused by the modernist philosophy of "the enlightenment" but merely one tiny element of all that makes up nature and the universe. In fact, our "objective" view of life is the product of construction processes and in particular the dominating processes of rationality and reductionist "scientific" exploration (Cooper, 1987, 1990; Chia, 2000, 2003). As Chia (2003, p. 127) stated, a post- [structural] critique:

> attempts to reveal modern rationality as the consequent effect of a reductionist operation whereby the phenomenal flux of lived experiences are [sic] forcibly carved up, conceptually fixed, and systematically subjugated by the widely practised organizing impulses of division, naming, classification, and represent- tation. Through this method of reduction and representation our otherwise intractable and amorphous life experiences are then made more amenable to instrumental manipulation and control.

What is overlooked in much of conventional social research is a rigorous and critical reflection on the underlying social, cultural, political, and historical forces shaping the way we see, understand, and behave within the institutionalised and organised structures of the modern world (Chia, 2003). For example, the work of

Deleuze and Guattari (1987) provides an exemplar of poststructural thinking by engaging in rhizomic, nomadic, and multiple modes of thinking. But who would use this kind of theorising in their work? Although the work of Gareth Morgan is wide-ranging, he is not well known for being a poststructuralist thinker. Yet in his text Imaginization (1993) he wrote about "strategic termites", a metaphor which in many ways alludes to the concept of rhizomic forms of organisation as described by Deleuze and Guattari. A key passage that links these two concepts is:

> One exciting theory emerging from the study of termite behaviour is that working the termite colony reflects a self-organizing process where *order emerges out of chaos* [and] ... [w]hile the nest always has a familiar pattern, *it is infinitely variable in terms of detailed form.* (Morgan, 1993, p. 44) [our emphases]

Our discussion above suggests that an understanding of three basic but key concepts is necessary to drive poststructural research inquiry, namely language, subjectivity, and difference. We now briefly describe and explain these concepts.

Language

Poststructuralists argue that it is the structured nature of language (and subsequent discourses) that creates the impression that reality itself is stable, pre-organised, and law-like in character. They insist that without the social acts of differentiating, identifying, naming, classifying, and the creation of a subject-predicate structure through language, lived reality is but a "shapeless and indistinct mass" (de Saussure, 1966, p. 111). Language thus provides one of the first systematic ordering impulses and is intimately linked to the rise of human civilizations throughout the world (Hatch & Cunliffe, 2006).

Conventional language contains significant portions of tacit and embodied forms of knowing that are suppressed, marginalised, or denied legitimacy in the modernist scheme of things (Legge, 1995; Chia, 2003). Without this embodied and tacit knowledge we are only partially informed. Chia (p. 127) argued that much of what is tacit and embodied is resistant to linguistic translation:

> There is an extensive realm of subliminal comprehension that resists and defies linguistic translation. Such subliminal and oftentimes subconscious forms of knowing can only be accessed indirectly and alluded to elliptically.

It is these "elliptic" approaches to social science inquiry that are captured by poststructural analysis. Indeed, Derrida argued that "language is a structure of material marks or sounds which are in themselves undecidable and upon which meaning has to be imposed" (Cooper, 1989, p. 480). This is in contrast to the more popular belief that language is a container of information and meaning. Derrida claimed that language is a process that "reflexively includes its own antithesis" as in organisation/disorganisation (Cooper, 1989).

Subjectivity

Although language is the common factor in the analysis of social organisation, social meanings, power, and individual consciousness (Weedon, 1987), it is also the place where subjectivity is constructed. The nature of subjectivity is yet another of the central assumptions made within the realm of the poststructural. Here subjectivity is constructed and is closely linked to language and discourse. Subjectivity is understood in this way through the ontological and epistemological status of poststructuralism.

For example, by using an adaptation of "Tamara"[1], Boje (1995, 2001) showed how people have multiple subjectivities that are continuously constructed as each of us moves through the different facets of life. As an example, in a work organisation our subjectivity is formally constructed for us in the form of a position description, title, role, etc. However, apart from the formal role, we also have multiple constructed subjectivities (many of which are informal in nature) based on the context at the time. In Boje's (2001, p. 5) view, these subjectivities are constructed through the processes of fragmented, storytelling narratives. "There is no whole unitary story" but only fragments where individuals are "only tracing story fragments, inventing bits and pieces to glue it all together, but never able to visit all the stages and see the whole". Therefore there is for each individual a "Tamara of stages happening simultaneously"; we do not get to "participate in all the performances", yet any one may affect our subjectivity at any point in time.

Although the earlier work of Foucault was mainly concerned with looking at discourse, his later work relates to subjectivity (see e.g. History of Sexuality vol 1, 1978, and Discipline and Punish, 1979). Foucault's work was concerned with the ways that power, knowledge, and the legal and other administrative processes sustain the institutionalised construction of subjectivity (Patton, 1998). In this context subjectivity is determined by these institutional processes which result in the "more or less fixed modalities of power over individuals" (Patton, 1998, p. 71). This, Foucault believed, constituted impediments for some individuals to experiencing their human capacities and or fulfilling their potential, because of the "ways in which certain human capacities become identified and finalized within particular forms of subjectivity" (Patton, 1998, p. 71). In other words, the institutionalisation process impedes our capacity to experience all of our "Tamara" stages. This, Foucault argued, was the process of domination.

Subjectivity is central to poststructural research approaches. Subjectivity is not singular but plural, and is in a constant state of flux. However, modern institutionalisation processes that are based on so-called rational thinking and supported by a reductionist scientific methodology serve to thwart the individual from experiencing life as a heterogeneous set of subjectivities.

Difference

Discussing Derrida's view of process, Cooper (1989) stated that difference is fundamental to understanding poststructural process analysis. Cooper (1990, 1989) argued that difference is like, or equivalent to, understanding information as a binary structure based on the idea of division (difference). Seen as a fundamental organiser of human philosophy, culture and language within the modernist paradigm, the concept of binary opposition (theoretical opposites) is a fundamental tenet of structuralism, which posits that the world is constituted by these oppositions, such as man/woman, management/workers, night/day. You will note that in every set of binary terms, one term invariably dominates the other (or is more privileged).

Cooper (1987, 1989, 1990) contended that there are two ways of interpreting this binary structure or boundary division. First, as in the structuralist approach, the emphasis is placed on the two separate terms. According to Cooper, most structuralists tend to adopt this perspective, then seeing the world through what he termed the "disjunctive mode of systemic-functionalism" (1987, p. 399) – an objective mode recognisable, for example, in mainstream human resource management systems. Second, as in the poststructural approach, the emphasis is placed on the actual process of division itself. This requires a conscious effort (a change in mindset) to see that "division is not merely an act of separation, but is also an undifferentiated state (or flux)" (Chia, 2000). In this approach the two terms are perceived as actually joined together – a viewpoint wherein the concept of a boundary or division is regarded as both separating and joining (Cooper, 1990). Cooper called this the "separation–wholeness paradox", where the opposing terms "[continuously] inhabit each other"; in fact, division is the "sharing of a whole between two terms in a continuous process of differentiation or active alternation" (Cooper, 1989, p. 488).

Difference can now be understood in two ways: first, as two different and independent terms and second, as a continuous differentiating process, which Derrida called différance.[2] It is the exploration and analysis of this process that is at the heart of poststructuralist approaches to social research.

In the following section we describe a number of research approaches that encompass the principles and assumptions presented above.

APPROACHES TO SOCIAL RESEARCH

Poststructural approaches to social research are many and varied because, as we discussed above, the field is not homogeneous. In fact, due to this non-unitary nature many of the scholars in this field would deny that what we present below constitute methodologies, as this would go against the principle of non-location (Linstead, 2004). Although we acknowledge that poststructural research is anti-methodology in a scientific sense, in this section we explore two approaches that have produced research findings in this field. First, we examine probably the most popular and widely known approach, namely "deconstruction". Many scholars have used this approach to some effect. Second, we examine a lesser known approach within the subject area of organisation studies, called "nomadic writing practices".

Deconstruction

Jacques Derrida pioneered the concept of deconstruction with the aim of revealing the "self contradictions and double binds that lie latent in any text" (Cooper, 1989, pp. 481/2). It is important to note that deconstruction is not a methodology as such but more a way of thinking. Boje (2001, p. 18) wrote, "deconstruction is a poststructuralist epistemology not a formula-method with steps and procedures", and Jones (2004, p. 36) described deconstruction as "a tool for identifying and questioning logocentric binaries".[3] Such an approach acts to problematise logocentrism, and prevents the possibility of logocentric incorporation. Linstead (2004, p. 5) stated that a post-structural approach using deconstruction seeks out the "fissures ... the failures, the immanences, the bursts of energy, the collapses [and lapses], the silences, and the refusal of the unsaid and the not-known to become the said or the known". Earlier, Martin (1990, p. 340) wrote that "deconstruction can be defined as an analytic strategy that exposes, in a systematic way, [the] multiple ways ... [any] text can be interpreted". Here she alluded to the binary oppositions which are set up to privilege one term over its opposite and thus set up power dynamics within the relationships. She argued that "deconstruction is able to reveal ideological assumptions in a way that is particularly sensitive to the suppressed interests of members of disempowered, marginalised groups". The sources of these dominant ideologies can be contemporary but are more often historical in nature. How do these dominant ideologies work their suppression? They reduce conflict between the terms by "eliding existing power relationships and creating myths of harmony, unity, and caring that conceal the opposite" (Martin, p. 340). Drawing on the work of White (1986), Martin (p. 340), further argued that "deconstruction attempts to peel away the layers of ideological obscuration, to expose the conflict that has been suppressed"; the devalued "other" (the underprivileged term) is made visible. Thus deconstruction reveals "power operating in structures of thinking and behaviour that previously seemed devoid of power relations".

The point of departure for deconstruction, therefore, is the understanding that human experience is pervaded by an "existential ambivalence" (Cooper, 1989, 1990) or what Chia (2000, 2003) called "undifferentiated flux". This, in turn, motivates us to stabilise or organise our world around us. In doing this we include some things while excluding others, which is our way of dealing with ambivalence or flux. In short, there is always something else that is omitted from the here and now: we can never fully capture everything in our stabilising processes. It is these "others" that are of interest to the poststructuralist, who seeks to include that which is excluded or elided.

David Boje is a contemporary scholar in poststructural thinking with a particular focus on narrative analysis and deconstruction. In particular, he has focused on exploring the text and searching for the fragmented, silenced, and marginalised voices trying to be heard (Boje, 2001). Martin (1990) also provided an engaging example of deconstruction by taking as her object of analysis a statement made in public from a senior executive officer of a large multinational corporation about a pregnant female employee who was a key member of a new product launch team:

> We have a young woman who is extraordinarily important to the launching of a new (product). We will be talking about it next Tuesday in its first world wide introduction. She has arranged to have her Caesarean yesterday in order to be prepared for this event. We have insisted that she stay home and this is going to be televised in a closed circuit television, so we're having this done by TV for her, and she is staying home three months and we are finding ways of filling in to create this void for us because we think it's an important thing for her to do (Martin, 1990, p. 339).

For those with a mindset of positivism the above statement would not be worrying or threatening. In fact, it would read as a sensible, rational disclosure of an organisation's intentions. However, a deconstructive analysis of the organizational efforts to help women reveals how these efforts have suppressed gender conflict and transgressed public and private dichotomies in the field of endeavour. To begin with, the organisation has not only taken upon itself to speak for the woman as employee but has also spoken for the woman as mother, and for the unborn child. This speech, couched not in intimate family terms but in "organisation-speak", thus transgresses the public/private boundary of this binary.

Nomadic Writing Practices

Nomadic thought owes no allegiance to any particular systems, established patterns, or traditional boundaries. As such, nomadism challenges institutional authority. Nomads have no points, paths, or land (Sim & Van Loon, 2009). In contrast, authority is inherently territorial. It is this deterritorialised nature of nomadism that destroys the basis of authority (Sim & Van Loon, p. 120). Nomadic writing practices follow this basic anti-authoritarian focus by postulating the principle that writing is a method of enquiry, in contrast to writing as a form of "telling" (Richardson, 1994). It is not just something that you do at the end of your data collection and analysis, but is also a form of data from which you learn more about your project (St Pierre, 1997). In essence, writing as a method of inquiry departs from the dominant social science practices to add an additional or alternative research practice. Writing as inquiry is about language in use; that is how we "word the world into existence ... then we reword the world" (Richardson, 1994, p. 923). As usual in a poststructural world of multiplicities, words can never fully capture the world we study, so continuous writing and rewriting about a subject is necessary, while at the same time interrogating the processes through which we construct the world (Richardson, 1994).

St Pierre (1997) employed Deleuze and Guattari's (1987, 1983) figurations of the rhizome, the fold, the normal, and haecceity to address the construction of subjectivity of a group of older, white, southern women in her hometown. She revealed how the use of these figurations in her writing shifted her understanding of subjectivity. In pursuing the notion of writing as a method of inquiry in research, St Pierre stated, "writing is thinking ... I believe that my writing about my participants has become an ethical practice of poststructural inquiry in ways I have only begun to understand" (p. 404). One of the central elements of St Pierre's approach to inquiry was to attempt to get free of herself and to think differently to previous thinking as an ethical principle. This ethic, she noted, is not found in basic texts on qualitative inquiry.

Grey's (2009) used a poststructural approach in her research in higher education, based around the concepts of "nomadic practices", "disruptive becomings", and "critical moments of difference". She allowed the multi-voiced experiences of her students to become the central element of expression by letting them speak for themselves. In so doing she attempted to liberate the multiplicities within her students and to explore them as a way of creating a richer understanding of subjectivity construction and its impact on experience. This also allowed Grey to use her writing as a method of inquiry that investigated how she constructed her world. For example, in a coursework exercise her students produced a picture of a face comprising different parts of faces taken from pictures of faces of multiple students. From exploration of this singular image emerged multiple constructs and assumptions based on differences. During this process, "points of significance" ("when somebody gets it; where someone throws out a comment that shifts the discourse" (Pennycook, 2004, cited in Grey 2009, p. 123)) and "critical moments" were identified. This enabled a self-reflexive ethnographic account to be given, driven by the critical moments of difference identified by the students.

REFLECTIONS

In this brief chapter we have tried to explain some of the assumptions, principles, practices, and processes that are underpinned by poststructural thinking. In doing this we are aware of the multiplicities that abound and that we have not included everything about the field. Much has been excluded. This is a difficult position to be in, but we are comforted by the belief that every time we read and re-read a text it will be different and therefore enriching. When writing narratives we get the sense that everything should be centred and given equivalent status, yet we know that some sections and examples in this text are more centred than others. This is not by choice but is a reflection of our thought processes, where some items resonate more than others in our constructions. We hope that you will now address your research, at least, by adopting a wider framework that includes more of the "other", that is difference, but also with the awareness that it is not possible to include everything.

NOTES

[1] A particularly long-running play in Los Angeles where the actors acted out the story on multiple sets and stages. The audience followed the story by choosing which set to visit and/or which actors to follow as they moved through the sets and interacted with other actors. This resulted in multiple versions of the same play.
[2] Différance is a term used by Derrida to embody two meanings in the same spacio-temporal term; the first is to defer, that is to postpone or delay in time; the second is to differ in space (Cooper, 1987).
[3] Logocentrism is a term used by Derrida to describe the mental strategy of centring experience around a presupposed metaphysical structure (Cooper, 1989). In short it describes a stabilising function.

REFERENCES

Boje, D. (2001). *Narrative methods for organizational and communication research*. London: Sage.
Boje, D. M. (1995). Stories of the storytelling organization: A postmodern analysis of Disney as "Tamara-Land". *Academy of Management Journal, 38*(4), 997–1035.
Chia, R. (2000). Discourse analysis as organizational analysis. *Organization, 7*(3), 513–518.
Chia, R. (2003). Organization theory as a postmodern science. In H. Tsoukas & C. Knudson (Eds.) *The Oxford handbook of organization theory: Meta-theoretical perspectives* (pp. 113–140). Oxford: Oxford University Press.
Cooper, R. (1987). Information, communication and organization: A post-structural revision. *Journal of Mind and Behaviour, 8*(3), 395–416.
Cooper, R. (1989). Modernism, postmodernism and organizational analysis 3: The contribution of Jacques Derrida. *Organization Studies, 10*(4), 479–502.

Cooper, R. (1990). Organization/disorganization. In J. P. Hassard & D. Pym (Eds.), *The theory and philosophy of organizations: Critical issues and new perspectives* (pp. 167–197). London: Routledge.
Cooper, R., & Law, J. (1995). Organization: Distal and proximal views. In S. Bacharach (Ed.), *Research in the sociology of organizations* (pp. 237–274). Greenwich, CT: JAI Press.
Deleuze, G., & Guattari, F. (1983). *Anti-Oedipus: Capitalism and schizophrenia*. Minneapolis, MN: University of Minnesota Press. (Original work published in 1972)
Deleuze, G., & Guattari, F. (1987). *A thousand plateaus: Capitalism and schizophrenia* (B Massumi, Trans.). Minneapolis, MN: University of Minnesota Press.
Derrida, J. (1973). *Speech and phenomena*. Evanston, IL: Northwestern University Press.
de Saussure, F. (1966). *Course in general linguistics*. London: Fontana/Collins.
Foucault, M. (1978). *The history of sexuality. Volume 1: An introduction*. New York: Random House.
Foucault, M. (1979). *Discipline and punish – the birth of the prison*. New York: Vintage Books.
Grey, M. (2009). Ethnographers of difference in critical EAP community – becoming. *Journal of English for Academic Purposes, 8*, 121–133.
Hatch, M., & Cunliffe, A. (2006). *Organization theory: Modern, symbolic, and postmodern perspectives* (2nd ed.). Oxford: Oxford University Press.
Jones, C. (2004). Jacques Derrida. In S. Linstead (Ed.), *Organization theory and postmodern thought* (pp. 34–63). London: Sage.
Lacan, J. (1977). *Ecrits*. London: Tavistock.
Legge, K. (1995). *Human resource management – Rhetorics and realities*. London: Macmillan.
Linstead, S. (Ed.). (2004). *Organization theory and postmodern thought*. London: Sage.
Martin, J. (1990). Deconstructing organizational taboos: The suppression of gender conflict in organizations. *Organization Science, 1*(4), 339–359.
Morgan, G. (1993). *Imaginization: The art of creative management*. London: Sage.
Patton, P. (1998). Foucault's subject of power. In J. E. Moss (Ed.), *The later Foucault* (pp. 64–77). London: Sage.
Pennycook, A. (2004). Critical moments in a TESOL praxicum. In B. Norton & K. Toohey (Eds.), *Critical pedagogies and language learning* (pp. 327–345). Cambridge: Cambridge University Press.
Richardson, L. (1994). Writing: A method of inquiry. In N. K. Denzin & Y. S. E. Lincoln (Eds.), *Handbook of qualitative research* (pp. 516–529). Thousand Oaks, CA: Sage.
Sim, S., & Van Loon, B. (2009). *Introducing critical theory*. London: Icon.
St Pierre, E. (1997). Circling the text: Nomadic writing practices. *Qualitative Inquiry, 3*(4), 403–415.
Weedon, C. (1987). *Feminist practice and poststructuralist theory*. Oxford: Basil Blackwell.
White, S. K. (1986). Foucault's challenge to critical theory. *American Political Science Review, 80*(2), 419–431.

AFFILIATIONS

James Latham PhD
Faculty of Business and Enterprise
Swinburne University of Technology
Australia

Robert Jones PhD
Professor of Human Resource Management and Organisation Studies
Faculty of Business and Enterprise
Swinburne University of Technology
Australia

BRANKA KRIVOKAPIC-SKOKO AND GRANT O'NEILL

29. DOING MIXED METHODS RESEARCH

BACKGROUND, POPULARITY AND RATIONALE

Doing mixed methods research means employing both qualitative and quantitative methods of data collection and analysis in a single study. More specifically, a mixed methods approach involves

> the collection or analysis of both quantitative and/or qualitative data in a single study in which the data are collected concurrently or sequentially, are given a priority, and involve the integration of the data at one or more stages in the process of research (Creswell, 2003, p. 212).

A number of scholars have discussed mixed research methods within the context of the two major research paradigms, qualitative and quantitative, and argued that mixed methods can be considered as a third research paradigm (Johnson, Onwuegbuzie, & Turner, 2007; Denscombe, 2008), a third methodological movement (Tashakkori & Teddlie, 2003), and even "a research paradigm whose time has come" (Johnson & Onwuegbuzie, 2004, p. 14). Although issues and questions around mixed methods research and its benefits continue to be debated, interest in and acceptance of mixed methods is growing strongly, as evidenced by the increasing number of books, papers and academic journals devoted to mixed methods research.

Mixed methods research is very powerful for gaining new insights into phenomena being researched, and a more comprehensive understanding. As an intellectual and practical synthesis of qualitative and quantitative research, mixed methods research can provide highly informative, exhaustive, balanced and useful research results (Johnson et al., 2007). It provides rich data, can initiate new lines of thinking and, by intentionally engaging multiple perspectives and presenting a greater diversity of views, mixed methods research is inclusive, pluralistic and complementary (Maxwell & Loomis, 2003). Further, as argued by many in the mixed methods research movement, it is more ethical to mix methods in order to represent a plurality of interests, voices and perspectives (Greene & Caracelli, 1997). As a research approach, mixed methods is most strongly underpinned by the philosophical approach known as pragmatism, which advocates a practical and outcome-oriented method of inquiry and need-based approach to research methods and concept selection (Bazeley, 2003a; Maxcy, 2003; Denscombe, 2008). That noted, there is growing concern that epistemological and ontological issues associated with mixed methods need to be reconsidered in light of an appreciation of the complexity and variability of qualitative and quantitative methods and reductive philosophical thinking (see e.g. Bergman, 2008).

After reviewing empirical studies which applied a mixed methods research design, Greene, Caracelli, and Graham (1989) identified five reasons for adopting mixed methods research: (a) Triangulation (i.e. intentional use of more than one method in studying the same phenomenon in order to seek convergence and confirmation of results – this can substantially increase the credibility of research); (b) Complementarity (i.e. elaboration, enhancement, illustration, or clarification of the results from one method with the results from another method – this can assist in understanding the overlapping and different facets of the phenomenon); (c) Development (i.e. using the result from one method to help inform another method); (d) Initiation (i.e. looking for paradoxes, contradictions and new perspectives that may lead to a reframing of research questions and results); and (e) Expansion (i.e. seeking to extend the breadth and range of inquiry by using different methods for different inquiry components). Clearly, collecting different kinds of data through different methods provides a wider range of coverage that may result in a more detailed analysis of the phenomenon (Tashakkori & Teddlie, 2003). Bazeley (2003b) tightly summarised the reasons for adopting a mixed methods approach, noting that they are typically employed for the purpose of verification (i.e. whether the results of different methods support each other), expansion (i.e. the use of different methods can add to our understanding) and initiation (i.e. generating new ideas).

Many qualitatively-oriented researchers (e.g. Bryman, 2006; Mason, 2006) suggest that qualitative research is prominent in mixed methods designs, and that a "qualitatively driven" approach to mixing methods offers enormous potential for enhancing our capacities for social explanation and generalisation (Mason, 2006). Others, such as Denzin and Lincoln (2005) and particularly Howe (2004), are rather critical of this approach, arguing that qualitative and quantitative paradigms cannot and should not be mixed. Further, based on claims that mixed methods designs are direct descendants of classical experimentalism, a presumed methodological hierarchy is posited that sees quantitative methods as dominant. With too little space to go into the detail of philosophical debates around quantitative and qualitative methods, it must suffice to note that the authors of this chapter do not accept the assumption that qualitative research should have secondary status in mixed methods inquiry. Indeed, this chapter is written from the perspective of a qualitative researcher seeking to explore some innovative and productive ways of combining qualitative and quantitative research methods.

When researchers propose a mixed methods study, most of them think of mixed methods as a parallel or sequential use of qualitative and quantitative approaches to data collection and analysis, whereas the "more adventurous" (Bazeley, 2003a, p. 387) refer to a full integration of these two approaches. We believe that Bazeley and Fielding and Schreier (2001) offer a useful framework for thinking about mixed methods research. They suggest two approaches to mixed methods: a basic approach to method combination and "hybrid" or inherently integrated methods. This chapter follows that framework and first outlines a basic qualitative– quantitative design where the components remain separate in the mixed methods research.

The discussion then moves to explain a full integration of the methods, which can occur on a number of levels and is facilitated by the use of computer software (Bazeley, 2006).

HOW TO COMBINE QUALITATIVE AND QUANTITATIVE RESEARCH METHODS

Researchers commencing exploration of mixed methods research will be surprised by the number of different typologies of mixed methods designs (Creswell, 2003; Morse, 2003; Johnson & Christensen, 2004; Leech & Onwuegbuzie, 2006). Tashakkori and Teddlie (2003) referred to almost 40 types of mixed methods design that were identified in the literature. Most of the authors developing a typology of mixed methods tend to focus on the relative importance of quantitative and qualitative components and how they are sequenced. Following Morse (2003), the ways of combining the methods may be based on two decisions a researcher has to make: (a) the priority decision which determines the extent to which the qualitative or quantitative methods will be the principal component of the design; and (b) the sequence decision which refers to the order in which the qualitative and quantitative methods are used.

Table 29.1 The Priority–Sequence Model (adapted from Morse, 2003)

1. Qualitative Preliminary	2. Quantitative Preliminary
Purpose: Smaller qualitative study (focus groups or in-depth interviews) helps guide the data collection in a large quantitative study; usually used for generating hypotheses and developing content for questionnaires; often used in large scale survey research for identifying context-specific variables and for improvement of the measurements **Example**: Krivokapic-Skoko & O'Neill, 2008	**Purpose:** Smaller quantitative study helps guide the data collection in a principally qualitative study; an initial small scale quantitative study provides a demographic portrait of participants and can be instrumental in developing in-depth questions for interviews; a preliminary survey of the empirical settings can help to select the sites for the in-depth research **Example**: Crump & Logan. 2008
3. Qualitative Follow-up	**4. Quantitative Follow up**
Purpose: Smaller qualitative study helps interpret results from a large quantitative study; for instance, a quantitative study explores statistical relationships across a large sample and a follow-up qualitative study looks at specific case studies to better understand these relationships; can be especially useful when provocative or contradictory results are found in quantitative research **Example**: Orhan & Scott, 2001	**Purpose:** Smaller quantitative study helps evaluate and interpret results from a major qualitative study; a survey can follow up the findings of case study research to explore generalisability of the findings from the qualitative research **Example:** Esteves & Pastor, 2004

When undertaking a mixed method study, a researcher may decide to give equal emphasis to the qualitative and quantitative phases of the study, or decide to complete a study based largely on a single method with small components drawn from another (e.g. conduct an ethnographic study which can be supplemented by a statistical study). In terms of timing, the researcher has to decide whether the qualitative and quantitative phases of the study will occur at approximately the same time, or whether the qualitative phase will be followed by the quantitative phase (or vice versa).

The Priority–Sequence model (Table 29.1) summaries four basic types of mixed methods research design based on whether the principal method is qualitative or quantitative and whether the complementary method occurs as a preliminary or a follow-up stage. The most frequently used mixed method designs start with a qualitative study followed up by quantitative research (Sale, Lohfeld, & Brazil, 2002). For example, a common sequential exploratory strategy commences with an initial phase of qualitative data collection and analysis, followed by quantitative data collection, frequently a large-scale survey (Quadrant 1, Table 1). Occasionally, focus group analysis (with a semi-structured format) is chosen as it is known to be useful in the identification of issues and themes that can subsequently be drawn upon to assist in the development of relevant survey questions. Another common way of combining methods is a quantitative preliminary type (Quadrant 2) where an initial small-scale quantitative study helps guide the data collection in a principally qualitative study. This design gives qualitative researchers the opportunity to select cases based on knowledge of representative samples. A qualitative follow-up design (Quadrant 3) may benefit quantitative researchers by achieving better and in-depth understanding of statistical associations between the variables within a large-scale quantitative study. According to Morse (2003), this type of mixed methods design is most frequently used when the results of the main quantitative study are unexpected or unanticipated, and a qualitative study is then conducted to find the reasons for the occurrence of such results. Finally, in order to enhance the generalisability of findings from qualitative research, some researchers carry out a "smaller" quantitative study as a follow-up (Quadrant 4) to a major qualitative study as a means of evaluating results from the qualitative phase. This "quantitative follow-up" research design is often used to support development of a conceptual model and then to empirically assess it within a particular setting; or in some instances, researchers may want to go beyond individual cases and say something about a more "representative" sample.

QUALITATIVELY DRIVEN MIXED METHOD RESEARCH AND "HYBRID" METHODS

There is a tendency among mixed methods researchers to include a much larger volume of unstructured data (that is, for example, used for hermeneutic analysis) than is the norm among researchers working within the qualitative tradition (Bazeley, 2004). Further, there is a growing trend of quantifying qualitative research (Sale et al., 2002). This so called "quantitizing" of data (Johnson & Christensen, 2004) involves converting qualitative data into numerical codes that can be quantified and analysed statistically. Others, such as Mason (2006), note increasing "mixing [of] methods in a qualitatively driven way" which sees the combination of hermeneutic methods for understanding the meaning of texts with techniques aimed at the reduction and standardisation of information contained in large amounts of textual data, where qualitative coding is converted into quantitative variables that can be further statistically analysed.

Some developments in qualitative research methods outlined below, such as Ragin's (1987) qualitative comparative analysis, Heise's (1991) and Griffin's (1993) event structure analysis, or Kuckartz's (1995) approach of case-oriented quantification, support these "quantifying" tendencies. Such developments allow for qualitative analysis to be systematic, formal, rigorous and procedurally replicable, and, importantly, it becomes possible to achieve a richness and intensity commonly associated with qualitative research while dealing with more than a handful of cases. These approaches are referred to as "hybrid methods" (Fielding & Schreier, 2001), approaches that constitute an integration of qualitative and quantitative elements, approaches where these elements may be so closely packed as to be practically indistinguishable.

(a) Case-Oriented Quantification

This method, developed by Udo Kuckartz and associates from Humboldt University, Berlin (Kuckartz, 1995), is appropriate for qualitative research dealing explicitly with a large number of individual cases and using semi-structured interviews. The case-oriented quantification combines qualitative and quantitative approaches during the evaluation of qualitative research data. The method includes a specific mathematical procedure for analysing qualitative data which can be used to classify the cases and construct a typology. The process starts with qualitative research where the goal is to unpack the subjective meaning of textual data and identify the relevant dimensions of whole cases. The dimensions developed from the data are then transformed into case-oriented variable and case-specific variable values. After that, formalised methods of comparison, such as cluster analysis and correspondence analysis, are applied to generate an empirically-based typology.

(b) Hermeneutic-Classificatory Content Analysis

Edeltraund Roller and associates from the Free University, Berlin (Roller, Mathes, & Eckert, 1995) endorsed combining quantitative and qualitative content analyses. With this method, a large quantity of information embedded in texts is reduced through a process of formal coding and the creation of a conceptual network of categories. Relevant information contained in the text segments is transformed into a quantitative data matrix which is then statistically analysed to find the frequency distribution of certain codes or code patterns.

(c) Qualitative Comparative Analysis (QCA)

Charles Ragin proposed a relatively new method for the formalisation and extension of the comparative case-study approach and conceptualised it as moving beyond qualitative and quantitative research (Ragin, 1987). Introduced as a "synthetic strategy", this method complements qualitative and quantitative analyses by providing a more complex approach than most quantitative research methods, and it is more "systematic" than most qualitative research methods. QCA also brings a form of rigour and a variable concept of quantitative methods to qualitative ones. Additionally, it offers to quantitative research some of the causal complexity and in-depth analysis of qualitative methods.

QCA is essentially case-oriented comparative research which provides a systematic and holistic analysis of a moderate number of cases. The method builds on the strengths of explanatory and interpretive research by primarily bringing complexity and intensity of in-depth investigation to a moderate number of cases, while maintaining rigour, replicable procedures and the use of formal logic. In terms of technical procedure, QCA systematises and transforms empirical evidence into algebraic forms, and then uses Boolean algebra to do comparisons. The dialogue between theory and evidence is well structured. Starting from theoretical arguments that determine the minimum set of case attributes, QCA proceeds indicatively by simplifying the complexity of the evidence in a systematic, stepwise manner. In QCA, cases are transformed into the unique combinations of selected causal conditions and associated outcomes, and then compared and interpreted holistically, focusing on their attributes. Thus, in applying QCA, each case remains contextualised as a whole – a meaningful, interpretable and specific configuration of causal conditions/attributes and outcome variables (Krivokapic-Skoko, 2003). QCA appears to be of substantial utility in research sites with contextual and multiple causal relations. The method assumes that causal variables are effective only when operating in conjunction with each other; consequently the impact of each causal variable should be discussed only in a particular context.

QCA has become increasingly popular among social science researchers and has been applied to different academic disciplines such as political science (Berg-Schlosser & De Meur, 1994), sociology (Wickham-Crowley, 1991), forestry science (Hellström, 1998), and areas of management science such as organisational management (Romme, 1995) and public management (Kithener, Beynon, & Harrington, 2002).

A common concern with the employment of QCA and Boolean algebra is that it requires dichotomous variables and does not allow for fine-grained measures of the attributes in question. To overcome that limitation, Ragin (2000) recently incorporated ideas of fuzzy-set logic into qualitative comparative analysis (QCA). The fuzzy-sets allow for continuously coding variables according to the degree of their association with the qualitative categories of interest. With fuzzy-sets, set membership is not restricted to the binary values of 0 and 1, but may instead be defined using membership scores ranging from ordinal up to continuous values.

(d) Event Structure Analysis (ESA)

Event Structure Analysis, or "a qualitative model of quantitative research" as David Heise referred to it, is a formal and replicable technique of qualitative data research that is used for analysing and interpreting events (Heise, 1991). This method is deemed more rigorous than a case study approach and focuses on the temporal order and sequencing of actions. It provides narrative explanation, and goes inside singular events and systematically organises information about events so as to explain how something happens. The method is formal as it uses a set of logical rules to analyse cases. The formal rules produce results that can be replicated and generalised to other cases. The method is qualitative in the sense that it draws on some subjective criteria and the understanding of the researcher, and it seeks to preserve the context of circumstances in which events take place. ESA is considered appropriate for causal analysis with an emphasis on process and contingency, and it can be used to interpret cases or events holistically (Griffin & Ragin, 1994).

ESA focuses on a single culturally or historically specific event; more precisely, it focuses on a narrative of the event. Here a narrative is an analytic construct that is used to identify a group of events and incorporate them into a single story (Stevenson & Greenberg, 1998). Narratives have a specific beginning, a series of intervening actions, and an end point which can be based upon a number of paths and interconnections between the actors. ESA is a formal technique of narrative analysis, and it tracks the temporal ordering and sequencing of actions in order to explain a singular event (Griffin, 1993).

Although ESA was originally developed to study cultural routines (Corsaro & Heise, 1990), it has since been applied to a study of racial conflicts in the USA (Griffin, 1993) and labour strikes and causal consequences of labour union campaigns (Brown, 2000). ESA is deemed to be very appropriate for analysing complex social processes and collaborative actions (Stevenson, Zinzow, & Sridharan, 2003) as well as examining the processes of organisational formation (Hager & Galaskiewicz, 2002).

(e) Q Methodology

Q methodology (QM) has been used by a number of qualitative researchers for eliciting, evaluating and comparing human subjectivity. It has been conceptualised as a hybrid approach, an approach that Stenner and Stainton Rogers (2004) have labelled "qualiquantology" to reflect its qualitative and quantitative features. QM allows for a "scientific" study of people's perspectives, meanings and opinions (Previte, Pini, & Haslam-McKenzie, 2007); as McKeown and Thomas (1988) noted, it is "a method for the scientific study of human subjectivity". Originally developing within a positivist tradition, QM is increasingly seen as providing an innovative approach to qualitative analysis that strengthens conceptual categorisation through the quantification of patterned subjectivities, using Q-sorts. Q-sorts are statements that are broadly representative of the discourse on the topic to be researched; they enable participants to respond to issues based on their individual experience (Previte et al., 2007). Individual responses captured by Q-sorts are then factor-analysed to identify patterns of subjective perspectives across individuals. The input of subjective data results in the production of "objective structures" (Previte et al., 2007). Application of QM can be found in psychology (Shemmings, 2006), landscape and tourism research (Fairweather & Swaffield, 2002), management science (Steelman & Maguire, 1999) and political science (Brown, 1980).

REFLECTIONS

Although a mixed methods approach to research will not allow you to readily transcend the philosophical divisions and debates associated with qualitative versus quantitative research methods, mixed methods research can be a highly useful and appropriate means of accessing and interpreting the social world and the problems and issues that confront us as researchers. They can facilitate the generation of knowledge that is rich and nuanced, as researchers can variously apply methods that may offer opportunities to achieve greater insight and understanding than would be the case pursuing solely qualitative or quantitative methods.

As should be clear from the foregoing discussion, mixed methods research abounds with complexity, not least because of the multiple approaches to parallel, sequential or integrative mixed methods research. Approaching mixed methods research you should be clear about your research aims and objectives so that you can carefully consider and justify the benefits, limitations and appropriateness of the methods you adopt. With well selected and applied mixed methods you will be able to respond to complex questions in ways that are sophisticated and insightful. It is for such reasons that we, like so many others, have frequently adopted mixed methods in our own research.

REFERENCES

Bazeley, P. (2003a). Computerized data analysis for mixed methods research. In A. Tashakkori & C. Teddlie (Eds.), *Handbook of mixed methods in social and behavioural research* (pp. 385–422). Thousand Oaks, CA: Sage.

Bazeley, P. (2003b). Teaching mixed methods. *Qualitative Research Journal, 3*, 117–126.

Bazeley, P. (2004). Issues in mixing qualitative and quantitative approaches to research. In R. Buber, J. Gadner, & L. Richards (Eds.), *Applying qualitative methods to marketing management research* (pp. 141–156). Basingstoke, UK: Palgrave Macmillan.

Bazeley, P. (2006). The contribution of computer software to integrating qualitative and quantitative data analyses. *Research in the Schools, 13*(1), 63–73.

Bergman, M. M. (2008). The straw men of the qualitative-quantitative divide and their influence on mixed methods research. In M. M. Bergman (Ed.), *Advances in mixed methods research* (pp. 11–21). London: Sage.

Berg-Schlosser, D., & De Meur, G. (1994). Conditions of democracy in interwar Europe: A Boolean test of major hypotheses. *Comparative Politics, 26*(3), 253–278.

Brown, C. (2000). The role of employers in split labour market: An event-structure analysis of racial conflict and AFL organizing, 1917–1919. *Social Forces, 79*(2), 653–681.

Brown, S. R. (1980). *Political subjectivity: Application of Q-methodology in political science*. New Haven, CT: Yale University Press.

Bryman, A. (2006). Integrating quantitative and qualitative research: How is it done? *Qualitative Research, 6*(1), 97–113.

Corsaro, W. A., & Heise, D. R. (1990). Event structure models from ethnographic data. In C. Clogg (Ed.), *Sociological methodology* (pp. 1–57). Cambridge, MA: Basil Blackwell.

Creswell, J. W. (2003). *Research design: Qualitative, quantitative and mixed methods approaches* (2nd ed.). Thousand Oaks, CA: Sage.

Crump, B., & Logan, K. (2008, June). *A framework for mixed stakeholders and mixed methods*. Paper presented at the 7th European conference on Research methodologies for business and management studies, Regent's College (ECRM 2008), London.

Denscombe, M. (2008). Communities of practice: A researcher paradigm for the mixed methods approach. *Journal of Mixed Methods Research*, 2(3), 270–283.

Denzin, N. K., & Lincoln, Y. S. (2005). Introduction: The discipline and practice of qualitative research. In N. K. Denzin & Y. S. Lincoln (Eds.), *The Sage handbook of qualitative research* (pp. 1–32). Thousands Oaks, CA: Sage.

Esteves, J., & Pastor, J. (2004). Using a multimethod approach to research enterprise systems implementation. *Electronic Journal of Business Research Methods*, 2(2), 69–82.

Fairweather, J., & Swaffield, S. (2002). Visitors' and locals' experiences of Rotorua, New Zealand: An interpretative study using photographs of landscapes and Q method. *International Journal of Tourism Research*, 4, 283–297.

Fielding, N., & Schreier, M. (2001). Introduction: On compatibility between qualitative and quantitative research methods. *Forum: Qualitative Social Research Sozialforschung*, 2(1). Retrieved September 19, 2009, from http://www.qualitative-research.net/fqs/

Greene, J. C., & Caracelli, V. J. (1997). Defying and describing the paradigm issue in mixed methods evaluation. In J. C. Greene & V. J. Caracelli (Eds.), *Advances in mixed methods evaluation: The challenges and benefits of integrating diverse paradigms* (pp. 5–18). San Francisco: Jossey-Bass.

Greene, J. C., Caracelli, V. J., & Graham, W. F. (1989). Towards a conceptual framework for mixed-methods evaluation designs. *Educational Evaluation and Policy Analysis*, 11, 255–274.

Griffin, L. J. (1993). Narrative, event-structure analysis, and causal interpretation in historical sociology. *American Journal of Sociology*, 98(5), 1094–1134.

Griffin, L., & Ragin, C. (1994). Some observations on formal methods of qualitative analysis. *Sociological Methods & Research*, 23(1), 4–21.

Hager, M., & Galaskiewicz, J. (2002). *Studying closure among non-profit organisations using event structure analysis and network methods*. Paper presented at HCOC4 (Health Care Organisation Conference), University of California, Berkeley.

Heise, D. R. (1991). Event structure analysis: A qualitative model of quantitative research. In N. G. Fielding & R. M. Lee (Eds.), *Using computers in qualitative research* (pp. 136–163). London: Sage.

Hellström, E. (1998). Qualitative comparative analysis: A useful tool for research into forest policy and forestry conflicts. *Forest Science*, 44(2), 254–265.

Howe, K. R. (2004). A critique of experimentalism. *Qualitative Inquiry*, 10(1), 42–61.

Johnson, R. B., & Onwuegbuzie, A. J. (2004). Mixed methods research: A research paradigm whose time has come. *Educational Researcher*, 33(7), 14–26.

Johnson, R. B., Onwuegbuzie, A. J., & Turner, L. A. (2007). Toward a definition of mixed methods research. *Journal of Mixed Methods Research*, 1(2), 112–133.

Johnson, R. N., & Christensen, L. B. (2004). *Educational research: Quantitative, qualitative, and mixed approaches*. Boston: Allyn & Bacon.

Kithener, M., Beynon, M., & Harrington, C. (2002). Qualitative comparative analysis and public services research. *Public Management Review*, 4(2), 485–504.

Krivokapic-Skoko, B. (2003, June). *Boolean algebra and the comparative method: Features and applications to social sciences*. Paper presented at the Second Workshop on Research Methodology, Amsterdam, organised by the Royal Netherlands Academy of Art and Science.

Krivokapic-Skoko, B., & O'Neill, G. (2008). University academics' psychological contracts in Australia: A mixed method research approach. *Electronic Journal of Business Research Methods*, 6(1), 61–71.

Kuckartz, U. (1995). Case-oriented quantification. In U. Kelle (Ed.), *Computer-aided qualitative data analysis: Theory, methods and practice* (pp. 158–166). London: Sage.

Leech, N. L., & Onwuegbuzie, A. J. (2007). A typology of mixed methods research designs. *Quality and Quantity*. DOI: 10.1007/s11135-007-9105-3. Retrieved September 19, 2009, from http://www.springerlink.com/content/2j645617056776735/fulltext.pdf

Mason, J. (2006). Mixing methods in a qualitative driven way. *Qualitative Research*, 6(1), 9–25.

Maxcy, S. (2003). Pragmatic threads in mixed methods research in the social sciences: The search for multiple models of inquiry and the end of the philosophy of formalism. In A. Tashakkori & C. Teddlie (Eds.), *Handbook of mixed methods in social and behavioural research* (pp. 51–90). Thousand Oaks, CA: Sage.

Maxwell, J. A., & Loomis, D. M. (2003). Mixed methods design: An alternative approach. In A. Tashakkori & C. Teddlie (Eds.), *Handbook of mixed methods in social and behavioural research* (pp. 241–273). Thousand Oaks, CA: Sage.

McKeown, B., & Thomas, D. (1988). *Q methodology*. Newbury Park, CA: Sage.

Morse, L. (2003). Principles in mixed methods and multi-method research design. In A.Tashakkori & C. Teddlie (Eds.), *Handbook of mixed methods in social and behavioural research* (pp. 189–208). Thousand Oaks, CA: Sage.

Orhan, M., & Scott, D. (2001). Why women enter into entrepreneurship: An explanatory model. *Women in Management Review, 20*, 15–24.

Previte, J., Pini, B., & Haslam-McKenzie, F. (2007). Q methodology and rural research. *Sociologia Ruralis, 47*(2), 135–147.

Ragin, C. (1987). *The comparative method: Moving beyond qualitative and quantitative strategies*. Berkeley, CA: University of California Press.

Ragin, C. (2000). *Fuzzy-set social science*. Chicago: University of Chicago Press.

Roller, E., Mathes, R., & Eckert, T. (1995). Hermeneutic-classificatory content analysis. In U. Kelle (Ed.), *Computer-aided qualitative data analysis: Theory, methods and practice* (pp. 167–177). London: Sage.

Romme, A. G. (1995). Self-organising processes in top management teams: A Boolean comparative approach. *Journal of Business Research, 34*, 11–34.

Sale, J. E., Lohfeld, L. H., & Brazil, K. (2002). Revisiting the quantitative-qualitative debate: Implications for mixed-methods research. *Quality & Quantity, 36*, 43–53.

Shemmings, D. (2006). "Quantifying" qualitative data: An illustrative example of the use of Q methodology in psychosocial research. *Qualitative Research in Psychology, 3*(2), 147–165.

Steelman, T., & Maguire, L. (1999). Understanding participants perspectives: Q-methodology in national forest management. *Journal of Policy Analysis and Management, 18*(3), 361–388.

Stenner, P., & Stainton Rogers, R. (2004). Q methodology and qualiquantology: The example of discriminating between emotions. In Z. Todd, B. Nerlich, S. McKeown, & D. D. Clarke (Eds.), *Mixing methods in psychology: The integration of qualitative and quantitative methods in theory and practice* (pp. 157–189). New York: Psychology Press, Taylor & Francis Group.

Stevenson, W., Zinzow, H., & Sridharan, S. (2003). Using event structure analysis to understand planned social change. *International Journal of Qualitative Methods, 2*(2). Article 5. Retrieved December 8, 2009, from http://www.ualberta.ca/~iiqm/backissues/2_2/html/stevensonetal.htm

Stevenson, W. B., & Greenberg, D. N. (1998). The formal analysis of narratives of organizational change. *Journal of Management, 24*(6), 741–762.

Tashakkori, A., & Teddlie, C. (Eds.). (2003). *Handbook of mixed methods in social and behavioural research*. Thousand Oaks, CA: Sage.

Wickham-Crowley, T. P. (1991). A qualitative comparative approach to Latin American revolutions. *International Journal of Comparative Sociology, 32*(1–2), 82–109.

AFFILIATIONS

Branka Krivokapic-Skoko PhD
Faculty of Business
Charles Sturt University
Australia

Grant O'Neill PhD
Faculty of Business
Charles Sturt University
Australia

ANITA MONRO

30. PURSUING FEMINIST RESEARCH:

Perspectives and Methodologies

INTRODUCTION

Feminism is perhaps best described as an ideology or world view with methodological implications rather than as a complete methodology in its own right. Feminist researchers work within a range of methodologies. These methodologies depend on the particular feminist perspectives or approaches adopted, the particular research disciplines within which feminist researchers work, and the particular subjects investigated. Ramazanoglu and Holland (2002, p. 2) noted that:

> debates on feminist methodology are framed by disagreements ... over how ideas about the social world can possibly be related to people's experiences of social life, and to actual social realities.

Feminist perspectives differ widely according to their ontological (how the world is understood) and epistemological (how knowledge is understood) approaches. Some examples of these disagreements are described later in this chapter. Although Ramazanoglu and Holland were particularly concerned with feminist researchers working within Western philosophical frameworks, their statement also applies when feminist researchers using non-Western philosophical frameworks are taken into account.

As an ideology or perspective, feminism is concerned with critiquing patriarchal influences wherever they occur in and around the subject being investigated, and in envisaging alternative possibilities that address such influences. In this respect, Karen Offen (1998, p. 151) described feminism as "both an ideology and a movement for sociopolitical change based on a critical analysis of male privilege and women's subordination". This twofold focus strongly influences the methodologies adopted by feminist researchers and the ways in which those methodologies are put into practice, although the manner in which patriarchy is understood to operate depends on the particular type of feminist perspective or approach used.

This chapter explores feminism as an ideology, and the implications of feminism and feminist perspectives for qualitative research methodologies. It does not investigate particular feminist perspectives in any detail, due to the extensive range of material that would need to be covered. The exploration of feminism as ideology outlines a general approach to a feminist analysis of patriarchy. This exploration is followed by a discussion of the methodological significance of the twofold focus of feminist analysis. This discussion sketches the way in which emphasis is placed on women's experiences, knowledges and perceptions as sources and subjects for research, and identifies an integrated, interdisciplinary *praxis* as the overall shape and objective of feminist approaches to research. The final section of this chapter raises particular issues for researchers working from feminist perspectives and within qualitative methodologies. A range of examples of feminist scholarship from a variety of perspectives is highlighted throughout the various discussions.

Given the varieties of feminist perspectives taken by researchers, it is appropriate that this researcher divulges that she works within the discipline of Christian theology and a feminist poststructuralist methodological framework (Monro, 2006), particularly influenced by the work of French feminist and psychoanalyst, Julia Kristeva (1982, 1984). This disclosure also signals an important element of feminism generally—the acknowledgement of the situatedness of the researcher.

DEFINING FEMINISM

There are many definitions of feminism. Ramazanoglu and Holland (2002, p. 7) reminded researchers that "any definition of feminism can ... be contested". The particular definition presented here is one which encompasses many of the markers discussed below. It is not the final word on defining feminism, but it may be a helpful summary of some of the core concerns of feminism across methodologies, disciplines and research subjects. Feminism is:

> a comprehensive ideology, rooted in women's experience of sexual oppression, which engages in a critique of patriarchy, embraces an alternative vision for humanity and the earth, and actively seeks to bring this vision to realization (Johnson, Ross, & Hilkert, 1995, p. 327).

This definition highlights the twofold focus of feminism as an ideology and suggests the shape that feminist perspectives give to methodologies.

FEMINISM AS IDEOLOGY

Critiquing Patriarchy

Feminism is a self-consciously political approach, aware that all knowledge is situated knowledge, i.e. affected by the context and perspective of the researcher and involved in the power relations which it seeks to examine. In that awareness, the claim is made that, in the history of human epistemologies, most knowledges (and certainly the dominant knowledges) have been situated patriarchally. They have been developed by men, about men and for the benefit of men with the inevitable result that knowledges produced by women, about women and for the benefit of women have been hidden, ignored, disparaged, skewed, suppressed or simply never allowed to develop. In this respect, patriarchy is the patterned or institutionalised legitimation of men's, male or masculine superiority. The fundamental concern of feminism is the influence of patriarchy.

The word "patriarchy" is derived from Greek roots which produce the meaning "the rule of the father". Patriarchy originally referred to the way in which the "father" or eldest male functioned as the head of a family or household, with the family/household being the significant social grouping in ancient societies.

Because of the recognition of the way in which many factors contribute to the situatedness of knowledges, some feminist scholars (e.g. Elisabeth Schüssler Fiorenza, biblical scholar and Christian theologian) choose to use the word "kyriarchy" rather than "patriarchy". Kyriarchy is also derived from Greek roots, in this case producing the meaning "the law of the master/Lord". The use of the word kyriarchy signals that a researcher is interested in the way in which many factors interact in producing a system of power relations that is structural, pyramidal, incremental and hierarchical. Schüssler Fiorenza (1992) provided a very readable account of the complex development and dynamics of patriarchal/kyriarchal structures from ancient familial practice through Greek democracy to modern capitalist structures.

Patriarchy or kyriarchy is regarded as a structural reality. That is, it is not simply about individual relationships but about the way in which societies and communities operate (consciously and/or unconsciously). That structured reality is highly complex. The differences in situations are affected by many small attributes and factors which produce subtle increments in the power differences between individuals, groups and communities. For example, although women generally might be observed to have limited access to political power as measured by the number of women parliamentarians in a society, certain women will be understood to have more access to political power than others—by reason of their socio-economic status or their social networks, etc. This structural reality is a hierarchy: some people have more access to power (of various kinds than others); and it is a pyramidal hierarchy. That is, there are more people with less access to power than there are who enjoy the greatest amount of power. The base of the power structure is much larger than its apex: those who are most powerless are also most numerous.

Feminist analysis is concerned with such power disparity not simply because of the disparity, but because it allows those with less power to be dominated and manipulated by those with more power. A feminist analysis of patriarchy/kyriarchy investigates the way in which power exists and operates for men, the male and the masculine and against women, the female and the feminine.

Envisaging New Paradigms

Feminist analysis does not stop with investigation. Patriarchal power relations are understood as inappropriate models, and accordingly alternatives are sought. The search for alternative models is the second aspect of a feminist approach to research, although not all research projects include both steps. Some projects may focus on investigation only, leaving the development of alternative models for others. Other projects may rely on investigation done previously to propose new paradigms.

FEMINISM AS METHODOLOGY

Critiquing Patriarchy

Essentially, the critique of patriarchy is an analysis of the way power relations operate in favour of men, the male and/or the masculine and against women, the female and the feminine. Feminist analysis is interested in the way in which such hierarchies of binary oppositions (e.g. male/female) function in language, social relations, values, symbolism, theories, philosophy, beliefs, construction of history, environmental interactions, epistemological perspectives, etc. Feminism seeks to analyse differential power relations on the basis of sex and/or gender, or sexed and/or gendered constructs (e.g. "nature" as feminine) against the background of the experience, perception and knowledge of women that one side of the binary is generally favoured over the other. Feminists are particularly interested in the way series of binary oppositions correspond, e.g. male/female, public/private, culture/nature. Feminist approaches may also challenge the validity of these binary definitions, and particularly the tendency for such binaries to be treated as polarised dualisms. The work of ecofeminist Val Plumwood (1993) provided an excellent example of such attention to binary oppositions and the way in which these oppositions coincide to produce a network of bias against that which is cast as "feminine" and, therefore, "other".

Awareness of such differential power relations on the basis of sex/gender is often accompanied by awareness of differential power relations on the basis of other factors such as class or socioeconomic status, race or ethnicity, age and ability. Ecofeminist scholars add species to this list. For example, Plumwood (1993, p. 5) described the focus of concern as "the multiple, complex cultural identity of the master formed in the context of class, race species and gender domination"—the "master model".

Inevitably, any approach to understanding the world betrays researchers' particular ontologies or world views and their epistemologies or approaches to gaining knowledge about the world. Feminist qualitative research will usually include a disclosure of the situation of the researcher in relation to the subject being studied and the methodology being used.

Envisaging New Paradigms

In the proposal of new paradigms, feminist researchers are concerned with addressing the power, existential and operational imbalances. Feminist researchers privilege the knowledge, experience and perceptions of women and/or those with less power both, in the critique of patriarchy and in the development of alternative options. For example, Carol Gilligan (1982) offered a systematic critique of the work of moral development theorist, Lawrence Kohlberg, by arguing that his approach valued autonomy and independence over relationality. Against the background of sociocultural pressure for males to develop autonomy and females to fit in relationally, any moral development theory that emphasises one more than another will be inherently biased towards the gender associated with it. Thus, Gilligan argued, under Kohlberg's theory, women will be understood as less morally mature than men. Gilligan's work prompted other researchers to explore further ethical decision making and practice when considered from women's perspectives (e.g. Ruddick, 1995; Slee, 2004).

The importance of relationality in women's experiences, perceptions and knowledges influences other aspects of feminist approaches. Feminist approaches assume that theory and practice are intimately connected, and cannot be treated in isolation from one another. Feminist research thus generally assumes a praxis model. A praxis approach to research assumes an ongoing dialogue between action and reflection, practice and theory, activity and thought. Feminist researchers are not unique in using this approach; it is integral to a range of perspectives that seek to work with knowledges that have existed outside recognised epistemologies (e.g. the knowledges of colonised and/or indigenous peoples). Such an approach is the outcome of the recognition that not all knowledge or understanding is intellectual knowledge, and that some knowledges have remained "unvoiced"; that is, they have not been theorised or reflected upon with the same rigour as others. Specifically, from a feminist perspective, women's knowledges, perceptions and experiences have not been brought into the realm of "public" or recognised knowledges throughout much of human history.

A praxis approach also recognises that theory must make sense in practice. Feminist approaches refuse to understand the "public" as separate from the "private"; the academy as separate from practicality; theory as separate from practice. One of the most important catch-phrases of the "second wave" of feminism (1950s–1970s) was "The personal is political". Where women's lives and their experiences have been relegated to home and family ("the private"), feminists argue for the relevance of home and family to the life of society and community, as well as seeking the entry of women into "the public" (government, professions, educational institutions etc.). The "first wave" of feminism (19th century; early 20th century) was concerned with matters such as women's right to vote (suffrage), access to education and improvement of working conditions, highlighting how the supposedly "private" interacts with the "public" and vice versa.

Because differently situated knowledges (e.g. public, private) are not understood as separate from each other, feminist researchers are often engaged in interdisciplinary research by way of collaboration or by eclectic use of methodologies and methods. Research participants may also be understood as research partners, as qualitative methods such as participant observation, unstructured interviews, discourse analysis and historical reconstructions through diaries, papers and artefacts are used to access women's experiences, perceptions and knowledges. Philosopher Moira Gatens wrote about the "feminist theorist" as a "patchwork-quilter, taking bits and pieces from here and there in an attempt to offer an account of women's social and political being" (1991, p. 1). Other metaphors such as spinning and weaving (e.g. Keller, 1986), braiding (e.g. Johnson, 2002) and kaleidoscopes (e.g. Schaab, 2001) have also been used to describe the eclecticism that feminist research promotes and perhaps necessitates.

Different types of knowledge are regarded as interconnected. Consequently, the use of methods and sources that have previously been overlooked or ignored in academic contexts may be a feature of feminist research. Qualitative methodologies can be particularly helpful in providing frameworks for such methods and accessing such sources. Because women's knowledges, perceptions and experiences have been hidden, ignored or forgotten, the search for new paradigms also involves the reclamation of work by, about and for women that might have been hidden, ignored or forgotten. Christ and Plaskow (1979, pp. 3–7) described the task of feminist scholarship as threefold for this reason: critique; reclamation; and reconstruction or re-creation. Many examples of such reclamative research are found in historical studies (e.g. Frymer-Kensky, 1992; Miles, 1988).

CRITICAL ISSUES FOR FEMINIST RESEARCH

In the second edition of *Feminist Thought*, Rosemarie Tong (1998) identified eight strands of feminism: liberal, radical (libertarian and cultural), Marxist and socialist, psychoanalytic and "gender", existentialist, postmodern, multicultural and global, and ecofeminism. Even so, it is arguable that she conflated too many different perspectives under at least some of these headings. In particular, assigning a range of non-Western and/or ethnicity-based feminist perspectives into the category "multicultural and global" hides a multiplicity of approaches. This concealed diversity is particularly apparent in a Christian theological context, where quite distinctive African, Asian, *mujerista* (South American liberationist), black (womanist) and indigenous feminist perspectives have emerged (see Kwok, 2000; Mitchem, 2002; Oduyoye, 2001).

Feminism is a diverse ideology; or rather series of ideologies. It is generally mixed with other Western and non-Western philosophies, ideologies, and methodologies to form particular feminist perspectives. Feminism's diversity, its interdependence on other philosophies, its eclecticism and its acknowledgement of its own situated knowledge are all targets for critique of feminist approaches. Some of these critiques come from within feminism and some from beyond.

That feminism recognises its own situatedness is actually a source and focus for criticism by dominant knowledges which claim objectivity.

> Feminists have been criticized for failing to produce adequately rational, scientific or unbiased knowledge (on the understanding that their critics use methodologies that are adequate in these respects) (Ramazanoglu & Holland, 2002, p. 3).

It is difficult to respond to such criticism except by continuing to highlight alternative knowledges. That feminist approaches offer and produce alternative perspectives, results and understandings is sufficient to call them into question in any environment which such alternatives explicitly question. The use of qualitative methodologies, regarded as less "rational, scientific and unbiased" and more interpretative, may exacerbate this criticism.

This recognition of situatedness and the coincident criticism of it are unsettling for feminist researchers who are often hyper-aware of the tenuousness of any situated knowledge. It is further complicated by women's varied experiences and the recognition of the network of factors which influence power relations in any society. Where feminist researchers have struggled to gain recognition, critiques from within feminism may be particularly confronting. An example of this destabilising influence from within may be found in the tension between "second wave" and "third wave" feminists described by Althaus-Reid and Isherwood (2007, p. 125) as a contrast between focusing on "equality" for women and focusing on "difference" between many different subjectivities/ identities.

"Second wave" feminists (1950s–1970s) struggled to gain recognition for women in their own right. The validity of women's subjectivity was a key feature of many second wave approaches. Conversely, the recognition that much of the gendered construction of women's subjectivity contained patriarchal bias further emphasised the necessity for women's self-determination, i.e. the development and control of their own subjectivity.

Against the background of postmodernism and postmodern theories, "third wave" feminists (1980s onwards) challenge both the possibility that any subjectivity is self-determined and the assertion that any particular subjectivity should be regarded as the ideal for which to aim, while at the same time continuing to explore the assigned "otherness" of women that was so integral to "second wave" theorists. The complexity of incremental differences across subjectivities is observed and valorised (see Gillis, Howie, & Munford, 2007). Ecofeminist Maria Mies (1993) offered an interesting account of a transition between "second wave" and "third wave" feminist thinking in the face of confrontation with the global complexities of women's lives. However, the conversation between these two groups of approaches is not always respectful. Accusations of essentialism (i.e. of a predetermined feminine nature) are often exchanged.

Although this broad picture of some aspects of the tension lacks the nuance which would be required for a more detailed analysis, it serves to highlight the differences that emerge between feminist perspectives. Differences in approaches and knowledges become targets for critique because of both the concern for scientific, rational and objective research focuses and methodologies and the tendency to expect non-dominant peoples and perspectives to be singular in their articulation. That both of these grounds for critique may be assigned to patriarchal/kyriarchal influences ensures that generalised criticism of feminist approaches and responses to it usually fall quickly into impasse.

Against the weight of existing epistemologies, feminist researchers can find it difficult to make themselves heard. Ramazanoglu and Holland noted:

> Feminists have had to contest what counts as reliable knowledge (in the sense of what can be replicated by other researchers) and valid knowledge (in the sense of representing reality), and how (or whether) such knowledge can be achieved.

There are two approaches to tackling this perennial issue: the validation of "claims to knowledge of social life/gender through existing scientific methods" and the proposal of "other criteria for justifying knowledge and how it is produced

(Ramazanoglu & Holland, 2002, p. 13). For some feminist perspectives, the first approach is not an option. In an essay entitled "The master's tools will never dismantle the master's house", Audre Lorde (1984), feminist essayist and poet, questioned the possibility of feminists operating within existing patriarchally constructed methodologies and academies. For other feminist perspectives, the complete vacation of existing academies, methodologies and/or epistemologies is not required, although radical overhaul of those sites is. Schüssler Fiorenza (2006, p. 370) wrote:

> Feminist students continue to be socialized into the hegemonic, kyriocentric paradigm of the discipline while feminist faculty are forced to prove their academic excellence and good citizenship in terms of positivistic scholarly or doctrinal standards.

She cautioned against feminist researchers losing the activist, practical dimension of feminist praxis as they move towards "the interests of the academy and publishing houses" rather than "transglobal movements for change".

A final caution about the fate of feminist research should be offered. Because of the suppression of women's knowledges and women as the owners/ originators of such knowledge, research material that is controversial when first produced by feminist researchers may still find its way into some mainstream acceptance through later male research. Often this route to integration into the mainstream is accompanied by the loss of the genealogy of the knowledge. In one respect, the integration of feminist research into mainstream approaches is an aim of feminist research. From another perspective, this situation is yet another example of the continuing co-opting and moulding of women's work in a patriarchal/kyriarchal context. In the context of biblical studies and Christian theology, important work by scholars such as Elisabeth Schüssler Fiorenza (1983) and Elizabeth Johnson (2002) is often overshadowed by later work by male scholars in similar areas in the academy's historical memory.

CONCLUSION

Although feminism encompasses a range of epistemological and methodological approaches, there are certain key features that may be regarded as common to most feminist approaches:
- the recognition of knowledges as situated
- the critique of patriarchal or kyriarchal power dynamics
- the privileging of women's knowledges, perceptions and experiences
- the proposing of alternative paradigms for understanding and acting
- the integration of action and reflection, theory and practice.

It is precisely the recognition of the situatedness of knowledges and of the biases against certain knowledges that ensures that feminist researchers must work hard to justify their approaches, to ensure that their voices are heard and to maintain the history of women's research. For this reason, this brief overview can only be regarded as a pointer to the wide variety of significant feminist research that has been produced.

REFERENCES

Althaus-Reid, M., & Isherwood, I. (2007). *Controversies in feminist theology*. Controversies in contextual theology series. London: SCM Press.

Christ, C., & Plaskow, J. (1979). *Womanspirit rising: A feminist reader in religion*. San Francisco: Harper & Row.

Frymer-Kensky, T. (1992). *In the wake of the goddesses: Women, culture and the Biblical transformation of pagan myth*. New York: The Free Press.

Gatens, M. (1991). *Feminism and philosophy: Perspectives on difference and equality*. Bloomington, IN: Indiana University Press.

Gilligan, C. (1982). *In a different voice: Psychological theory and women's development*. Cambridge, MA: Harvard University Press.

Gillis, S., Howie, G., & Munford, R. (Eds.). (2007). *Third wave feminism: A critical exploration* (expanded 2nd ed.). Basingstoke, Hampshire: Palgrave Macmillan.

Johnson, E. A. (2002). *She who is: The mystery of god in feminist theological discourse* (10th anniversary ed.). New York: Crossroad.

Johnson, E. A., Ross, S. A., & Hilkert, M. C. (1995). Current theology – feminist theology: A review of literature. *Theological Studies, 56*, 327–352.

Keller, C. (1986). *From a broken web: Separation, sexism, and self*. Boston: Beacon Press.

Kristeva, J. (1982). *Powers of horror: An essay on abjection* (L. S. Roudiez, Trans.). European perspective series. New York: Columbia University Press.

Kristeva, J. (1984). *Revolution in poetic language* (M. Waller, Trans.). New York: Columbia University Press.

Kwok, P.-L. (2000). *Introducing Asian feminist theology*. Introductions in feminist theology. Sheffield: Sheffield Academic Press.

Lorde, A. (1984). *Sister outsider: Essays and speeches*. Freedom, CA: The Crossing Press.

Mies, M. (1993). Self-determination: The end of a utopia? In M. Mies & V. Shiva (Eds.), *Ecofeminism* (pp. 2188–2230). Melbourne: Spinifex.

Miles, R. (1988). *The women's history of the world*. London: Paladin.

Mitchem, S. Y. (2002). *Introducing womanist theology*. Maryknoll, NY: Orbis.

Monro, A. J. (2006). *Resurrecting erotic transgression: Subjecting ambiguity in theology*. Gender, theology and spirituality series. London: Equinox.

Oduyoye, M. A. (2001). *Introducing African women's theology*. Introductions in feminist theology series. Maryknoll, NY: Orbis.

Offen, K. (1988). Defining feminism: A comparative historical approach. *Signs, 14*, 119–157.

Plumwood, V. (1993). *Feminism and the mastery of nature*. Feminism for today series. London: Routledge.

Ramazanoglu, C., & Holland, J. (2002). *Feminist methodology: Challenges and choices*. London: Sage.

Ruddick, S. (1995). *Maternal thinking: Toward a politics of peace*. Boston: Beacon Press.

Schaab, G. L. (2001). Feminist theological methodology: Toward a kaleidoscopic model. *Theological studies, 62*, 341–365.

Schüssler Fiorenza, E. (1983). *In memory of her: A feminist theological reconstruction of Christian origins*. London: SCM Press.

Schüssler Fiorenza, E. (1992). Justa – Constructing common ground; To speak in public: A feminist political hermeneutics. In E. Schüssler Fiorenza (Ed.), *But she said: Feminist practices of Biblical interpretation* (pp. 102–132). Boston: Beacon Press.

Schüssler Fiorenza, E. (2006). Reaffirming feminist/womanist biblical scholarship. *Encounter, 67*(4), 261–373.
Slee, N. (2004). *Women's faith development: Patterns and processes.* Explorations in practical, pastoral and empirical theology series. Aldershot, England: Ashgate.
Tong, R. P. (1998). *Feminist thought: A more comprehensive introduction* (2nd ed.). Boulder, CO: Westview Press.

AFFILIATION

Anita Monro PhD
United Theological College
School of Theology
Charles Sturt University
Australia

M. ELAINE DUFFY AND WAYNE (COLIN) RIGBY

31. RESEARCH IN INDIGENOUS SPACES

PERSONAL POSITIONING

This chapter represents the reflections of two colleagues on research in Indigenous spaces, Indigenous research methodologies, engaging Indigenous communities, values, ethics and principles in Indigenous research and building research capacity in Indigenous research spaces.

To contextualise this chapter and the authors writing it, we believe it is important to position ourselves. My views (Duffy) are shaped and inscribed by my different and continually changing subject positions, as a non-Indigenous, middle class, female academic on the one hand and on the other, as a nurse privileged to work and live in Indigenous communities in the Northern Territory, Australia, interacting on a daily basis with Indigenous peoples, creating opportunities to evaluate my own racist and anti-racist practices. My experiences, however, do not allow me the privilege to "talk about" or "on behalf" of Indigenous peoples, nor do they bestow on me expert knowledge about Indigenous peoples and cultures. My experiences and my embodied consciousness do enable me to speak with my own voice and with the awareness that I too am socially constructed as "white", "woman", "nurse" and "academic".

From my position (Rigby), whilst sharing the writing of this chapter, I reflected on many years of working as a nurse with both Indigenous and non-Indigenous people in mental health and social and emotional wellbeing. I am an Aboriginal man and so my views are shaped by my experiences and heritage, living and working in many communities across New South Wales, Australia. I do not speak on behalf of all Aboriginal peoples but only from my head and heart. However, it is an honour to show that Aboriginal peoples can achieve if they are focused and determined and proud of their heritage.

DECOLONISING RESEARCH IN INDIGENOUS SPACES

Research, knowledge production and knowledge translation have been and continue to be seen as the domain of the expert disciplines in the academy, who speak authoritatively about Indigenous issues. Research methods and approaches have evolved from dominant Western hegemonic values and paradigms. Research in Indigenous spaces has been and continues to be, to a large degree, dominated by white, male, Western scientific discourses that are incongruous with Indigenous ways of knowing. Hence, from the perspectives of Indigenous peoples, research in

Indigenous spaces has been viewed as another strategy of colonial domination. Martin (2002, p. 203) has referred to the notion of "*terra nullius* research", in which Aboriginal peoples are seen only as objects of curiosity and subjects of research, to be observed but never consulted or respected. The knowledge and ways of knowing of Aboriginal peoples are subjugated within the traditional research frame. Consequently, the notion of research in Indigenous spaces evokes an array of emotions, questions, challenges, paradigms and counter-paradigms for Indigenous peoples.

Colonial practices maintained strict regimes of control, and Western research was imposed on Aboriginal peoples with no regard for ethical principles, cultural beliefs, human rights and usefulness of research. Indeed, much of the research was beneficial only to the researchers, not to those researched or to their communities. Thus Western research practices *re*present colonial attitudes and practices, though subtly and insidiously, but at the same time always centring "whiteness" as the norm. However, there is increasing interest in research that confronts whiteness by both non-Indigenous (Frankenberg, 1993; 1996; Dyer, 1997; Fine, Weiss, Powell, & Wong, 1997) and more recently Indigenous (Moreton-Robinson, 1999, 2004; Fee & Russell, 2007) scholars. Naming whiteness has the effect of displacing it from its unmarked and unnamed status, which is itself an effect of its dominance. As Frankenberg (1993, p. 6) suggests, to look at the social construction of whiteness is to look head-on at a site of dominance. It can thus give rise to discomfort and to challenging new ways of producing knowledge and confronting entrenched political interests. A poststructuralist perspective challenges researchers to be reflexive and to examine their own position of power and truth claims.

Critique of Western research by Aboriginal academics (Fejo-King, n.d.; Rigney, 1997; Smith, 1999; Martin, 2002; Moreton-Robinson, 2004) has led to discourses about Indigenist research frameworks and theories, with the aim of decolonising methodologies in Indigenous research spaces. In her book *Decolonising methodologies: Research and Indigenous peoples*, Smith (1999), a Maori Indigenous scholar, argues that research and knowledge production dehumanises Indigenous peoples and privileges Western ways of knowing:

> Research is implicated in the production of Western knowledge, in the nature of academic work, in the production of theories which have dehumanised Maori and in practices which have continued to privilege Western ways of knowing, while denying the validity for Maori of Maori knowledge, language and culture. (p. 183)

Indigenous spaces, however, also provide sites of resistance that produce counter-discourses to those that dominate research. Indigenous knowledges, beliefs and ways of knowing have been subjugated by privileged researchers. Decolonising research in Indigenous spaces requires a reconceptualisation of research so that it incorporates Indigenous voices and discourses within a culturally safe context that respects difference. The discourses of Indigenous peoples about research provide spaces for resistance because their meanings allow for different positionings than those represented in dominant Western discourses. Resistance becomes possible when a space between the positions offered by a discourse and individual interests is recognised:

> We are conscious of a dominant subject position that we actively resist through the deployment of a variety of subject positions. Our resistances are therefore not reducible to overtly defiant behaviours. They are multifaceted. Our resistances can be visible and invisible, conscious and unconscious, explicit and covert, partial and incomplete and intentional and unintentional. They are profoundly political acts that are neither one dimensional or fixed and they do not always lead to conflict or self-destruction. (Moreton-Robinson, 2000, p. xxiii)

In the process of decolonising methodologies it is important to reposition Indigenous voices and knowledges. Indigenist research has been defined by Rigney (1997, 2006) as culturally safe and culturally respectful research that is comprised of three principles: resistance as an emancipatory imperative, political integrity in Indigenous research, and privileging Indigenous voices in Indigenist research. This is a direct challenge to non-Indigenous researchers, who are in a privileged position to speak about all aspects of the research process. Rigney (1997) points out, however, that critical research by non-Indigenous researchers should continue and has the capacity to inform the struggles of Australian Indigenous peoples for self-determination. To achieve self-determination and empowerment through research, Denzin, Lincoln, and Smith (2008, p. 6) call for the development of "culturally responsive research practices" that would position Aboriginal peoples and communities centrally in determining and defining what acceptable/non-acceptable research is.

Specific methodologies have been created that work with marginalised communities, facilitate the expression of marginalised voices, and attempt to represent their experiences in genuine and authentic ways. Some examples include critical research; social justice research; participatory action research; Kaupapa Maori research; oral histories; critical race theory; and, more recently, testimonio (Beverley, 2004; Smith, 2006, p. 160). Fejo-King (n.d.) has adopted the position of naming and claiming a space for decolonising methodologies named by other Indigenous researchers, for example, Aboriginal Grounded Theory research, which is a counter-claim to Western Grounded Theory research.

ENGAGING INDIGENOUS COMMUNITIES

It is only recently that Aboriginal peoples have been involved in researching their people and communities. Previously, Aboriginal peoples had no say in the development of the research question, issues of concern, participation in the research or the impact of the study. In the absence of involvement of Indigenous researchers and appropriate engagement with Indigenous communities there is the real possibility that research about Indigenous matters and peoples could miss key issues, report inaccurate perceptions and findings, and have little or no benefit to the very communities that were studied.

Humphery (2001) claimed that it was widely accepted that the concept and practice of research, as long observed with Indigenous peoples in Australia and elsewhere, is intimately bound up with histories of colonisation. Across the globe Indigenous peoples, particularly throughout the last century, have been relentlessly studied by non-Indigenous researchers such as medical practitioners and health scientists, anthropologists and linguists, historians and sociologists. As both Indigenous and non-Indigenous critics of this process have argued, this effort has more often than not resulted in a gross exploitation of Indigenous peoples involving invasive and disrespectful "experimentation", the theft of their beliefs and knowledge, and the portrayal of their societies and cultures in ways that merely reflect the values, prejudices and reoccupations of the non-Indigenous researchers.

As an Aboriginal person having experienced the education system at universities, I (Rigby) have come across a number of experts, particularly in regard to Aboriginal peoples. Most of those experts have come to their area of expertise, not necessarily from a will or a desire to "own" Indigenous peoples, but within a European notion of an investigation, posing questions, having them resolved, and finding new knowledge. It is only in recent times that we have been able to change this approach. It has come about through Aboriginal peoples posing those questions, also by those who are engaging in these endeavours changing the way in which they acquire and express knowledge. There has also been a desire to work in a coalition or collaboration with those of us who were formerly only the subjects or objects of investigation (Brady, 1999; Humphery, 2001).

Humphery (2001) noted that over the past decade, Indigenous Australians have strengthened their attacks on the inadequacies of medical research and contemporary scientific studies. Moreover, Indigenous writers have both encouraged and reflected upon the promotion and adoption of research guidelines with a continuing emphasis on Aboriginal communities and organisations undertaking research themselves.

Engagement with Indigenous communities must go beyond the superficial. McKennitt (2007) argued that seeking a mutually beneficial relationship, whether or not it leads to identifiable initiatives and arrangements, is a crucial step in engaging Aboriginal communities in research. This mutual relationship must be equitable and have shared goals. This will involve "yarns" with key Indigenous stakeholders in the identified communities. The most culturally appropriate means of eliciting information from Indigenous Australians is through narratives allowing community members to voice the priorities, importance and range of issues important to the community. Process is as important as outcomes, and since relationships are highly important to Indigenous peoples, outcomes are difficult without good relationships. It is imperative for researchers to understand each community's culture, values, histories, geography, community composition and leadership. It is vital to compare interests and seek common interests. For instance, traditional land owners are focused on meeting customary responsibilities and obligations to look after their land. The processes of engagement and decision making adopted must suit Indigenous decision-making structures and timeframes, rather than be imposed by non-Indigenous agencies. Some Aboriginal communities work well with researchers using informal arrangements whereas others may seek more formal arrangements.

VALUES, ETHICS AND PRINCIPLES IN INDIGENOUS RESEARCH

Research that involves Indigenous peoples, communities or cultures must be based on the importance of trust, recognition, values and ethics. Trustworthiness lays the foundation and is dependent on the open engagement between people. It involves transparent and honest dealings, with recognised values and ethics and without prejudice, maintaining respect and human dignity. This has not been the case in the past, and history records the perpetuation over couple of centuries of colonial inequality and injustice. Indeed, Carsons, Dunbar, Chehall, and Bailie (2007) argued that the circumstances of Indigenous peoples made them uniquely brutalised:

> I had seen white babies starve and not be fed, I had seen white men fall sick and not be treated, I had seen white women sell themselves for a few shillings worth of groceries. But no white man, even in the depths of the depression, had suffered as much as the black man suffers now in the height of the nation's boom (p. 60).

The significance of developing trusting relationships for Indigenous Australians in research cannot be undervalued. Ball (2008) advised that responsibility for maintaining trust and ethics should not be solely dependent on rules or guidelines. The development of a shared language for engagement between Indigenous peoples and researchers is an important first step in negotiations over research and whether Indigenous peoples have an interest in the research question. One way of ensuring that the interests of local Indigenous community members are not overlooked in the design and ethical review of research is to include them in the study. However, when academic researchers and Indigenous peoples discuss research and ethics, they do not always have the same meanings; therefore researchers need to consider the principles of protection, partnership and participation.

In a review conducted by the National Health and Medical Research Council (NHMRC, 2003) concerns were raised by Aboriginal and Torres Strait Islander peoples about poor consultation, lack of communication, and infringement of deeply held values arising from cross-cultural insensitivity, despite researchers' compliance with the legal requirements of ethical guidelines. Much of research is tied up with Indigenous history and there is a need for balancing rules, values and ethical guidelines. Further concerns were highlighted by Penman (2006) regarding the types of issues and questions Indigenous peoples might raise, such as how consultation will occur, how research participation will affect them and how research findings will be interpreted and used. Scougall (2006) acknowledged the cultural and linguistic barriers and competing expectations that might arise when non-Indigenous workers undertook program evaluations in Indigenous communities. Davidson, Sanson, and Gridley (2000) asked about Indigenous peoples' understanding of intellectual ownership of all aspects of their knowledge and experience, and how it might differ from non-Indigenous people's conceptions of rights over intellectual property.

Concerns persist in many Indigenous communities about the ethical quality of research involving them, reinforcing the importance of trust and integrity and recognising that building partnerships is central. Carsons et al. (2007) summarised the values underpinning the NHMRC guidelines (2003, p. 8), for ethical conduct in Aboriginal and Torres Strait Islander research which are defined as:

- *Spirit and Integrity* which is not only central but crucial to understanding and working with Australian Indigenous cultures;
- *Reciprocity* which is a mutual obligation that exists among Aboriginal and Torres Strait Islander communities, and extends to the land and social order – for researchers this value means ensuring that there are clear benefits to Indigenous communities as a result of participating in research;
- *Respect* in relationships which leads to trust and co-operation, thus research requires the involvement of Indigenous peoples in ways that are appropriate to their culture;
- *Equality* in research which should make Australian society fairer for Indigenous peoples – survival and protection values are demonstrated through ethical negotiation, conduct and dissemination of research that they are trustworthy and will not repeat the mistakes of the past; and
- *Responsibility* which acknowledges that Indigenous peoples value kinship bonds, caring for others and the maintenance of harmony and balance within and between the physical and spiritual realms.

Ethical research thus occurs when harmony between the sets of responsibilities above is established. Participants are protected, trust is maintained and accountability is clear. These are understood as being bound together over time by spirit and integrity.

To ensure the quality of communication and the researchers' understanding of the community, Aboriginal peoples need to be involved in research projects. Community engagement is one strategy for developing trust and building on the strengths of individuals and communities in order to identify and find solutions to community concerns. Collaborative research requires building the capacity of both community and academics in equal partnerships, recognising that each brings to the process unique but equally valuable skills and knowledge.

BUILDING RESEARCH CAPACITY IN INDIGENOUS RESEARCH SPACES

The number of Aboriginal researchers is limited, and there is historically a widespread distrust of researchers by many Aboriginal peoples throughout Australia. There is also a need to recognise that there are two very different worlds of Aboriginal and non-Aboriginal Australians. Fundamentally, engaging Aboriginal peoples in their own research and building a sustainable capacity to continue building on their own projects is particularly important. This will lead to Aboriginal peoples actively searching for solutions to growing social and economic problems that continually affect them, solutions which can in turn promote self-determination and self-management.

According to Smith (2007), the social capital for Aboriginal peoples is a requirement for a healthy community that may assist rural communities to find a way forward. It originates with people forming social connections and networks based on principles of trust, mutual reciprocity and norms of action. Accumulated social trust allows groups and organisations, even nations, to develop the tolerance sometimes needed to deal with conflicts and differing interests. Social capital refers to networks, norms and trustworthiness that increase a community's productive potential and is often referred to as the "glue that holds people together". Insufficient social networks, caused by isolation, marginalisation, cultural issues or geographic location, are known risk factors. Strong social capital in a community provides people with a sense of purpose and a sense of community, which is fundamental to building knowledge and improving the effectiveness of the workforce. Thus if social capacity is the glue that holds people together, research capacity building must include acquisition of the knowledge and skills to empower Aboriginal peoples to carry out their own research within their own communities.

The process of research capacity building involves formal training of Aboriginal peoples and communities in question development; research methodologies; method utilization; analysis and critiquing; and validation of findings. The development of research questions can be vexed, as closed questions can be intimidating for Indigenous peoples and open-ended questions are often overwhelming. The requisite skill is to organise questions appropriately. For example, a leading statement utilised in a focus group can achieve richness of data. As outlined earlier in this chapter, several critical methodologies are acknowledged as appropriate for research in Indigenous spaces.

Davidson et al. (2008) claimed that a major source of concern in Indigenous research has been the lack of adequate ethical procedures and the inappropriate processes sometimes employed. Ethics committees need to be more stringent and culturally sensitive in the criteria and procedures they follow in giving approval to Indigenous research. Most important, however, is the need to ensure that approval is given by the community. An honest and open dialogue with Indigenous peoples and communities is essential to ensure the appropriateness of the process, content and methodology of research. Ethical considerations are imperative, and the involvement of Elders is paramount, especially in the development process. Their contribution as to the initial background, insights and stories about past and current histories can be invaluable. Creating reciprocity in these relationships is important; as in all partnerships, both parties must have something to offer.

Research capacity building is not a simple matter, as there are processes to be thought through, such as shifting control from non-Aboriginal people to Aboriginal peoples. Furthermore, Gooda (2008) stated that Aboriginal health problems could be improved through research to discover new ways to apply existing knowledge to Aboriginal health; for example, shifting from a thematic approach to a programmatic approach with a focus on action; building partnerships between Aboriginal communities through a systems approach that builds linkages and integrates respectful medical, scientific, social science and cultural knowledge, health services, research institutions and governments. This would encourage a two-way exchange of skills and knowledge between Aboriginal and non-Aboriginal partners, allowing each the use of research and data to improve the effectiveness of their own organisations. This may also increase the involvement of Aboriginal peoples in research leadership.

REFLECTIONS

We believe that research in Indigenous spaces calls for a dialogue between Indigenous and non-Indigenous researchers. Culturally receptive research practices are required for research in Indigenous spaces; practices that locate Indigenous communities and peoples as the key decision makers in the research process. For both Indigenous and non-Indigenous researchers, research practices must be meaningful, ethical, critical, empowering, respectful and humble. All research in Indigenous spaces is political; it must therefore be framed in a social justice framework. Indigenous peoples, as the drivers of the research process from question development to the discovery of new knowledge, must have first access to the research findings and must make decisions about the distribution and translation of knowledge.

REFERENCES

Ball, B. (2008). Enacting research ethics in partnerships with Indigenous communities in Canada: "Do it in a good way". *Journal of Empirical Research on Human Research Ethics, 3*(2), 33–51.

Beverley, J. (2004). *Testimonio: On the politics of truth.* Minneapolis, MN: University of Minnesota Press.

Brady, M. (1999). The politics of space and mobility: Controlling the Ooldea/Yalata Aborigines 1952–1982. *Aboriginal History, 23,* 1–14.

Carsons, B., Dunbar, T., Chehall, R. D., & Bailie, R. (2007). *Social determinants of Indigenous health.* Crows Nest, NSW: Allen & Unwin.

Davidson, B., Spooner, C., Fisher, K. R., Newton, B. J., Dadich, A., Smyth, C., et al. (2008). *Indigenous research strategy: Working better with Aboriginal and Torres Strait Islander people and communities.* SPRC Report 14/08, University of New South Wales, Social Policy Research Centre.

Davidson, G., Sanson, A., & Gridley, H. (2000). Australian psychology and Australia's Indigenous people: Existing and emerging narratives. *Australian Psychologist, 35*(2), 92–99.

Denzin, N. K., Lincoln, Y. S., & Smith, L. T. (2008). *Handbook of critical and Indigenous methodologies.* Los Angeles: Sage Publications.

Dyer, R. (1997). *White.* London: Routledge.

Fee, M., & Russell, L. (2007). "Whiteness" and "Aboriginality" in Canada and Australia. *Feminist Theory, 8*(2), 187–208.

Fejo-King, C. (n.d.). *Decolonising research from an Australian Indigenous research perspective* [Electronic version]. The National Coalition of Aboriginal and Torres Strait Islanders Social Workers Association. Retrieved September 24, 2009, from http://trabajosocialalternativo.googlepages.com/Decolonising20Research20from20and20Australian20Indigenous20Perspective.pdf

Fine, M., Weiss, L., Powell, L. C., & Wong, L. M. (Eds.). (1997). *Off white: Readings on race, power and society.* New York: Routledge.

Frankenberg, R. (1993). *White women, race matters: The social construction of whiteness.* Minneapolis, MN: Routledge, University of Minnesota Press.

Frankenberg, R. (1996). When we are capable of stopping, we begin to see: Being white, seeing whiteness. In B. Thompson & S. Tyagi (Eds.), *Names we call home: Autobiography on racial identity* (pp. 3–17). New York: Routledge.

Gooda, M. (2008). *Listening to Aboriginal voices: Valuing Aboriginal solutions to Aboriginal health.* Submission to Review of the National Innovation System. Casuarina, NT: Co-operative Research Centre for Aboriginal Health. Retrieved December 8, 2009, from www.innovation.gov.au/innovationreview/Documents/267-CRCAH.pdf

Humphery, K. (2001). Dirty questions: Indigenous health and "Western research". *Australia and New Zealand Journal of Public Health, 25*(3), 197–202.

Martin, K. (2002). Ways of knowing, being and doing: A theoretical framework and methods for Indigenous and Indigenist re-search. *Journal of Australian Studies, 76*, 204–214.

McKennitt, D. W. (2007). Engaging with Aboriginal communities in collaborative research. *University of Alberta Health Sciences Journal, 4*(1), 30–33.

Moreton-Robinson, A. (1999). Duggaibah, or 'Place of Whiteness': Australian feminists and race. In J. Docker & G. Fischer (Eds.), *Race, colour and identity in Australia and New Zealand* (pp. 240–255). Sydney: UNSW Press.

Moreton-Robinson, A. (2000). *Talkin' up to the white woman – Indigenous women and feminism.* St. Lucia: University of Queensland Press.

Moreton-Robinson, A. (Ed.). (2004). *Whitening race: Essays in social and cultural criticism in Australia.* Canberra: Aboriginal Studies Press.

National Health and Medical Research Council. (2003). *Values and ethics – Guidelines for ethical conduct in Aboriginal and Torres Strait Islander health research.* Canberra: Commonwealth of Australia. Retrieved December 3, 2009, from www.nhmrc.gov.au/_files_nhmrc/file/health_ethics/human/conduct/guidelines/e52.pdf

Penman, R. (2006). *Aboriginal and Torres Strait Islander views on research in their communities.* Canberra: Australian Government Department of Families, Community Services and Indigenous Affairs.

Rigney, L.-I. (1997). Internationalisation of an Indigenous anti-colonial cultural critique of research methodologies: A guide to Indigenist research methodology and its principles. In *HERDSA Annual International Conference proceedings; Research and development in higher education: Advancing international perspectives* (pp. 632–639). Retrieved December 3, 2009, from www.herdsa.org.au/wp-content/uploads/conference/1997/rigney01.pdf

Rigney, L.-I. (2006). Indigenist research and Aboriginal Australia. In J. E. Kunnie & N. I. Goduka (Eds.), *Indigenous peoples' wisdoms and power: Affirming our knowledge through narrative* (pp. 32–50). London: Ashgate Publishing.

Scougall, J. (2006). Reconciling tensions between principles and practices in Indigenous evaluation. *Evaluation Journal of Australasia, 6*(2), 49–55.

Smith, J. D. (2007). *Australia's rural and remote health: A social justice perspective* (2nd ed.). Croydon, VIC: Tertiary Press.

Smith, L. T. (1999). *Decolonising methodologies: Research and Indigenous peoples.* London: Zed Books.

Smith, L. T. (2006). Choosing the margins: The role of research in Indigenous struggles for social justice. In N. K. Denzin & M. D. Giardina (Eds.), *Qualitative inquiry and the conservative challenge* (pp. 151–174). Walnut Creek, CA: Left Coast Press.

AFFILIATIONS

M. Elaine Duffy PhD
School of Nursing, Midwifery and Indigenous Health
The Research Institute for Professional Practice, Learning & Education
Education for Practice Institute
Charles Sturt University
Australia

Wayne (Colin) Rigby
School of Nursing, Midwifery and Indigenous Health
Director, Djirruwang program
Charles Sturt University
Australia

JOY HIGGS

32. HERMENEUTICS AS META-STRATEGY

INTRODUCTION

Hermeneutics is as an overarching means of meaning making in practice. This chapter presents the following arguments:
- Meaning making is a fundamental way of making sense of the world across many endeavours, including professional practice,[1] researching, teaching and self-directed learning.
- Meaning making involves decision making or reasoning, knowing and knowledge generation.
- In advanced practices subjectivity is naturally present since these practices involve human beings. Subjectivity requires interpretation.
- Even in objective practices like scientific research and meta-analyses of empirical research reports, despite claims of high level objectivity and reliability, there is considerable interpretation (e.g. of comparability of research contexts and methods, research credibility).
- Texts in their multiple forms (visual, text, text analogue) and narratives are tools for organising meaning at many levels.
- Hermeneutics emphasises the social, cultural and historical nature of inquiry and rests on the assumption that understanding cannot be separated from the social interests and the standpoints assumed by individuals, within a particular culture (Thompson, 1990).
- Hermeneutics, a strategy built around interpretation of texts about particular phenomena, is a way of implementing meaning making. Hermeneutics can serve as a meta-strategy for achieving reasoning, decision making and problem solving as the core feature(s) of advanced practice across research, professional practice and education.
- Further, hermeneutics serves as a meta-interpretation and meta-strategy for research in its different modes and paradigms. In using the term *meta-interpretation* a key argument is that this process is not merely one of understanding what the author of a text intended to convey; it also produces new knowledge, a new way of interpreting the phenomenon that is the subject of the text.

MEANING MAKING IN PRACTICE, LEARNING AND RESEARCH

Meaning making is a core dimension of being human and of human endeavours. People are essentially sense-making beings. Meaning making involves interpreting

and understanding a mass of information (sought and unsought) encountered in given situations in relation to a number of key factors, including:
- the time, place and people of the current situation
- the data, information and resources of the situation
- the goals, tasks and interests of the situation
- the context (goals, purpose, circumstances) of the tasks and setting
- the frames of reference (lenses, culture, values, interests, philosophy) of the participants engaged in the situation and task(s)
- the tools and capabilities (e.g. language, knowledge base) of the participants.

In the context of advanced practices such as research, teaching and professional practice, meaning making underpins three key responsibilities: to be self-directed in learning to pursue ongoing professional development and service responsibilities (i.e. one's professional duty of care), to test and construct knowledge, and to make practice decisions in responsible, informed ways best suited to clients' needs and interests.

Professional decision making (whether in practice, research or teaching) can be understood more fundamentally, deeply and richly if it is seen as a "languaged" and contextualised phenomenon rather than as the processing of information or a task of problem solving. Language is central to understanding and communicating understanding, as it "shapes our expectations and our dealings with things in the world" (Bontekoe, 1996, p. 123). Language is regarded as the "tool of tools" (Dewey, 1925/1981, Vygotsky, cited in Cole & Wertsch, 1996); it is a situated and living means of making sense of human needs, experiences and activities.

MEANING MAKING, DECISION MAKING AND KNOWING IN PRACTICE

In the advanced practices of research, teaching and professional practice, the researcher/educator/practitioner employs reasoning and knowledge to make decisions and take actions in the interests of the goals, tasks and clients pertaining to the given situation. A great deal of research and theoretical literature has addressed the different features and types of reasoning, knowledge and practice actions. In meaning making these processes and choices are indivisible.

Meaning making involves interpreting, creating, understanding, acquiring, questioning, expanding and using knowledge. In situations where the dualism between knowledge and practice (including reasoning) is broken down, meaning making is enhanced. According to Bereiter (2002), sociocultural theory (situated cognition, situativity theory) provides one way of dealing with this dualism. Bereiter contends that "knowledge does not exist either in a world of its own or as stuff in individual minds but as an aspect of cultural practice. Knowledge is neither produced or acquired but is constituted in communities of practice and embodied in the tools of such practice" (p. 58). For Bereiter these purposeful human creations or artefacts range from theories and designs to concepts, and are relevant to the knowledge society age which reflects Popper's (1972) "World 3", the world of ideas (as opposed to the physical and subjective/mental Worlds 1 and 2). World 3 contains entirely human creations that are fallible but improvable, and have a life of their own independent of their creators. Meaning making in advanced practices, therefore, requires recognition of this amazing potential of knowledge to grow, to be challenged and to be born out of practice, and yet to surprise us as practitioners with its own development. In creating knowledge, in a sense, we send it out into the world of practice to pursue its own journey; in using knowledge we embody it and it reframes us; and in critically appraising it we seek to understand it anew and ascertain its usefulness to enter the world of ideas.

MEANING MAKING, INTERESTS AND PARADIGMS

Meaning making in professional contexts is grounded in the meaning maker's (or shared meaning makers') interests and acculturation, regardless of whether this meaning making occurs through reasoning and decision making, through learning or through research. Professional practice and practice/research/ education communities are embodiments of interests and paradigms in action. Technical competence and the unquestioned acceptance and adoption of hegemonic norms and expectations are inadequate approaches for addressing complex context, ethical, human, power and social construction issues of practice. Instead, we need to recognise and understand the epistemological and ontological frameworks and issues underpinning our own practices and the practices of others.

In his theory of cognitive interests, Habermas (1972) argued that ideas shape our interests and actions, and he identified the way that technical, practical and emancipatory interests can frame practice knowledge and practice strategies. The term *interests* refers to those things that a person needs, or that are conducive to his or her flourishing and success (Blackburn, 1994). The importance of interests is that meaning making is referential. It is essentially a process whereby meaning maker(s) make sense of their reality, their experiences, and the puzzles, problems and challenges that arise in their lives and practices. And in this process they refer to their existing norms, standards, points of truth, interests and values, to help determine what they consider to be the best solution for the given situation; that is, the choice or outcome that makes best sense to them and is most defensible.

Much of the personal and disciplinary frame of reference that guides an individual's (or group's) meaning making is crafted and inculcated through acculturation. We are who we are, and we hold certain values, interests and positions, in part due to being members of our various social, cultural, educational and disciplinary groups. For professionals, the traditions of the field or discipline in which they have been educated and the language and concepts they develop profoundly influence the way they conceptualise and see the reality of their world. Being educated within a discipline promotes the adoption of particular views about the origins of knowledge, ways of seeing truth, what counts as evidence (ways of handling proof), and the nature of theory and practice (Higgs, Andresen, & Fish, 2004).

Chapter 4 presents an interpretation of research paradigms. It is valuable in exploring meaning making to extend the notion of paradigms beyond research communities (see Table 32.1). Broadly speaking, in research communities the goal is to generate knowledge. In learning communities the goal is to acquire knowledge. In professional practice communities the goal is to use knowledge in the service of others. Yet in each case these goals and processes (research, learning, practice) overlap, particularly in today's world of rapid knowledge growth and widespread rapid access to knowledge advances. All three processes are part of successfully dealing with the explicit and external as well as with the more implicit and self-regulatory demands for accountability that professionals face. For example, in professional practice advanced practitioners critically combine learned, received knowledge with knowledge of their clients' needs and interests, and they would critique the adequacy of their existing knowledge in the face of the situational parameters encountered. From their practice and critical appraisal of their knowledge they reflexively develop new knowledge for future practice. Thus they combine the acts of learning, using and generating knowledge.

In Table 32.1 the term *paradigm* refers to a way of knowing and a broad way of doing; it reflects the common underlying philosophical stance across the various columns in any row. However, given that the term more precisely refers to the way a community of practice functions and is framed (whether this occurs in an educational, research or practice context), it is important to recognise that the common assumptions of practice, the shared practices and behaviour norms that characterise these communities of practice, differ in each of these contexts. Therefore it is useful to clarify how the term is used by employing the terms research paradigms, practice paradigms, learning paradigms, etc.

MEANING MAKING AND HERMENEUTICS

Hermeneutics is first and foremost a process of construction and interpretation of texts. As such, the process is one of intent, an act of seeking meaning and understanding. Beyond the origins of hermeneutics as the interpretation of sacred and biblical texts (Powers & Knapp, 1995), it is now used more broadly in the interpretation of human action (Crotty, 1998). The extension of hermeneutics to the interpretation of human action arose from the argument by Ricoeur that human action and text share similar features (Hekman, 1984; Ricoeur 1979). "Human behavior becomes a text analogue that is studied and interpreted in order to discover its hidden or obscured meaning" (Leonard, 1989, p. 52). Almost any artefact produced or used meaningfully by human beings can be regarded as a text or a text analogue, and is therefore available for and susceptible to interpretation.

Hence, hermeneutics, the interpretation of lived, received and constructed texts, provides a valuable approach to meaning making in advanced practices. According to Svenaeus (2000), professional practice requires relevant information to be interpretively synthesised into a coherent narrative. He argued that the philosophical hermeneutics of Gadamer (1989) provides a powerful theoretical framework for conceptualising practice encounters.

Table 32.1. *A comparison of learning, researching, practising and professional decision making across paradigms*

	Learning	Researching	Practising	Professional decision making	Common features
Empirico-analytical paradigm	Learning is acquiring received truth and discovering objective truth	Using the scientific method (of the natural sciences). Quality is judged by objectivity, rigour, reliability, validity	The biomedical model of clinical practice	Hypothetico-deductive reasoning	Technical knowledge; focus on physical world; objective external reality
Interpretive paradigm	Learning is a search for understanding and meaning	Using hermeneutic and phenomenological research approaches to explore the lived world. Quality is judged by credibility, trustworthiness, rigour and ethics	Models include the biopsychosocial model, the wellness model, occupational performance (within and beyond health care contexts)	Narrative reasoning	Practical knowledge; focus on human world; multiple realities
Critical paradigm	Learning is the pursuit of empowerment and change through doing, knowing and becoming	Using action research and collaborative strategies to understand and change the lived world. Quality is judged by value of the change to the people involved	Models of health care and social practices based on the critical social sciences	Collaborative reasoning and decision making	Emancipatory knowledge; focus on the human world; sociocultural historical realities

Wilber (2000) portrayed hermeneutic inquiry as quintessentially concerned with the interpretation and appreciation of meaning. The interpretation or "reading" of the text provides the means for understanding the phenomenon (Crotty, 1998). This purposeful interpretation occurs within a context that is personal, social, cultural and historical. In each of these frames of reference, knowledge is shaped and shapes us. We understand through the lenses that have shaped our social and cultural journeys or histories.

One view of history is of a repository of knowledge about what it means to be human and what humans are capable of thinking, feeling and being. It is important to remember that "much of our knowledge and understanding is relative to where we happen to be living in history" (Stanford, 1998, p. 159). As researchers we may not initially find texts meaningful when we set out to interpret them due to their being located in different cultural or historical contexts. Our task is to seek a fusion of horizons between our traditions and those of the text authors and users.

Understanding is a fluid process. Woolfolk, Sass, and Messer (1988, p. 17) argued that "understanding, and especially understanding through language, is a primary form of being-in-the-world. Human beings not only come to know through the hermeneutic process, but are formed and constituted by it. This process of self-formation and self-understanding or self-development can never be final or complete". Such a growth in self-understanding is labelled transformative learning, and it has been described as

> a deep, structural shift in basic premises of thought, feelings and actions ... a shift of consciousness that dramatically and permanently alters our way of being in the world. Such a shift involves our understanding of ourselves and our self-locations; our relationships with other humans and with the natural world; our understanding of relations of power in interlocking structures of class, race, and gender; our body awareness, our visions of alternative approaches to living; and our sense of possibilities for social justice and peace and personal joy. (Morrell & O'Connor, 2002, p. xvii)

This being-in-the-world through understanding requires reflexive awareness (metacognition). Reflexivity is a crucial part of being a capable learner, practitioner and researcher. Armstrong and Horsfall (2007) contended that reflexivity is based on the narrative assumption that we not only story the world, we story ourselves in the world, and our social world influences how we story the worlds of others. We interpret the worlds of others through our personal narratives. We achieve this knowingly, with due respect to those whose lives, experiences or ideas we portray, by acting reflexively, reflecting on ourselves and acting from a position in relationship to others as we act. Ethically, in practice, research and education, reflexivity involves making transparent how we position others (and ourselves) in the world, through their/our culture, history, power and personal narratives.

A conundrum in this discussion is consideration of the focus on ontology and epistemology in hermeneutics and meaning making. Hermeneutics has been used to denote ontological inquiry in focusing on the exploration of existence of human beings who view their world as an object of understanding (rather than sense perception) (Mautner, 2000). Yet hermeneutics as a strategy of text construction and interpretation provides a powerful means of interpreting many human experiences and pursuits, including the epistemological task or goal of creating knowing. Gadamer emphasised that the practice of understanding and theoretical reflection on that practice are inseparable. Meaning making about meaning making lends itself to hermeneutic inquiry strategies. This chapter views meaning making as both a way of understanding the world (epistemology) and a way of being (ontology) a meaning making human being in a socio-culturally, historically constructed world.

HERMENEUTIC MODES OF INQUIRY

Contributions to hermeneutic philosophy and to the interpretation of human action, have come from a number of philosophers, significantly from Friedrich Schleiermacher (1768–1834), Wilhelm Dilthey (1833–1911), Martin Heidegger (1889–1976), Hans-Georg Gadamer (1900–2002), Paul Ricoeur (1913–2005) and Jürgen Habermas (1929–). Research strategies building on the work of these writers are numerous. All, however, share the core processes of text construction and interpretation, and researchers share the aim to "uncover meanings and intentions that are, in a sense, hidden in the text" (Crotty, 1998, p. 91). All build these interpretations on pre-judgements and pre-understandings of the phenomenon or situation being studied. All involve the negotiation of meaning between the inquirer and the text in the act of interpretation.

Understanding of the whole text is dynamic and is open to revision based on new insights gained through a deeper examination of its parts (Bontekoe, 1996), while the parts of the text are understood in relation to the whole. This is referred to as *the hermeneutic circle*. The outcome of hermeneutic inquiry is necessarily reflective of the unique interpretation of the individual who has engaged with the text. As Geanellos (1998, p. 160) suggested, "interpretive diversity results because interpreter pre-understandings give rise to textual plurality and multiplicity and because interpreters question the text from particular perspectives".

Each research paradigm involves interpretation of texts of some sort (including numerical data sets, received stories, constructed narratives or artwork), whether interpretation is an overt and core process as in the interpretive paradigm or a less evident process often obscured by words like "objectivity" as in the empirico-analytical paradigm. Bontekoe (1996) contended that there is a single unified fabric of understanding that joins the two core traditions of knowledge creation: the scientific method's pursuit of causal relationships and the humanities' recognition of relative value and significance, and that this conjunction is supported by the growing acceptance that both traditions are inherently interpretive.

The empirico-analytical practice paradigm involves technical interests, knowledge and language used in the processing of data texts using probabilistic reasoning. For example, in the health professions, existing texts (e.g. from research and theory) are combined with the construction of a case history (text) to provide a biomedical interpretation of the patient's medical needs.

Using an interpretive practice paradigm involves placing a greater emphasis on practical knowledge and language to address issues and problems in the lived world. In this approach, text construction can occur in the blending of discipline-based texts with participants' lived experiences. Such blended perspectives produce narratives that can interpret or provide interpretations and proposed actions, and produce a reconstruction of people's lives to provide alternative interpretations to those arising from use of the scientific method. The process of text construction and interpretation is ongoing and iterative, with a resulting expansion of meaning (as the basis for action and understanding).

In the critical paradigm the focus shifts to emancipatory practice language, goals and strategies, such as critical, collaborative decision-making dialogues. Texts are more commonly negotiated without coercion and misuse of professional dominance, rather than being delivered by an authority, and the dynamic, self-critical, interactive processes of text construction and interpretation occur throughout the decision-making process. In this paradigm the value of critical and creative conversations (see Higgs, 2006) in fostering shared meaning, negotiation and decision making in learning, research, practice and professional decision making is particularly evident.

Figure 32.1 illustrates a hermeneutic interpretation of different inquiry modes or approaches inherent in different research strategies, traditions and paradigms. This categorisation is both a reflection of the evolution of hermeneutics (see also Chapter 20) and an interpretation of how other research paradigms merge into a meta-interpretation of research in its many hues as hermeneutic inquiry.

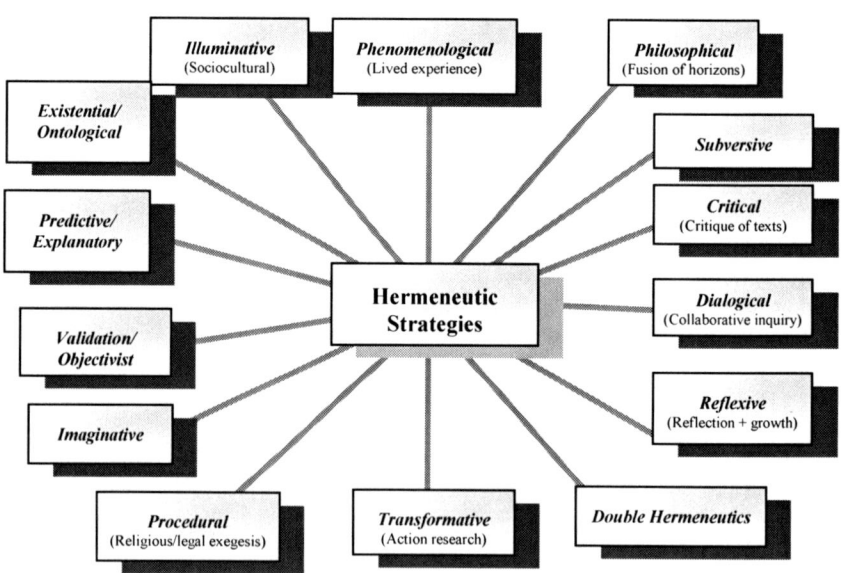

Figure 32.1. Modes of hermeneutic inquiry.

In essence these modes of hermeneutics can be described as follows:

- **Procedural (traditional) hermeneutics – the use of interpretive procedures to provide correct (theology) or authoritative (law) interpretation of texts**
  "There has be reflection on the art of interpreting texts since ancient times, but the word 'hermeneutics' was first used by J. C. Dannhauer in the mid-seventeenth century. He noted that texts for which a theory of interpretation was needed fell into three classes: Holy Scripture, legal texts ... and the literature of classical antiquity" (Mautner, 2000, p. 248). Linguistic and historical processes informed this mode of interpretation.

- **Imaginative hermeneutics – placing a text in its imagined historical setting**
  Schleiermacher proposed a general theory of interpretation that involved an imaginative reconstruction of how the text arose as well as an appropriate grasp of the linguistic and historical facts.

- **Validation hermeneutics – confirming fixed meaning in the text**
  Legal historian Emilio Betti and literature professor E. D. Hirsch contended that the text author's meaning is fixed, an object that can be accurately portrayed. The external point of reference is the author's intent and the validity of the interpretation is judged against this point (Schwandt, 1997).

- **Predictive/explanatory hermeneutics – the scientific method**
  The hermeneutics of the natural sciences deals with scientists' theories and discourse, and involves analysing an objective world that does not construct and interpret the meanings of its activities (Giddens, 1982). This category recognises that empirico-analytical paradigm research is a process of interpretive inquiry or hermeneutics. The scientific method involves creating a text (a set of empirical data) around a hypothesis that itself has arisen from interpretation, a chosen set of variables, insight and imagination (even if these are called analysis, deduction and hypothesising), and testing this hypothesis through quantitative analysis (which involves interpretation and choices such as point of reference/analysis, focus of inquiry, level of significance, implications).

- **Existential hermeneutics – understanding as being in the world**
  Heidegger moved hermeneutics from a theory of interpretation to a theory of existential understanding (Mallery, Hurwitz, & Duffy, 1987). Heidegger viewed hermeneutics as "the existential-phenomenological analysis of the constitution of Dasein ('existence' or 'Being-in-the-world')" (Schwandt, 1997, p. 63). For Heidegger, hermeneutics or understanding is a fundamental concept of ontology and a core feature of human existence.

- **Illuminative hermeneutics – interpretations of sociocultural, historical realms**
  Dilthey contrasted understanding (*Verstehen*) and explanation (*Erklären*) linked respectively to the human or cultural sciences (*Geisteswissenschaften*) and the natural sciences (*Naturwissenschaften*) (Mautner, 2000).

- **Phenomenological hermeneutics – interpreting lived experiences**
  This approach blends the thick descriptions of lived experience from phenomenology with the interpretive strategies of hermeneutics. Phenomen-ology seeks to be attentive to how things appear and aims to let things (human phenomena) speak for themselves. Hermeneutics claims that there are no such things as uninterpreted phenomena. Meaningful experiences are meaningful because they are captured in language. This strategy seeks to interpret people's lived experiences.

- **Philosophical hermeneutics – fusion of horizons**
  This method was developed by Gadamer; it is built on the assumption that understanding and interpreting the object/text/human action are the same endeavour. For Gadamer, hermeneutics is "the philosophical theory of knowledge that claims all cases of understanding necessarily involve both interpretation and action" (Schmidt, 2006, p. 2). According to Gadamer (1985), hermeneutics describes understanding as the interplay of the movement of tradition and the interpreter. Gadamer's hermeneutics is an ontological (since understanding is our way of being in the world), universal (in that understanding underpins all human activity), and conversational (dialogical) encounter (Schwandt, 1997). We interpret (using the tool of language) in the light of pre-judgements that come from our traditions, perspectives or horizons in which we do our thinking. The term *fusion of horizons* refers to the process whereby inquirers test their horizons through the process of interpreting another's text and horizon, and through the critical appraisal of both texts reach greater understanding (Bontekoe, 1996).

- **Subversive hermeneutics**
  Ricoeur differentiated between traditional hermeneutics (that sought the message in the text) and a hermeneutics of suspicion that is a subversive strategy seeking the hidden drives, class interests, etc. beneath texts (see also Nietzsche, Freud, Foucault).

- **Critical hermeneutics – critique of ideologies and social conditions**
  Habermas took a view of hermeneutics that is highly sceptical of the status quo and givens (interpretations, meanings, claims to truth, knowledge). The aim of this approach is to critique existing social, cultural and political conditions through interpretation and demystification of texts of current circumstances.

- **Dialogical hermeneutics – collaborative interpretations**
  Collaborative inquiry is inherently a dialogue between researchers throughout the research process, including interpretation of findings. Reason and Rowan (1981) reflected on multiple collaboration strategies in new paradigm research.

- **Reflexive hermeneutics – self challenge and growth**
  Finlay (2003, p. 108) described reflexivity as the "process of continually reflecting upon our interpretations of both our experience and the phenomena being studied so as to move beyond the partiality of our previous understandings and our investment in particular research outcomes". Reflexive hermeneutics research pursues understanding through critical reflection on the phenomenon and through critical self-reflection on the research process and of the researcher's decisions and actions. This process leads to a growth in understanding or interpretation, and a growth in being (of the researcher).

- **Double hermeneutics – adjusting dual pre-understandings**
  In this model (Nørreklit, 2006) there are two types of hermeneutic circle: the inner circle, in which an actor's pre-understandings inform the interpretation of incoming information, and the outer circle, in which reflexive understanding by researchers allows their pre-understanding to "meet" and "adjust to" the pre-understandings of the other(s) (i.e. the research participant(s)). Double hermeneutics focuses on the person behind, rather than the on actions of the players, asking, for example, why an actor has or uses a particular form of pre-understanding. Double hermeneutics involves one outer circle and two inner circles (the researcher's and the participant's).

- **Transformative hermeneutics – changing self and practices**
  Although all interpretive inquiry directly or indirectly implies the desire to change there is an explicit goal of transformation of practice and situations in critical paradigm research. This category recognises the important place of this research in the spectrum of research possibilities. All research changes the researchers who pursue it, to a greater or lesser extent. Yet in working intensively with others to change practice, this research category provides a genuine arena for changing oneself as researcher, person and practitioner.

CONCLUSION

I have argued in this chapter that hermeneutics serves as a meta-strategy for advanced practices including teaching/education, self-directed learning, research and professional practice. *Meta* in meta-strategy has three meanings: that this strategy transcends (is above/across) other strategies and contributes to each, that it requires and engages in metacognition, and that this understanding is seeking to create a pervasive, meta or dialectical term.

In dealing with human issues and human beings professionals need to acknowledge the inherent subjectivity of being in the world. In seeking to understand, learn and change, there is a need to pursue an interpretive dialogue between the various human texts and conversations that are present. Hermeneutic dialogue provides the overarching strategy, metaphor and meta-interpretation of meaning-making in personal, professional and practice advancement (Higgs, 2006). Advanced practices in professional inquiry endeavours are essentially complex meaning-making processes that can ideally be understood as hermeneutic dialogues. Such dialogues or conversations between the text and the inquirer construct or reconstruct knowledge and (shared) understanding. A "unique characteristic of hermeneutics is its openly dialogical nature: the returning to the object of inquiry again and again, each time with an increased understanding and a more complete interpretive account" (Packer, 1985, p. 1091).

In relation to research across different paradigms and methodologies it is valuable to understand the differences between them in order to pursue them authentically. However, it is also valuable to see the shared reality across these research positions; that is, that researchers make meaning from their texts using the interpretive tools of their paradigm.

As a final point, the interpretation of texts is not an endpoint but a delivery of new understanding into discourse and practice and the creation of new narratives of practice that themselves become texts for others to interpret into practice, learning, and new knowledge practices through research.

REFLECTIONS

Hermeneutics as a process of critical interpretive inquiry is central to human experience and what it means to be human.

Contemporary hermeneutics can be thought of as being polarised between those who view hermeneutics as a set of methodological principles (in the traditions of Schleiermacher) and those who follow Heidegger and view hermeneutics as "a philosophical exploration of the character and requisite conditions for all understanding" (Palmer, 1969, p. 46). In labelling this chapter as meta-strategy, I have avoided any notion of there being a set way of pursuing hermeneutics, rather the reverse. And I have embraced a situational or referential perspective, thus avoiding the methodologists' pursuit of objectivity. I have argued in favour of human meaning making in its many forms being a hermeneutic process. I am pursing a view of hermeneutics as meta-method as well as human understanding.

A second point of reflection about this chapter concerns the Gadamer–Habermas debates (see Ormiston & Shrift, 1990; Johnson, 2000). A key aspect of this debate is Gadamer's (1989) claim to the universality of hermeneutics "which needs to be understood as the claim that all understanding is bound to language" (Johnson, 2000, p. 57). This claim was debated by Habermas (1971), who argued that science can arrive at knowledge claims without the use of language but conceded the advantage of philosophical hermeneutics in helping translate scientific findings into lifeworld language. Gadamer countered with the argument that "rather than function within the misconception that it is independent from the lived experience of daily life, science requires a hermeneutic reflection that will examine the presuppositions that it embodies" (Johnson, 2000, p. 57). The importance of tradition as an influence on understanding and behaviour and the place of critique of assumptions, influences and power also underpin these debates. In particular, Habermas contended that hermeneutics must include a critique of ideology.

In this chapter hermeneutics is both critical and interpretive, and it is broadly context rather than specifically language that is presented as the reference point for interpretation. People make meaning and make sense of their worlds in relation to their contexts (including traditions, culture, language, interests, values, current circumstances). They make changes to their knowledge, practices and circumstances through critical appraisal, interpretations and actions to modify the status quo. They bring credibility to their research by owning, explicating, critiquing and justifying the assumptions, philosophical stances and interests underpinning their inquiry strategies. They make positive contributions to their communities through the pursuit of understanding and change that is driven by social responsibility. They transform themselves as people and researchers through critical self-appraisal in addition to the critique and interpretation of practice that is the stated goal of their inquiry. As a critical point, it can be argued that not all inquirers do each of these things, or pursue these motivations. In consideration of this, what then is missing from the inquiry process, product and credibility?

NOTES

[1] It is recognised that research and education are forms of practice, alongside professional (service-to-society) practice.

REFERENCES

Armstrong, H., & Horsfall, D. (2007). Ethics in critical, creative research. In J. Higgs, A. Titchen, D. Horsfall, & H. Armstrong (Eds.), *Being critical and creative in qualitative research* (pp. 78–87). Sydney: Hampden Press.
Bereiter, C. (2002). *Education and mind in the knowledge age*. Mahwah, NJ: Lawrence Erlbaum.
Blackburn, S. (1994). *The Oxford dictionary of philosophy*. Oxford: Oxford University Press.
Bontekoe, R. (1996). *Dimensions of the hermeneutic circle*. Atlantic Highlands, NJ: Humanities Press International.
Cole, M., & Wertsch, J. V. (1996). Beyond the social-individual antimony in discussions of Piaget and Vygotsky. *Human Development, 39*(5), 250–256.
Crotty, M. (1998). *The foundations of social research: Meaning and perspective in the research process*. Sydney: Allen & Unwin.
Dewey, J. (1925/1981). Experience and nature. In J. A. Boydston (Ed.). (1981) *John Dewey: The later works, Volume 1: 1925*. Carbondale, IL: Southern Illinois University Press.
Finlay, L. (2003). Through the looking glass: Intersubjectivity and hermeneutic reflection. In L. Finlay & B. Gough (Eds.), *Reflexivity: A practical guide for researchers in health and social sciences* (pp. 105–119). Oxford: Blackwell Science.
Gadamer, H.-G. (1985). The historicity of understanding. In K. Mueller-Vollmer (Ed.), *The Hermeneutics reader: Texts of the German tradition from the enlightenment to the present* (pp. 256–292). New York: Continuum.
Gadamer, H.-G. (1989). *Truth and method* (2nd Rev. ed.). New York: Continuum.
Geanellos, R. (1998). Hermeneutic philosophy. Part 1: Implications of its use as methodology in interpretive nursing research. *Nursing Inquiry, 5*, 154–163.
Giddens, A. (1982). *Profiles and critiques in social theory*. London: Macmillan Press.
Habermas, J. (1971). The hermeneutic claim to universality. In G. L. Ormiston & A. D. Scrift (Eds.), *The Hermeneutic tradition: From Ast to Ricoeur* (pp. 245–272). Albany, NY: State University of New York Press.
Habermas, J. (1972). *Knowledge and human interest* (J. J. Shapiro, Trans.). London: Heinemann.
Hekman, S. (1984). Action as text: Gadamer's hermeneutics and the social scientific analysis of action. *Journal for the Theory of Social Behaviour, 14*(3), 333–354.

Higgs, J., Andresen, L., & Fish, D. (2004). Practice knowledge – its nature, sources and contexts. In J. Higgs, B. Richardson, & M. Abrandt Dahlgren (Eds.), *Developing practice knowledge for health professionals* (pp. 51–69). Edinburgh: Butterworth-Heinemann.

Higgs, J. (2006). *Realising hermeneutic dialogues: Creating spaces for critical, creative conversations in learning, research, clinical decision making and practice advancement.* CPEA, Occasional Paper 5. Collaborations in Practice and Education Advancement, The University of Sydney, Australia.

Johnson, P. A. (2000). *On Gadamer*. Belmont, CA: Wadsworth Thomson Learning.

Leonard, V. W. (1989). A Heideggerian phenomenologic perspective on the concept of the person. *Advances in Nursing Science, 11*, 40–55.

Mallery, J. C., Hurwitz, R., & Duffy, G. (1987). Hermeneutics: From textual explication to computer understanding? In S. Shapiro (Ed.), *The encyclopaedia of artificial intelligence* (pp. 1–32). New York: John Wiley and Sons.

Mautner, T. (Ed.). (2000). *The Penguin dictionary of philosophy* (Rev. ed.). London: Penguin.

Morrell, A., & O'Connor, M. A. (2002). Introduction. In E. O'Sullivan, A. Morrell, & M. A. O'Connor (Eds.), *Expanding the boundaries of transformative learning: Essays on theory and practice* (pp. xv–xx). New York: Palgrave.

Nørreklit, L. (2006). The double hermeneutics of life world: A perspective on the social, dialogue and interpretation. *Philosophy and Science Studies, 5*, 1–13. Retrieved October 10, 2009, from www.filosofi.aau.dk/2008-coaching/5-Double%20hermeneutics.doc

Ormiston, G. L., & Schrift, A. D. (1990). *The hermeneutic tradition: From Ast to Ricoeur*. Albany, NY: State University of New York Press.

Packer, M. J. (1985). Hermeneutic inquiry in the study of human conduct. *American Psychologist, 40*(10), 108–193.

Palmer, R. E. (1969). *Hermeneutics: Interpretation theory in Schleiermacher, Dilthey, Heidegger and Gadamer*. Evanston, IL: Northwestern University Press.

Popper, K. R. (1972). *Objective knowledge: An evolutionary approach*. Oxford: Clarendon Press.

Powers, B. A., & Knapp, T. R. (1995). *A dictionary of nursing theory and research* (2nd ed.). Thousand Oaks, CA: Sage.

Reason, P., & Rowan, J. (Eds.). (1981). *Human inquiry: A sourcebook of new paradigm research*. London: John Wiley & Sons.

Ricoeur, P. (1979). The model of the text: Meaningful action considered as text. In P. Rabinow & W. M. Sullivan (Eds.), *Interpretive social science: A reader* (pp. 73–101). Berkeley, CA: University of California Press.

Schmidt, L. K. (2006). *Understanding hermeneutics*. Stocksfield: Acumen.

Schwandt, T. A. (1997). *Qualitative inquiry: A dictionary of terms*. Thousand Oaks, CA: Sage.

Stanford, M. (1998). *An introduction to the philosophy of history*. Oxford: Blackwell.

Svenaeus, F. (2000). *The hermeneutics of medicine and the phenomenology of health: Steps towards a philosophy of medical practice*. Dordrecht: Kluwer Academic.

Thompson, J. L. (1990). Hermeneutic inquiry. In L. E. Moody (Ed.), *Advancing nursing science through research, Vol. 2* (pp. 223–286). Newbury Park, CA: Sage.

Wilber, K. (2000). *The collected works of Ken Wilber. Volume 6: Sex, ecology, spirituality: The spirit of evolution* (2nd Rev. ed.). Boston: Shambala.

Woolfolk, R. L., Sass, L. A., & Messer, S. B. (1988). Introduction to hermeneutics. In S. B. Messer, L. A. Sass & R. L. Woolfolk (Eds.), *Hermeneutics and psychological theory: Interpretive perspectives on personality, psychotherapy, and psychopathology* (pp. 2–26). London: Rutgers University Press.

AFFILIATION

Joy Higgs AM PhD
The Education for Practice Institute
Charles Sturt University
Australia

NITA CHERRY

33. FUTURE POSITIVE?

This book, in a number of ways, reflects Denzin and Lincoln's (2005) framing of the seventh – and present – moment in research as being methodologically contested and involving moral discourse. Like each of the previous moments, the seventh moment is a way of characterising the particular dynamic that seems to be currently in play in world conversations about what research is and how it is done.

Firstly, in keeping with a major characteristic of the seventh moment, the book depicts the very broad range of sophisticated choices now available to researchers as they design their methodology and craft the specific techniques they will use to create and explore data; the ways they will work with others; and the texts used to present the work. Secondly, it reflects the ways in which new "takes" on research design challenge old and perhaps simplistic ways of classifying research approaches. Blended methods, mixed methods and new angles on qualitative research allow us to overcome the limitations of previous ways of thinking, while challenging us to develop new protocols for ensuring the robustness and credibility of our work. Thirdly, the book suggests ways in which the voices of those formerly marginalised from the research dialogue might now be heard, and how those formerly unacknowledged can take up their own authority in the research process.

The time of this seventh (current) moment opens up many possibilities. Denzin and Lincoln point to the positive energy of this time, reflecting the passion of many, many people to engage fully with the world in which we live. This is a world in which we must all deal with the serious implications of rapid transition and globalisation. It is a time in which they exhort us to be prepared and able to go to previously unexplored places and domains.

THE CHALLENGES

The seventh moment has been labelled by Denzin and Lincoln (2005) as the methodologically contested present. For all the possibilities available to us, this time is also subject to the pressures of conservatism, to calls for the return to conventional standards of what constitutes validated knowledge creation: large-scale, randomised, representative sampling, standardised measures and scales, and comparative interventions. These trends are part of the global trend of demands for accountability and are perhaps clearest in demands for evidence-based funding of social and community initiatives, and the arguably narrowing range of methodologies mandated through competitive research grants and ethics committees.

Denzin and Lincoln predict that this tension between new possibilities and conservative restriction will continue through the eighth and ninth moments. The eighth moment is framed around the recommitment and reconnection of social science to social justice, "reciprocal and reciprocating rather than objective and objectifying" (Denzin & Lincoln, 2005, p. 1118); the strengthening of Indigenous social sciences; and the increasingly diversified demographic of the academy itself. The ninth moment they have labelled the fractured future:

> a future in which, unless an intervention we cannot currently imagine takes place, methodologists will line up on two opposing sides of a great divide. Randomized field trials, touted as the "gold standard" of scientific educational research, will occupy the time of one group of researchers while the pursuit of a socially and culturally responsive, communitarian, justice-oriented set of studies will consume the meaningful working moments of another. A world in which both sides might be heard, and their results carefully considered as differently produced and differently purposed views on social realities, now seems somewhat far away, mixed-methods advocates notwithstanding. (Denzin & Lincoln, 2005, p. 1123).

In this respect, they admit to being more pessimistic than in their previous writing. They still hold to the vision that research methodology will not have truly come of age until we have developed a new collective praxis that is "deeply responsive and accountable to those it serves" (ibid.). But for the moment, they worry that previously courteous disagreement within the academy between methodologies has escalated to become a fierce battle for resources, for control of policy and for political power.

It is impossible to read Lincoln and Denzin's Epilogue to the latest version of their *Handbook of qualitative research* (Denzin & Lincoln, 2005) without the realisation that in many places the dynamics of research policy, funding and practice are, and will continue to be, essentially political battles. When Denzin and Lincoln refer to the politics of research policy and funding, it is easy to think of prominent figures engaged in well-publicised power plays, systematic lobbying, strong coalitions and cliques, and conspiracies of one kind or another. There are certainly times when coalitions – formal and informal – might seem to determine what is accepted for consideration and review (and who reviews it) for various scholarly journals and competitive grant processes. There are certainly times when powerful interests seem to capture and dominate the formulation of policy that creates the context for resource allocation.

Unlike the dynamics of high-profile party politics, however, the challenge of the politics of research is its lack of high-profile publicity focused on defining or pivotal decisions; and, arguably, its lack of clear accountability. Once entrenched, the ruling coalitions can dominate accepted practices and can be hard to dislodge.

These are sobering issues. The metaphor of battle implies something spectacular and widely acknowledged. Perhaps the word *struggle* (against the unquestioned hegemony, and against the unquestioning of hegemony) is more appropriate in this case, because here the contest is ongoing, playing out in many ways, in many places, and at many levels. This struggle is seldom carried out in spectacular and obvious public debates – and perhaps it would be more helpful if it was, because attention would then be drawn to it, and people would have a chance to become part of an active and vigorous conversation. The danger of the current struggle might well be that it is more incremental, taking place over many sites, with no formal declaration of hostilities, and therefore not seen for the struggle that it is. When a committee makes a decision not to support a particular research proposal because of the methodology employed, or a teacher of a research methods subject denigrates an approach that does not fit with his or her own view of robust research, the contest is playing out even though no battle trumpets are sounding. Yet this is dangerous territory, where important principles are conceded inch by inch in everyday decision making, where it is easier simply to take the line of least resistance when confronted by the views of others. Even more dangerous are the institutional practices and formal decision rules that limit the range of ways that things can be thought about at all.

BACK TO BASICS: WHAT WE CAN DO

However, we argue that if battles can be lost inch by inch, they can also be won in the same way. Individuals do make a difference. Perhaps the key to this is not to miss the small or modest opportunities that present themselves, so that richer and mutually respectful dialogues become the norm rather than the exception. Saving the debate for the day when the big decisions need to be made is to make the task doubly difficult.

Anyone who participates in a staff meeting can make a difference; anyone who applies for funding for a research project of any size, anyone seeking ethics approval, anyone giving guidance to doctoral and master's candidates, anyone teaching in a research methods subject, anyone training students about what constitutes knowledge, can make a difference. And any student or novice, asking a question or asking experienced researchers to make their research reasoning and strategies transparent, can also make a difference. Too often disputes and controversies lie in the silences and the lack of challenge to taken-for-granted research practices as well as the over-specification and articulation of "accepted" or "approved" practices.

It is particularly important for supervisors to understand the influence they have on their candidates, shaping the way that they, in their turn, come to think about what constitutes scholarship in knowledge creation, and its social and ethical dimensions. For it is that cohort who will create the context for knowledge creation in the generation of researchers to follow. (See History of Ideas, Chapter 1.)

Despite their frank acknowledgment of the challenges of what they call the contested present and fractured future, Denzin and Lincoln (2005) themselves offer much practical advice about how we might engage with those challenges. For example, in the face of rapid change, they write about the need to be adaptive and to work in the mode of *bricolage*. To be a bricoleur means to be resourceful, to work with what is to hand, to be inventive and to look again, with fresh eyes, at familiar things. It also means to be prepared to craft a new approach in response to what is confronting us, whether it is an opportunity or a problem. An example of that is the researcher who wants to engage with something as it is happening, not relying solely on the memory or reconstructions made by people after the event. A rich exploration of something as it is happening opens up many options that can be combined in interesting and novel ways. When we don't know what will happen next, we might pay closer attention to what is actually happening now, not simply viewing it through the filter of whether it was later judged as a success or as a failure.

Research approaches that encourage us to pay attention to a phenomenon as it is developing need to give us tools for doing that, in a range of ways. Researchers can invite participants in the action to keep individual but anonymous journals or learning logs; or to have reflective conversations about their collective experience of what is happening. They might use wikis, blogs or other on-line interactions. They might write a collective story. They might use forecasting techniques to predict what is likely to happen next or to make sense of what is happening now. They might use numbers and photos, poems and management reports. They might invite participants to be interviewed by people who are the ultimate clients or users of their work.

Mixed methods approaches (see Chapter 29) also afford many opportunities to work in more nuanced and sensitive ways with emerging phenomena. At the same time, considered use of mixed methods can challenge the simplistic and rigid categorisation of approaches as being "either this or that" (e.g. qualitative or quantitative). One element of mixed methods research might involve the collection of large-scale data; another might encourage a close-up engagement with individual cases or examples of interest. Or the researchers might create quite different kinds of text to communicate and explore a particular issue, event or world view.

Adaptive bricolage and inventive use of mixed or innovative methods challenge researchers to craft or design methods rather than simply taking methods "off the shelf". This inventiveness opens up many methodological opportunities. At the point of design, it is possible to invite into the research journey, at a much earlier stage, voices that might have appeared much later in the journey or not at all (see Chapter 13). Empowerment, taken as a deliberate intent in research, requires rather more than just asking a lot of different people what they think of the research findings, or even working arm-in-arm with them during the implementation of the research design. It means asking them what questions need to be tackled, and what issues need to be explored, when, where and how. It means shared design of the whole research strategy. It means serious consideration of who owns the data and the wisdom generated through the study, along with where and how it might be reported and published.

The seventh moment also illuminates the way we develop vibrant communities of practice. Cultivating communities of research practice could, of course, be understood as seeking out like-minded colleagues and working with a shared philosophy about research and how it should be conducted. In the spirit of the seventh moment, however, a community of practice might be developed with a view to deliberately including people whose perspectives are quite different from each another. In the world of complexity, transition and global scope that we live in, it is clear to us that many issues demand multi- and cross-disciplinary inquiry, with all the differences in methods and protocols that this entails. Indeed, it can be argued from a postmodern perspective that we live in a postdisciplinary (or at least transdisciplinary) age, in which knowledge domains intersect, boundaries blur, and life in separate ivory towers is simply not sustainable.

What might be less obvious is that the framing of issues through a single lens has led researchers to oversimplify complex issues from the past. The practice of medicine as science, detached from holistic understanding of human beings as emotional and spiritual beings, is a case in point. The practice of education without the benefit of the perspectives of psychobiology is another.

The strategies we have identified are all approaches that can help us deal with the contested present and the fractured future identified by Denzin and Lincoln. However, the application of these innovative approaches depends upon the will, ingenuity and skill of individuals, groups and communities of practice to experiment, to take action themselves and, at times, to educate, advocate and join in the debate with others. The success of these strategies also depends on the capacity and commitment of the researchers to pursue quality research and to demonstrate this quality, thereby giving credibility to their research.

GETTING BACK INTO THE DEEP END

The eighth and ninth moments of qualitative research challenge us to reconnect and re-engage with the important human issues of our time, issues of economic and social justice and security, of freedom from hunger, poverty, illness and war. Many writers have complained of the progressive sanitisation of research agendas as those who pay for research seek to control research strategies and agendas. A conspicuous example of this sanitisation is the adoption of action research as a tool for assisting organisational change when the nature of change has already been determined and the research, posing as consultation, is really about its systematic implementation (Zuber-Skerritt, 1991).

The escalating demand for doctoral studies and other postgraduate studies has created an enormous appetite for a range of research topics as well as a volume of research opportunities. However, the depth and usefulness of that research could well be argued to have been in inverse proportion to its quantity. Studies that consist of interviews with representative samples of so-called experts, opinionating at a safe distance, after the event, have become a common form of inquiry in business and other discipline areas, while inquiry into complex and evolving practice itself – and its impacts for better or worse – has become more scarce (see Chapter 2).

What is needed are individuals – and preferably teams of people working in co-operative collective inquiry who are prepared to pose generative, juicy questions that take us to the heart of urgent, significant human dilemmas. Of particular importance are the dilemmas associated with sustainable communities and economies, endemic poverty, mental health, food production/distribution; with the use of biotechnologies, global communication, armaments and surveillance technology. These are issues calling for multidisciplinary frames, extended fieldwork, and concurrent development and testing of policy, practice and theory.

Researchers need the skill and confidence to work in research mode with a range of people who are prepared, in turn, to work with them. Serving police officers, nurses and teachers can and do become part of research projects, writing papers and presenting them at scholarly conferences as part of research teams. This happens because they have taken up the invitation to work closely in defining the research questions and crafting the research design, or because they were the ones who invited the researchers in to work with them.

Engagement with these issues calls for methods that are crafted with all the care and ingenuity of committed bricolage. These are methods that do not cramp the space of practitioners, do not ask them to so simplify the practice issues so that they become useless or jaded, and do not confuse scholarship with detachment, lack of care or empathy, or with political neutrality. They are methods that demand high levels of reflexivity; in other words, that take responsibility for the lenses used, deploy a diversity of such lenses, and design processes that are so sensitive to impact that they register and reflect back to us the effect of our interventions, both intended and unintended.

Such research practice needs the additional dimension of constant finely tuned ethical and moral awareness (see Chapters 9 and 11). Curiously, it is possibly moments of contest and fracture that make the deeper ethical dimensions of research practice more obvious as well as more critical. These deeper dimensions are not usually addressed in ethics applications. Ethics applications do not usually ask: Whose voice is omitted or restricted in this research? Who is making all the key decisions? Who controls the budget? Whose language has been colonised or superseded by the language of the researchers? Who is invited to consider the meanings that others impose on their words?

Arguably, the more stable and uncontested a research approach appears to be, the less likely it is to be examined or challenged by its practitioners in terms of its ethical assumptions. Honourable intent is assumed to translate into honourable practice, and it can take a new generation and the passage of many years to expose the ways in which human dignity and wellbeing have been compromised. At the time of writing, an apology has been issued by one of the oldest and most distinguished universities in Australia for its association with researchers undertaking experimentation with children in state care 50 years ago. That children in care could be treated that way beggars belief today, but must have seemed quite reasonable at the time, to one of Australia's most prestigious university communities.

For individual researchers and for the communities of research practice to which they belong, the questions to be posed are: What do you think is perfectly reasonable? What do you take absolutely for granted as being acceptable? Whose life experience do you presume or claim to represent to others? Whom do you judge to be suitable as participants for your investigation, and whom do you exclude? Why? How articulate and complete does a response need to be before you count it in your data set? And having asked these questions, how do you answer your own questions? What guiding coalitions or stakeholders influence the ways you make judgments about what is appropriate or not?

RESEARCH AS PRAXIS

An innovative and ethical research stance requires care, skill and imagination. This is further encouragement to think of ourselves as research practitioners, responsible for self-consciously and deliberately cultivating our individual and collective praxis. Such reflective self-examination powerfully reframes the opportunities and the obligations of the serial researcher. To be a researcher is not simply to undertake a series of projects over a period of years, or to be an academic who does research. It is to regard research as a journey of professional practice, in which the researcher matures and gains confidence to speak, to challenge and, at the very least, to offer sensitive, well-crafted and resourceful options that enrich the way we co-create knowledge.

This sounds, perhaps, somewhat grandiose and heroic. But in practice it is something quite humble. It might begin with having a few techniques for holding open the conversation and decision spaces for a bit longer, so that other options can be considered. Next we might ask for input from everyone around a table, not just the usual contributors, taking the trouble to find really good examples of adaptive crafted approaches that have been published or funded or have helped to shape policy. It could involve looking to the ways other disciplines have approached methodologies and approaches and supporting others who are putting forward fresh thinking; then framing proposals in ways that are persuasive as well as clear.

Whatever specific strategies we use, we make a choice to take up the authority we do have, based on the lived experience of research and practice that is undisputedly our own, that cannot be taken away without our own consent. Taking up this authority effectively goes beyond having the confidence to speak up. It implies that we can describe that experience, that we can articulate our view of things, that our own theory of research practice is something we can clearly communicate to others. It involves making the tacit wisdom and skill that we possess quite explicit.

Doing all these things can be demanding, and not just for early career researchers. Sometimes it is the most experienced researchers who have the most difficulty expressing what they do, because their practice has long ago passed into the realm of unconscious competence. Inviting or allowing someone else to interview you is one way to try to realise and unpack what you know and believe about research practice. Reading what others have written about your research practice, from perspectives different from your own, can help to sharpen – or extend – your self-understanding and your practice descriptions.

STAYING AWAKE

There is an old story that is told of the Buddha. He was interviewed one day by a group of people anxious to find a label for his profession. "Are you a warrior?" they asked. "No, I am not a warrior. I have no weapons. I wage no war". They asked again: "Are you a teacher, Buddha?" "No, I am not a teacher. I have no books. I have no classroom". And again they challenged him: "Are you a doctor?" "No", he replied. "I have no medicines. I have no prescriptions". Exasperated, they finally asked: "Then what are you?" He replied: "I am awake".

To cultivate research as praxis, whether personal or collective, we need to be awake, alert, eyes and ears, hearts and minds wide open (see Chapter 10). This chapter began with Denzin and Lincoln, so let's end it with their notion of what it means to be awake(Denzin & Lincoln, 2005, p. 1116):

> We believe that that there are genuine ruptures in the fabric of our own histories, precise or fuzzy points at which we are irrevocably changed. A sentence, a luminous argument, a compelling paper, a personal incident – any of these can create a breach between what we practiced previously and what we can no longer practice, what we believed about the world and what we can longer hold on to, who we will be as field-workers as distinct from who we have been in previous research. Indeed, we would argue that what we call moments are themselves the appearance of new sensibilities, times when qualitative researchers become aware of issues they had not imagined before. They are the 'ah-ha' moments, the epiphanies

To recognise and fully realise, through practice, these moments – whether in the history and practice of qualitative research across the world or in the context of our personal professional histories – one certainly needs to be awake. These are the times when practice can be transformed.

REFERENCES

Lincoln, Y. S., & Denzin, N. K. (2005). Epilogue: The eighth and ninth moments – qualitative research in/and the fractured future. In N. K. Denzin & Y. S. Lincoln (Eds.), *The Sage handbook of qualitative research* (pp. 1115–1126). Thousand Oaks, CA: Sage Publications.

Zuber-Skerritt, O. (1991). Action research as a model of professional development. In O. Zuber-Skerritt (Ed.), *Action research for change and development* (pp. 112–135). Avebury: Aldershott.

AFFILIATION

Nita Cherry PhD
Faculty of Business and Enterprise
Swinburne University of Technology
Australia

CONTRIBUTORS

Rola Ajjawi PhD
The Education For Practice Institute
Charles Sturt University
Australia

Robyn Barnacle PhD
School of Graduate Research
RMIT University
Australia

John A Bowden PhD
Swinburne Research, Swinburne University of Technology
Australia

Donna Bridges PhD
The Education For Practice Institute
Charles Sturt University
Australia

Stacy M Carter PhD
Centre for Values, Ethics and the Law in Medicine and the School of Public Health
The University of Sydney
Australia

Nita Cherry PhD
Faculty of Business and Enterprise
Swinburne University of Technology
Australia

M. Elaine Duffy PhD
School of Nursing, Midwifery and Indigenous Health
The Research Institute for Professional Practice, Learning & Education
Education for Practice Institute
Charles Sturt University
Australia

Jill Franz PhD
School of Design
Queensland University of Technology
Australia

Sandra Grace PhD
The Education For Practice Institute
Charles Sturt University
Australia

CONTRIBUTORS

Carol Grbich PhD
School of Medicine Flinders University
South Australia

Pamela J Green PhD
Swinburne Research, Swinburne University of Technology
Australia

Susan Groundwater-Smith PhD
Faculty of Education and Social Work
University of Sydney
Australia

Joy Higgs AM PhD
The Research Institute for Professional Practice, Learning & Education
The Education For Practice Institute
Charles Sturt University
Australia

Debbie Horsfall PhD
Social Justice and Social Change Research Centre
University of Western Sydney
Australia

Robert Jones PhD
Professor of Human Resource Management and Organisation Studies
Faculty of Business and Enterprise
Swinburne University of Technology
Australia

Branka Krivokapic-Skoko PhD
Faculty of Business
Charles Sturt University
Australia

James Latham PhD
Faculty of Business and Enterprise
Swinburne University of Technology
Australia

Rosemary Leonard PhD
Social Justice and Social Change Research Centre
University of Western Sydney
Australia

Stephen Loftus PhD
The Education For Practice Institute
Charles Sturt University
Australia

CONTRIBUTORS

Robert Macklin, PhD
The Research Institute for Professional Practice, Learning & Education
Faculty of Business, Charles Sturt University
Australia

Sharyn McGee
The School of Social Sciences
The University of Western Sydney
Australia

Gavin Melles PhD
Faculty of Design
Swinburne University of Technology
Australia

Inger Mewburn PhD
School of Graduate Research
RMIT University
Australia

Anita Monro PhD
United Theological College
School of Theology
Charles Sturt University
Australia

Grant O'Neill PhD
Faculty of Business
Charles Sturt University
Australia

Wayne (Colin) Rigby
School of Nursing, Midwifery and Indigenous Health
Director, Djirruwang Program
Charles Sturt University
Australia

Rodd Rothwell PhD
Faculty of Health Sciences
The University of Sydney
Australia

Sue Saltmarsh PhD
School of Teacher Education
Charles Sturt University
Australia

CONTRIBUTORS

Angie Titchen PhD
Knowledge Centre for Evidence-Based Practice
Fontys University of Applied Sciences
The Netherlands

Franziska Trede PhD
The Education For Practice Institute
Charles Sturt University
Australia

Natasha Wardman
School of Teacher Education
Charles Sturt University
Australia